GRANDMOTHER IN THE KITCHEN

By the same author

GRANDMOTHER'S HOUSEHOLD HINTS

•

With COLONEL HANS CHRISTIAN ADAMSON, USAF (R)

THE SPORTSMAN'S GAME AND FISH COOK BOOK

THE GALLEY COOK BOOK

GRANDMOTHER IN THE KITCHEN

A Cook's Tour
of American Household Recipes
from the
Early 1800s to the
Late 1890s

by

HELEN LYON ADAMSON

CROWN PUBLISHERS, INC.
New York

To
BELLA'S
Four Great-Granddaughters

NATALIE LYON CHRISTOPHER
JANET LYON CROSBY

and

BEVERLEY LYON WILLIAMS
BARBARA LYON COURSON

•

BELLA
Would Share My Pride in Them

TABLE OF CONTENTS

INTRODUCTION

Frankly, I do not believe that this book needs a lengthy introduction, because I have made a sincere effort to express its purpose in the text. Briefly, its object is to convey a word picture of that engine room of the home called the kitchen, in which nineteenth-century housewives worked diligently to stoke the culinary fires of their respective households. I have tried to depict the laborious, often dangerous, labors they had to perform, and to show the end results of these labors in the types of food they sent to their tables. As mentioned in the book, these recipes came to me from my grandmother, Bella Lyon, who—from girlhood days in pre-Civil War Boston and throughout the years to the 1890s—collected cook books and individual recipes, all of which she gave to me decades later. As a unit of Kitchen and Culinary Americana, this collection forms a fairly complete panorama of virtually every phase of food preparation from the closing era of open-fireplace cookery down through the bewildering and frustrating years of the Kitchen Revolution, the time when cumbersome, tricky and temperamental flame-throwers called Kitchen Ranges and Cooking Stoves made kitchens veritable Hells for housewives, days when nearly all the old reliable cooking recipes went by the board, as new, and largely untested, "receipts" for cooking on the Fiery Monsters inundated households. This chaos was launched in the early 1800s; not until the mid-1800s did order and efficient cooking methods take hold. Many uncertainties faced women in those years in the shape of flocks of untried recipes in circulation, and I have used some of them to illustrate the pitfalls they represented. Also, since the mid-1800s form the bull's-eye of my target, I have concentrated on that era and given attention to candle making and details of kitchen equipment, its use and how it was kept clean; I have listed formulas for Three Square Meals a day and tables of weights and measures that cover the spread of a century. Some of these listings are obsolete, but the majority are as good in 1965 as they were in 1865. In conclusion, I want to extend my hearty appreciation to Mrs. Jane Humphreys of San Jose for her enthusiasm and efficiency in putting complicated and hard-to-read material into readable type.

HELEN LYON ADAMSON
The Francesca
San Francisco, California

July 1st, 1965

A Note to the Reader

The asterisks that follow many of the recipes denote the following: * practical; ** impractical; *** obsolete museum piece. Recipes signed by individual contributors date from the late 1850s to the early 1870s, and are not graded.

1. *A Word on the Wise Way to Use This Cook Book*

One Thing at a Time
And that done well;
Is a very good Rule
As Many can tell.
                    —GRANDMOTHER RHYME

At the outset, I should like to explain that I have tried to accomplish two things in this book. One is to give a well-rounded picture of what families in the northeastern states ate in the 1800s. In passing, let me note that wives of Yankees who migrated westward during that period naturally clung to the cooking lore they had acquired in their eastern homes. Thus, in time, their cooking habits spread from Atlantic shores to the Mississippi and beyond. I also want to make it clear that the recipes which follow represent the fare of ordinary, well-to-do families. They include neither the quite fanciful dishes indulged in by the very rich nor the rather spartan fare of the very poor.

In selecting recipes, I have tried to balance the various categories on the same scale on which they appeared in the old cook books. Actually, the number of recipes for soups, meat, fish, fowl, etc. in these cook books is vastly outweighed by those for breads, biscuits, puddings and custards. This is because the nineteenth-century housewife set great store on her status as a baker, pudding maker and custard creator. So if the reader becomes more than a little weary of the seemingly endless array of biscuits, puddings and custards that vary little from each other except in name, please remember that they were important milestones along the road to dyspepsia in bygone years.

Next, my aim has been to draw the recipes from two representative sources, one being the cook and household books referred to earlier, the other being the "favorite receipts" of housewives who, more or less, regarded themselves as expert cooks. The former recipes can be identified by the time references—such as early, late or mid-1800s—which follow the individual titles; the latter carry the name of the contributor at the end of each recipe. All recipes of the second sort date from the late 1850s to the mid-1870s. All material in parenthesis in the text is mine; all weights and measures, except where otherwise noted, are those of our day.

THEY GAVE AWAY SECRETS AND KEPT THEM TOO—The amusing and also amazing attitude of many nineteenth-century housewives who were recipe writers is that of wanting to reveal their culinary secrets and keep them too. They accomplished this by giving only sketchy descriptions of quantities and procedures, as demonstrated in the following recipe from the treasures of a Mrs. Houghteling:

1

VEAL PIE— Take 2 or 3 pounds of lean veal, a couple of slices of salt pork chopped fine, 1 coffee cup of bread crumbs, 2 eggs, salt, pepper and herbs to taste; mix thoroughly and bake; use cold as a relish.

Another gem, chockful of misguidance, was contributed by Mrs. Anna Marble in the form of a receipt for:

PICKLED ONIONS—Peel your onions and let them lie in a weak brine made of salt and water over night; then put them in a jar; cover them with boiling white wine and vinegar. Cover close and tie down when cold.

Other recipe writers, such as a certain Mrs. Oswald M. Parker, held that such fiddle-faddle as giving exact quantities of ingredients was a lot of highfaluting nonsense. A strong exponent of the "by guess and by gosh" method of culinary artistry, Mrs. Parker wrote: "By practicing the same recipes carefully, the procedures will fix themselves in your mind, so that success is certain. In making pies, for instance, one very heaping handful of flour will make a common-sized pie; not, however, allowing for the flour to be used in rolling the paste. When a woman with an average-sized hand dips it into a flour barrel and comes up with a heaping handful, the amount usually equals ½ pint; contrarily, a small hand will hold only about 1½ gills (¾ cup)."

With recipe guidance as flimsy as that to lean on, a newly hatched housekeeper had no place to send her husband but back home to Mother's cooking. Her only alternative was to steel herself to attend the cooking school of bitter experience. There was no royal road to kitchen expertise; only the rutty and rocky one of trial and error. To be sure, once women reached the secure haven reserved only for good cooks, they looked down their noses at the unchosen and untrained many.

Having, so to speak, put things in their proper place and perspective, let us turn to the bill of fare. Even a cursory glance will reveal that there is little there to tickle the jaded palate of the gourmet. On the other hand, the dishes—though plain—had nose- as well as taste-appeal and united in forming that feat of fattening plenty which came to be known as "a square meal."

But first, an important message about the culinary assembly line.

WEIGHTS AND MEASURES (1800s–1900s)—Always use the graduated 8-ounce measuring cup whenever the word "cup" is used, except where the small teacup (4 ounce) and small coffee cup (6 ounce) are specified. The mark *** means the item is no longer commonly used as a measure.

1 pennyweight***=	1/20 ounce	16 tablespoons=	1 cup
1 drachm***=	1/8 ounce	1 cup=	½ pint
1 small pinch=	1/16 teaspoon	1 small coffee cup***=	¾ cup
1 large pinch=	1/8 teaspoon	1 large teacup***=	1 cup
1 saltspoon***=	¼ teaspoon	1 small teacup***=	½ cup
4 saltspoons***=	1 teaspoon	1 wineglass***=	¼ cup
3 teaspoons=	1 tablespoon	1 tumbler***=	1 cup
1 dessertspoon***=	2 teaspoons	1 pint=	½ quart
4 tablespoons=	¼ cup	4 quarts=	1 gallon
		1 gill***=	½ cup

SEASONINGS AND FLAVORINGS —The standard measurement of these changed from ounces to tablespoons in the late 1800s.

1 ounce allspice, powdered=	4½ tablespoons
1 ounce almond extract=	2 tablespoons
1 ounce cinnamon, powdered=	4½ tablespoons
1 ounce cloves, powdered=	4 tablespoons (¼ cup)
1 ounce curry, powdered=	4½ tablespoons
1 ounce ginger, powdered=	5 tablespoons
1 ounce lemon juice=	2 tablespoons
2 to 3 lemons, juice of=	8 tablespoons (½ cup)
1 lemon, rind of, grated=	4 tablespoons (¼ cup)
1 ounce mustard, powdered=	4½ tablespoons
1 ounce mustard, prepared=	4 tablespoons (¼ cup)
1 ounce nutmeg, powdered=	3½ tablespoons
1 ounce orange juice=	2 tablespoons
3 oranges, average, juice of=	16 tablespoons (1 cup)
1 orange, rind of, grated=	4 tablespoons (¼ cup)
1 ounce paprika, powdered=	4½ tablespoons
3 ounces parsley, minced or chopped=	16 tablespoons (1 cup)
1 ounce pepper, ground=	3½ tablespoons
1 ounce sage, powdered=	3 tablespoons
1 ounce salt (table), powdered=	2 tablespoons
1 ounce vanilla extract=	2 tablespoons

NEVER SPARE THE PARSLEY (mid-1800s)—Of all seasonings that lend flavor to dishes that stretch from soup to sauce to salad, parsley leads the procession. It not only gives zest and flavor to foods, but it is also good for the nerves, helps sufferers from rheumatism and sits well on the stomach. Use it in as many dishes as you can and as often as possible. Our forefathers held it in high regard.*

EGG AND BUTTER EQUIVALENTS (mid-1800s)—

1 egg, raw=	3 tablespoons
10 eggs, raw=	14–16 ounces or 1 pint
18 egg whites, raw=	14–16 ounces or 1 pint
24 egg yolks, raw=	14–16 ounces or 1 pint
10 eggs, hard-cooked, chopped=	1-1/3 pints (2-2/3 cups)
1 teaspoon butter=	1/6 ounce
1 tablespoon butter=	½ ounce
½ pound butter=	½ pint (1 cup)
Butter the size of a filbert=	1 teaspoon, rounded
Butter the size of a hazelnut=	1 teaspoon, rounded
Butter the size of a butternut=	1 dessertspoon, rounded
Butter the size of a walnut (English)=	1 tablespoon, rounded
Butter the size of a pullet's egg=	1½ ounces
Butter the size of a hen's egg=	2 ounces

EQUIVALENTS OF STAPLE ITEMS (late 1800s)—

1 ounce baking powder=	2½ tablespoons
1 pound beans, uncooked=	2½ cups
1 pound beans, cooked=	1½ quarts
¼ pound bread crumbs, white, fresh=	2 cups
1 pound cabbage, shredded or chopped=	4 cups
1 pound carrots, cooked and diced=	3 cups
½ pound celery, raw and diced=	2 cups
½ pound cheese, grated=	2 cups
2 pounds chicken, cooked, cubed or minced=	¾ quart (3 cups)
1 ounce chocolate, grated=	¼ cup
1 quart clams, average to small=	50 to 100
1 quart clams, large=	25 to 50
1 pound coconut, fresh, shredded=	1¾ quarts (7 cups)
1 pound coffee, coarse-ground=	4¾ cups
1 pound coffee, fine-ground=	4½ cups
1 pound cornmeal=	3 cups
1 ounce cornstarch=	3 tablespoons
1 pound cranberries, raw or cooked=	4 cups
1 ounce cream of tartar=	3 tablespoons
1 pound flour (wheat)=	1 quart (4 cups)
1 ounce horse-radish, shredded=	2 tablespoons
1 pound meat, cooked, chopped=	2 cups
½ pound mushrooms, raw, sliced=	3½ cups
½ pound onions, raw, sliced=	1½ cups
1 quart oysters, small=	50 to 100
1 quart oysters, large=	25 to 50
½ pound peas, split, cooked=	2¾ cups
1 pound potatoes, raw, diced=	2½ cups
1 pound potatoes, cooked, mashed=	2 cups
¼ pound rice, cooked=	2 cups
1 pound sugar, white, granulated=	2¼ cups
1 pound sugar, white, powdered=	2-1/3 cups
1 pound sugar, brown=	2¼ cups
1 pound tomatoes, raw, chopped=	2 cups

TESTING OVEN HEATS BY HAND (early and mid-1800s)—Stick one of your hands into the center of a going oven and count the seconds in time with the ticks of your kitchen clock. If the hand feels uncomfortably hot in 12 seconds, the oven is *hot* (450°F.); if the heat is felt at 18, the oven is *quick* (400°F.); if at the count of 24, the oven is *moderate* (350°F.); if at 30 it is *slow* (300°F.); if at 30 or over, it is *low* or merely *warm*.

TESTING OVEN HEATS WITH FLOUR OR PAPER (mid- and late 1800s) —Spread flour over a small pie-plate and place it on the middle rack of the oven; watch the following table of time: If in 3 minutes the flour turns black, the oven is hot (450°F.); if it turns dark brown, the oven is quick (400°F.); if brown as a filbert, the oven is moderate (350°F.); if light brown, the oven is slow (300°F.); if it merely tans, the oven is very slow (250–75°F.) This test can be conducted with a sheet of unglazed white paper also, but do not use a newspaper.

HEATING FAT FOR DEEP FRYING (late 1800s)—Gauge the heat of the fat by dropping a 1-inch cube of stale bread into it. If the cube browns in 35 to 45 seconds, the fat is hot (380°F.), as required for crullers, doughnuts, asparagus, cauliflower and some potatoes; when the cube browns in 55 to 60 seconds, the fat is about 375°F. and right for fin fish, fritters and croquettes; when the cube shows color in 65 to 70 seconds, the fat is ready for shellfish, oysters, breaded meats, French toast, onions.

HOW TO SAVE DEEP-FRYING FAT (late 1800s)—All but fat used for fish can be used again if you treat it by the following method: Put a layer of muslin in a strainer and sieve the fat while it is still hot; pour strained fat back into cleaned kettle and reheat it until a bread cube browns in 70 seconds (350°F); put a large, raw, peeled and sliced potato in the fat; remove it when a light brown. This clarifies the fat and removes all traces of taste and smell—except those of fish.

2. *A Roast Is a Roast Is a Roast*

GRANDMOTHER WAS A BEEFEATER—"Heavens to Betsy!" exclaimed Grandmother Lyon with a note of exasperation. "What is the world coming to when they serve up a slice of *Baked Meat* and call it *Roast Beef!*"

As she spoke, an angry glint flashed from her usually serene pansy-brown eyes. But it vanished in a fraction of a second and her world was at peace again. She motioned to the waiter to remove our plates and smiled pleasantly. I noticed with interest that, despite the outbreak, Bella Lyon's plate had been polished as clean as my own. Not a shred of the offending meat remained upon it. Just a touch of old New England—"waste not, want not."

We were having lunch in the sedately ornate dining room of the old and long-departed Adams House on Boston's Washington Street, part of a regular Saturday routine that started with shopping, was broken by lunch and ended at a movie. As we waited for Henry—a white-haired veteran on the hotel's dining-room staff—to bring Grandmother's coffee and my dessert, she continued on the subject of Roast Beef.

"The trouble is," she was saying, "that nowadays they bake beef in ovens everywhere instead of doing it to a turn on a spit. And that's no way to roast a roast. Baked Beef—bah! The only one I know who does a roast the *right way*—on a spit—is your Great-Aunt Ville's Mary down in Portland. There's a *real* cook!"

A dreamy look came into Grandmother's eyes as she made a quick mental journey to Aunt Ville, who had an old-fashioned pride in setting a wonderful table. I have since concluded that it was Mary's cooking rather than Aunt Ville's company that lured Grandmother on summer visits to Portland. Despite my tender years, I, too, regarded meals at Aunt Ville's as very special occasions.

"This summer, when school is out," said Grandmother suddenly, "I'll ask your parents if I can take you to Portland. I want to show you, myself, how a roast is done on a spit. I was no older than you are now when your Great-Grandmother Chapin taught me how to spit a roast, how to flour, baste and froth it."

True to her promise, when Girl's Latin School closed for the summer a few weeks later, Grandmother and I went to visit Aunt Ville. The number-one item on the agenda was to initiate me into the arts and mysteries of roasting beef on a rotating spit before a bed of glowing coals on the hearth of a kitchen fireplace.

Like Grandmother, a widow, Aunt Ville lived in a venerable mansion-like house that overlooked Casco Bay. She was a cheerful, roly-poly little lady whose kitchen was under the command of Mary, a gaunt, craggy-faced Swiss who had grown old and bossy in Aunt Ville's service. Bella Lyon, probably because of her broad knowledge and deep enjoyment of food, was a privileged character in Mary's kitchen. For reasons I cannot explain, I was also a welcome visitor in Mary's otherwise forbidden precincts.

If I live to be a hundred, I will never forget Mary's kitchen and that particular roast-beef demonstration staged by Grandmother, with Mary as an approving and cooperative assistant.

The kitchen itself, large and light, was made cheerful by potted geraniums in the windows, before which hung gay red and white checkered curtains. In the center of the floor, which was covered by linoleum, stood a deal table, its scoured surface white as snow, as was the woodwork that flanked the kitchen sink with its gleaming copper pipes and brass faucets. On one wall, a big-mouthed, full-throated fireplace held a commanding position. Normally it was covered by a meat-screen, of which more later; but on that day the screen had been moved aside and the grate, the kettle crane and the spits were in full view. A blaze of hardwood fire flickered in the cast-iron grate and a small pile of logs lay on the floor nearby. To the left of the fireplace stood a bake-oven, its cheerful pattern of red bricks and white mortar broken by a big and heavy iron door that shone like patent leather. On the opposite side, a massive wood- and coal-burning kitchen stove gleamed like polished ebony, and its nickel trimmings glittered like silver. A soft rosy glow from the firebox gave proof of a carefully banked fire.

On the wide mantel that ran the length of the fireplace stood a steadily ticking kitchen clock, whose pendulum swung with a steady beat. On one side of the clock stood an hour glass; on the other a half-hour glass graduated into minutes. I looked at them with interest and my fingers itched to turn them upside down so that the sand would start running.

"Go ahead, set them going," said Mary, with a smile that seemed oddly out of place on her usually morose face. I turned the glasses and two tiny streams of sand began to flow.

Grandmother thumped me on the shoulder and said, "You've heard people say that 'a roast has been done to a turn'?" When I nodded, she told me:

HOW A ROAST IS DONE TO A TURN (mid-1800s)—A roast is done to a turn at the precise point at which the time taken by even one more turn of the spit will spoil perfection. Next to the quality of the meat and the perfection of the fire, the timing is most important. For tender, rosy-red beef, a roast should be done 16 minutes to the pound; the time set for the roast to be done is the moment when the roast actually goes to the table and not merely the hour set for dinner.*

DESCRIPTION OF ROASTING-SPIT MECHANISM (mid-1800s)—Above the mantel, on brackets that extended from the wall, were rods from which endless chains hung on grooved spools. The spit itself was a long, slim metal dagger which stretched across the fireplace level with the fire; it had a two-pronged sliding skewer for holding the roast in place and rested on one of a series of graduated racks that extended from the wall. Thus the spit could be set at varying distances from the fire. The spit was rotated by the chains that hung from the spools; these, in turn, were driven by a windmill hidden in the chimney and operated by the air that rushed through it. On the hearth, in front of the grate, stood a dripping pan. And that completed the equipment.

Frankly, I felt a little troubled. For the life of me, I could not see how anyone could roast beef with it. Grandmother brought me out of my musings.

"The only time you can get a good rib roast is when you order it for Sunday. We'll have it next Sunday and dinner at 2 o'clock. That means that, allowing for delays, soup and small talk, the roast will be timed and ready to be served 20 minutes past the hour. On the dot, like an express train."

When the roast arrived on Saturday morning, it was found to weigh 12 pounds. At 16 minutes per pound, it would need 3 hours and 12 minutes of roasting time.

"We'll have the roast spitted and the hickory coals at white heat at 11 o'clock Sunday morning," said Grandmother. "That'll leave us just the right time to get the beef greased, floured and in warming position at 8 minutes past."

I wondered what warming the meat could mean, but I found out when I entered the kitchen on Sunday forenoon, eager-eyed and expectant as a bride. Grandmother was there in one of Mary's huge white aprons that folded around her slim figure like a tent, all set to show me. Today, there were no flames flickering from the fire in the grate. There was, instead, a fiercely hot, solid mass of glowing coals which radiated a constant blast of searing heat.

THE BLAZE AS IMPORTANT AS THE BEEF (early 1800s)—Start your fire in good time, so that it will be just right when you have to use it—a bed of white-hot hickory, oak or other hardwood coals. Do not use hemlock or chestnut; they snap. Unless the fire is at fierce heat, you simply bake the beef. Your fire must be long enough to extend at least 3 inches beyond the ends of the beef, or the ends will not cook and brown. One must learn by practice just when a fire reaches its peak and how long it will remain at that stage. Never start roasting over a fresh fire or an old one.

THE USES OF A MEAT-SCREEN (early 1800s)—To save coals from dying into embers too soon, use a meat-screen to hold off drafts and help reflect the heat toward the side of the meat that is away from the coals. It should stand squarely upon the floor and be a foot wider than the fireplace at each end. Four to 5 feet is the average height, and it should be placed a similar distance from the fire. A lot of people put shelves on their meat-screens to warm plates and to keep cooked things, such as vegetables and gravies, hot. Meat-screens can also be employed with advantage out of doors to screen and concentrate fires used in making soap and maple-syrup sugar or washing clothes.***

PREPARING A BEEF FOR ROASTING (early 1800s)—Have the beef at room temperature when you spit it, and never season a roast with salt until it is well browned. Salt draws the juices out of the meat and dries it. Before you lay the beef near the fire, rub it with unsalted grease or butter; dredge it lightly and evenly with flour.*

THE OLD-TIME WAY OF ROASTING (early 1800s)—Start a roast turning before a steady, strong and flame-free fire some 10 to 12 inches from the coals. This gives the heat a chance to enter the meat clear through so that it cooks in its own juices. Baste at 15-minute intervals, preferably with unsalted butter, until there is grease enough in the dripping-pan to serve for basting. Watch your beef lest juices start to seep out. The timing, as always in roasting, depends upon the heat of the fire and the size of the roast. The moment it begins to sweat move the beef to roasting distance. That usually means within 6 to 8 inches of the fire. Make certain that the meat rotates slowly and evenly. When the roast is half-way done and ready for browning, stir up the coals to freshen the blaze; sprinkle fine salt on the meat and such other seasonings as powdered marjoram. Now bring your beef closer to the fire for browning and baste at 5-minute intervals. Again, the distance from the fire depends upon the heat of your fire and the size of your roast. There is just no way of telling anyone what that distance is. The experienced cook knows her way by the looks of the roast and the feel of the fire on the backs of her hands.**

I watched with interest as Grandmother and Mary guided the roast through its various stages, and even took a hand at basting. Throughout the operation—as the beef turned from raw meat to a lusciously browned roast whose odors filled the kitchen—Bella Lyon ran an almost continuous narrative. Much of it I have forgotten, but some of the vital points registered in my mind forever.

AVOID COOKING A ROAST WITH WATER (mid-1800s)—The practice of pouring water, hot or cold, into basting-pans that go under beef that is being oven-roasted is vile and uncivilized. This method became common in the years that followed the Civil War, when most women, and many writers of cook books, had poor understanding of roasts and ovens. They steamed the poor roasts to death.*

TO FROTH A ROAST THE OLD WAY (early 1800s)—Half an hour before the roast is ready, dredge the beef very evenly and very thinly with flour and baste it lavishly with melted butter. Before a hot fire, this combination raises a fine froth which gives the roast a smooth-as-satin golden-brown finish.*

While Grandmother kept an eye on the roast, Mary put a Yorkshire Pudding together according to a recipe Grandmother had given her. Even as she had decided ideas when it came to roasting beef, so Grandmother took a well-defined stand on the subjects of Yorkshire Puddings and gravies (see also Index). She believed that no beefeater worth his salt would spoil a slice of roast with any kind of sauce or gravy other than that made by the meat's own natural juices. To be sure, she condescended to give Mother Nature a helping hand in producing these juices, and I will have a few hints on that in a moment.

As for Yorkshire Puddings, she maintained that there were many kinds of them and that few were worth eating. She used a formula given by Dr. William Kitchener in his *Cook's Oracle*, published in London in 1827. The book had passed into her possession from Great-Grandmother Chapin's, and she regarded Dr. Kitchener as an infallible culinary oracle and the high priest of beefeaters. Here is the recipe:

YORKSHIRE PUDDING UNDER ROAST MEAT, THE GYPSY'S WAY (early 1800s)—Six tablespoons of flour, 3 eggs, a teaspoon of salt and a pint of milk, so as to make a middling-stiff batter, a little stiffer than you would for pancakes. Beat it up well and take care that it is not lumpy; let it stand for 1 hour. Put a dripping-dish under the meat and let the drippings drop into it until it is quite hot and well greased; then pour in the batter; when the upper surface is brown and set, turn it so that both sides may be browned alike; if you wish it to cut firm and the pudding to be an inch thick, it will take ¾ hour at a good fire. The true Yorkshire Pudding is about ½ inch thick when done. But it is our habit to make them full twice that thickness.* (In a moderate 350° F. oven, 25 minutes under the beef rack to catch the drippings on the pudding—HLA.)

Many years later, when I classified the clippings and notes in Grandmother's boxes of recipes, I came upon a maybe impractical, but certainly unusual, Yorkshire Pudding. I say maybe, because I never got around to trying it. But, for whatever it may be worth, here it is:

RISING YORKSHIRE PUDDING (late 1800s)—An hour before you bake it, blend 4 tablespoons and 1 teaspoon of flour into ⅓ cup of cold milk with ½ saltspoon of salt; drop 2 unbeaten eggs into this mixture and beat thoroughly; let it rest a few moments, then add slowly as you beat vigorously ⅔ cup of cold milk. Just before you pour it into a pan greased with dripping, whip the batter with 4 teaspoons of cold water and a pinch of powdered tarragon. Baking time: about 20 minutes in a moderate 350° F. oven until done.**

After this excursion from that Sunday in Aunt Ville's Mary's kitchen, let us return and find Grandmother in the act of removing the roast from the spit and placing it—brown and fragrant—on a platter.

"At this point," said Grandmother, "I could make a *Meat Gravy,* but I am not going to because I believe that *Platter Juice* is better." However, for those interested in making Meat Gravy from spitted beef, the method follows:

MEAT GRAVY OR SAUCE AU JUS (early 1800s)—When you stand the roast on its platter after the spit has been withdrawn, stick a small funnel into the opening made by the spit. Have a gill (½ cup) of well-salted hot Beef Broth ready; pour it through the funnel slowly and give the soup time to seep through the spit hole and onto the platter. This is a good and quick way to make Meat Gravy.*

PLATTER JUICE FOR ROAST BEEF (early 1800s)—At the table, on the carver's right side, should be a gravy boat well filled with boiling hot water into which ¾ teaspoon of salt has been dissolved. As he cuts a slice of rare and rosy beef and puts it on a platter, the carver ladles 1 tablespoon of this liquid upon each slice. In moments, the saline water will extract a flow of rich, natural juices without damage to the beef.*

Before it becomes too late for me to do so, let me report hastily that that Sunday Roast Beef Dinner at Aunt Ville's was wonderful! I still have vivid recall of every heavenly bite.

THE MAKING OF A NINETEENTH-CENTURY GOURMET—As time went on and the years sped by, Grandmother and I became increasingly closer. She had been denied the blessing of having a sister or a daughter and, since I was the only girl in the family, she always lavished her stored-up knowledge, attentions and affections upon me. We became even closer after Bella sold her house on Woodbine Street. Rena, her faithful housekeeper, and Silas, her coachman and man-of-all-work, died, and she made her home with my parents in their house on Schuyler Street, in Roxbury, a part of Greater Boston.

There, on the second floor, she occupied a living room, a bedroom and bathroom, plus a guest room that had been converted into a fully equipped kitchen where she liked to putter around. Food had always been one of her main interests and she was a full-out gourmet; but in a peculiar, academic sort of way. Her approach to cookery was that of an understanding and inquiring student. However, it was in no way stimulated by a palate that had to be pleased or an appetite that must be satisfied. In fact, beef was the only kind of food—when it came to meats—she was interested in. She had an idea that it met every demand the human body could make in the realm of nutrition.

"There is nothing in the world better than beef to feed your body and brain," she would say. "This new idea that fish is a brain-food—tush! Any kind of beef is better for one than fish, flesh or Rhode Island Reds and that goes for lamb, mutton, veal and pork."

Naturally, there was always a place at our table for Grandmother. All of us—Father, Mother, my Annapolis-bound brothers, Melville and Rupert —adored her and enjoyed the sparkle of her company. However, through close liaison with Hannah, our cook, Grandmother only appeared when beef was for dinner. Otherwise, she fended for herself upstairs in her own kitchen. I well remember the rich and savory odors that would come whiffing down the stairs when Bella was in a cooking mood. In this connection, it must be remembered that Grandmother was brought up at a time when cooking and keeping house were part of a girl's education, when Boston ladies were not only gracious hostesses but kitchen-wise housewives who could show the best "hired cook" in town how to do anything over the coals of a fireplace, the fiery grate of a kitchen range or the closed-in firebox of a cooking-stove.

Grandmother Lyon came of New England ship-owning, seafaring stock. Her father and three brothers went down to the sea in their respective ships and never returned. She was born in Boston in 1848 and was named Isabella Aurelia. In 1866, she married Albert Melville Lyon, owner of a Maine paper mill that had been family property for many generations. Thanks to her training, Bella was fully qualified to take charge of his Boston mansion, as well as of a summer home in Skowhegan, when she became a bride at the age of eighteen years.

That first summer in Skowhegan, Bella acquired a brand-new hobby when she visited Grandfather's paper mill. In those days, thrifty housewives listened for the call of the ragman, to whom they sold castoff clothing and linen. In time, some of those articles found their way to paper mills, including my Grandfather's, where they were transformed into various grades of paper. In the sorting process, all types of buttons were removed and collected. The result was that Grandmother, at Cumberland, discovered a young mountain of buttons—round, square, octagonal, triangular and other shapes; ancient steel-cut buttons and almost equally old ones of hand-painted china —buttons, buttons, buttons, and, presto, Bella had them all.

Little by little she culled a collection any woman might envy, and in those days every woman had a well-cherished button bag. As the decades went by, the collection grew in size and scope. When I was old enough to be intrigued by buttons they were stored in an immense sea-bag, which served as my favorite treasure-trove. For years on end, I found untold delight in arranging yards on yards of beautiful and unusual buttons strung as neatly as if they were strands of pearls. One of the never-to-be-explained mysteries in my life is: what happened to the collection? By the time I was old enough to value its worth truly, the button bag had vanished—gone—buttons, buttons, buttons, who had Bella's buttons? To this day neither I nor any member of my family knows the answer.

But let us return to the 1860s, when Grandmother had to be more than a bride with a penchant for pretty buttons. There were household duties to perform, but she was equal to them. From the time Bella was old enough, her mother had made cook and household books parts of her routine reading. In addition, she spent hours each day in the kitchen and at other kinds of housework. Looking back over the years, she could remember when nearly all cooking was done over the open fireplace and when the first stoves and ranges appeared in Boston from England. When one looks into the matter it becomes immediately clear that English kitchens and cookery exerted great influence in Boston and New England from earliest Colonial times until far into the nineteenth century. This is proven by numerous English cook books used by Great-Grandmother Chapin, and Bella too. Other influences upon Boston cooking were the strange foodstuffs, fruits, flavorings, wines and spices—plus ideas about how to use them—that were brought home by Yankee vessels from far-off ports.

As a matter of fact, these directions on their use were vitally important. Grandmother told me about a stove brought back from London before she was born. It was the pride, but an unproductive one, of her mother's kitchen. The trouble was that no one knew how to cook on it. The situation was not corrected until the captain made another passage to England and returned with cook books adapted to the use of ranges. When Grandmother became head of her own household, kitchen stoves, in the East at least, were in common use. Always interested in subjects that applied to home management and cookery, she treasured cook books and recipes collected by her mother and as the years went on, kept the collection up to date by the purchase of new cook books and by clipping items of interest to housewives from American and English periodicals and newspapers. Thus, by the end of the 1800s, she had a line-up of household, kitchen and cookery hints that covered the entire century. These were not only useful and/or interesting, but they also reflected the changes brought about in American kitchens by radical, dramatic and even painful evolutions in the nation's kitchen equipment and cookery procedures.

The helpful hints in those old books ran all the way from setting tables, entertaining guests, carving, and etiquette for folding linen napkins, to cookery of all kinds, brewing beer, and concocting a vast variety of catsups and other seasonings for the scads of rich and pungent gravies and sauces which were so popular in the early 1800s. Proof that eating for the sake of eating ranked high in those days in affluent circles is found in receipts associated with eating but not with cookery. In this chapter we have taken quite a few steps down Memory Lane away from the straight and narrow storyline, so why not take a few more of them here—or it could be that I just feel a recipe or two coming on? The three I have in mind express concern for Gourmets, Gastronomers and Grand Gourmands whose gustatory processes and digestive slumbers are disturbed by aching teeth or stomach aches.

TOOTHACHE EMBROCATION (early 1800s)—In no branch of the practice of Physic, is there more dangerous quackery, than in the dental department. To all, a toothache is an intolerable torment, but what an overcoming agony it must be to a Grand Gourmand when a toothache deprives him of food, the grand solace for all his sublunary cares. When this affliction befalls him, the following specific is recommended: R. Sal volatile, 3 parts; laudanum, 1 part; mix and apply.***

STOMACHIC TINCTURE (early 1800s)—Let 1½ ounces of bruised Peruvian bark and 1 ounce of orange peel, mashed, steep for 10 days in 1 pint of brandy. Shake the bottle daily for 8 days, let it remain quiet 2 days, then decant the clear liquor. A teaspoonful in a wineglass of water is to be taken twice daily before meals. This agreeable tonic is an effective help to concoction and restores stomachs to good Temper, good Appetites and good Digestion.***

PAREGORIC ELIXIR IN TEWAHDIDDLE (early 1800s)—Steep a drachm each of purified opium, flowers of Benjamin and oil of aniseed with 2 scruples of camphor in 1 pint of brandy; let it stand 10 days, shake occasionally and strain. Take a teaspoonful at night in a Tewahdiddle, which you make as a regular "night cap" by mixing a tablespoonful of good brandy, a teaspoonful of brown sugar and a pinch of nutmeg into a pint of ale or beer. The elixir, itself, is good for children when given in doses of from 5 to 20 drops on a bit of sugar.***

One volume proudly announced that every reader, by using the wisdom spread upon its pages, would become a veritable *Magnus Coquus,* or Master Kitchener, and thus join the ranks of the High and Mighty Masters of the Alimentary Art. One will notice that most of these books were written by men, although nearly all kitchen mechanics were women. Maybe the redoubtable Dr. Samuel Johnson—whom Boswell describes as "a man of very nice discernment in the science of cookery"—spoke for the era when he said: "Women can spin very well,—but they cannot make a good book of cookery."

Since neither a recipe nor Rome was built in a day, it is quite likely that many of the household books of the early 1800s reflect kitchen practices that date back to the eighteenth century. After all, there were no truly sweeping changes in food preparation while the fireplace, and its open fire, held undisputed sway in the kitchen. With her mother's old books to build on, Bella Lyon extended the collection during her lifetime so that it reached into the early days of the twentieth century. It is timely here to refer to the clippings Grandmother collected from newspapers and periodicals when these mediums of communication began to extend their reading appeal to housewives. Besides recipes of all sorts, they offer a wide array of information that reveals the struggles that faced the wives of the early settlers in turning out even the simplest of meals or in performing the most fundamental of household tasks. That was when the New England maxim "eat it up, wear it out; make it do, or do without" really was born, as was the know-how, show-how and do-how of Yankee wives.

It is, alas, impossible to list the sources of these clippings. Some are from the very earliest of American and English publications devoted to the affairs of housewives, such as *Godey's Lady's Book* and *The Family Friend*, plus numerous American publications. Yes, Grandmother was a dyed-in-the-wool clip-tomaniac.

As for Grandmother's books, while they are representative of cook and household books of the entire nineteenth century, they do not by any means constitute a complete collection. For instance, I regret that they do not include Amelia Simmons' book *American Cookery*. Published in Hartford, Connecticut, in 1796, it was actually the first American cook book, and please note that it was written by a woman, despite Sam Johnson's pessimistic attitude some years earlier. The author, quaintly, identifies herself as "an American orphan." Having seen it, I can testify that the book lives up to the tone of quaintness established by this introduction of its author.

While I was working on *Grandmother's Household Hints*, a friend of mine sent me a Syllabub recipe from *American Cookery*. I give it here because it demonstrates the rustic simplicity, or tongue-in-cheekness, of this perhaps not so simple Simmons:

SYLLABUB FROM THE COW (pre-1800s)—Sweeten a quarter of cyder with double-refined sugar, grate nutmeg into it, then milk your cow into the liquor; when you have thus added what quantity of milk you think proper, pour ½ pint or more, in proportion to the quantity of Syllabub you make, of the sweetest cream you can get, all over it.***

Since it is not always easy for a modern housewife to reach for a milch cow when a Sillabub or Syllabub mood sweeps upon her, here is one more representative of a type of refreshment which, in its day, enjoyed great popularity on both sides of the ocean. Actually, it was not a drink but a curd-like dish generally served as a dessert. Here is one worth trying:

SHERRY OR CIDER SILLABUB (early 1800s)—Pour 1 pint of good, dry sherry into a bowl; add ½ nutmeg, grated, and pounded sugar to taste; froth 1½ pints of milk by beating it. The milk may be warm or cold, but it should always be poured with a circular motion of the hand, not in a straight stream, from a spouted jug or teapot held very high. If cider is used instead of wine, use 3 gills (1½ cups) of cider and 1 gill (½ cup) of brandy. Whipped cream may be laid on top, with powdered cinnamon or nutmeg and sugar. Flavoring the cream with a bit of brandy also helps.*

But here I go again, meandering. Still, it is awfully difficult to follow a straight and narrow course when one succumbs to the temptation of reading through those venerable recipes. And yet, follow the path one must, so I will swing back to the subject of the book sources of recipes.

Early 1800s: *Cook's Oracle* by Dr. William Kitchener; *The Housewife's Directory* by John Edward Watson; *Common-Sense Housekeeping* by Phyllis Browne; *The Housekeeper's Oracle* by Dr. William Kitchener; *Bills of Fare* by Isabella Beeton; *Essays* by Count Rumford, on ranges and cooking.

Mid-1800s: *Home and Its Duties* by J. W. Laurie; *The Practical Housewife* by the Editors of *Family Friend; The Boston Kitchen School Text Book* by Mrs. D. A. Lincoln; *The American Woman's Home* by Catherine E. Beecher and Harriet Beecher Stowe; *The Young Housekeeper's Friend* by Mrs. M. H. Cornelius; *The Home Cook Book* by J. F. Waggoner; *The Model Housekeeper* by Ross Murray; Ward & Lock's *Home Book;* Parks and Webster's *Encyclopedia of Domestic Economy.*

Late 1800s: *Maria W. Howard's Cook Book; Practical Recipes* by R. A. Beal; *Cooking Recipes* compiled by the Young Ladies' Cooking Club of Skowhegan, Maine; *Domestic Life and Affairs* by Delia McNair Wright; *Practical Housekeeping*, a publication devoted to home management.

LUNCHING WITH GRANDMOTHER WAS FUN—Grandmother Lyon not only had a memory like a bear trap but was well informed, observant and fluent on all things that dealt with the economics of and practices related to housekeeping. She was fun to listen to, fun to be with; I admired and adored her and my principal wish was to be exactly like her when I grew up. To me, those Saturday trips to town were gala occasions. I loved to walk with her and always tried to keep my back as straight as hers. Although Grandmother was a slim and tiny little lady she seemed taller than she was because she held herself as erect as a grenadier, and there were drum beats in the firm steps of her small feet. At all times, she was dressed in the regimentals of a Boston dowager—practical black shoes; black garments, conservatively cut, well made and of materials guaranteed to outlast Methuselah; a black hat, equally timeless, set squarely on the top of her head. The few ornaments she wore were either cameo or jet, trimmed with gold. A small watch, suspended from a black ribbon, hung over her heart.

What with the healthy appetite of a growing girl, to me the peak of the Boston trip was always reached at lunchtime, when we entered the dining room of the Adams House, Hotel Touraine or Parker House. I had whatever my heart desired, but Grandmother always ordered beef in one form or another, and took Roast Beef only when no other form of beef was available. To me she always was as much of a Beefeater as the famous warders of the Tower of London. On rare—but only on very rare—occasions Bella would have a yen for Chicken Pie. But she ate this dish only at Thompson's Spa on Washington Street, famous for that item. Usually, like Mary's little lamb, wherever Bella went, recipes were sure to follow. Not so at Thompson's Spa. But she compensated for this defeat by acquiring the recipe for Aunt Ville's Mary's own Chicken Pie, which, I am certain, would set the mouth of even the most addicted Beefeater drooling. My, it was good! Try it sometimes, particularly in the merry month of May (for other chicken pies, see Index).

SPRING GARDEN CHICKEN PIE (late 1800s)—Have as many 2½-pound broilers as you may need, kitchen-ready, and count on half a broiler per person. Place the halved chickens in a large pot, cover with water and let them simmer slowly, covered, for about 1 hour or until done. Remove the birds from the liquid, skin them and set them aside. Toss the skins into the pot liquor and for each serving boil in this liquor, unpeeled, 3 tiny new potatoes, 3 tiny new onions (or the small white bulbs of scallions), 3 tiny young carrots. When they are cooked, peel the potatoes and onions, but do not cut the roots of the onions too close or they will separate. Scrape and rub the carrots with a rough cloth, but do not peel them. Set the vegetables aside and simmer the liquid down to 1½ cups.

Make a gravy by rubbing 3 tablespoons of flour into 3 tablespoons of melted butter in a large skillet; add the pot liquor slowly and rub out the lumps. Add a tablespoon per serving of tender new peas and of paper-thin slices of raw mushroom (do not use the mushroom stems), plus 4 ounces of good, dry sherry, 2 coarsely chopped 10-minute eggs, a small whisk of parsley and a fragment of a bay leaf. As the gravy heats, add cream to suit if it is too thick. It should have the consistency of good cream. Season to taste with white pepper, salt and a small dash of powdered sage. After simmering for 10 minutes to kill the flour taste and to blend the flavors, remove the bay leaf and parsley and set the gravy aside. Make a good short pie crust (see Index) that will fill the circumference of your chicken-pie pan top and bottom. Do not grease the pan.

Put the bottom crust into the pan and bounce the pan lightly against the table so that the crust will settle into the bottom, leaving no air holes. To make the crust moisture-resistant, paint it with the white of an egg slightly stirred with a fork, not beaten. Arrange chickens and vegetables in layers and spoon some gravy over each layer. As you do this, be sure to stir the gravy, to prevent the peas and mushrooms from settling on the bottom. As a final touch, pour the remaining gravy over the lot.

Remember, the filling must be slightly higher in the center and slope toward the edges of the pan. The reason for this is that the top crust must rest on a solid base or it will become soggy. In fact it is a good idea to paint the underside of the top crust, as well as the bottom crust, with white of egg to make it resist moisture. This pie can be made richer by mixing and adding the boiled, mashed chicken livers with 1 tablespoon of chicken dressing for each liver (for Chicken Dressing, see Index). Cut steam vents in the crust and bake in a moderate to hot (400°F.) oven for about 15 minutes or until brown.*

One thing that always used to set me wondering about Grandmother's collection of clippings—they ran from long articles to short recipes—was its contradiction of Bella's firm and active sense of order and system. To keep them in shoe boxes was to me—a frustrated librarian—a most unmethodical way of treating them. However, when I offered to sort the material out and paste it up, Bella's answer was that she knew exactly where to find what she wanted. To tell the truth, the way she could reach unerringly for whatever she wanted in those boxes was most uncanny. Years later, when my Grandmother's health was failing, she gave me her books and boxes of recipes with perfect freedom to arrange them as I liked. Somehow, I never had the heart to do that; so they have remained heaped up in shoe boxes until now, and it is from those that they emerge like faded visitors from bygone days.

3. Useful or Unique Beef Recipes

LEAVES FROM A BEEFEATER'S BOOK—Although Grandmother made a rule of not sorting or classifying her clippings and notes, there was to this, as to all rules, an exception. In a notebook she had assembled a collection of recipes based upon her favorite food—beef. Some of these are good, some a bit odd, some distinctly off-beat. She had a cute way of using astericks to classify them and I have followed that method here. Most of the recipes in this book close with astericks that serve as a means of classification. Thus, * means practical and acceptable; ** probably practical but needs adjustment; *** impractical, obsolete but interesting and/or amusing. Also, all comments, notations and observations in parenthesis, including oven temperatures, are mine.

When viewed as a whole, the ** and *** classifications reflect changes in food acceptance from one generation to other generations. Dishes which at one time—and not too long ago, at that—were consumed with acclamation, today are rejected as abominations. Oddities also were introduced, especially in early nineteenth-century cook books. Many of these were written by penny-a-line hacks who did not know a Rabbit Stew from a harelip and dreamed up their formulas. In the mid-1800s—when the change from fireplaces to kitchen ranges and cooking-stoves finally blew long-cherished mother-to-daughter recipes into limbo—many housewives permitted their new recipes to be published in books, periodicals and newspapers, usually for a few pieces of silver. The trouble was that many of these women were so proud of their personal culinary skills that they falsified their recipes just a little to prevent other women from being able to prepare dishes as appealingly as they did. In fact, it can be said that not until the end of the nineteenth century did factual integrity prevail in the publication of cooking and baking recipes offered by lay contributors.

After this short but necessary explanation, I will settle down to the very pleasant task of presenting some random selections from Grandmother's beef book. Other beef recipes will be found under Meats. The one I tee off with is truly what in journalese would be called a scoop. It is the only recipe for a one-man roast of beef that I have ever seen. It does, I believe, fill a very real need in families of two—or in the lives of singletons—to whom a regular cut of rib roast is too much meat to dispose of:

ONE-RIB ROAST OF BEEF (late 1800s)—Buy a 1-rib cut that weighs about 2½ pounds; trim away surplus fat; wipe it dry and then rub with lard or butter; season with a pinch of sage or marjoram and dust lightly all around with flour from a sifter. Heat the oven to low (250°F.); put the meat on a rack over the stripping-pan and place it in the oven to warm it through to the bone. After 5 minutes, raise the heat to moderate (350°F.). Baste every 5 minutes as it roasts at this temperature; 30 minutes for rare, 40 minutes for medium, 50 minutes for well done. Now salt the meat on both sides; baste it with melted butter and an ever so thin flurry of sifted flour. Raise the heat to very hot (475°F.), so that flour and butter will form a froth that turns into a brown glaze.* (For Platter Juice, see Index.)

As readers will notice, this was actually Grandmother's adjustment to roasting beef in an oven in the way she used to roast it before a fire and on a spit—first warming, then roasting, lastly browning. To use modern methods, reverse the procedure and roast beef in a 350°F. oven 15 minutes for rare, 18 minutes for medium and 23 minutes for well done, per pound. Omit the flour, but baste often. Save the drippings in the pan. In the foregoing, as in many of the beef recipes that follow, Grandmother's method—of never salting beef while it is still uncooked for fear of drying it—is followed; however, I urge the reader to heed his or her own dictates in that connection.

WINE-CRUMB SAUCE FOR ROASTS (pre-1800s)—Heat slowly together 1½ gills (¾ cup) of red wine and 1 tablespoon each of vinegar, molasses and butter thickened with ¼ pint (½ cup) of white crumbs from fresh bread; season with 1 saltspoon (¼ teaspoon) of cinnamon and ditto of ginger. Goes well with nearly any kind of roasted meat or game.*

If one wishes, a Yorkshire Pudding (see Index) can be baked under the roast if it is started early enough. Those who dread waste—and it takes quite a few helpings to dispose of a whole Yorkshire—may be interested in the following small pudding which was also one of Bella Lyon's favorites:

POTATO YORKSHIRE PUDDING (late 1800s)—Moisten a pint or so of cold, cooked, peeled and sliced potatoes with a little cold milk and give them a good shaking in a grocery bag into which you have put a little powdered thyme or grated nutmeg, salt, pepper and a ¼ cup of flour. The idea is to produce a coating of seasonings on the potato slices. Mince enough onion to fill ½ cup and cook it—together with the potatoes—in ½ pint of good milk until the potatoes are hot but not mushy. Now, whip the potatoes solid and creamy with as much onion-milk as you need. Don't use butter; it is apt to make them heavy. Instead, add 2 well-beaten egg yolks and the shipped white of 1 egg. These make the pudding rise and eat light. Pour the mixture onto a greased pan and put it into the oven under the beef so that it catches the drippings. When the top is brown, drain the excess fat away. This is a satisfying dish for one-woman cookery; make patties of what is left and have them with Roast Beef Hash, which follows. (For note on waxy and mealy potatoes, see Index.)*

TO HASH BEEF AND MAKE GRAVY (early 1800s)—Mince the rarest portions of left-over roast of beef so fine that the pieces are almost as short and thin as pine needles. To do this, cut the slices thin with a knife so sharp that it will split a hair. Next, cut these slices thin as ribbons and slice these ribbons of meat so that they become mere threads. Chop these into inch-long bits and you have the foundation of a masterly hash. Cook in very little butter until tender about 4 tablespoons (¼ cup) of sliced mushrooms and of sliced onions per ½ pint (1 cup) of meat; then pour this mixture into whatever heated platter juice or gravy you have left from Sunday's roast. If you need more moisture—but you never need much because the hash must not be wet—dissolve ¼ teaspoon of arrowroot in 1 tablespoon of cold water and let it thicken over the fire in 2 ounces of water, milk or broth; when it is ready, blend it into the onions and mushrooms. These are added to the beef, with salt and pepper to taste. Shape the mixture into a cake the size of your skillet.

Now heat 1 tablespoon of butter or drippings in the skillet and when it is good and hot lay the meat into it. Let it lie until the bottom is brown, but do not let the hash get more than pleasantly warm. If the hash is cooked and starts to steam, the beef sheds its freshness and flavor. It is fashionable to top each serving of this dish with a fried egg.*

BEEF PALATES (pre-1800s)—Take ½ dozen beef palates, soak them in cold water, rub them with salt and let them simmer in water for a few minutes that the external skin may be removed; then divide them into convenient portions. Blend in a stew-pan some butter and flour and moisten this with beef gravy or good soup stock; when this mixture is of proper thickness—like thin porridge—let the pieces of palate stew slowly in it until tender. Season with fine salt and good, fresh pepper.***

BEEF STEAKS THE LONDON WAY (early 1800s)—Those who are nice about steaks never attempt to have them broiled except at seasons when the meat can be hung until it is tender, that is, from late fall to early spring. The best beef steaks are those cut from the middle of a rump of an ox that has been hung at least 4 days in moderately cold weather, much longer in really cold weather; otherwise the meat does not age properly and sometimes not at all. The steaks should be cut about 6 inches long, 4 inches wide and ½ inch thick. Do not salt them and do not beat them with a meat hammer, which vulgar trick breaks the cells in which the meat juices are contained, and the steaks become dry and tasteless. However, if your butcher sends meat that is not tender, do not object to him being beaten. Also browbeat him into giving you cuts of equal size and thickness. Take care to have a new, clear and brisk fire under a red-hot gridiron; put into a good amount of butter cooking slowly in a dish-pan before the blaze enough minced parsley and shallots (or spring onions, known also as scallions) to allow a heaping tablespoon for each steak. While they are cooking, turn the steaks almost constantly with a pair of meat tongs (no forks allowed) for 6 to 8 minutes, when the steaks should be done unless you favor them very rare or well done. Spoon the butter, parsley and onion combination over each steak as it goes to the table.***

The following dish of yams or sweet potatoes offers a quite unusual touch and fits in well with Beef Steaks as given above.

RUM AND YAM RAISED PUDDING (late 1800s)—Heat ½ cup of cream with ¼ cup of dark Jamaica rum and 3 tablespoons of butter. Whip this into 2 cups of mashed yams or sweet potatoes over a low fire. Let it cool. Beat 3 egg yolks; add a squirt of lemon juice, large pinches of table salt and grated nutmeg, small pinches of powdered ginger and pepper; blend all these items in a saucepan; set the saucepan in boiling water and keep stirring the mixture until 5 minutes after it has become hot. Remove it from the heat and let it cool for 10 minutes. After this well-earned pause, whip the whites of 5 eggs; when they start to peak but still droop, they are just right, for the whites should not be too stiff and dry. Fold the whites carefully into the mixture so as to preserve their "lift." Have your oven at a moderate heat (350°F.); pour the pudding into a 1½-quart greased bake-dish and let it stay in the oven exactly 40 minutes. (If done right, this dish will be all puffed up and brown as a berry when you serve it.)*

ROASTED OX-TONGUE (early 1800s)—Parboil a tongue that has been salted only about 10 days; roast it before a fairly soft fire (or in a 325°F. oven) so that the outside does not get too well done before the tongue is cooked right through. Baste it with butter, a little ginger and red wine. Peel it and serve it with a sauce made from left-over bastings, minced parsley and stoned raisins. Tongue is best when sliced very thin and served with boiled and chopped spinach. The latter may be made more interesting by adding chopped watercress, cream sauce, chopped hard-boiled eggs, nutmeg, salt and pepper.*

COLD ROAST BEEF OR STEAK WITH MASHED POTATOES (mid-1800s) —Blend the yolks of 2 eggs, 2 tablespoons of melted butter and ½ teaspoon of salt into 1 pint (2 cups) of cold mashed potatoes with ½ gill (¼ cup) of warm milk. Lay thinly sliced meat, the rarer the better, in the bottom of a greased baking pan; sprinkle some thin quartered and parted onion slices over the meat, also pepper, salt and a slight touch of rosemary. Add some meat gravy if on hand; if not, use a tablespoon or 2 of soup stock or melted beef drippings. Cover the whole with a crust of the potato mixture; score the potato into squares and dribble some butter or beef drippings over it. Bake uncovered for ½ hour in an old-fashioned Dutch Oven (see Index) at baking distance from a good fire, or in a moderate (350°F.) cooking-stove oven.*

HOW TO MAKE TOUGH STEAKS TENDER (early 1800s)—If you suspect steaks of being tough—especially during months when it is too warm for meat to hang—soak them in ½ pint of red wine wherein a blade or 2 of mace, 2 mashed cloves, 2 large anchovies, a small sliced onion, a chipped celery stalk, a few sprigs of parsley and a bay leaf are swimming. Let the steaks bask in this bath for 1½ to 2 hours.*

GOOD WAY TO COOK TENDERIZED STEAKS (early 1800s)—Put the wine mixture given above and the steaks into a large stew-pan and cover with a good tight lid. When the mixture boils, remove the pan to a place where it will simmer gently. From here on, it must not boil. Skim when necessary and add a little more wine if called for. After an hour, test the steaks for tenderness. If they show promise of becoming ready, add 2 wal-nut-sized balls of butter (1 tablespoon) into each of which a heaping table-spoon of flour has been blended. Stir this into the beef liquid until it is smooth and thick. Replace the lid and let the steaks simmer until they can be cut by the dullest of knives. If before serving you will add a measure of great Cape Cod oysters, this good steak stew will become even better. Decorate with fingers of sweet and sour pickles.*

TO TAME A TOUGH PIECE OF BEEF (mid-1800s)—Braising is the best method of handling inexpensive and less tender cuts of beef. For a 6-pound piece of such meat, dice ½ pint (1 cup) of salt pork and try it out in your stew-kettle—be sure it has a solid, well-fitting lid. While the pork is frying, prepare ½ pint (1 cup) each of chopped turnips, carrots, onions and celery and toss them into the pot. Season the meat with pepper and nutmeg, dredge in flour and put it in the pot on top of the vegetables. Cover and cook for 20 minutes. Then add 1 quart (4 cups) of hot water and cook all slowly about 4 hours. The meat should be turned occasionally and the liquid in the pot should never be less than 1½ pints (3 cups), so add hot water if needed. After 3½ hours of cooking, add a thickening made by blending 4 tablespoons (¼ cup) of flour into 3 tablespoons of drippings or butter.*

ROASTED COW'S UDDER (pre-1800s)—This, for those who deem it a delicacy, is usually served with an ox-tongue that has been pickled about 3 days. They are parboiled together, the udder stuffed with parsley. After parboiling, the parsley is removed; the udder is stuck thick all over with cloves and tied to the tongue; they are spitted together and basted with butter while browning.***

MEDALLIONS OF BEEF WITH OYSTERS (late 1800s)—Have as many slices as you may require cut 2 inches thick from the top of a filet of beef. Shape them into circles by beating them lightly with the edge of a plate; brown on both sides in butter over high heat and turn constantly with meat tongs 6 to 8 minutes. Place the medallions on a hot earthenware platter; sprinkle with salt and pepper, coat with melted butter and chopped chives, cover with small pyramids of raw, well-drained oysters and bake in a hot oven (425°F.) during a few watchful moments until the oysters curl around their edges.*

CABIN BEEF STEW OR QUARTERDECK LOBSCOVS (early 1800s)—Trim away most of the meat left on a roasted joint of beef but leave some on the bones. For 4 persons (with seagoing appetites), chop enough meat, quite coarsely, to fill a quart (4 cups) measure. Crack the beef bones, put them into a pot and add 2 or 3 very small fragments of bay leaf. Pour in enough boiling water to cover this. Next, add the following: 8 pieces of very lean parboiled salted pork diced into 2-inch squares, 1½ pints (3 cups) of peeled and quartered raw potatoes, ¾ pint (1½ cups) of raw onions, also peeled and quartered. Let this cook slowly and skim often. When the meat has cooked off the bones and—with the other items—has been incorporated with the liquid and become a lumpy mush, fish out the bones and bits of bay leaf; add the chopped beef gently, so that the lumps in the dish are not broken. Let it warm slowly. Just before the Lobscovs goes aft, galley cooks sprinkle it with minced parsley.*

BOSTON BOILED BEEF IN TWO ACTS (early 1800s)—Act One: Sunday dinner. Set enough water to cover a 4-pound cut of lean brisket boiling in a large pot and season it with ¼ gill (2 tablespoons) of cider vinegar, half that of sugar (1 tablespoon), 6 peppercorns, a dessertspoon (2 teaspoons) of salt, a small piece of bay leaf or blade of mace, and a whisk made of 1 stalk of celery and 1 branch of parsley. Add the brisket. Allow the water to boil up after the meat has cooled it off; then place the pot where the water therein will merely simmer. Cover the pot tightly and let the beef cook for 2 hours; skim as needed. Prepare the following vegetables. Peel 6 medium-sized, waxy potatoes (see Index for note on waxy and mealy potatoes), the same number of medium-to-small onions and 2 similar-sized turnips; clean and quarter 4 carrots and a smallish head of cabbage. Have ready 6 egg-sized cooked and peeled beets. After 2¼ hours of simmering, add the vegetables—excepting the beets—to the beef and let them cook for 45 minutes or until the meat and vegetables are tender. Before adding the vegetables, it is well to test the meat for its stage of doneness. Just before serving add the heated beets. Serve with Horse-Radish Sauce, which follows. (Act Two, Vermont Red Flannel Hash, follows after Horse-Radish Sauce and Parsley Dumplings.)*

HORSE-RADISH SAUCE FOR BOILED BEEF (early 1800s)—In a sauce-pan, melt 2 tablespoons of butter and blend 2 tablespoons of flour and 1 cup of milk into it. When this is smooth, add a generous ½ gill (¼ cup) each of freshly grated horse-radish and fresh white bread crumbs; season with salt and pepper to taste. Lastly, add 1 tablespoon each of vinegar and lemon juice.*

Among Grandmother's favorite companion-dishes for a Boiled Beef dinner was Parsley Dumplings. They follow.

PARSLEY DUMPLINGS (late 1800s)—Chop 1/3 cup of parsley fine and mix it with 1 pinch each of sage, thyme, nutmeg and cloves; blend in 2 cups of flour sifted with 4 teaspoons of baking powder and ¾ teaspoon of salt; cut in 4 teaspoons of butter and drip in ¾ cup of boiling water. Drop the batter by the tablespoonful into the beef pot and steam, tightly covered, for 12 minutes.*

VERMONT RED FLANNEL HASH (early 1800s)—Act Two: Monday supper. As New Year follows Christmas, so this Monday hash followed the Sunday boiled dinner. For every ½ pint (1 cup) of chopped boiled beef, ¼ pint (½ cup) each of chopped boiled potatoes and diced cooked beets were added, and the whole was browned in drippings or butter in a frying pan over a lively fire. As a crowning touch, a couple of tablespoons of cream were mixed into the fat and brownings—after the hash, now a lush red, thanks to the beets, had been removed to a platter—this sauce was poured upon the hash.

BROWN STEW (late 1800s)—Take 1½ pounds of "stew meat" beef, cut in pieces the size of large eggs. Place this in a kettle, laying all the fatty pieces at the bottom, and let the fat fry out. Cut in 1 large onion and let it brown. Add salt and pepper, and, when it is all browned, put in about 1 quart (4 cups) of water and all the bones, knuckle bones last. Stew until done; remove the bones and thicken the juices with 1 teaspoon of cornstarch moistened in a little cold water. If it is not brown enough, the stew can be colored with burnt sugar, which can be made slowly on a spider. Serve with carrots, boiled separately, and mashed turnips.*

With Brown Stew Grandmother usually produced Maizemeal Bread.

MAIZEMEAL SIDE-DISH BREAD (mid-1800s)—Grandmother plucked this dish from its native Southern hearth (where it was called Spoon Bread) and modified it to New England ways. Beat 4 eggs after you have set 1 pint (2 cups) of water to boiling; when the water is boiling vigorously add ½ teaspoon of salt and a pinch of nutmeg stirred into ½ pint (1 cup) of yellow water-ground maize. Pour in the maize so slowly that the water keeps boiling; stir as you count to 60 seconds; lower the heat and blend in 2 tablespoons of butter; count to 30 slowly; then stir in the eggs; count to 60 again and add ½ pint (1 cup) of good milk. Pour this dough into a really well-greased baking dish and bake in a hot (450°F.) oven for ½ hour. This bread is put into side dishes and served with the meat. Do not pour gravy over it, but lots of butter.*

BEEF SHORTCAKES (late 1800s)—Cut 1 pound of tender beef in small, thick slices; simmer them slowly in butter until tender. Have ready a Cream Sauce (see Index) and give it an extra seasoning with a pinch of sage. The proportions for the sauce in this instance are about 3 tablespoons each of flour and butter to 2 gills (1 cup) of soup stock, milk or water. Be sure to add the liquid slowly and to stir constantly; let the resulting sauce bake in the pan about 10 minutes to kill the paste-like taste of the flour. Keep the sauce hot over warm water. For the Shortcake use a good biscuit crust, such as:

OLD-FASHIONED SODA BISCUITS (mid-1800s)—With a quart (4 cups) of flour use 1 tablespoon of melted shortening, ½ teaspoon of salt, 1 teaspoon of baking soda and 2 teaspoons of cream of tartar. Mix the soda (saleratus) and cream of tartar thoroughly through the flour; then add the other ingredients plus 1½ cups of rich milk. Do not knead, but shape into 2½-inch by ¼-inch cakes and bake for 10 minutes in a hot (450°F.) oven.

While the biscuits are baking, remove the meat from the pan; pour the Cream Sauce into the drippings (this to give it flavor and color). If you have time, it is a good idea to brown the flour for the Cream Sauce in a pan over a very low fire, stirring constantly. It even helps to brown the butter before the flour is blended into it; the dark gravy on the snowy biscuit makes quite a handsome effect. When the gravy is thoroughly mixed, add the meat to it.

But on with the Shortcakes. Be sure to time the blending of the meat and the gravy with the baking of the Shortcakes. These should be opened quickly with a fork and well-buttered. Pour some of the meat and gravy mixture over the butter, replace the top of the biscuit, and cover this with more meat and gravy. Work fast so that you can serve them piping hot.*

Because many of our grandmothers were inordinately proud of their Baking Powder Biscuits, I submit the following as an interesting example of the "short-change" techniques often used in recipe writing by housewives. Please notice that I give it a ** rating.

OLD-FASHIONED BAKING POWDER BISCUITS (mid-1800s)—Use 1 quart (4 cups) of flour, 2 teaspoons of baking powder, 1 tablespoon of softened butter. Rub these together well; mix with a little cold water, stirring quickly with a knife; when well mixed add flour enough to mold out smoothly; roll the dough about 1 inch thick, cut it with a tumbler or tin cutter, place the biscuits in a pan and bake quickly in a well-heated oven. If made properly they will be as light and white as foam.**

This recipe was written by a Mrs. M. G. Adams, who probably was known throughout her county for her delicious biscuits. It is typical of the cheating and half-truths common among housewives who liked to see their names in print but were so jealous of their own reputations that they never gave the full and complete measures and procedures. That was probably why Mrs. Adams did not say how much cold water to use. Too much or too little could tilt the biscuit scale the wrong way; nor did she state the oven heat that was to be used.

ROASTED BEEF TENDERLOIN (early 1800s)—For this tempting morsel, one needs a large and well-dressed loin of beef, which many marinate in port wine for an hour or so before cooking time, turning it often so that the wine reaches all sides. When it is ready, place it on a spit and roast it before a peak fire in the grate (see Index under Roast Beef).

Since loyal subjects of this king of meats prefer it rare and well browned, it should rotate before the fire at roasting distance for about 15 minutes per pound. For medium rare, time the beef 5 minutes more per pound, and for well done—if anyone should ever commit this desecration—10 minutes more per pound. Baste with butter continually. (If spit and fire grate do not happen to be handy, roast a 2¼- to 2½-pound fillet in a 425°F. oven for 15 minutes and then at 350°F. for 15 minutes.)

Place the beef on a roasting rack and save the drippings. If the fillet is not larded, baste it generously with butter, having wrapped it in a thin blanket of butter before you put it in the oven. To keep the drippings moist, add ½ cup of water and replenish it as necessary.*

The following sauce did not exist in spit-and-grate days; however, it is one of the best for this princely dish.

MADEIRA SAUCE SUPREME (late 1800s)—Slice 1 pound of large, cleaned mushrooms (caps only). From the drippings of the fillet make a brown Béchamel Sauce (see Index). Cook the mushrooms in 3 tablespoons of butter; season with salt and pepper; when the mushrooms are done, add 2 teaspoons of minced shallots or ditto of white ends of scallions or of sweet onion. Add this to the mushrooms with 1 glass (2 ounces) of Madeira wine or sherry; then blend all into the brown Béchamel Sauce. Pour the sauce into a sauce boat and decorate it with a small teaspoon of finely minced chives.*

BEEF À LA MODE (mid-1800s)—In the eyes of gourmets, some of the aspects of this dish make it rank with manslaughter or worse. To quote the receipt, one takes a cheap cut of meat about 4 to 5 inches thick and, with an awl or screwdriver, drills holes entirely through it at small distances apart. Then one fills these holes with strips of fat salt pork, rolled in pepper, garlic juice and cloves, lays the meat in a pan, covers it closely, puts the pan over a steamer and lets it steam for 3 hours. When the meat is done, the gravy is thickened in the pan with 1 or 2 teaspoons of browned flour, flavored with curry and thinned down with cream.**

LEFT-OVER BEEF RAGOUT (mid-1800s)—Dice 1½ cups of lean cooked meat. Brown 1½ tablespoons of flour in 1½ tablespoons of butter slowly over a low fire; stir frequently and look out for sticking. Add 1 cup of warm beef broth, stir the mixture until it is thick and smooth and let it simmer for 15 minutes. Then add 1 medium-sized chopped onion, a medium bay leaf, 4 cloves, 6 black peppers, and a bouquet of parsley, summer savory or sweet basil; let the sauce simmer ½ hour longer, stirring from time to time, then strain it. Half an hour before serving, add ½ teaspoon of lemon juice, and 6 slices of sweet and 6 slices of sour pickles. Now put the cubed cooked meat into the sauce, of which there should be enough to cover the meat completely. If not, add beef stock. If the gravy becomes too thin, thicken it with ¼ teaspoon of arrowroot moistened in 1 tablespoon of water. Make sure that the stew does not boil after the meat is added; this makes it tough.*

POTATOES ARE NOT JUST POTATOES (mid-1800s)—For some meals housewives need waxy potatoes and for other occasions the mealy kind. The former are best in stews because they boil well and cut smoothly; the latter are best for puddings, Potato puffs (for which see Index) because they have a soft, not a firm, texture.

TO TEST WAXY AND MEALY POTATOES (mid-1800s)—First, the mealy potatoes are always heavier and denser than the waxy ones. To tell them apart, put them into a strong solution of salted water. The mealy ones will sink; the waxy will float. This trial never fails.***

TO BOIL POTATOES (mid-1800s)—The potatoes all should be the same size so that they cook equally. Wash them but do not pare or cut them, especially the mealy kind. Put them in a pot and pour in cold water until it clears the potatoes by 1 inch; they should be just covered with water when finished. Set them over a moderate fire to boil; when they boil, set them at the side to simmer slowly until they are soft enough to admit of a fork. Pour the water off and let them stand in the pot over a warm spot so that they will dry quickly. Although the potato is covered with a skin of cork, some moisture does seep through. Sprinkle some salt on them and cover them with a napkin as they dry. This method of managing potatoes is equal to steaming and dresses them much more quickly—15 to 20 minutes depending on size. The proper way to serve boiled potatoes is in a wooden bowl covered with a cloth, peeled or not as you prefer. Never peel new potatoes; use a scrubbing brush or a piece of coarse flannel. Incidentally, kidney potatoes, so called because of their shape, serve better all-around purposes than do the waxier round or "Irish Apple" potatoes.*

LET THE SKY RAIN POTATOES, LET IT HAIL KISSING COMFITS (early 1800s)—As Falstaff exclaims in *The Merry Wives of Windsor,* potatoes may have invigorating aspects; still, the whole of the family are suspicious; a great number are narcotic and some are deleterious. It is generally assumed that water in which potatoes are boiled is injurious; and as instances are on record where cattle, having drunk it, fared badly, it may be well to err on the safe side and avoid its use for any alimentary purpose. It is, further, well known that potatoes that have turned from brown to green on being exposed to air are very unwholesome and to be avoided.***

A FEW KIND WORDS ABOUT THE POOR POTATO (mid-1800s)—So many people regard the potato not as a fruit but as a veritable Borgia; and yet, it brings greater blessings to Man than even the Arctic seal does to the Esquimaux. A bright light, so powerful as to enable a person to read by it, issues from the common potato when in a state of putrefaction. When ripe, they foment and yield vinegar or wine; the stalks produce a cottony flax, also potash; its tubercles made into pulp are a substitute for soap in bleaching; sugar and sweet spirits are extracted from the roots; liquor from making potato starch will clean silk, woolen and cotton articles without damaging them and is also useful in cleaning paint; the substance of the potato answers the purpose of farina and the best soufflés are made with it; hair powder has also been produced from the potato's farina; as has size for coating paper and cloth, as well as yeast for the use of either brewer or baker. Since its introduction into England by Thomas Herriott in 1586, time has given truth to this great mathematician's statement to Queen Elizabeth, at Court on July 27th, that they are good food boiled or roasted.*

As we know, the humble potato fought its way from the realms of the proscribed to first row, center aisle, in the global theatre of the culinary arts. And it was brought into focus at this particular point by the frequent references to firm and mealy potatoes among these beef recipes. I simply cannot leave the poor potato standing here alone and unsupported by a single potato recipe to keep it company. So here goes:

POTATO CHEESECAKES (mid-1800s)—To 1 pound of mealy mashed potatoes add ½ pound of good, well-grated and mild Cheddar cheese, ¼ pound each of currants, sugar (½ cup plus 1 tablespoon) and butter (1 stick), 5 egg yolks, and 4 egg whites well beaten together. Mix well and pour into patty tins lined with Puff Paste (see Index). Bake in a hot (425°F.) oven for 10 to 12 minutes; then in a moderate oven (360° F.) for 20 to 25 minutes.*

Now let us turn to Mashed Potatoes, because they should be served with Stewed Beef Steaks, next on the beefeater's menu:

MASHED POTATOES (mid-1800s)—For every pound of mealy mashed potatoes allow 1 ounce (2 tablespoons) of butter, 2 tablespoons of fresh, unskimmed milk, and pepper and salt to taste. Boil the potatoes in their skins; let them dry on the side of the fire; peel them and beat to a paste with a large fork in a saucepan; add butter, milk, pepper and salt in the above proportions and stir until well heated directly over the fire—but avoid burning them. Dish them lightly and draw the fork back and forth over the potatoes to make the surface rough. When dressed in this manner, they may be browned at the top with a salamander, or before the fire. Some cooks press the mixture into molds, then turn them out and bake them brown in a bake-oven; this—although a pretty mode—makes them heavy. But in whatever way they are sent to table, care must be taken to have them absolutely smooth and free from lumps.*

Or one could try a very old variation of Mashed Potatoes, an early number called:

VERY THIN-MASHED POTATOES (early 1800s)—Boil, dry, peel and mash about 1 pint (2 cups) of mealy potatoes (mashed measure); add 2 tablespoons of melted butter and 1/3 pint (2/3 cup) of good broth or light soup stock. Stir this mixture through a sieve to remove all lumps. Put the mixture into a well-buttered saucepan and stir constantly with a wooden spoon as you hold the saucepan by hand over the fire; cease the moment the potatoes start to bubble; season to taste with pepper, salt and nutmeg; transfer to a serving dish and dress with minced chives, parsley or a mixture of both.*

STEWED BEEF STEAKS (mid-1800s)—Start by boiling ¾ pound of white onions and draining them (see Index); grill 2 slices of bacon and break them into bits; shred 2 large carrots very fine; clean, slice and pan-fry ½ pound of mushrooms. For 4 persons, have ready as many 8-ounce lean top-round beef steaks; dress them lightly with garlic, dredge in flour and fry them quickly on both sides in butter until they are a light brown; season them with salt and pepper. Now season each steak with a small pinch of thyme and sprinkle some onion, bacon, carrot and mushroom over it as you stack the steaks in a heated saucepan. Boil up ½ gill (¼ cup) of beef stock with 1½ gills (¾ cup) of white wine or hard cider and a small bay leaf; when the liquid boils, remove the bay leaf and pour the liquid over the steaks, let it boil up again and remove immediately to a lower fire to simmer, covered, for 25 to 30 minutes, depending on the goodness of the steaks.*

BOILED FLANK "SAUSAGE" (mid-1800s)—Take a nice 5-pound flank; trim it, clean it, and wipe it with vinegar. Brush its surface thinly with mustard and sprinkle it lightly with powdered thyme, ginger and cloves, a small bay leaf broken into many tiny bits and black pepper. Please pass up the salt. Roll the meat into a sausage and tie it firmly with cooking cord (see Kitchen Twine, below) or button thread. It is better to tie short pieces of individual cord closely together round the meat than to string a long piece along the sausage. When ready, drop the sausage into boiling water; the water will cool off, but when boiling is resumed, put the pot over a simmering fire; let the meat stand thus, covered, 5½ hours or until tender; never let it boil; skim as called for. After 5 hours of cooking, add 1 teaspoon of salt to the water, which should be standing above the meat at all times and is therefore added to when necessary. Always add simmering water in such cases. Many cooks weight the meat down with a stone, an old brick or a discarded iron.* With this dish goes a Sharp Sauce:

SHARP SAUCE FOR BOILED MEATS (mid-1800s)—In a saucepot, cook 1 tablespoon each of minced capers, chives, olives, pickles and green peppers in 2 tablespoons of cider vinegar. As they simmer slowly, blend 2 tablespoons of flour with 2 tablespoons of butter in a spider until well browned, then add ¾ pint (1½ cups) of meat stock, a good ½ teaspoon of salt and a big pinch of pepper. Mix 1 tablespoon of sherry or rum into the seasoning mixture and add the whole to the brown cream gravy in the spider; stir well and keep it simmering gently 15 to 20 minutes.*

KITCHEN TWINE, HOW TO PREPARE (early 1800s)—Often, when even the strongest thread is not good enough to use in cookery, one must turn to the use of twine or cord. However, since twine sold in stores contains all manner of unsavory adjuncts that kill flavors in cooking and impart ghastly seasonings of their own, it behooves the wise housewife to act as follows. When you buy twine for the kitchen, measure lengths of 5 to 6 feet off the ball; run these into rings around two fingers and tie them. Drop the cords into salted boiling water and let them boil for an hour or so. After that, stretch them and hang them up to dry; wind them into rings and use them as they are needed.***

CORNED BEEF AND CABBAGE (early 1800s)—Wash a 5- to 6-pound brisket piece carefully and put it into a pot that will hold plenty of water. The water should be cold; the same care is necessary in skimming as for fresh meat. It is not too much to allow 40 minutes per pound, from the time when it begins to boil. The goodness of Corned Beef depends much on it being boiled gently and long. Lay it into a coarse earthen dish and place over it a piece of board of the same size. Upon this board put a clean stone or some other heavy weight. All salt meat is much improved by being pressed and ripened around the clock after being cooked. Next day, put the meat to boil in cold water with a shredded or quartered head of green cabbage and peeled or halved large potatoes (quartered carrots are optional). Dinner is ready when the potatoes are done. Serve this with a sauce boat brimming with Melted Butter Sauce (see Index). (Try flavoring the sauce with 1 teaspoon of mild mustard.)*

DAMN YANKEE PEPPER POT (mid-1800s)—This rather simple concoction of tripe, potatoes and seasonings is usually associated with Philadelphia. It was, however, concocted by a Yankee quartermaster in General Sheridan's Army Corps as an appetizer for the foot-weary soldiers who campaigned in the Shenandoah Valley on a monotonous diet of pale, mushy boiled tripe. As it reached New England fresh from Virginia, the recipe called for 1 pound of tripe chopped into small pieces, 2½ cups of diced raw potatoes, 1 cup of green peppers, ½ cup each of onion and celery, all well chopped, and ¼ cup of barley. Cook the vegetables in a good amount (about 2/3 cup) of butter about ¼ hour over a moderate fire or until tender. The vegetables must not fry. Meanwhile blend ¾ cup of flour into 1 cup of cold beef soup; mix this into the vegetables; see that the butter is well absorbed. Then add 1½ pints (3 cups) of hot soup stock (beef), add the tripe, dust in pepper, salt and cayenne to taste and cook about 3 hours or until the tripe is tender. In handling tripe, housewives cannot be too careful in cleaning it, after making sure that it is fresh and wholesome; a regular pattern of honeycombs tells the story. Some women boil the tripe for 20 minutes before they dice it. To please the folks, some cooks add ½ cup of heavy cream and a lump of butter as big as a plum just before the dish is served. Serve with Hoe Cakes, (see below).*

"Little Phil's" Boys in Blue were not the only Federals who brought back new ideas to the kitchens of the North. For instance, in bivouacs as they paused during General Sherman's march through Georgia, colored camp followers taught the Northerners how to make Hoe Cakes on field equipment, ranging from spades to mess gear, over their open campfires.

DAMN YANKEE HOE CAKES (mid-1800s)—Blend 1½ cups of fine, firm cornmeal with ¾ teaspoon of salt; then work in about 1½ tablespoons of any kind of good fat—lard is best. To this add 2/3 cup of boiling water— more or less depending on the quality of the cornmeal. Grease your spade or mess tin well; bake in close proximity to the blaze at a distance where you can count slowly to 8 without your hands feeling seared (375° F. oven); let the cakes bake 10 to 15 minutes on each side. Any Boy in Gray will assure you that Hoe Cakes beat the pants off Corn Pone when it comes to sopping up pot likker. (They can be made on buttered baking tins, too.)*

BEEF AND BIRD FOR FOREFATHERS' DAY (mid-1800s)—This, although it was a standard dish way back in Colonial days, is usually served in New England as a *must* on December 21st, the day the Pilgrims reached Plymouth after their short stop-over on Cape Cod. In ancient days, the great feast began with the consumption of a gigantic whortleberry pudding; made the Indian way originally, it has been "improved" by many generations of inventive cooks to a point where it repels boarders. On the other hand, the Boiled-Beef-and-Bird main course is easy as falling off a log.

The day before the big feast, set aboiling about 4 pounds of lean corned brisket that has been soaked in cold water over night, but the moment the water comes to a boil, put the kettle some place where it will simmer. Now add a fat old hen that weighs about as much as the beef and let that simmer with the beef, skin on, for about 3½ hours until both are tender. Skim for scum when necessary. When done, let bird and beef cool in their bath and then put them under a weighted board until they are wanted the next day; soak 1¼ quarts (5 cups) of pea beans over night. Dice as many waxy potatoes as you will need, slice 1 peeled turnip for each 2 persons and hull enough corn (see Index) to fill a quart (4-cup) measure. Mash the beans in a mortar after picking them over carefully for culls. Put the vegetables into the chicken-beef water and add the hen-beef. Thanks to the corned beef, no seasoning is necessary, except perhaps ½ teaspoon of mustard powder dissolved in cold water. Let all simmer slowly about 20 to 30 minutes until potatoes and turnips are tender. Serve like a stew, and with dumplings (see below) if you like.*

LIGHTNING-FAST AND LIGHT DUMPLINGS (late 1800s)—Sift 2 cups of flour, 3 teaspoons of baking powder and a good ½ teaspoon of salt three times together; add 1 cup of fresh whole milk and stir well for 5 minutes. The trick is to drop these dumplings on solid meat and not into the stew juice or gravy. Cover tightly and let them steam for 12 minutes.*

YANKEE POT ROAST (mid-1800s)—This recipe gives best results if the roast is cooked in a heavy cast-iron Dutch Oven with a closely fitting lid; however, any similar cast-iron or heavy kitchen kettle will do. First, melt 2 to 3 tablespoons of drippings in the pot or oven; brown in them 2 large thickly sliced onions. Give the onions a good tanning, but watch out for burning them, since that is ruinous; next, put the meat in and turn it regularly to give it a brown crust all around; have ready 2 medium-large peeled and quartered tomatoes, toss them in and add 1¼ cups of hot, strong beef stock (bouillon will do); as a final gesture, dust in a saltspoon (¼ teaspoon) of powdered ginger and a pinch of caraway seeds. Season to taste after 5 minutes of simmering. Cover tightly and let all cook ever so gently for about 3 hours; then check for tenderness.*

In Chapter 1, I took the liberty of swinging off course from the delights of Roast Beef to a Chicken Pie that attracted Grandmother Lyon's fancy. And suddenly, in this book of beef, I discover the red and roguish look of a Chicken Lobster Stew. No true New Englander could ever turn her back on "shore dishes," as they were called, and, in the proper season, Bella developed a yen for Maine lobster which nothing could douse or deter. This is Aunt Ville's Mary's receipt for:

CHICKEN LOBSTER STEW IN THE BRAVA MANNER (mid-1800s)—First kill 3 hen lobsters that weigh about a pound apiece. This is done by inserting a knife into the back between the body shell and the tail and cutting the spinal cord. Hen lobsters can be distinguished from male lobsters because their tails are narrower. Chop the claws off close to the body with a cleaver; split the lobsters open lengthwise from head to tail; now remove the tails and cut the chests into pieces; trim the legs down a bit, but throw nothing away. Set aside the coral and the tomalle (when cooked the former becomes red and the latter green); leave all the meat in the shell but crack the claws. Salt the lobster meat lightly and simmer it gently in oil, of which freshly kegged spermacetti is best and oiled butter (see Index) next best; set it aside. Now cook 2 chopped shallots or 1 small onion in a bit of butter and add 4 ounces (½ cup) of dry, not sweet, white wine. Stir the lobster pieces into this and have ready 4 ounces (½ cup) of real cognac heated to the temperature of shaving water; set it aflame with a match after you have poured it over the lobster. At this point, add 2/3 cup of fish stock if you have it; plain water, if not; at any rate, add 1 gill (½ cup) of tomato juice fortified with 1 dessertspoon (2 teaspoons) of arrowroot and 4 small peeled and diced tomatoes. (By the way, dropping tomatoes into boiling water and keeping them there to the count of 10 expedites peeling no end, especially if you start from the "blossom" atop the tomato.) Let this cook about 10 minutes to unite the flavors; then remove the pieces of lobster, which should be served in their shells. Now for the stew. Strain the liquid through a coarse sieve into a smaller spider; add the coral and tomalle, a bit of butter no larger than a hazelnut (1 rounded teaspoon), a clove of crushed garlic and some finely mortarized tarragon. Simmer this—do not boil—and add the lobster servings. (Chances are that the Portuguese "bravas" on Cape Cod used olive and not whale oil. I would prefer that, too.) The best accompaniment to this dish is Saffron Rice.*

SAFFRON RICE (mid-1800s)—Pour ½ pint (1 cup) of rice into 1½ pints (3 cups) of furiously boiling water and let it cook, covered, until tender, which should be about the time all the moisture has been absorbed by the rice. Do not stir the rice while it is cooking; when it is done, stir in 1 teaspoon of powdered saffron, 2 tablespoons of butter and 1 teaspoon of salt, with a 2-pronged fork. If need be, keep the rice hot in a basin stood in a pot of simmering water. This recipe can also be used for rice rings cast in molds and filled with flesh, fish or fowl.*

BEEF DUMPLINGS AS MAIN COURSE (mid-1800s)—In a big bowl or basin mix ½ pound of minced beef, ¼ pound of minced lean pork, ¼ pint (½ cup) of bread soaked in milk and squeezed dry, 1 beaten whole egg; mix these together well. Next, add 1 tablespoon of minced parsley, ½ gill (¼ cup) of barley and ¼ teaspoon of thyme or tarragon or sage and/or mace. Shape into balls like ducks' eggs and simmer in beef stock about 1 hour uncovered. Serve with Macaroni.*

HEAVENLY MACARONI IN A HURRY (late 1800s)—The title of this recipe reveals that even in 1880, when it first appeared, women felt a certain impatience with the demands the kitchen made on their time. Cook the macaroni for as long as the package directs in salted water with an onion stuck with a pair of cloves and a lump of butter. When it is tender, drain it well and place it in a kettle; add a piece of butter as big as a walnut (1 tablespoon), 1½ gills (¾ cup) of grated Swiss cheese, a dash of nutmeg, a pinch of newly ground pepper and a tablespoon of heavy cream. Shake vigorously over the fire until the butter has been melted, the cream absorbed and the cheese made invisible. You can now serve it or, if you like, line a dish with puff paste, fill it with the macaroni mixture, cover with 1 gill (½ cup) of light cream, cover the whole with puff paste and bake in a medium low oven (325°F.) about 1 hour or until the paste turns brown.*

WHALEMEN'S LOBSCOUS (early 1800s)—Have the ship's cook dice anything of lean, cooked meat from ox, cow or calf so long as it is fresh and enough to make a pint (2 cups); have him chop enough cold boiled potato to make 1½ pints (3 cups), and chop enough onion coarsely to make ¾ pint (1½ cups). Let him brown the onions slowly in a small hunk of drippings, upon which he will remove the onions and brown the meat; next he removes the meat and blends in 3 tablespoons of flour and adds 1 pint of soup stock or water; let him add more liquid if the gravy is too thick. Have him make a cream sauce by thickening any soup stock in the galley; when timely let him season it with salt and pepper. He returns the onions and meat to the pan and lets them simmer some 8 to 10 minutes, but so slowly that it would not match the heat of a hawser running through a hawse-hole. Then he adds the potatoes, and, when they are warm, have him bring it back to the cabin, where the skipper can enliven it with a hot noggin (2 ounces) of Medford rum.**

POT ROAST WITH CRANBERRIES (early 1800s)—Sprinkle a 4-pound rump roast with a very little flour and brown it in 3 tablespoons of fat. Next toss in 1 pint (2 cups) of raw cranberries, 1½ pints (3 cups) of boiling water, ½ gill (¼ cup) each of minced onions and celery, 6 whole peppercorns and ditto sprigs of parsley, 3 whole cloves and 1 medium bay leaf. Cover the kettle and let it come to a boiling point; simmer for 2 hours; then turn the meat and check for doneness and also add a short 2 teaspoons of salt. From that point on, watch for the point of cooking perfection. When it has been reached, thicken the gravy with 1 teaspoon of arrowroot for every ¼ pint (½ cup) of liquid. A point of caution: do not forget to dissolve the arrowroot in 1 tablespoon of cold water before it is added to the meat sauce. Also, some city folks at this point add a wineglass or 2 of heavy port if the sauce seems small.*

FILETS MIGNON THE BOSTON WAY (late 1800s)—Allow one ¾-inch-thick filet of the mid-tenderloin section per person. Have ready an adequate quantity of fresh Potato Snow (see below), kept hot over simmering water. Halve and quarter 1 banana per serving; dip the pieces twice into a beaten egg with a short tablespoon of cold water added and into very fine stale bread crumbs; fry in butter; place the bananas on a sheet of brown paper so that the fat drains away and keep them hot over simmering water. Now place the filets in a frying pan with hot melted butter that has passed the frothing point. After searing for 1 minute, turn and sear for 1 minute on the other side. Repeat this turning at minute intervals for 6 minutes for rare, 8 minutes for medium, 10 minutes for well done. Serve this meal with Potato Snow and alacrity.*

POTATO SNOW (mid-1800s)—Cook the potatoes in their skins until mealy; dry them well and keep them warm as you peel each potato and rub it through a sieve into a hot serving dish. Let the potato flakes fall like a gentle snow; use no butter and do not stir them, or they will collapse.*

RED WINE SAUCE FOR BEEF (mid-1800s)—Pound a 2-inch stick of cinnamon with 12 whole cloves (about 1 teaspoon each in powdered form); put this into a saucepan with 3 tablespoons of sugar, the shaved and minced outer skin of a lemon and 2/3 cup of port or burgundy; let them simmer, covered, for 15 minutes. Remove from the fire to a large gravy boat and, just before serving, stir in 1½ gills (¾ cup) of red-currant jelly. With burgundy some use only 6 cloves and black-currant jelly instead of red. The ease with which this sauce is put together belies its culinary majesty.*

ALL-IN-ONE BEEF LOAF (late 1800s)—To make this large meat loaf takes a lot of doing, but—since it makes grand eating, be it hot, warmed up or cold—the results justify the labor. On the day you make it, begin with stringing 1 pound of string beans; remove the ends but do not cut the beans before you boil them.

THE SECRET OF BOILING STRING BEANS (early 1800s)—To boil a mess of truly fine string beans, bring them to a fast and furious boil. For this, try the ancient trick of heating a poker or some similar tool white hot; drop the beans into boiling water and, the same instant, stick the poker into the beans. Instead of bubbling out, the water will boil up instantly; keep it boiling for about 15 minutes, when the beans should be tender.*

Building the meat loaf starts with cutting the cooked beans lengthwise and dicing them with a knife; fry 2 sliced and chopped onions lightly in butter; skin 2 big tomatoes by dipping them into boiling water for 10 seconds and chop them fine; grate 2 raw carrots not too coarsely; cook ½ pound of chopped mushrooms in butter for a few minutes; chop 4 stalks of young celery rather fine and mash 1 clove of garlic; add ¾ teaspoon of salt, ¼ teaspoon of pepper, ¼ teaspoon of oregano, 1 pinch of powdered bay leaf and ¼ teaspoon of dry mustard to 2 beaten egg yolks and blend all of this into ½ gill (¼ cup) each of sherry, soy sauce and beef broth. Have 3 pounds of ground top round of beef at hand. Lay the meat in a large basin and add the items in the order already given, or any way you like so long as the egg mixture comes last. Work this diligently with a fork to give it lightness; the longer you work, the lighter the loaf. Pack the mixture into a well-buttered baking dish or bread pan and bake it for 15 minutes uncovered in a quite hot oven (425°F.); then reduce the oven to moderate (350°F.) and bake, covered, for 1¾ hours.*

BEEF LOAF GRAVY (mid-1800s)—Half an hour before the Beef Loaf is to be served, drain off the juices and spoon the fat off the top. Melt 2 tablespoons of butter in a pan and brown 3 tablespoons of flour in it; blend in the fat from the loaf and, when the dough is smooth, add the remainder of the loaf juice and test for seasoning. If this does not provide enough volume, add as much milk as may be needed to furnish a smooth cream sauce that is not too thick. A real touch of gourmet elegance is brought to this sauce by adding truffles and sherry, as follows:*

TRUFFLES AND SHERRY IN SOUPS AND SAUCES (early 1800s)—Wash ½ ounce of truffles; then slice them and simmer in 2 or 3 tablespoons of sherry for a few minutes; put them with their liquor into the soup or gravy. They thicken broth and give a fine flavor, but should be allowed at least 15 minutes of cooking time.*

HASHED BEEF CAKES (early 1800s)—Bathe two ½-inch slices of raw rump of beef in ½ pint of burgundy over night; hack the meat into small bits. Cook ½ cup each of minced onion and mushroom caps in 2 tablespoons of butter; stir 2 egg yolks into 1 gill (½ cup) of bread crumbs, ½ teaspoon of dry mustard and 1 tablespoon of flour; add a pinch of powdered mace, salt and pepper. Stir all the foregoing items into a meat batter and shape it into balls as big as hen's eggs, press them flat, roll them in flour and fry them slowly in fresh suet or roast-beef drippings. Make the following sauce.*

BURGUNDY SAUCE FOR HASHED BEEF CAKES (early 1800s)—Heat ½ pint (1 cup) of the burgundy used as a marinade in the above recipe and add 1 tablespoon of jelly to sweeten it. Skim if necessary. In 1½ tablespoons (4½ teaspoons) of cold vinegar moisten 1 teaspoon of arrowroot; stir this into the wine until it thickens. Drain the fat off the meat, pour the sauce over the cakes and let it boil up once and simmer a few minutes.*

TO TOSS UP COLD BEEF (early 1800s)—Cut the beef into little bits; grate a little nutmeg over them and add a little salt and pepper. Now, to ½ pint (1 cup) of milk add the yolks of 2 eggs well beaten and a spoonful of chopped mushroom or some minced pickle; heat this slowly and stir so that it thickens smoothly. Put the beef into it, remove it from the fire after counting to 30, take it to table and toss it up and about with a fork. Cold beef done this way eats well, especially if it is rare.*

COW'S HEEL WITH FRIED ONIONS (pre-1800s)—Get one that has been only scalded, not a heel that has had all the good boiled out of it and most of the jelly extracted. Boil it covered for 7 to 8 hours in 1 quart (4 cups) of water and renew the quantity as water boils away. Skim when called for. Later, this broth can be made into fine jelly or delicious soup. When cooked to the point of tenderness wanted, cut the heel into handsome slices, dip them into a beaten egg and fine breadcrumbs, and fry each slice a light brown on both sides. Also fry a great number of onion rings. These are to be piled in the center of the serving platter with the slices of cow's heel around it.***

RICH SHEPHERD'S MEAT CAKE (mid-1800s)—Fill a 1-pint (2-cup) measure with chopped cooked beef and mash a similar amount of boiled potatoes. Beat separately the whites and yolks of 2 large or 3 small eggs. Give 1 tablespoon each of chopped onions and parsley a light frying in 1 tablespoon of butter and blend them with the meat, potatoes, a little salt and pepper and 2/3 cup of milk. Stir in the thick, yellow yolks and fold in the well-whipped whites very lightly. Pour into a buttered baking dish and for 1 hour bake it uncovered in a moderate (350°F.) oven. Serve with Caper Sauce (see Index).*

BEEF CAKES AND CREAMED ONIONS (mid-1800s)—Blend 1 pound of raw minced rump of beef with ¼ pound of minced broiled bacon or boiled ham. Add a small pinch of mixed and powdered savory herbs, such as thyme, sweet basil and marjoram; season with pepper and salt. Bind this together with 1 yolk and 1 whole egg beaten with a small handful of flour. Fashion into square cakes about ½ inch thick and fry them in hot drippings or butter very slowly so that they do not burn. Have cooked, drained and ready ¾ pint (1½ cups) of small white onions (see Index). Heat them over boiling water in a white sauce made of 2 tablespoons of butter into which 2 tablespoons of flour has been blended and 1 cup of warm milk added. When the cakes are removed from the skillet, pour the creamed onions into the pan gravy and thus add to their flavor and coloring. It is best to scrape the brownings in the skillet loose before the creamed onions are poured in. The latter are very fragile, and the less handling, the better.*

STEAK AND KIDNEY PIE (mid-1800s)—Have 2 pounds of round of beef sliced ½ inch thick; cut these pieces into finger lengths; clean and trim a ½-pound beef, calf or veal kidney and slice it into thin strips; mix the meats well; season with salt, pepper, a whiff of nutmeg and a pinch of thyme; add enough gravy or beef stock to just cover the meat. Use a largish, rather flat baking pan and make a crust for a meat or chicken pie (see Index). In placing the top and bottom crusts follow the directions given for Spring Garden Chicken Pie (see Index). After the top crust is in place and gashed, bake 1 hour in a moderate (350°F.) oven.*

BAKED MEAT CAKES AND CELERY ROOTS (late 1800s)—Scrub 1 large or 2 medium celery roots and boil them in 1 cup of water until tender; peel them and dice them coarsely; return them to the celery water and keep them warm. Mix 1 pound of nicely chopped beef with 1 teaspoon of salt and 1 tablespoon of minced onion. Soak ½ cup of bread crumbs free from crust in ½ cup of milk seasoned with ½ teaspoon of freshly ground black pepper; squeeze the crumbs dry by hand, blend them into the meat mixture. If it seems too dry, add more soaked crumbs. Form the mixture into cakes. Using lard or butter, fry the cakes rapidly in an iron frying pan to give them a good outside browning. Put them into a baking dish. Melt 2 tablespoons of butter and blend 2 tablespoons of potato flour into it; stir in the celery water; if too thick, add good milk or light cream to suit; season to taste. Put the celery pieces with the meat cakes in the baking dish, pour the sauce over all and bake, uncovered, in a medium-low (300°F.) oven for 15 minutes. This dish is not expected to brown.*

MOCK DUCK OF BEEF (mid-1800s)—Take a large and not too thin round of beef (about ½ inch thick) and season it with salt, pepper and a flick of powdered ginger. Prepare bread or crackers as for poultry stuffing (see Index); use ¼ pint of oysters or not, as you prefer. Lay the stuffing in the center of the meat, which first should be dredged on both sides with flour seasoned with salt and pepper. Sew the beef up with needle and thread, using a tight cross-stitch. Roast the meat a good hour in a moderate to hot (400°F.) oven; baste with butter almost constantly. Even if the folks do not see any wings and legs on these queer birds, they'll think that there is roast duck for dinner. Béarnaise Sauce is just the goose for this duck, and so are Potato Pancakes—see below.*

BÉARNAISE SAUCE (SO-CALLED) (late 1800s)—Just before it is time to serve dinner, mix 5 raw egg yolks with 1 tablespoon of warm water in a saucepan; place the pan in very hot but not boiling water; stir constantly until the yolks thicken; season with salt and pepper to taste plus a small pinch each of powdered oregano and thyme. In a few minutes add ¼ cup of cider vinegar and ¼ cup of dry white wine which has been reduced to half by boiling and given a chance to cool a bit.*

POTATO PANCAKES FOR BEEF COURSES (late 1800s)—Pick 4 round, firm and white potatoes; peel them and soak 1 hour in cold salted water. Dry them carefully, grate them rather coarsely into a sieve and wring dry in a cloth so that all moisture vanishes. Have ready a small grated onion, also dried in a cloth, 2 beaten eggs and 2 pieces of cooked bacon saved from breakfast. Mix the onion and bacon bits into the potatoes and follow with 1 teaspoon of salt, a pinch of pepper, ditto of mace or nutmeg, 1 tablespoon of minced parsley and 2 of melted—but not hot—butter; blend 4½ teaspoons of flour into the eggs; add this to the rest and stir vigorously. Drop the tablespoonful onto a hot buttered spider and turn as you would pancakes to brown on each side.*

THE BEST CORNED BEEF HASH THERE IS (mid-1800s)—There is but one way to challenge that label, and that is to try it. To ¾ pint (1½ cups) of finely hashed corned beef, add ½ pint (1 cup) of finely hashed waxy boiled potatoes (see Index) blended with ¼ pint (½ cup) of corned beef juice. The beef should be leanest of the lean and hashed the old way, that is, cut into thin slices, shredded with your fingers and then minced. The potatoes must be firm and not mealy. Mince very fine, and mix with the beef and potatoes, 1 tablespoon each of raw carrots, onions and green cabbage. Heat a 9-inch skillet, bring 1 tablespoon each of lard and fresh (unsalted) butter or well-washed barrel butter to a sizzling boil and pour the hash into it. The skillet is now placed over a low heat so that the hash barely cooks and the bottom browns evenly and slowly. Meanwhile, poach 1 egg for each person in just enough half-and-half vinegar and water to cover the eggs. When the yolks look blind on top, the eggs are poached. They will keep hot in the liquid away from the fire. Meanwhile, keep an eye on the hash to see how it is browning. When it is nearly ready, pour ½ gill (¼ cup) of ordinary cream on its top and tilt the skillet quickly so that the cream spreads over the entire surface of the hash. A few minutes later, run the point of a knife across the center of the hash from edge to edge but do not cut clear through to the bottom. Turn one half of the hash on top of the other—it is best to use two spatulas. At the table, place a poached egg on each individual serving. Baptize each egg with this sauce:*

BURNT BUTTER SAUCE (early 1800s)—Put 2 ounces (4 tablespoons) of fresh, unsalted butter into a small frying pan; eye it carefully as it passes the frothing point and turns from yellow to brown; when its shade is that of dark chewing tobacco, add 1½ teaspoons of vinegar and season with a little pepper and salt. Serve very hot.*

The next presentation has two separate stages of preparation and is apt to seem a little too time-consuming to busy housewives. However, on a day when you happen to have time on your hands before dinner—and the remnants of a rare roast and some beef gravy in the refrigerator—here is an unusual and bound-to-please hash dinner.

ROAST BEEF HASH WITH SHERRY (early 1800s)—Collect 1 pint (2 cups) of loosely packed shredded roast beef (for procedure in this see Index, To Hash Beef and Make Gravy). These nubbins of beef are now to be browned in 4 tablespoons of beef drippings (butter will do), yet they must not be allowed either to harden or boil. When the meat is done, remove it from the pan in which it was cooked and pour into the pan ½ gill (¼ cup) each of good beef gravy and good sherry. Let this simmer until reduced to half and, meanwhile, turn to stage two:

HASHED POTATOES WITH ONIONS (late 1800s)—Cook in 2 tablespoons of butter until they are golden and soft 2 gills (1 cup) of sliced onions. They should be sliced the thickness of 50¢ pieces, cut in quarters and pulled into separate strips. Have ready 2 cups of waxy potatoes, boiled but far from soft enough for mashing. Cut the potatoes into slices as thick as silver dollars and mince 3 tablespoons of parsley—no stalks, no branches, just the green leaves. Mix the potato, parsley and onion in a bowl and season to taste with salt and pepper. In one of two twin skillets, heat a piece of butter the size of a pullet's egg (3 tablespoons); when it ceases to bubble and starts to brown, pour the potato mixture into it and stir to make sure that all is well distributed; place the pan so that the mixture slowly takes on a bottom that is delicately brown and yet quite firm and thick. Now return to stage one.

Make up for the loss of half of the sherry-gravy mixture by whipping up a small cream sauce of ½ gill (¼ cup) of good milk and a like amount of cream. Thicken this in a skillet with 2 tablespoons of flour blended into 2 tablespoons of butter. Add the sherry gravy, which now should have boiled down to ½ gill (¼ cup). Season this with 1 saltspoon (¼ teaspoon) of salt and ½ saltspoon (⅛ teaspoon) of white pepper, a big pinch of powdered ginger and a small one of cayenne. Let this simmer slowly for 10 minutes and add the shredded beef.

Now melt a lump of butter about the size of a walnut (1 tablespoon) in the empty skillet. When it stops bubbling, turn the potato mixture into it, upside down, so that it will brown on the uncooked side. Do this quickly, turn the potato hash out on a platter and spread the meat over it as you would the frosting on a cake. The gravy will probably run down the sides of the potato, but that is as it should be.*

BEEF AND EGG BALLS IN CURRY SAUCE   (early 1800s)—Beef Balls: Chop and mash in a mortar 1½ pounds of pure, red beef with a bit of rosemary. Make sure that not a scrap of fat goes into the mortar. Roll the mixture into balls a bit smaller than apples, weighing about 3 ounces each. Fry these quickly in butter until they are well browned but still rare inside; pure meat like this is inclined to stick to the pan at the start, so always loosen the balls with the tip of a knife before you try to roll them.

Egg Balls: Egg Balls are made by putting 4 chilled hard-boiled eggs into a mortar or bowl with the yolk of 1 raw egg, 1 teaspoon of flour, 1 ditto of chopped parsley, ¼ teaspoon of salt and a little sage. Mash these well and roll into balls the size of hazelnuts (since they swell in boiling). Let them simmer in water a few minutes, just enough to set.*

CURRY SAUCE (early 1800s)—Curry Sauce should be quite thick. Put 1 teaspoon of curry or more—depending on how *hot* you like it—into a basin with 2 tablespoons of flour and ½ teaspoon salt; make the mixture smooth with 2 tablespoons of cold beef soup or broth. Run this through a sieve into a large flat stew-pan and shake it well about until it boils, add ½ pint (1 cup) of warm beef soup or broth and let it simmer 20 minutes, stirring often. When thick, sieve the sauce again to remove lumps; add ¼ cup of cream and the Beef and Egg Balls; give it all a boil up; let it ripen over low heat about 5 minutes at most.*

There were times when a housewife, in order to serve curry dishes, had to know how to make her own curry powder. Here are two receipts; the main trouble is that it would be easier to buy the curry today than to locate the items in a twentieth-century kitchen:

HOME-MADE EAST INDIAN CURRY (early 1800s)—Put the following ingredients in a cool bake-oven (250°F.) over night. The next morning, mash them in a mortar and rub them through a fine sieve. Three ounces each of coriander seed and turmeric root, 1 ounce each of whole black pepper, mustard seed and ginger root, ½ ounce each of allspice and cardamon seeds, ¼ ounce of cummin seed. Bottle and seal this well.***

DOWN ON THE FARM CURRY POWDER (mid-1800s)—Mix 1 ounce of ginger, 1 of freshly ground black pepper, 1 of mustard, 3 of coriander seed, 3 of turmeric, ¼ ounce of cayenne pepper, ½ ounce of cardamon, ½ ounce of cummin seed and ½ ounce of cinnamon. Pound the whole into a fine powder, sift in through a hair-sieve and keep it in a bottle corked tight.***

CORKING KITCHEN BOTTLES (early 1800s)—It is a vulgar error that anything is gained by the purchase of cheap corks and another that a bottle is well stopped when the cork is forced down level with the mouth of the bottle. This latter is rather a sign that the cork is too small for the neck.

Following is a cement of great use in preserving such things as curry and other pungencies which, without its help, would soon spoil from clumsy and ineffectual corking.

BOTTLE CEMENT, TO MAKE (early 1800s)—Melt ½ pound of black resin with ½ pound of red sealing wax and ¼ ounce of beeswax in an iron or earthen pot; when it froths up, before all is melted and apt to boil over, stir it with a tallow candle, which will settle the froth until all is melted and fit for use.**

Lest I stretch these excerpts from Grandmother's beef book into a whole meat department, I would like to close on the culinary high note of steaks and the sauces that went with them. In the old days, there were two principal kinds of steaks—broiled or fried and boiled or stewed. Only young, tender and well-aged beef could be used for the former; older and tougher meats went into the latter. But truly tender, juicy, tasty steaks—as we know them today—did not exist in earlier times, before the art of raising beef cattle had come into its own.

For this reason, it was necessary to dress steaks up with sauces to give them life and flavor. Here are a few.

BEEFSTEAKS OR BIFTECK (early 1800s)—If you wish to entertain your mouth with a superlative beefsteak, you must have the inside of the sirloin (tenderloin) cut into steaks. Some settle for steaks that are cut from the middle of a rump but a steak, to be superlative, must be from the sirloin's inside. The meat should have hung at least 4 days. Desire the butcher to cut them of even thickness; if he does not, divide the thicker from the thinner steaks and give them time accordingly. Take care to have a very brisk, clear fire of hardwood. Charcoal is not to be considered. Throw a little salt on the coals to ginger them up a little; make the gridiron hot and set it slanting, to prevent the fat from dropping into the fire, slowing the blaze down and making it smoke. It requires more practice and care than is generally supposed to do steaks to a nicety. Sear them quickly; turn them frequently; do not use forks; serve rare. Cooking time depends on heat of fire, thickness of steaks and the good common sense of the cook.***

FLANK STEAKS (mid-1800s)—A good way to serve flank steak is to broil it. However, to do so you need a hot fire, a sharp knife and a good "cutting eye." Take as much flank as you will need, allowing about 2/3 pound per person to be served. Remove the membranes, dry it thoroughly and coat its top with a thin blanket of drippings—those from roast beef are the best. Have your fire hot and steady and place the beef as near it as you can without burning it. Broil on the first side for 4 minutes; on the second for 3 minutes. A flank steak must be so rare that one can still hear the mooing of the critter it came from. Put the steak on a meat-board and slice it paper-thin across the grain, or the meat will not chew well; the same applies if it is done beyond the point of rosy rare.*

So little time and trouble is required in handling a broiled flank steak —in modern ovens it should be placed under a high-fire broiler in close proximity to the blaze—that a housewife can well afford to spend a little time on a sauce that seems just made for it:

CHAMPAGNE SAUCE (mid-1800s)—Just before the meat is ready for serving, make a brown gravy dough by browning 4 tablespoons of flour in 3 tablespoons of melted butter, stirring all the while. When it is brown, add a good gill (2/3 cup) of warm strong soup or broth; when well blended, move the pan to the back of the range and let it cook, but stir constantly and beware of it sticking, as this dough will be very thick. After 5 minutes, add 2 wineglasses of champagne (4 ounces) and 2 teaspoons of minced sweet red peppers (now called pimientos) as it heats. It must not boil. If the sauce is too thick, add more champagne until it has the texture you want.*

BEEFSTEAK SMOTHERED IN ONIONS (late 1800s)—Sear a slice of rump, sirloin or round 1½ to 2 inches thick on a red-hot skillet which has been lightly greased by being rubbed with a piece of beef suet; do this searing quickly, and turn the beef every 10 seconds for 5 minutes; then brown for 5 minutes on each side; season to taste. Have ready and well drained 1½ dozen small white onions of uniform size peeled and boiled for 1 hour in salted water. Pour these and 1 tablespoon of butter on the meat in the pan; cover closely and let the steak cook slowly, without turning it, for 15 to 20 minutes.*

BOILED ONIONS FOR STEAKS (early 1800s)—Peel a pint (2 cups) of button onions and keep them in 1 quart (4 cups) of cold water an hour before you boil them; let them boil until tender; drain them, add a little butter and keep them hot. Those who like the full flavor of onions cut off only the strings and tops before soaking and boiling them in their skins. Onions gain flavor by soaking.*

BROWN ONION GRAVY STEW FOR STEAKS (early 1800s)—Brown 1 pint (2 cups) of drained boiled onions (cooked as in the above recipe) in 4 tablespoons of butter in a frying pan over a slow fire and turn them well about until completely browned. Remove the onions and stir in 4 tablespoons of flour; add ½ pint (1 cup) of broth and make the gravy smooth; season with pepper and salt; when done, the gravy should have a dark-golden color; if it has not, darken it slightly with a touch of burnt sugar; now add 2 tablespoons of good heavy port and ½ teaspoon of lemon juice. In some homes, the onions are served separately; in others they are rubbed through a fine sieve with the gravy and kept hot over warm water.*

ONION BASE FOR CURRY SAUCE (early 1800s)—Brown Onion Gravy also makes a fine base for a Curry Sauce. Add 1 teaspoon of curry, or a little more or less, according to taste. Use sherry, not port, when the gravy is used for curry sauce.*

PAN-FRIED STEAKS (early 1800s)—Put a good lump of butter with a smidge of powdered ginger into a frying pan, and when it is hot lay in the steaks; keep turning them until they are done enough. Do not season them with salt until they are cooked. Combine the steaks with Boiled Onions or Browned Onions (see Index), or use the Brown Onion Gravy Stew (above), if that is your preference.*

WINE SAUCE FOR PAN-FRIED STEAKS (mid-1800s)—Remove the steaks from the frying pan and add about 1 ounce (2 tablespoons) of butter to whatever fat is there; rub in as much flour as will make a paste and let it bake until brown; add enough hot soup stock to make it into a cream; add 2 tablespoons each of minced onions and Burgundy. Some beefeaters like Chopped Shallots as a side dish.*

A WELL-OILED NIFTY NINETIES STEAK (late 1800s)—For a 1½-pound 1-inch porterhouse, pour 4 ounces of fine olive oil into a cup and, using a long-haired brush, paint the broiler and the steak with oil. For a rare steak, place your broiler near enough to the fire to sear the steak thoroughly in 2 minutes on one side and 1¾ minutes on the other. Widen the distance between steak and fire by about an inch to reduce the heat. Now oil both sides of the steak again and let it broil 3 minutes on one side and 2½ minutes on the other. Finally, oil the steak on the top side and place that side so close to the fire that it becomes a crusty dark brown. The secret of this steak is to keep it well oiled. For serving the steak, heat a platter as hot as a flatiron and put a piece of butter the size of a walnut (1 tablespoon) on it.*

GRILLED BEEFSTEAK WITH PLATTER JUICE (mid-1800s)—Lay a thick, tender steak upon a greased gridiron over hot coals. Use a gridiron with slender bars that will leave only thin black lines on the steak; broad bars act as miniature frying pans and scorch the meat. Heat a metal or china platter and pour on it about 2 tablespoons of melted butter into which some salt and pepper has been blended. When one side of the steak is cooked, lay it on a platter cooked side up so that the juices which escape may run freely upon the platter; you can stimulate this process by pouring 1 dessertspoon (2 teaspoons) of boiling salted water upon it; return your steak to the gridiron fairly quickly and cook the other side. When done, place the meat in the platter juice, season with salt and pepper, spread the top with butter and dust with finely minced parsley.*

It is quite natural that Grandmother, with her dedication to beef and steaks, should have been interested in the sauces that go with them. I include a few here as a closing touch to this chapter, and lead off with a very, very old-time Butter Sauce and a few that were old when Escoffier's great-grandfather was young; and yet, they have never been surpassed.

BASIC MELTED BUTTER SAUCE (pre-1800s)—Cut 4 ounces (½ cup) of butter into bits that it may melt more easily and mix more readily; put it into a small stew-pan with a large teaspoon of flour and 2 tablespoons of milk. Stir over a gentle fire until you have a smooth, velvety dough; now add 6 tablespoons of water; hold the pan over the fire and shake it so that the contents swirl in a clockwise motion until they just begin to simmer. The sauce should be of the thickness of good cream and it should not be manhandled with a stirring spoon. This is the best way to make Butter Sauce. Milk and butter take to each other like lover and sweetheart and they soon join in perfect union.*

MAÎTRE D'HÔTEL SAUCE (mid-1800s)—Put 1 small teacup (2/3 cup) of butter in an earthenware dish and heat it; have ready 2 large tablespoons of finely minced parsley—it must have been boiled before it was minced. Add the parsley to the melted butter with the juice of 2 lemons, a pinch of cayenne and pepper and salt to taste; let the butter come to the bubbling boil and remove it from the fire immediately.*

GARLICKE BUTTER SAUCE (pre-1800s)—Pound 2 cloves of garlicke with a piece of fresh butter as large as a nutmeg; rub it through a sieve and add it to ½ pint (1 cup) of Melted Butter Sauce.*

SHALLOT BUTTER SAUCE (pre-1800s)—Mince as minutely as you can 2 nice firm shallots and boil them lightly without having them turn color in 2 tablespoons of butter. Drain the butter off and add the shallots to ½ pint (1 cup) of Melted Butter Sauce.*

CUTTING CAPERS FOR BUTTER SAUCE (pre-1800s)—To make ¼ pint (½ cup) of Caper Sauce, take 1 heaping tablespoon of capers and 2 teaspoons of vinegar. The present fashion is to cut capers in the following manner: mince 1/3 of them very fine and divide the remaining 2/3 in halves. Blend capers and vinegar into ½ pint (1 cup) of Melted Butter Sauce.*

YOUNG ONION BUTTER SAUCE (early 1800s)—Peel ½ pint (1 cup) of button onions and put them in a quart (4 cups) of cold water 1 hour before boiling. If you like a strong onion taste, do not peel them until after they are boiled, which takes about 30 minutes. Add this to ½ pint (1 cup) of Melted Butter Sauce.*

OILED BUTTER FOR COOKERY (early 1800s)—If you are short of oil for steak frying, you can turn butter into an oil by placing the amount you need in a frying pan and setting the pan at such a distance from the fire that the butter melts slowly until it becomes an oil; pour it off quietly from the dregs. (This is also called Clarified Butter.)*

WHITE CREAM SAUCE (pre-1800s)—Blend 1 tablespoon of flour into 1 tablespoon of melted butter; let this simmer briefly without browning;

thicken with ½ pint (1 cup) of milk; add 3 tablespoons of minced onions, a flake of mace and a spray or 2 of parsley; season with salt and pepper. Let this cook 15 minutes and strain it. This is the basic white cream consistency (thin). To make a thicker sauce, double the flour and butter; for a truly thick sauce, treble the flour and butter. The measure of milk remains constant. This is a French method; nonetheless it is very good.*

OYSTER SAUCE CAPE COD (early 1800s)—Keep 1½ dozen plump and juicy oysters in their shells until it is time to cook 12 of them in a stew-pan with their own liquor, well strained. Before that time, you take the preparatory step of making Essence of Oysters (see below) from 6 of them. Put the remaining dozen oysters into a stew-pan with their own juices, well strained. As soon as they plump, turn them into a sieve and let the juices run into a bowl. Rinse the pan; measure the oyster liquor into it, plus an equal quantity of milk; rub 1 tablespoon of flour into a ball with 1 tablespoon of butter. Stir it into the oyster juice until smooth, give it a boil up and let it simmer slowly. Now trim the oysters of their grisly parts; if they are very large, cut them in half; put the oysters into the sauce to heat, but if they boil they will toughen up. Lastly, blend in the Essence of Oysters, and your ship is at anchor with a savory cargo.*

SAUCE PIQUANT (late 1800s)—Brown and blend 3 tablespoons each of flour and butter; when they are done, blend in 1¼ cups of soup stock. Set the sauce to simmer. In another pan, put 2 tablespoons of tarragon vinegar to heat and in it cook 1 tablespoon each of minced capers, chives, green peppers, stoned olives and pickled sour cucumbers; let these cook 5 minutes after it comes to a boil; add them to the sauce and cook slowly an additional 20 minutes, stirring almost constantly.*

ESSENCE OF OYSTERS (early 1800s)—Pound the soft parts of oysters and rub them through a sieve. If the liquor thus produced seems very thin, beat the yolk of an egg into it.*

OYSTER CATSUP (early 1800s)—Take fresh, fat oysters and wash them in their own liquor; pound them in a mortar; to a pint (2 cups) of oyster paste, add 1 pint (2 cups) of sherry; boil them up and add 1 teaspoon of salt, 1½ teaspoons of pounded mace and a small pinch of cayenne; let the mixture boil up again, skim it and rub it through a hair-sieve. When it is cold, bottle it, cork it well and seal it down with Bottle Cement (see Index). A superior seasoning for meats and gravies.*

GARLICKE VINEGAR (pre-1800s)—Peel and chop 2 ounces of garlicke cloves and add them to 1 quart (4 cups) of superior cider vinegar; stop the bottle closely and let the garlicke steep for 10 days; shake it well daily. Finally, pour the liquid into small bottles, because the fewer times you open a bottle and expose its contents to the air, the longer its quality will last. Be very careful not to use too much of this; a few drops go a long way in flavoring steaks and seasoning gravies and sauces.***

MILD SHALLOT AND LEEK VINEGARS (pre-1800s)—These may be made the same way as Garlicke Vinegar by using 3 ounces (¼ cup) of chopped shallots and 3 ounces (¼ cup) of minced bottoms of leek, but of leek use only the firm white part. Of these flavoring vinegars, leek is the mildest on the breath of the beef eater, next come shallots and lastly garlicke.*

Attached to this recipe Grandmother had an old tongue-in-cheek remedy for curing "conspicuous breath" caused by these three members of the onion breed. It dates back to the seventeenth century and runs as follows:

> "If leekes you like but do their smell dis-like,
> Eat onions and you shall not smell the leeke;
> If you of onions would the scent expell,
> Eat Garlicke, *that* will drown the onion's smell."

And that reminds me of a little rhyme that Grandmother liked to recite because it warns housewives that when they boil or otherwise cook anything, the size of the pot should be adapted to the bulk of whatever it is to contain; the larger the pot, the more room it takes upon the fire without really earning its keep; also, small pots keep housewives from spending time boiling more water than necessary. Pin this on your cupboard; it may help you save time and keep your fuel bills down:

> "A little pot
> Is soon hot!"

4. A Helping of Historical Stuffing

IN THE DAYS OF FIREPLACE COOKERY—At this rather late hour, I would like to make it clear that this book is not a full-out treatment of New England cooking. It is, rather, a record of changes in the preparation of meals in Boston kitchens wrought in the course of the nineteenth century by outside influences and shifts in taste and cooking equipment. Except in Boston and a few other large and prosperous New England communities, there could not—in the pre-1800s—be an absolute definition of regional cooking in the area.

There was *country cooking* for hard-working, patient farmers who wrested meager livings from flinty soil, men whose wives had the industry, initiative and imagination to transform spartan basic foods into dishes that often reached heavenly heights.

There was *coastal cooking,* based upon the fish and shellfish which bold and hardy husbands snatched from a far from friendly sea. Here, too, wives brought touches of genius to foods that otherwise could have been monotonous, though nourishing.

In early days, when transportation was poor, there was very little overlapping of coastal and country cooking. It was, in the main, a two-pronged fork, the points of which reached into Boston and other cities where fishermen and farmers disposed of their wares for cash or barter. It was here, where products from sea and soil joined in a flow of abundance, that New England cookery was born. From here—when prosperity and networks of roads and country lanes spread after the Revolution—country dishes migrated up and down the coast, and coastal dishes ventured inland.

But something was added in the process. Many old recipes were changed by the injection of strange seasonings and foreign ideas brought to New England harbors—but principally Boston—by Yankee skippers from ports all around the world. New recipes, reflecting culinary practices of many lands and adapted to American usage in city homes, also fluttered into country and coastal kitchens. From this union of many factors New England cooking was born, and it was the first cosmopolitan cookery in North America.

As the nineteenth century got well under way, the hands of Time made even further changes. Before the 1820s, all New England meals were prepared before open fireplaces. After the 1820s, cooking was done over a confusing variety of kitchen stoves or ranges as well as over open fires on hearths. Then followed the decades of the Great Kitchen Revolution—forty years of hectic conflict and radical change. The revolt started in harbor cities up and down the Atlantic coast from the Canadian border to the Mexican Gulf and spread by river, canal and highway westward to the Mississippi. As a matter of fact, it actually took more than half a century to put an end to the squabble over the superiority or otherwise of the hideous kitchen range, with its open fire-grate that spread smoke and heat like a smith's furnace, and the cumbersome cooking stove, with its firebox which was enclosed but which could neither roast nor broil. Not until the 1870s were the best features of these pieces of equipment united into truly acceptable kitchen stoves that could handle the whole range of cookery. I believe that it can be truthfully said that no greater changes ever took place in American households than those that rose from the dead ashes of the open kitchen fireplace. First, the new equipment demanded new knowledge in the handling and use of cooking and baking fires. Second, it tossed traditional fireplace cookery—on which all recipes had been based—to the winds. Thousands of carefully cherished books, on the pages of which women had written their "receipts" laboriously and handed them down from mother to daughter, suddenly became as outdated as Eve's fig leaf.

But, as Grandmother would say, "First things first; everything in its place and a place for everything." I have, so to speak, put the bread pan before the yeast. This chapter should really start in the Pilgrim days, the days when Colonial wives—hard pressed by food scarcities and inadequate equipment for cooking—learned a few tricks from Indian squaws when their husbands were not fighting Indian warriors. As is well known, wives of the early New England settlers had a difficult time because they needed so much, had so little and could acquire hardly anything. Shipping facilities between the Old Country and the New were unsatisfactory—slow and unreliable. Incurable shortages appeared at every turn and in every place, including the kitchen. The so essential cast-iron cooking utensils were scarcer than even hens' teeth. True, the newcomers learned from Indians how to make wooden kitchen- and table-ware. But none of that could be used over flaming kitchen fires.

Those who were lucky enough to own iron pots lived on one-dish meals, and this was the birth of the New England Boiled Dinner.

ONE-POT BOILED DINNER (pre-1800s)—Take 3 pounds of salted meat and a small pound of the leanest of salt pork from the brine at night and soak it in cold water until morning. Put the meat into cold fresh water and let it cook slowly until the sun is high. Then take the pork out of soak, trim it nicely and cut it into squares. Let it cook with the meat until the sun is westering. As the meats cook, wash and quarter, according to your needs, turnips, onions and cabbage. Lay them with the meat in this order at ½-hour intervals by the glass. When the turnips are almost done, add whole carrots and potatoes in their skins. If you have beets, boil them apart and put them on the table with dinner.**

Roasting any kind of flesh or fowl in those days was a primitive affair. And yet even those simple methods would work as well today—when a multitude of chimneys on suburban homes reveal the presence of fireplaces —as they did then. There is, however, one basic principle that must be followed: When roasted before an open fire, meat must be kept turning in order to be cooked right through. Well, believe it or not, this can be accomplished without electric power, manpower, child-labor or the spending of a nickel, with nothing more than a nail, a string and something heavy, such as a brick. Our forebears performed the trick in this manner.

ROASTING MEAT ON A STRING (pre-1800s)—Drive a peg (or a nail) into the mantel directly over the center of the fire. Tie to this one end of a stout worsted string (any strong twine will do). Truss the thing to be roasted (weighing up to about 6 pounds) and fasten it in the middle of the string; tie a stone at the other end to hold it down. Depending on the fire, hang the roast near or away from the blaze. Set it turning slowly by twisting the string as taut as the catgut on a fiddle; the meat will turn as the string unwinds and then rewinds under its own momentum. The string must be twisted when it runs down (about 5 minutes) and it is work that any child can be set to do and work he will enjoy. In roasting meat this way, it is well to up-end it when half done so that the juice does not gather in one end. Place a dripping-pan under the roast and, before you start, rub the roast with fat and sprinkle it with flour or cornmeal. Baste from the drippings in the pan.***

Birds, as well as small game and meat, can be roasted in this fashion. The method could amuse guests and provide an object of occupation as well as a subject for conversation, if nothing else. To be sure, one could also copy the example set by early New England housewives after they acquired spits. First they or their children turned them laboriously by hand—a most tedious job. Then treadles, whereby one rotated the spit by foot like an old-time sewing machine, came along; later, miniature treadmills, which even dogs could operate, appeared. Could it be here that the phrase "a dog's life" began? Why not try it on your own bored pooch sometime?

However, let me remind the reader that roasting before a live log-fire eats into the woodpile. It is, therefore, the most expensive of all modes of cooking, unless one uses uranium. Of course, the cost of wood did not worry early or even late settlers. There were plenty of hardwood stands. From Rhode Island to the Canadian border, the woods were full of them until the mid-1800s, when scarcities of hardwood led to mean pinching and coal gained ground.

Meat was a great problem in those early days, if one excludes game, of which there was plenty. There were no closed seasons, either. But when winter set in and snows sealed the countryside, housewives had to rely on their salt-meat barrels. Often as not, these casks contained pork, because hogs were easier to raise and more prolific than other meat-providing animals. There were many methods of curing; here is one.

SALTING PORK (pre-1800s)—Cover the bottom of your barrel with coarse salt an inch deep; put down 1 layer of pork and cover that with salt 1 inch thick; continue this until all your pork is disposed of; then cover the whole with strong brine; pack as tightly as possible, the rind side down or next to the barrel; keep the pork always under brine by using an inner cover and well-scrubbed weighting stones. Should any scum rise, pour off the brine, scald it and add more salt. Old brine can be boiled down, skimmed and used for another salting down. The brine, of thickly salted water, should always be heavy enough to float an uncooked hen's egg.***

Early settlers soon discovered that there was a long stretch between the setting in of winter and the end of the chilly spring. This meant long abstinence from fresh field and garden greens and sent New England women into the woods in search of them as soon as the rills began to chatter like old women on their diet of melting snow. Mainly, they looked for the newly sprouted fronds of ferns called fiddleheads, so called because in their coiled-up state they looked so much like the heads of miniature fiddles.

BOILED SALAD OF FIDDLEHEADS (pre-1800s)—Pick a mess of 20 fiddleheads and keep them moist until ½ hour before dinner. Then scrape off the hairs and scales with a dull knife. In doing this, try to unroll their coils as well as you can without breaking them, since they, too, must be cleaned; chop off the coarse bottoms. Boil them whole for 30 minutes in salted water. They make a very pretty and welcome dish.***

In the springtime, these industrious women gathered leaves and flowers of various kinds of greens for medicines, for wines and vinegar. Let us turn to the dandelion. We have all heard about dandelion wine; but this weed was also prized because of its medicinal properties, and pioneer women knew a thing or two about home cures. They had to.

DANDELION EXTRACT (pre-1800s)—Infusions and decoctions may be made of roots and leaves. But an extract thus prepared is the best. Take up the roots in September, clean them, bruise them in a mortar and press out the juice; strain the root paste and put it upon a plate in a warm room to evaporate and render it thick and solid. Give in small doses 3 times daily for liver complaints.***

DANDELION BEER (pre-1800s)—Use ½ pound of dandelion root to 1 gallon of water; boil it well and, when new-milk warm, add 1 pound of maple sugar, 1 ounce of ginger, 1 teaspoon of good vinegar and a little yeast. It is very good for the digestion.***

Those gallant girls also walked down the primrose path, but not for reasons commonly associated with such excursions. On the contrary, they gathered primroses by the pack in order to make Primrose Wine and Primrose Vinegar. First, the wine.

PRIMROSE WINE (pre-1800s)—Gather 7 pecks of primroses while 30 pounds of honey is boiled in 15 gallons of water until 1 gallon be boiled away. Skim it and withdraw it from the fire. Have ready 16 lemons cut into halves; take a gallon of the liquor and put it to the lemons. Put the primrose flowers into the remainder and let them steep in it all night. Add the lemonade and 8 spoonsful of new yeast, stir it well together and let it work 3 or 4 days. Then strain it, put it into a cask, and after it has stood for 6 months, bottle it off.***

PRIMROSE VINEGAR (pre-1800s)—To 15 quarts of water put 6 pounds of brown or maple sugar and take the scum off while it boils 10 minutes. Pour on it ½ peck of primroses; before it is cold, add a little fresh yeast and let it work in a warm place all night; keep it in a barrel in the kitchen, and when it has done working, close the barrel, still keeping it in a warm place.***

CIDER AND HONEY VINEGAR (pre-1800s)—Mix cider and honey in the measure of 1 pound of honey to a gallon of cold hard or soft cider; let it stand in a vessel for some months well covered in a warm place, and vinegar will be produced so powerful that water must be mixed with it for common use.***

Pilgrim wives and those of early settlers learned about quite a few foods from Indians, particularly the use of maize, or corn. It was used whole with other vegetables, such as beans, or boiled into a porridge, or it was pounded to a meal in a mortar. One of the oldest boiled maize dishes is:

HULLED MAIZE PORRIDGE (pre-1800s)—Just how Indians removed the hard hulls of corn so as to cook the soft kernel is not known. But it has been claimed that an early New England way of dealing with this problem was to add a bit of ash-lye to the water in which the corn, stripped off the ears, was soaked. It was then rinsed and rinsed, and then boiled and boiled until it became a porridge. When soda came into use, it was tried and found satisfactory as a means of hulling corn. This is how that was done. Stir 1 teaspoon of soda into 2 pints of yellow corn covered by cold water. In about an hour the hulls should begin to separate from the kernels. When they have, drain the water and wash away the hulls. Now boil for 2 to 4 hours in slightly salted water; drain off the water and boil the corn in fresh water another 45 minutes. By then the porridge should be ready. Eat hot or cold with molasses or maple syrup. (Not exactly an item for a breakfast quickie, but it could be an amusing supper surprise).***

Most of the Indians the pioneers made friends with were generous and not "Indian givers." One of their greatest gifts was the secret of how to collect sap from maple trees in buckets and how to turn it into syrup and/or sugar. Elsewhere in this book are maple sugar and syrup recipes, but let's take a quick look here at how to "sugar off."

SUGARING-OFF FOR MAPLE SYRUP (pre-1800s)—Always use a cauldron that is deeper than it is wide and never fill it more than half full with sap to leave room for the boil-up. Except during odd winters, the sap runs best soon after Candlemas Day (early February). Always build a thick bed of faggots for fast and hot kindling, and since very few folks have those new-fangled "sugaring houses," pile some brush up to break the wind. This makes the flames burn more evenly and keeps your sap boiling steadily. Anyone who figures on less than 32 gallons of sap for 1 gallon of maple syrup is not good at figuring or at making maple syrup.***

MAPLE SNOW SUGAR CANDY (pre-1800s)—Stuff some snow tightly into a sap bucket and make the top smooth; when the boiling syrup is at the point where it starts to wax, drop it by the tablespoonful on the snow, where it will splatter into fancy shapes. Remove these while they are still soft and roll them into curls. (Our great-great-grandmothers enjoyed these candies made out of doors in the sugaring-off season. We can enjoy them today by heating maple syrup very hot until it balls up, that is, when drops turn into little yellow pills when plunged into cold water. Then drop the syrup from a spoon onto a bucket of snow; even a cake of ice will do. Ice cubes are also good if they are frozen smooth in the top of the refrigerator. Children will just love this.*

Cornmeal, the staff of life for the settlers in the New World, lends itself easily to fill the human need for sustenance. It makes wonderful breads and puddings and is as untemperamental to handle as the Old Gray Mare. Take a look at:

HEARTH HOT BREAD OR ASH CAKES (early 1800s)—For this, the cook needs nothing but a hearth that has remained hot over night, ½ pint each of boiling salted water and yellow cornmeal and 1 tablespoon of maple sugar, syrup or molasses. Make a dough of the water, sweetening and cornmeal and let it stand in a warm place while you clean away embers and ashes from a hot spot on the hearthstone. It does no harm to rub the stone with a rind of fat salt pork. When you are ready—and take your time because the dough improves with waiting—form the dough into tiny loaves 3 inches long, 2 inches wide and 1 inch thick. Put them on the stone and bury them under hot live ashes. When the time is ripe for the cakes to be ready, set some water boiling; and, when they are nice and brown and baked, remove them, brush off the ashes and give each a quick dip in the boiling water. Take to the table at once.***

STIR-ABOUT POT PUDDING (pre-1800s)—Some cooks while away too much time fixing their Hasty Puddings and put on airs by adding this and that. A real Stir-About Pudding is easy and quick to make, good to eat, and cheap, too. Set 1 pint and 1 gill (2½ cups) of water to boiling; when it boils up slip ¼ pint (½ cup) of cornmeal in slowly from the palm of your left hand while you stir with a wooden spoon in your right. Add 1 small tea-spoon of salt. Let the pudding bubble slowly for 30 minutes and never let up stirring for one second. Some women grease their pots, believing that this prevents sticking; this is not so. Use a good, heavy iron pot, stir and stir, and you will have no sticking or scorching. (Today one would cook this for an hour in a double boiler and stir often.)*

JOHNNYCAKE OR JOURNEY CAKE (pre-1800s)—For a small meal, meas-ure ½ pint (1 cup) of boiling water, in which a piece of shortening as big as a hazelnut (1 rounded teaspoon) and a heaping saltspoon (¼ teaspoon) of salt are melted. Pour this on ½ pint (1 cup) of cornmeal and whip it smooth. Spread this fairly thick batter on a board or pan, put it in a slant-ing position before the fire and let it bake until done, about ¾ hour. (See Index for other cornbreads.)***

This bread was called Journey Cake because it was so easily made by travelers before camp fires.

But, returning to the lack of kitchen iron-ware in early times, it must have seemed to the women of that period as if much needed implements could be produced only by a miracle. And who dares say miracles never happen? They do! And one did in the Old Bay Colony.

PILGRIMS DISCOVER BOG ORE— This miracle was wrought through the discovery of bog ore, or iron pellets and tiny pancakes of iron, in ponds at Middleboro, Carver and Assawamsett in Massachusetts not too many years after the *Mayflower* came to anchor off Plymouth. The name of the first finder and the time and place of discovery are unknown. This is unfortunate, because the ore "strike" was as important to Americans of that day as was the discovery of gold at Sutter's Mill in California to the nineteenth century. It was treasure that became veritable pots of gold at the end of Pilgrim wives' kitchen rainbows.

Bog ore came in nuggets of almost pure iron frequently found in clusters, like grapes. The ore was mined by hand in the marshes along the edges of ponds or plucked from pond bottoms with long-handled wooden rakes. Some of these nuggets were round and the size of musket balls; others were in the shape of "turkey droppings," as one chronicler put it, or flat, like two of the King's shillings placed on top of each other. But—what to do with them?

There was not much to do with. Still, Yankee ingenuity was, even then, in the making. As mining boomed, make-do furnaces sprang into being; thick smoke belched from their stubby clay chimneys and spread in clouds over the countryside. Men became professional bogtrotters and made a good living at it. A "miner" might, with luck, hit a pocket and gather as much as 1,000 pounds of ore in a single day. Since it sold at $6.00 per ton, this was good income at a time when few men saw that much cash money in a year.

Numerous ponds—as far south as Rhode Island—yielded up to 600 tons a year, and rills of liquid cast-iron ran into molds for implements that found many uses. Not least among these were kitchen utensils. As a matter of fact, the first iron casting of a kettle was made by the Saugus Iron Works at Lynn, Massachusetts, in 1642. Soon the progenitors of the roving peddlers who were to become a Yankee institution cruised the mire, dust and muck of the country roads. They offered such unthinkable luxuries as andirons, mortars and kettles, pots, skillets and spiders—even candlesticks and candle molds. Women hardly dared believe their eyes and bought or traded for all that their scant means would allow.

The rivulets of molten bog iron flowed freely and fast in those early times, because it was generally believed that, in this stern but strange new country, the unique metal supply was not only unlimited but also self-perpetuating. It was held that the iron nuggets grew like some peculiar kind of New World berries. There is a story about one bogtrotting Yankee "miner" that illustrates this point of view. He bragged that it would soon be "as easy to raise a bed of bog ore as a row of cabbages." Alas, he was wrong. In time, the bogs ran dry of iron and the settlers had to depend on iron from British or other sources.

Wives of settlers bought cast-iron candlesticks while looking forward to another miracle—one that would enable them to light their kitchens come dark. We who take well-lighted kitchens for granted just cannot imagine the handicaps those women had to put up with. At first, the only lights they had were those cast by the flames in their fireplaces or by their Betty Lamps. The latter were nothing more than wicks stuck into cups of grease. Women made primitive candles by collecting rushes in the marshes, soaking them in grease and lighting the stalks like candles.

As time went on, enterprising settlers established small industries for making household-ware of such materials as metal, pottery and glass. Among these wares were a great variety of kitchen implements, including the Dutch Oven. While these articles were welcomed, they came nowhere near serving as adequate substitutes for the well-equipped cookeries, pungent brew-cellars and aromatic bake-houses women had left behind them in the Old Country. Still, they did much to alleviate the burdensome shortages and conditions that had called upon these brave souls to match New England's granite mountains with resolution and endurance. That was where and when the Dutch Oven acquired a leading role as a housewife's saving angel.

YE OLDE BRICK BAKE-OVEN— Skills and materials to make the old reliable brick bake-houses were lacking. They were difficult to build and took a lot of know-how to handle. But, oh what bread and pastries they could produce! These bake-ovens were queer-looking affairs, something like flattened beehives. Since this narrative seems to demand almost as many side dishes as main courses, let us take a quick look at the bake-oven. It was usually a squat structure made of brick. Low walls of brick rose from a circular stone or tile floor into a curved roof. The oven did not have a firebox. Short, split hardwood logs were heaped upon seasoned faggots for quick and hot kindling on the floor of the oven itself. They were set ablaze and left to start a roaring fire that burned briskly behind the oven's tightly closed iron door. (For Faggots for Starting Fires, see Index). The smoke escaped through the oven's own chimney. A good baker knew from practice just how much wood was needed and the length of time it took to raise the "soaking heat" for which the brick oven was justly famous. With the palm of her hand she would check the heat of the outside wall. At the proper time, the fire would be withdrawn, the ashes would be swept out, bread tins filled with dough and other "hot bakings"—such as beans—were pushed into place, chimney and oven doors were shut as tight as drums and, in time, out came brown crisp loaves and divinely baked beans. But that was just the start. After the "hot bakings" were done, the heat-retaining oven was used for baking that required lesser heat in proper sequence from biscuits to custards.

THE DUTCH OVEN OF PRE-1800s—But our detour from the New World *pièce de résistance,* the Dutch Oven, has been long enough. This creation of gleaming tin did much to improve baking conditions. When used for baking, skillets and spiders placed over or near the fire or on the hob (or back shelf) of the fireplace had severe limitations. The Dutch Oven of our day is radically different from those of pioneer days. We know it as a deep, wide, heavy-lidded glass or metal pot that can be used over open and closed fires. The original Dutch Oven was actually an ingenious and highly efficient heat reflector specially designed for roasting or baking in front of open fires. It is too bad that the old Dutch Oven is no longer to be had—it is made of tin and relatively simple to produce—because ovens of this type could be most useful in open-fireplace and out-of-doors cooking today.

The Dutch Oven of before 1800 was a semicircular box that stood about 18 inches high and measured about 20 inches across the open front and at its greatest depth. The shelf that sat in its center was made of a somewhat heavier tin than the rest. This shelf, used for baking, was removed for roasting. Small birds, cuts of meat and small game intended for roasting were hung on hooks, three of which ran through the top of the oven into its interior. The part of the hook that stuck up above the oven was formed into a loop, which was turned during the roasting process to insure that the meat was evenly cooked. The oven formed a reflector that produced a strong and steady heat from even low fires and that required some practice in its handling lest the foods be drained of moisture. There was room for a drip-pan in the bottom which could be used for certain kinds of cooking, too.***

Just to show the versatility of the old Dutch Oven as a baking implement, I will cite a recipe for Yorkshire Pudding that goes back to Colonial times.

DUTCH OVEN YORKSHIRE PUDDING (pre-1800s)—Beat up 3 eggs, strain them through a sieve and gradually add to them ½ pint (1 cup) of milk; stir these well; rub together in a mortar 2 ounces (generous 1/3 cup) of moist sugar and ½ teaspoon of grated nutmeg. Stir these into the eggs and milk; then put in 4 ounces (1 cup) of flour and beat these into a smooth batter; by degrees stir in ¾ cup of suet minced as fine as possible (or butter or lard) and 3 ounces (¾ cup) of bread crumbs. Mix all thoroughly together and leave it to stand for at least ½ hour before you bake it. This will take about an hour in a moderate (350°F.) oven.

This pudding can be baked under meat in the same way as ordinary Yorkshire Pudding. It can also be baked in an ordinary earthenware dish in a second run of the bake-oven after the bread is done (350°F.), or stood in a dish in boiling water for 3 hours, in which case tie a pudding cloth over it and make sure to tie it very tight. However, if you boil the pudding, use half the milk called for in this receipt.**

Although the original Dutch Oven as just described served nobly, a noticeable improvement was scored by the invention of:

THE AMERICAN PORTABLE BAKER (early 1800s)—The roasting hooks are removed from this oven, which was about the size of its ancestor but rectangular instead of semicircular. The top and bottom inside panels slanted in from the front to the back of the oven. The former slanted down some 5 inches; the latter slanted up a similar distance. The outcome was a greater concentration of heat. There was no drip-pan, but the oven's false back was a good place for warming dishes and keeping foods hot. This oven, too, was made of tin; a removable shelf of heavier metal—even equipped with handles!—ran through its center.*

Things were getting better in the kitchen but, whichever way one looks at it, the grindstone of necessity and the millstone of arduous labor kept American housewives squeezed between them until deep into the nineteenth century. In the gradual lessening of the grind, the One-Pot Boiled Dinner gave way to an open metal basket wherein various vegetables could be cooked in separate compartments at one and the same time. Bit by bit— even bite by bite—the variety of the menu expanded as fireplace implements grew in number and variety.

OLD AND NEW FIREPLACES IN THE 1800s— The old days of empty fireplaces where only a pot or two stood on the naked hearth gradually disappeared. The fireplace itself underwent drastic changes. In ancient days, the hearthstone ran along the back of the fireplace, forming a sort of shelf against the deeply recessed back. Here the baking was done. In time, back plates and sloping baking shelves of cast-iron supplanted the "hob." Also, cast-iron grates or "ranges" took the places of andirons, because they saved fuel and therefore some of the labor of lugging wood from the pile.

A movable crane extended—usually from the left-hand inside wall of the fireplace—over the fire. From it dangled chains and iron hooks, from which pots and kettles were suspended at various distances above the blaze, according to the needs of the cook. Often small trivets were fastened on the tops of andirons to provide additional cooking facilities. Brackets for spits extended from the walls, and roasts were turned by automatic roasting jacks driven by weights or springs. Eventually roasts were even turned by small windmills inserted in the chimney, such as Aunt Ville had. Hot air rushing through the chimney set the windmill spinning and the windmill turned the spit. On or near the hearth stood or hung a great variety of implements, some of which would intrigue even today's sophisticated gadgeteers.

TOOLS FOR FIREPLACE COOKERY— Let us take a quick look at this line-up. Copper, tin, cast-iron, earthen and other ware for the practice of cookery; numerous spiders, some on legs, others on portable tripods; pans for frying, for catching drippings, for baking small breads, cakes, pies and biscuits; large and small saucepots and pans; a huge boiling pot; a great kettle; a Dutch Oven or a Bottle-Jack, the latter being a portable rotating roaster; a wooden meat-screen to shield roasts from chilling drafts; a stand for sad irons to heat on; another for pokers, tongs and ash shovels. To those savvy cooks, the iron poker was right handy.

RED-HOT POKER FOR QUICK BOILING (pre-1800s)—When you will be needing boiling water in a hurry, prepare for this by cleaning 1 or 2 pokers of their ashes and placing them over the fire at its hottest point so that they get red as a rooster's comb. When you must bring water from a slow to a quick boil, stick the pokers into the water in the pot, and almost at once you will have boiling water.***

On the walls near the fireplace hung a rich variety of smaller implements. For instance, suspended over spoon drippers dangled iron basting ladles, stirring spoons and meat forks.

SPOON DRIPPERS IN PRE-1800s— These, because they are such practical and easy to make time- and trouble-savers, are worth knowing about. Buy a sheet of tin, the size depending on the number of spoons and other such implements with handles you use when you cook. For 4 implements it should be 12 inches wide and 24 inches long. With a bottle or a rolling pin curve up one of the long sides a half-turn; in other words, make one side of the sheet of tin into a shallow trough. Paint the tin a color that goes with your kitchen wall and nail it on the wall, trough end at the bottom, within easy reach of the stove; drive 4 large nails or hooks an equal distance apart

across the top of the tin and put a disposable rag into the trough. You hang
the implements you use while you cook on the hooks or nails and wash them
later. Whatever drips from them will be caught on the rag in the spoon
dripper.*

I mentioned the Bottle-Jack as an aid to open-fire cookery. It was a
portable roaster—and is as good now as it was then—and came in different
sizes, from small ones for small roasts to large affairs for big roasts. Again,
here is an interesting old-timer which virtually any modern Handy Andy
with proper tools and some ingenuity could put together. The following
description is for a small model.

BIRD BOTTLE-JACK (early 1800s)—This device was usually the size of,
and looked like, a dairyman's milk can. It was made of tin or some other
light metal, and was called a Bottle-Jack because it looked exactly like a
bottle cut in half from neck to bottom and stood upright. In the neck of
the bottle was a clockwork mechanism or spring that rotated a rod which
projected some 6 inches into the body of the bottle. To the end of this rod
a metal disc ringed by several sharply pointed hooks was fastened horizontally. The birds or other items to be roasted were hung on the hooks on this
disc and turned very slowly before a low fire. Basting was done from a drip-
pan placed at the bottom of the bottle.*

Just as an aside, New England wives had unique ways of keeping track
of time before the 1800s. Clocks were not easy to get, even if one had the
money to buy them. Some timed their cooking by guess, gosh or glass, others
by the place of the sun in the sky, and many whose windows faced in the
right direction had markings on the floor on which the sun denoted the
time of day. This situation was eased after 1810 when Eli Terry, a Connecticut clock maker, found a way to make cheap clocks by mass production.
They sold like hot cakes.

Before we leave the gentle warmth of wood-burning fireplaces and de-
part for other and hotter kitchens, I believe that a few hints on how to
handle problems connected with open fireplaces and what kinds of wood
to burn may be timely. If you have a fireplace, this will interest you.

HOW TO BUY FIREWOOD (early 1800s)—In buying a measure of firewood try to get a good blending of hickory and oak. Of all woods these two
give the best heat value. If you buy wood by the cord, see that you are not
cheated by crooked pieces, each of which fills the space of two straight logs.
You do not save money or get good results by buying the cheaper softwoods,
as the following facts will prove. A cord of well-dried hardwood, such as
hickory, apple, oak, cherry, locust, hard maple, beech, black or yellow birch
or long-leaf pine, will weigh about a ton. To equal such a cord, it would
take about 1½ cords of ash, black walnut, soft maple, hemlock or sycamore,
and 2 cords of ordinary pine, cypress, spruce, willow, poplar or basswood.
Reject green wood of all kinds. Such logs contain a lot of moisture, which
actually cuts down the heat of your fire because of the steam they release.
Also, their thick, black smoke is apt to foul your chimney.*

PLATE IN GRATE SAVES WOOD (mid-1800s)—It is cheaper to burn wood in a fireplace range or grate than on dogs (andirons), because the blaze runs its course more gradually and with even less use of wood than when the fire is built on the hearth itself. Economies in the use of ranges or grates can be worked by placing a perforated metal plate in the bottom of the grate; thereby the draught is reduced, the intensity of the fire is lowered and the wood burns longer.*

In European novels dealing with the olden days, one often reads about ancient, worn-out men and old crones, even children, making a meager living by collecting in the forests bundles of wood called faggots. These were sold in the towns to country dwellers or to housewives who used them for starting baking fires. Suburbanites whose own or whose neighbors' bushes, hedges or trees are being pruned will find it profitable fun to save these cut-offs and turn them into faggots; or they may enlist the interest of their youngsters in gathering such materials on tours through the woods. The following description of these lightning-fast blaze starters shows how handy they can be in giving any kind of a fire a quick and hot getaway.

FAGGOTS FOR STARTING FIRES (pre-1800s)—A faggot is a bundle made up of all sorts of small branches, including sprays and shoots, from bushes, hedges, underbrush and trees aged from 3 to 4 years old. In making up a faggot, one should trim the branches down to naked sticks. These are tied, with the trimmings at the center, into small or large bundles as may suit the case. They season quickly and kindle readily, give a great quantity of flame and are without peer where a clean, quick and hot blaze is wanted. As they burn away rapidly, faggots are not fit for ordinary durable fires; however, in conjunction with other wood, they supply the means of producing any fast and furious increase of heat that may be wanted.*

GATHER YE PINE CONES WHILE YE MAY (pre-1800s)—Almost any pine cone that has dropped from a tree of its own accord makes good kindling. However, those that have dried on the ground in the fall before the rains and snow set in have the most burning juice in them. They are amazing to have about for starting fires on cold winter mornings. Chop a cone into chunks and light all at the same time; some burn so readily that they will burst into flame from the light of a candle.*

Chimneys—thanks to building laws and construction methods, as well as to a better understanding among builders of good chimney design—are less troublesome today than they were as recently as a few score years ago. In those times, chimney fires and smoking chimneys were quite common, and every housewife had to be on the watch for, and ready to meet, such emergencies. If your chimney smokes, there is probably some structural flaw that can best be remedied by an expert. In the olden days, if one can believe what one reads, some housewives took this measure:

CURE FOR A SMOKING CHIMNEY (early 1800s)—Inflate a large ox or hog bladder by breathing into its neck (or fill it from the free air faucet at a service station). Tie the balloon by the neck to the middle of a stick so that it hangs loosely from the stick, climb to the roof and insert the stick across the chimney a few feet below its top; or push it up into the chimney's throat when you let the hearth go cold; but be sure that it is safely above the flames. The hot air that rises from the fire will keep the bladder in constant motion, and this will prevent air from the outside from driving smoke down into your kitchen.***

When it comes to chimney fires, I have two remedies to offer, one that is easy to apply and one that demands materials that are not always readily obtainable. They follow in that order.

TO PUT OUT A FIRE IN A CHIMNEY (early 1800s)—So many serious fires and losses of life and property have been caused by chimneys catching fire and not being quickly extinguished, that the following method of doing this should be made generally known. Throw some powdered brimstone (sulphur) on the fire or ignite some on the hob; then put a board or hang a blanket or rug in front of the fireplace to prevent the fumes descending into the kitchen. The vapor of the brimstone rising into the chimney will then effectively extinguish the soot on fire.***

A HORSE, A HORSE, MY KINGDOM FOR A HORSE (early 1800s)—Throw at once upon the fire a large forkful of wet horse litter from the stable or the manure pile. Ordinarily, the steam ascending from the litter will extinguish the chimney blaze in less than a minute. Care must be taken that the litter is neither too moist nor too dry; if the former, it may extinguish the fire on the hearth; if the latter, it may break out in flame and increase instead of lessen the fire danger.***

A YANKEE MERLIN AT KING GEORGE'S COURT—Fate left it in the hands of Benjamin Thompson, born on a farm at Rumford, New Hampshire, in 1753, to start the rumblings of the Great Kitchen Revolution that was to come. As an affable and able young man-about-Boston, he won the favorable attention of General Gage, the British commander, because of his mathematical genius; on the other hand, he met wide condemnation among Americans because of his outspoken Tory opinions. In fact, Thompson was so loyal to King and Crown that he set sail with General Gage for England aboard a British warship, just escaping being run out of town by the Liberty Boys. But Benjamin was to return to America, where he fought with the Redcoats as a colonel in His Majesty's army.

Although Thompson was a renegade in the Revolution, housewives in America—and, for that matter, throughout the Western world—should have niches in their kitchens wherein to burn candles in his memory. Because, before he died, Thompson had become the Einstein who found the formula for the harnessing of cooking heat, the Edison who invented a wide variety of cooking implements, and the Escoffier who led the development of a brand-new kind of cooking method.

It all began in Germany after the 1776 Revolution, when this Yankee's quick perception of Bavaria's economic problems and practical ideas for solving them caused him to become the right-hand man of Maximilian, the future king of that country. Maximilian offered Thompson the position of chief administrative officer of Bavaria; with the consent of King George of

England, Thompson accepted. He instituted sweeping social and military reforms and declared an all-out war on the conditions that made for the undernourishment, and even starvation, of a large part of the Bavarian population. His principal weapon was the potato, and with it he won his war.

His interest in food caused Thompson's methodical mind to probe into methods of cooking. He discovered that the open fireplace was woefully inadequate and wasteful of heat. In this manner Ben Thompson's studies of heat and its habits began. Later they were to bring him world fame as a physicist and make him a pioneer in bringing newer and better cooking methods into European and American kitchens.

RUMFORD'S GARGANTUAN STOVE (pre-1800s)—In 1789, he created the cooking stove. It was a cumbersome mammoth, shaped like a horseshoe and built of bricks and cast-iron. It measured about 8 feet in width and at least half that in depth. Instead of one large firebox, it had fourteen small ones, each with its own small blaze. Built into the stove above each fire was an iron container. These containers were actually the bottom parts of what we would now call double boilers. When in use they held boiling water, into which were inserted other containers holding the food to be cooked. The secret of Ben Thompson's device was that it used, instead of the direct flames of the fireplace, coal fires that threw concentrated heat upon the boiling water. By these means the steam was produced that did the cooking. This was a new and spectacular method. Major drawbacks were that the cooking stove could neither roast nor broil; nor could it bake, except in very limited amounts. But when it came to soups, stews, gravies and such, the stove was a thing of beauty and a work of art.

Almost over night it became a European sensation in great houses as well as in moderate homes, this despite the fact that its basic purpose had been to reduce cooking costs and improve food quality in public institutions—which, to be sure, it did. To make the stove usable, Thompson concocted a number of recipes, the first and most famous of which was a potato stew. Because of his contributions to culinary progress, Maximilian, now the ruler of Bavaria, lifted Ben Thompson into the nobility. In honor of his hometown in faraway New England, the stove-creating Yankee asked to become known as Count Rumford. His famous potato dish, therefore, went into kitchen history as:

COUNT RUMFORD'S POTATO SOUP (pre-1800s)—Soak 3 cups of dried peas over night; put them to cook with plenty of cold water; when they come to a boil, add ¾ pound of lean, fresh pork, 1 cup of barley and salt to taste. Peel and wash 4 large potatoes; slice them into ¼-inch pieces and cover them with cold water. Let the peas simmer, skimming them well, 3½ hours, and add the potatoes 45 minutes before meal-time. Add boiling water if necessary to thin the soup, but it should be rather thick. Just before serving, dice the pork, pour the soup through a colander and rub the potatoes through it with a wooden spoon. Sprinkle with finely minced parsley. (Since this soup is alleged to contain 148.7 carbohydrates and 40.5% fat, it has no place on a reducing diet. It is the kind which, as the Old Folks used to say, "sticks to your ribs.")**

One day in the 1790s, as often happens at courts, the Count found himself out of royal favor. Nothing loth, he packed his gear and started off for England. There King George received him warmly, encouraged his scientific research, approved his culinary probings and elevated him to knighthood. Thus Count Rumford became Sir Benjamin Thompson, and he liked it. Now his most productive years began. Yet, although he gained in both stature and shekels, a great longing for the homeland burdened his life. Repeated overtures to the United States for permission to return were rejected. He died in France in 1814, many claim of a broken heart — this despite the honors and acclaim he had won from British royalty and fellow physicists.

RUMFORD'S BEEF ROASTER (early 1800s)—During his productive years, Sir Ben was a go-getter. When he discovered that his cooking stove did not prove as popular in beef-loving England as he had expected it would be— it could never broil a steak or roast a joint—Rumford went to work and developed a beef roaster that has not been equalled in efficiency to this day. But, alas, no illustration of it is available. However, it was a unique apparatus and deserves description. Let him copy it who can. But, before any do-it-yourself specialist tries his hand at it, let me warn him that, after the few bricklayers and ironworkers who had been trained by Sir Ben died out, the beef roaster died with them. This is the place to note that Sir Benjamin neither patented his inventions nor claimed profits from their sale.

Rumford's first roaster cooked the forebears of more joints of oven-roasted beef than I would care to count. It was nothing more than a sheet-iron cylinder some 24 inches long and, generally, 18 inches in diameter, set horizontally in a square structure of brickwork. The rear of the cylinder was sealed; the front was provided with an iron door that had a reliable lock. Directly beneath the cylinder was a small closed firebox. From this, heat and flame enveloped the cylinder; the smoke escaped through a flue to a chimney. Within the cylinder there was a double dripping pan, part of which held drippings, part, water. On each side of the roasting tunnel ran, like rails, two tracks. The beef to be roasted was laid on a rack which slid like a sledge over the tracks. So far, there is nothing special—but now comes the kicker. It consists of the first application ever made of super-heated air to the art of cookery. Two small iron tubes closed with petcocks ran from outside the brickwork through the very body of the blaze in the firebox. They rose into the cylinder, where their mouths were aimed directly at the roast. After the beef was done to the desired rareness, it was browned by the red-hot super-heated air that entered through the pipes when the petcocks were opened. That air was hotter than the Devil's breath.

The invention created a furore among tradition-loving Beefeaters in the British Isles. In large numbers they greeted the Yankee's creation with catcalls, hoots and thundering denunciations. An Englishman's home, by the Lord Harry, was his castle, where his beef belonged on a rotating spit before a huge bed of glowing coals; roasts done in ovens were baked, and who—as Grandmother remarked much later—wanted baked beef?

Nonetheless, Rumford Roasters were installed by the thousand all over Britain from Land's End to the tip of Scotland. Some followed the Rumford cooking stove across the Atlantic. However, because they were so difficult to construct, they found little, if any, favor in American coastal cities, and none whatever in the country.

The roasters were wonderful while they lasted, which was only some 30 years. But Rumford had started something. His cooking stove had its points, all agreed. It was widely copied, modified, improved. As the stove trade expanded, some thought, "Why not unite the stove's advantages with those of the grate or 'range' in the open fireplace?" The outcome was that some bright person or persons lifted the range from the hearth and made it part and parcel of a reduced version of Sir Ben's stove. This invention became known as a Kitchen Range. Having a large and exposed firebox, this range could roast and broil in addition to boiling. But—and there was the rub—it could not bake. The first step toward eliminating this drawback was a hideously topheavy portable oven that could be perched on a specially constructed heating stove.

RUMBLES OF THE KITCHEN REVOLUTION—So, as the nineteenth century got under way, American and English housewives had three choices. They could take a cooking stove that could bake and boil but not roast; or they could favor a kitchen range that could roast, broil and boil but not bake; or they could stick to what they had—namely, the open fireplace with its spits and other means of cooking and the venerable brick bake-oven for bread, etc. Some wives settled the matter by adding a cooking stove to their kitchen equipment, letting the fireplace do the roasting and keeping the bake-oven for emergencies. The early kitchen ranges were smoking monsters that had to stand under the throat of the chimney. Thus they usurped the hearth that had belonged to the fireplace. The cooking stoves could be put in any part of the kitchen because pipes could carry their smoke to the chimney, but, in turn, they saturated the kitchen with their heat and filled the house with cooking odors. The same may be said of the unique gridiron ranges, which added confusion, clutter and heat to kitchens in which they were installed. Like dinosaurs, they headed for limbo.

This situation, with many changes but few real improvements, lasted throughout the first half of the nineteenth century. During this entire period, the kitchen revolution raged with increasing spread and fury. Women took sides for or against one type or the other. Even as today, when cars are traded for new models every year, just for the sake of appearances, so women then traded in old kitchen stoves for new ones. Many of these goods were trash and soon broken, burned out and thrown on the trash heap.

Always ready to tilt their lances in housekeeping causes, Catherine Beecher and her sister, Harriet Beecher Stowe, launched a resolute attack upon kitchen ranges as late as 1869 in their book *American Woman's Home*. "The kitchen range is inferior to the cooking stove!" they thundered from their Boston homes. "It is less economical; its open fire endangers the dress of the cook; it requires more stooping than the stove; it will not keep a fire at night; it will not burn coal and wood equally well."

The sisters then went on to describe the perfect answer to a woman's prayers for a suitable stove and praise its many virtues. This wondrous invention could bake and boil. And, lo, by merely removing a side panel, the fire could be exposed to enable the stove to roast and broil. This wonder of wonders had more gadgets than a modern auto's dashboard has dials. In addition to a seventeen-gallon reservoir for hot water, a removable roasting oven and an extension baking oven, it had warming closets, a place for heating flatirons and a number of enormous tin lids which could be placed on the stove's top and under which pies and cakes could be baked.

All that, and cooking, too!

But who washed the dishes?

Some of these cooking stoves were made abroad and brought to America as early as the 1820s. A very popular type was one developed in France by the Marquis de Chabannes and sold in England. Unlike the Rumford stove, it did not cook with steam; instead of numerous small fires, it had one large firebox and also a spacious oven for baking. Its top surface was a single large plate of metal. It was a range of this type that Bella's father had brought across the Atlantic aboard his clipper and for cooking on which Great-Grand-mother Chapin had no recipes. Competing with these makes were stoves made later in Pennsylvania and New York. These were adaptations and enlargements of the old-time Pennsylvania Dutch heating stove and, in many ways, superior to those developed abroad. All had one feature in common —they were hotter than the hinges of Hades. The science of insulation was not discovered until Civil War days when removable insulating panels were added. These could be taken off in winter, when kitchens were hard to keep warm, and installed in the summer, when cool kitchens were necessary.

PROGRESSIVE INVENTIONS BY-PASSED KITCHENS—When one reviews the contributions made in the 1800s by inventive geniuses to virtually every phase of American life, it becomes pitifully clear that few or none of those geniuses took an interest in kitchens. By mid-century—when industrial and agricultural activities were being widely mechanized—housewives still carried the wearisome load of long hours over hot stoves with kitchen equipment that had not kept step with the times. The kitchen ranges were hot, demanding and temperamental. Solid wood or cast-iron implements were heavy enough to break a woman's back or lame a dray-horse. Coal took the place of wood as the latter became increasingly hard to obtain, and with it came the twin nuisances of dirty smoke and ashes.

Although coal gas for lights was being manufactured as early as the 1840s, it took decades before a practical gas stove was developed. And while a tiny electric bulb powered by a wet cell shed its feeble light as early as 1847, more than half a century was to pass before pioneer electric lights and heating plates were to enter the kitchen.

Although stores springing into existence in cities, towns and villages offered an increasing variety of foods and household necessities, women as a class had to remain self-reliant and resourceful in making do with what they had or with what their various household skills could produce. To almost the very end of the nineteenth century, the American housewife was virtually a castaway on a desert island of neglect in an ocean that teemed with progress and invention.

Man's work was no longer the whole stretch from sun to sun; but it still held true that woman's work was never done.

5. *Adventures in Nineteenth-Century Kitchens*

LONG DAYS, AND DRAB ONES—Many cook books of the 1835 to 1875 period were aimed at brides, and their authors took great delight in winging out on flights of poetic fancy. Thus, one writer led off with a few lines from Longfellow to the effect that launching a new home is a glorious occasion. He wrote:

> "O fortunate, o happy day
> When a new household takes its birth
> And rolls on its harmonious way
> Among the myriad homes on earth!"

Fortunate and happy for whom? For the bridegroom? Certainly, in nine cases out of ten, he got an able and willing team-mate fully prepared to pull her share, and more, of the load. With respect to the bride, there was more poetry than truth in Longfellow's romantic conception. While love did not go by the board, the woman usually stepped from romance into harness. In fact, it could be that a fitting observation by the groom would be those lines from *Jabberwocky* by Lewis Carroll:

> " 'O frabjous day! Callooh! Callay!'
> He chortled in his joy."

For all that lay before the average bride of that period was a long hard road, a daily grind that hardly allowed her time off for having babies. Not that husbands were merciless drivers and hard taskmasters. On the contrary, the frenzy to acquire and exercise housewifely skills was whipped up by other women who regarded near-exhaustion as a desirable status symbol, and the Mrs. Grundys could gossip about uppity and lazy neighbors in ways that were both vicious and cunning.

There is no such thing as the typical New England wife of that era. They were either country, village, town, suburban or city women and they all traveled in different orbits. But even those who lived on the fringes of cities kept poultry, milch cows and porkers. However, for the sake of argument, let us leave the city minority out of this particular picture and turn to the young housewives in the other four categories as representing the brides who were to become our grandmothers. They made it a point of pride to start their work before sunup and to fold their tired hands long after sundown. They found a peculiar, almost fanatic delight in performing many highly diversified chores that ranged from kitchen work to running neat as pins houses; from making bread, butter, cheese, soap and maple syrup and sugar to boiling, scrubbing, wringing, drying and ironing the weekly wash; from concocting and administering medicinal remedies to putting up cider, beer, cordials and wines; from tending their milch cows and goats to collecting hen's eggs, harvesting down from domestic ducks and geese, and killing such fowl as were needed for the table; collecting faggots for bake-ovens, salting ham and pork for their smoke-houses, picking hops for their brew-houses, corning meats for brine barrels, with side excursions into mixing and applying house paint and whitewash, making stove and grate blacking, concocting leather, furniture, shoe and other kinds of polish —not forgetting the eternal duties of looking after their broods of young 'uns.

Yes, our grandmothers were any and all things, including one-armed paperhangers on tin roofs. They had tough rows to hoe, including those in their vegetable and herb gardens. But once more we must recognize the hard truth that most of them slaved to suit stupid rules and not to fill needs which only they could meet. They were afraid of what Mrs. Grundy would say if it was bruited about that they purchased "boughten" materials in stores instead of making them at home, and "boughten" was a dirty word.

Many of the women who wrote books or articles on housekeeping chores made open attacks on this behavior pattern. One, who identified herself as "Aunt Sophronia," had this to say about women who literally worked themselves into madhouses or early graves: "If a wife dies of overwork, a housekeeper will cost $5 per week plus found, and some of them can find a lot they are not entitled to; if a wife goes to an asylum, let her consider the expense. Or, if she dies, her husband takes another wife and her children become mere step-children. Don't be a dead hawk tied to the pole of a scarecrow."

The pride, joy and principal exasperation of the post-Civil War housewife was her cooking stove or kitchen range, which, often as not, occupied the place of honor that formerly belonged to cozy fires on grates or andirons, to cooking crane, roasting spits and other open-fire cookery gear that had cluttered the hearth prior to the arrival of the Iron Monster that had wrought such drastic changes in the lives of housewives. These ugly cast-iron contraptions robbed the kitchen of much of its warmly welcome glow. Gone was the bright-looking hearth rug which, when the kitchen had been tidied up after the evening meal, was usually spread before the fire; gone, too, was the rocking chair that had stood before the hearth. And in the corner near the window, where not so long ago the spinning wheel had stood, squat, ugly ice chests now began to appear.

While, in time, the kitchen stove was to become a fairly efficient and valued device, the fact is that the mid-century models were voracious fire-eaters. To keep them going, women had to make frequent trips to the wood pile or the coal shed; to keep them clean, they had to lug heavily loaded buckets of ashes to the heap. Women who had been expert at regulating cooking heats in fireplaces and knew just how to produce the whole gamut —from soft to quick, from sharp to soaking, fires—now found themselves utterly unable to control the blaze in the monster's firebox or to regulate the oven. Actually, it took above average ingenuity for a housewife to understand and operate the numerous controls, such as hearth valves, sliding ventilator panels, front and back dampers, plus other doodads. Astronomical was the number of breads that slumped, pies and cakes that were scorched or heavy as lead, and meats that were either baked to cinders or came out of the oven roaring raw, before our grandmothers got the hang of things and taught themselves how to make delicious meals on the Iron Monsters, which, in time, they actually learned to love.

Naturally, the hints for housewives that appeared in various guises during the two decades that followed the Civil War were crammed with hints on how to manage kitchen stoves. The subjects covered ranged from economy and efficiency of operation to advice on cooking and precautions against burns and flaming dresses. A few specimens—still sound and practical—follow:

REVIVING DYING COAL FIRES (mid-1800s)—A dull fire can often be revived by placing a poker across it, because the metal concentrates the heat and throws it on the fire; air drawn between the poker and the coals also creates a slight but reviving draft.*

TO SAVE KITCHEN COALS (mid-1800s)—See that cinders are properly sifted and the good pieces saved. Because they are so small, it is best to make a thick paste of the grains of coal dust that always gather in the bin. Use cold water, mix the bits of coal into a dough and shape it into small cakes or loaves. Let them dry in the sun and use them as coal.*

WHEAT PASTE TO START COAL FIRES (mid-1800s)—Gather the bottom dust in a wheat bin, mix it with water or very wet sawdust and a little moistened clay to help bind it; press the mixture into flat discs as big as buckwheat cakes and put them out to harden and dry. These make kindling just as good as the wheat-coffins our grandmothers made in the olden days.*

TO AVOID BURNING HANDS (mid-1800s)—Instead of using metal spoons, forks and the like when you work over the stove, turn to wooden utensils. You will like them once you get used to their lighter "feel." Buy good hardwood, the lasting kind; softwood is cheaper but apt to break, split or swell.*

WETTING COALS FOR BETTER FIRES (mid-1800s)—As you fill your bucket at the bin, sprinkle the coal lightly with water, because once the kindling is well started the red-hot scalding steam speeds the combustion and increases the heat. This method is particularly helpful when you want a soaking heat in a hurry.*

GRANDMOTHER'S WORKING DAY—But, before we venture deeper into our kitchen yesteryears, let us detour long enough to catch a quick glimpse of grandmother's working day. She would rise, winter or summer, about 5 to 5:30 A.M. En route to the kitchen she would, in favorable weather, open a window to let some air into the house. Next she would remove the stove lids, clean out the ashes beneath them and brush the ashes into the ash pan by way of the firebox. Then she would remove the ash pan and lay the fire, wood or coal, as the case might be. If the former, she would lay logs for a soft, quick, sharp or soaking fire, according to her needs. If she needed a fast starter she would use faggots (see Index) or "coffins," an odd name for a fire kindler made by plaiting ropes of a dozen straws "dry enough for making bricks" and tieing them into bundles with strands of straw called "withes."

Let us, on this make-believe morning, follow our grandmother as she prepares a far from make-believe morning meal. She had decided on its contents the day before—Oatmeal with cream and butter; Codfish Cakes with a helping of reheated Baked Beans; Crumb Omelet, Baking Powder Biscuits; left-over pie; coffee and/or milk.

BREAKFAST OATMEAL (mid-1800s)—This was started after supper the night before, when 1 cup of oatmeal was blended into 4 cups of boiling water with 1½ teaspoons of salt, put over a low fire and stirred frequently until bedtime, when pot and all were placed in a homemade hay heater (see Index) to continue cooking itself into a soft mush until morning. Oatmeal was usually served in a large soup-plate, where it appeared as a volcanic island, rising, lavishly sprinkled with sugar, out of a sea of thick cream, with a large lump of freshly churned butter melting in its crater.*

BAKING POWDER BISCUITS—Check with your hand to make sure you have a right hot oven (see Index). Now, sift together 3 cups of good flour and 3 tablespoons of baking powder with 1½ teaspoons of salt, and cut in with a knife a small ½ gill (¼ cup) of unsalted beef fat or unsalted butter. Have ready-mixed ¼ pint (½ cup) of equal parts of milk and water. Add this to the mixture; do not knead or stir the dough, but cut it with a knife until perfectly blended. Shape it into biscuits and bake them from 10 to 15 minutes, depending on the size of the biscuits and the heat of your oven. —Miss Mabel Wentworth

CODFISH CAKES—Give 1½ cups of shredded salted codfish a quick boil-up after supper if the cakes are to be used for breakfast; pick it well and soak it in cold water over night. In the morning, squeeze the fish dry with your hands and mix it with 1½ cups of chopped boiled potatoes; heat this in 1 gill (½ cup) of milk until it has absorbed the milk. Place the mixture in a mortar and pound it to a pulp with 4 teaspoons of fine as sand bread crumbs. Lastly, add 1 yolk from a large egg. Make your cakes, dip them in the beaten white of the egg, roll them in bread crumbs and let them stand to harden. The trick in making good Codfish Cakes is to have them just about ¾ inch thick and to fry them very quickly in smoking hot fat made from equal portions of fresh (unsalted) butter and lard. Greasy fishcakes are little more than hog fodder.—Mrs. William G. Fales

BAKED BEANS, TO REHEAT—Always let left-over beans remain in the crock in which they were baked. Since they have a tendency to dry up, they can be moistened in the following manner. First, place the crock, covered, in a hot oven, this to soften the beans so that they will not break when stirred. Next, depending on the amount of beans in the crock, blend a small quantity of melted butter and molasses in a skillet; when this is hot, add a tiny amount of good vinegar. Stir this mixture into the beans and return the crock to the oven for the blending of flavors.—Julia Simpson

CRUMB OMELET—Heat 1 cup of milk and have a similar measure of stale and not too fine bread crumbs in a bowl. Prepare 1 cup of cream sauce by blending 1 tablespoon of flour into 1 tablespoon of melted butter in a frying pan; when you have a paste, add the hot milk and crumbs; stir strongly; season well with salt and pepper. Work swiftly as you separate the yolks and whites of 3 eggs. Beat the yolks well and turn them into the bread-sauce mixture. Whip the whites until they are dry, stir them in gently and pour all upon a hot, heavily buttered frying pan. Do not turn the omelet, but let it cook over a gentle fire. Before serving, give it 5 minutes in a hot oven for a nice browning.—Mrs. Morton G. Olmsby

TO MAKE HEALTHY AND INEXPENSIVE COFFEE— With ¾ pound of rye grains use ¼ pound of coffee beans. Sort them separately and carefully and remove bad grains and beans; wash them separately in cold water; drain off the water for a moment as you take coffee or rye from the washing water with the hands; put each handful directly into the browning skillet; during browning stir carefully all the time to insure even browning and to prevent scorching. After the browning, blend the rye grains and coffee beans; grind only as needed; settle the brew with a beaten egg, or a 2-inch square of dried codfish skin, and serve with cream and sugar. I say sincerely that this coffee brew is better and healthier than pure coffee, which is enervating and de-bilitating. You may try barley, peas, parsnips, dandelion roots, etc., but none of their flavors are equal to rye, although all of them are used to a greater or a lesser degree in the making of coffee. Housewives who object to smelling their houses up at coffee roasting will do well to put a pan of glowing char-coal in the back yard on an up-ended boiling-pot; that is one good way of getting rid of the often persistent smell. A better idea is not to use coffee at all. Like all stimulants, it is unnecessary and dangerous.—Mrs. R. A. Beal

After the family had breakfasted—during which Grandmother usually found time to do the upstairs rooms—she would prepare and consume her own morning meal. To rid the kitchen of cooking odors in the winter she would pour 1 teaspoon of sugar into a pie-pan and leave it on a warm but not hot place on the stove, or plunk a piece of charcoal into the oven and leave the oven door open.

NO COFFEE-BREAKS IN ROCKING CHAIRS—One would think, after their menfolk had left for their appointed tasks and the children had trudged off to school, that our grandmothers would, in a body, have slumped into their rocking chairs as placid Grandma Moses types. But those energetic women would rather have been found dead on their feet than caught rock-ing in working hours. Remember—a time for everything! And so many things had to be done by a nineteenth-century housewife that there was little time for rest and even less for relaxation.

In addition to keeping the house clean and the routine tasks of plan-ning and preparing three hefty meals a day, cooking, scrubbing and cleaning afterward, every day had its special calendar of scheduled work. Monday was wash-day. Tuesday was "folding" and baking day. Wednesday was iron-ing day. Thursday was house-cleaning day. Friday was for odd chores rang-ing from making soap to molding candles. Saturday was baking day and Sunday was for whatever rest a body could find after the added chores of 'tending church and fixing the always demanding Sunday dinner.

Now we come to another interesting question: what kitchen aids did housewives have to work with in those days?

When one balances the multitudes of simple and complex kitchen aids of today, from mere gadgets to impressive appliances, without which the average housewife would feel completely frustrated and defeated, against those to be found in run-of-the-mill kitchens of a century ago, it becomes clear at once that kitchen equipment of that era was labor-demanding rather than labor-saving. In fact, the only mechanical devices on hand, as will be revealed in the following complete list of *essentials* in an ordinary mid-century kitchen, was a clothes wringer, an ice-cream freezer, an egg beater and a coffee mill.

Peruse the following line-up, and you will realize how the average kitchen of a hundred years ago was equipped to meet the needs of the housewife.

EQUIPMENT IN AVERAGE KITCHEN IN MID-1800s—

Wooden-ware: kitchen table, wash bench, wash tubs (3 sizes), wash board, skirt board, bosom board, bread board, towel roll, potato masher, spoons, clothes stick, flour barrel cover, flour sieve, chopping bowl, soap bowl, pails, lemon squeezer, clothes wringer, clothes bars, clothes pins, clothes baskets, mop, wood boxes (nests).

Tin-ware: one boiler for clothes, boiler for ham, bread pans, dish pans, preserving pan, 4 milk pans, 2 quart basins, 2 pint basins, 2 covered quart pails, 4-quart covered pail, saucepans with covers (2 sizes), 2 cups with handles, 4 jelly molds (½-pint), 2 pint molds (for rice, blancmange, etc.), skimmer, 2 dippers (different sizes); 2 funnels (one for jugs and one for cruets), quart, pint, ½-pint and gill measures (broad and low, as such are more easily kept clean), 3 scoops, bread pans, 2 round jelly-cake pans, 2 long pie-pans, coffee pot, tea steeper, colander, steamer, horse-radish grater, nut-meg grater, small salt-sieve, hair-sieve (for straining jelly), Dover egg beater, cake turner, cake cutter, apple corer, potato cutter, 12 muffin rings, soap shaker, ice filter, flour dredge, tea canister, coffee canister, cake, bread, cracker and cheese boxes, crumb tray, dust pan.

Iron-ware: range, pot with steamer to fit, soup kettle, preserving kettle, tea kettle, large and small frying pans, dripping-pans, gem pans, spoons of different sizes, gridiron, griddle, waffle iron, toasting rack, meat fork, jagging iron, can opener, coffee mill, flatirons, hammer, tack hammer, screwdriver, ice pick, ice-cream freezer.

Stone-ware: crocks of various sizes, 6-quart, 4-quart, 2-quart 1-pint bowls, 6 earthen baking dishes (different sizes).

Brushes: table brush, 2 dust brushes, 2 scrub brushes, blacking brush (for stove), shoe brush, hearth brush, brooms.

HIRED GIRLS WERE SCARCE—Women of our times, who entertain the highly erroneous belief that hired help was readily available in Grandmother's era, may wonder why housewives shouldered so many responsibilities alone. There are several answers to that question and I will try to give them briefly.

To begin with, many women were either too self-sufficient to want a helper underfoot or they were too afraid of what Mrs. Grundy would say if they were so extravagant and lazy that they had to have a hired girl around the house.

In addition, New England women who wanted assistance soon discovered that Yankee girls were loth to hire out, either because they did not want to enter domestic service or because there were other and better jobs. The amazing industrial expansion of New England offered good wages to "young females" and more personal freedom than any domestic ever had. Even "green" lassies, fresh from the Old Country, were attracted by factory work rather than housework.

It may be said here that one reason among the many why domestic service was disdained by young women was the attitude of housewives as mistresses. Because they demanded so much of themselves in terms of willingness and capacity to work, they were, as a class, difficult to please—slave-driving perfectionists. Heaven help the hired girl who took time out to rest when there was work to be done—and there always was.

I can testify from experience that Grandmother Lyon did not belong to that tartar strain. Rena and Silas gave ample proof of that, since each was in her service more than a quarter of a century. In earlier times, Grandmother had wandered in the desert of Boston's servant famine; but she had rolled with the punches and, as John L. Sullivan, also a Bostonian, might have said, kept her left up with a Roast of Beef and her right ready with a Yorkshire Pudding.

KITCHEN WORK WAS NOT DEMEANING—In my girlhood days, when I dreamt of Sir Galahad riding me off to matrimonial Utopia, Grandmother insisted that I must learn the rudiments of cooking—she would rather have seen me get a scholarship to the Boston Cooking School than the one I was awarded for voice training at the New England Conservatory of Music; as for myself, my true ambition had been to attend Simmons College, then famous for its course for librarians. While I love food and appreciate music, I adore books above everything else. And even to this day, I feel twinges of regret that I did not go. Father, always family conscious, wanted me to attend Mount Holyoke, a pioneer college for women, because its founder, Mary Lyon, was his father's cousin.

But let us come back to the kitchen. I remember Grandmother one day producing a copy of *American Woman's Home,* written in 1869 by Catherine Beecher and Harriet Beecher Stowe, both extremely proper and fiercely crusading Bostonians. In fact, "Hattie," author of *Uncle Tom's Cabin,* was named by Abraham Lincoln as the firebrand who ignited the Civil War with the issue of slavery. Grandmother opened the book at a certain page and read in her firm, clear voice: "Any bride who thinks that a woman demeans herself knowing anything about kitchen work and takes pride in not cooking an egg should know that all the ladies of King Louis XIV's court dabbled in cookery and that Madame de Sable (a great favorite) established a cooking school for the nobility and in which the Duc de La Rochefoucauld stood at the head of the class."

I was tempted to make an appropriately impertinent reply, but thought better of it. One just did not do things like that to Bella Lyon; when her temper was really up, it would have been more fitting to spell Lyon with an *i* than with a *y.*

GRANDPA WAS THE FATTED CALF—In the do-or-die race for first place in the cemetery—women slaved themselves into eternity and fed their husbands to premature death—breakfast was the first, and almost lethal, blast fired at the menfolk from the kitchen batteries. To us it would be a Brobdingnagian repast; to our grandfathers, it was merely routine. Here is such a breakfast. Try it on your husband for size if you have nothing better to do some bright and leisurely morning (see Index for recipes).

Hominy and Heavy Cream with Maple Sugar*
Breakfast Beefsteak with Hashed-in Cream Potatoes*
Buckwheat Cakes, Bacon, Hot Syrup and Melted Butter*
Apple Pandowdy with Sweet Sauce*
Tea or Coffee*

About the noon hour on weekdays (an hour or two later on Sundays and holidays) something like the following dinner would be served.

Green Pea Soup with Diced Salt Pork*
Boiled Ham with Cake Icing and Egg Sauce*
Potato Croquettes and Escalloped Tomatoes*
Home-made Bread and Freshly Churned Butter*
Coleslaw, Pickles, Sweet 'n' Sour, Catsup*
Dan'l Webster Pudding, Boston Cream Pie*
Tea or Coffee

The third and last culinary broadside would volley out of the kitchen at supper time about the hour of sunset. Yes, this was a lighter meal, but in a strictly relative sense. On the supper table one might expect to find:

Creamed Chicken Shortcake with Butter Sauce*
Cold Sliced Ham and Boiled Ox-tongue*
Baked Potatoes and Succotash*
Muskmelon Pickles, Chow-Chow, Spiced Peaches*
Buttered Tremont Biscuits and Cottage Cheese*
Almond-Vanilla Blancmange and Election Cake*
Milk or Tea*

Under this steady barrage of carbohydrates, cholesterols and calories, small wonder many husbands buckled under, went to their just rewards prematurely and left their wives clad in widows' weeds with the unpleasant prospect of having to fend for themselves.

6. Sunrise and Sunset Dishes

LEFT-OVER VEGETABLE HASH (early 1800s)—In a large frying pan heat 2½ tablespoons of suet fat or good drippings and have ready, chopped and mixed in a basin, ½ pint (1 cup) of cabbage, ¼ pint (½ cup) each of boiled beets and potatoes, ditto of turnips and carrots, to which 1 teaspoon of salt and ½ teaspoon of pepper have been added; stir in 4 tablespoons of boiling water. When the fat is smoking, pour the vegetables into it and blend the mixture with a fork to give it even distribution in the pan, like a large cake; pat it down gently with the blade of a knife; let it cook over a slow fire for 30 minutes, when it should be browned on the bottom and well heated. Fold the hash and slide it onto a serving plate.*

BAKED BEANS CROQUETTES (late 1800s)—Have ready 1 pint (2 cups) of baked beans into which ½ pint (1 cup) of boiled rice and ½ cup of mashed potatoes have been mixed; season to taste with pepper and salt; if the beans are on the sweet side, blend in 1 tablespoon or so of finely minced sour pickles. Make a simple Croquette Sauce by blending 1½ tablespoons each of melted butter and flour, but, instead of water or milk, add ½ cup of juice of tomatoes. Mix the sauce into the beans, shape them into croquettes and fry in deep, hot fat (see Index).*

EASY BOSTON BAKED BEANS—Soak over night 1 pint (2 cups) of Navy beans in clear water; in the morning parboil the beans, and at the same time, in another dish, parboil a piece of salt pork about 3 inches long and wide and thick. Drain off the water from the beans and pork; put both together in a deep crock with the pork on top; season with 1 tablespoon each of brown sugar and molasses and 1 teaspoon of dry mustard powder. Bake for 6 hours in a slow (275°F.) oven. Top with a little water when they have baked 3 hours—Anon.

YANKEE BAKED BEANS—Boil the beans in enough water to cover them until they begin to crack with a pound or two of parboiled salt fat pork. Put the beans in a baking pan in their own water; score the pork across the top and settle it in the middle; add 2 tablespoons each of brown sugar and molasses. Bake in a moderate oven 2 hours. The beans should be very moist when first put into the oven, or they will grow too dry in baking; do not forget the sweetening if you want Yankee Baked Beans.—Mrs. Higgins

BOILED BEANS POLENTA (early 1800s)—Although many Boston housewives turn up their dainty noses at this way of preparing beans, the fact is that beans are never so good even if baked the time-hallowed Boston way. Wash common white beans, put them into cold water and simmer about

2 hours until soft and mealy. For every quart (4 cups) of boiled beans, take 1½ tablespoons of molasses, 1 teaspoon each of salt and dry mustard, 1 table-spoon of butter, ¼ teaspoon of white pepper, 1 tablespoon of vinegar; stir these into the beans carefully and let them cook, under vigilant eyes, for 15 minutes. The beans, when done, should be quite dry. Take great care not to scorch them.*

BAKED BEANS CROQUETTES (mid-1800s)—Nothing better could happen to left-over baked beans than to be turned into croquettes. Mince, as fine as you can, 1 medium onion, ½ small green pepper and ½ red pepper; add ½ teaspoon of salt and ¼ teaspoon of nutmeg; mix these well as you cook them tender in a little butter. Mash 2½ cups of baked beans to a pulp, work in the onions and peppers and set them aside. Now make a Croquette Sauce (see Index) and stir it into the bean mixture. Mold the mixture into cro-quettes and brown them in butter in a frying pan or fry in deep fat after they have been dipped successively in crumbs, beaten egg and crumbs again. The fat should brown a bread cube 1 inch square in about 45 to 50 seconds (375–80°F.).*

CIVIL WAR VINTAGE BAKED BEANS (mid-1800s)—Friday night after supper, put 1 quart (4 cups) of whole picked-over pea beans and a few stalks of celery in enough cold water to cover them to soak over night. On Satur-day morning, after breakfast, bring this to a boil; let the beans simmer until the jackets spring open. Scald your bean pot and see that you have a nice slow (300°F.) oven. In the bottom of the pot place a not too large sliced and peeled onion. By the way, people who like a strong onion taste should leave the skin on. Remove the celery stalks from the beans and discard them. Drain the beans of their liquor and save it. Put the beans in a saucepan and season them with ¼ cup of molasses, 1 tablespoon each of vinegar and brown sugar, 1 teaspoon each of salt and dry mustard, ½ teaspoon of black pepper. Blend well and pour the beans into the bean pot. Poke 1 pound of par-boiled salt pork, well scored, into the beans, so that only the rind shows. Bake covered in a slow oven about 10 hours. At intervals see if the beans need more moisture; if they do add the heated bean broth in small quanti-ties. Instead of bean broth, many women use Tomato Catsup (see Index) thinned down with about 1/3 of bean broth. After 9 hours remove the cover to brown the pork and the top of the beans.*

LEFT-OVER MEAT AND TOMATO STEW (early 1800s)—When tomatoes are to be had, quarter several, according to the quantity of cold meat at hand; there may be twice as much tomato as there is meat. Put the tomatoes, which are nicer if they are peeled (see Index), in a saucepan with just enough water to cover the bottom of the pan; let the stew come to a slow boil, when you must remove it from the fire and lay the meat remnants, large and small, of cold roast beef, roast mutton or lamb or pork, or what-ever you have, into the tomatoes. Add ½ tablespoon of brown sugar; use also cold fat-free gravy if you have it, any good catsup (see Index) and a smallish piece of butter. Let the stew cook again, but only long enough, about 5 minutes, to heat the meat thoroughly.*

AN EARLY NINETEENTH-CENTURY HASH (early 1800s)—Chop fine some pieces of cold soup meat, or other boiled meat, be it salt or fresh; then chop a like amount of cold potatoes that have been cooked and peeled; mix them with the meat. In a spider, heat some cold gravy, or soup or water in which meat has been boiled. As it boils up, add the meat and potatoes; season with pepper and salt and add a small bay leaf; cover it close and let it cook 5 minutes; then stir in a piece of butter the size of a walnut (1 tablespoon); let it stand over the fire a minute or 2 longer and take it to table in a warm dish.*

CORN BANNOCKS (mid-1800s)—Mix 1 pint (2 cups) of yellow cornmeal with 1½ teaspoons of baking powder and cut in 4 teaspoons of lard or drippings with a good pinch of salt; add enough cold water to make a dough like that for biscuits. Drop the bannocks from a tablespoon onto a greased, uncovered skillet over a mild fire until they are brown; then flip them over and brown the other side. To test for doneness, pull a sharp splinter out of a log and stick it into the middle of a bannock; if the splinter comes out clean, it is time to break the bannocks into pieces and eat them with melted butter.*

GOOD BREAKFAST CAKES—Three eggs well beaten, 2½ cups of flour, 1 pint (2 cups) of sweet milk, a little salt. Make a batter of these; put in buttered cups or rings and bake in a quick (400°F.) oven 20 minutes.—Mrs. J. H. Brown

THRIFTY WIFE'S BANNOCKS— Mix 1 quart (4 cups) of Indian meal with a little salt; wet it quite soft with boiling water or milk—the liquid must be boiling; wet your hands; pat the mixture out in small flat cakes; fry on a skillet in hot lard, using not enough to cover the bannocks. Cook one side first, then turn and cook the other. Cheap and good for breakfast.—Mrs. R. A. Sibley

BUTTERMILK CORN CAKE (early 1800s)—Take 1 pint (2 cups) of buttermilk, break an egg into it, stir in a spoonful or 2 of flour and add Indian (corn) meal enough (about 2 cups) to make a thick batter; put in 1 teaspoon of salt and 2 tablespoons of molasses; stir for 5 minutes; then add a heaping teaspoon of saleratus (baking soda) dissolved in a teaspoon of boiling water. Mix all thoroughly and bake in a not too quick oven (350–75°F.) in a deep, buttered pan for 35 minutes. If it is the season for berries of any kind, put a gill (½ cup) or 2 (1 cup) into the dough at the very end. These cakes can also be baked on the griddle.*

CORNMEAL PONES—Scald a quart (4 cups) of milk; stir in 1 pint (2 cups) of meal and 6 eggs, whites and yolks beaten separately, a little salt, 1 tablespoon of flour, 2 teaspoons of baking powder. Bake in buttered white cups or small bowls and send to the table in the cups, so they may be hot to be turned out on to the plate and eaten with butter or syrup. Bake in a hot (425°F.) oven exactly 20 minutes.—Mrs. A. M. Gibbs

LAPLANDERS FOR BREAKFAST—Three eggs, 3 cups of flour, 3 cups of sweet milk, 1 teaspoon of melted butter and a little salt. Beat all well together, then bake in a hot (425°F.) oven for 15 minutes in greased iron molds.—Mrs. A. L. Chetlain

BREAKFAST GEMS—One cup of sweet milk, 1½ cups of flour, 1 egg, 1 teaspoon of salt, 1 teaspoon of baking powder. Beat these together for 5 minutes; bake in hot gem pans in a hot (400°F.) oven about 15 minutes.—Mrs. Brown

BREAKFAST BUNS—Two cups of flour, ¾ cup cornmeal, ¾ cup of butter, ½ cup of sugar, 2 beaten eggs, 1 cup of milk, 3 teaspoons of baking powder. Bake in a hot (400–25°F.) oven for 20 minutes.—Mrs. J. W. Preston

QUICK SALLY LUNN—One cup of sugar, ½ cup of butter; stir these well together and then add 1 or 2 eggs; put in 1 pint (2 cups) of sweet milk with sufficient flour to make a batter about as stiff as that for a cake; put in 3 teaspoons of baking powder. Bake in a hot (425°F.) oven and serve piping-hot with butter, for tea or breakfast.—Anon.

JOLLY BOYS—Scald and cool 1 quart (4 cups) of cornmeal; add 1 pint (2 cups) of flour, 2 eggs, 1 teaspoon of soda, 2 teaspoons of cream of tartar, a little milk, salt. Make as thick as pancakes and fry in hot lard. Nice for breakfast.—Jeannie Brayton

WHITE CORNBREAD—One pint of meal thoroughly scalded with hard-boiling water. Add a piece of butter the size of an egg (4 tablespoons) and 1 well-beaten egg; add as much milk as will make the batter just thin enough to flow over the pan. Have the batter an inch thick, and then bake in a hot (425°F.) oven for 20 minutes.—Mrs. E. S. Cheeseborough

A GOOD CORN BREAD (late 1800s)—One egg, 1 cup of sour milk, 1 teaspoon of soda, 1 tablespoon of molasses, 1 gill (½ cup) of flour, a little cream or butter and enough cornmeal to mix a quite stiff batter. Bake in a buttered pan in a hot (450°F.) oven about 20 minutes.*

SAMP PORRIDGE (pre-1800s)—Crack dried corn in a mortar until you have 1 pint (2 cups). Cover this with cold water; remove the splinters of the hulls as they rise and leave the samp on the bottom. Now boil the samp an hour or so until it pulps like hulled corn; add hot water as needed; eat hot with maple syrup and butter.***

STAGE-STATION CORN PONES (mid-1800s)—Blend 1 pint (2 cups) of fine Indian meal and 1 pint (2 cups) of milk; melt and add 1 tablespoon of butter; beat 2 eggs very light and add them together with 1 teaspoon of dry cream of tartar; beat the mixture and add 1 teaspoon of baking soda dissolved in a tablespoon of cold milk. Beat all the ingredients together, pour the mixture into a buttered baking pan sprinkled with dry meal; bake in a quick (425°F.) oven for about 20 minutes.*

HASTY PUDDING THE HARD, SLOW WAY (early 1800s)—Boil in a pot or kettle about 6 quarts (24 cups) of water, leaving room for the addition of the meal. Mix 1 pint (2 cups) of Indian (corn) meal and a dessertspoon of salt with enough cold water to form a dough. When the water boils, stir the dough into it. After ½ to ¾ hour, when the pudding is smooth and thickening, stir in 4 or 5 handfuls of dry meal and let it boil as much longer; then add as much more dry meal as your judgment dictates. Taste to see if it needs more salt. Stir the pudding very often to prevent it from burning. Most people make their Hasty Puddings too thick and do not boil them half long enough; they should boil at least 2½ hours. When taken out the pudding should be so soft that it will quickly settle down in the dish as smooth as silk. If you wish to fry it, put a tablespoon of cold water into each pan or dish wherein the pudding is put away. This prevents the pudding from sticking when you turn it out for slicing.***

HEAD CHEESE OF PORK (mid-1800s)—Take the feet, head, ears and tail of a fully dressed hog and boil them until all the bones fall out. Then take all the meat and throw the bones away; boil the meat up and stir in Indian meal, just as in making Hasty Pudding. Put in a great deal of salt and let the mixture boil very moderately about 1½ hours, stirring briskly nearly all the time. Then take it up in deep dishes and, when it is cold, cut it in slices and brown it on a griddle. A convenient article for people engaged in hard work, but too hearty for persons of sedentary habits.***

SOUSE (early 1800s)—Take off the horny parts of the feet and toes of a pig and clean the feet, ears and tail very thoroughly; then boil them until the large bones slip out easily. Pack the meat into a stone jar with good sprinklings of pepper, salt and allspice; mix some good cider vinegar with the liquor in which the meat was boiled, in the proportion of 1/3 vinegar to 2/3 liquor; strain this well through a hair-sieve and cheesecloth and fill up the jar.***

EGGS WITH CHEESE (mid-1800s)—Cut some hard-boiled eggs in slices and lay them on a well-buttered dish; next, put 1½ tablespoons of White Cream Sauce (see Index) into a stew-pan with 2 ounces (½ cup) of chopped cheese, a small piece of butter, the yolks of 2 or 3 eggs and a little pepper. Stir the sauce over the fire until it starts to thicken, pour it over the hard-boiled eggs, sprinkle bread crumbs over all, put the dish in the oven and serve as soon as the contents begin to color.*

BACON-AND-EGG PASTIES WITH POTATO PASTIES (mid-1800s)—Bacon-and-Egg Pasties: Make a simple and small pie dough with 1½ gills (¾ cup) of flour blended with ¼ teaspoon each of baking powder and salt; add ½ gill (¼ cup) of drippings and 2 tablespoons of cold water; work this into a dough and roll it thinly; cut the dough into 4-inch squares and shape them into cups. In each cup place 1 freshly broken egg and sprinkle each egg with 1 dessertspoon (2 teaspoons) of chopped well-done bacon; close each cup by pinching the edges of the dough together. Bake 10 to 15 minutes in a hot (425°F.) oven.

Potato Pasties: Lay a tablespoon of mashed potatoes, salted and peppered, on a slightly larger square of pastie dough; top it with a dab of butter,
seal it and bake 10 to 15 minutes in a hot (425°F.) oven.**

ESCALLOPED HAM AND EGGS (late 1800s)—Mix equal parts of minced
ham and bread crumbs; season with salt, pepper, a little mild mustard and
melted butter; moisten the mixture with cold milk until it is quite soft.
Fill small patty pans with this mixture; cover the tops with beaten egg and
cracker crumbs dusted with pepper and salt. Set in a moderate (350°F.) oven
until brown.*

HAM-AND-EGG CAKES (early 1800s)—Mince lean ham finely until you
have ½ pint (1 cup); mince the whites and yolks of 4 hard-boiled eggs; combine the eggs with the ham and season with ½ teaspoon of minced parsley
and a dash of nutmeg or powdered ginger, salt (unless the ham is salty) and
pepper to taste; beat in 2 whole raw eggs and bind with enough bread
crumbs to make a firm dough that will shape into flat cakes about 1 inch
thick and 3 inches across. Dredge in flour and fry in butter over a slow
fire until brown and heated through. A rasher or 2 of Baked Bacon (see
Index) enhances this.*

HAM AND EGG AND BAKED TOMATO (late 1800s)—Scald, skin and
scoop out 1 large red tomato per person. Fill the tomatoes with a mixture
based on the following proportions. Pour ¾ cup of Pea Soup (see Index) in
a bowl, add 2 well-beaten egg yolks well seasoned with salt and pepper; next
add 1 cup of lean, minced ham; mix thoroughly. Fill the tomatoes with
this mixture and bake in a moderate (350°F.) oven ½ hour or more or less,
depending on the size of the tomatoes.*

HAM AND APPLE TREAT (mid-1800s)—For this easy and pleasant dish
use enough thinly sliced cooked ham and raw sliced apples to make several
layers in a fairly large buttered baking dish. Sprinkle each layer with dashes
of molasses, a few dribbles of dark Jamaica rum, bits of butter and coarse
bread crumbs. Bake well covered for about ¾ hour in a medium hot (375°F.)
oven; leave the dish uncovered during the last 10 minutes of baking.*

COLD PORK AND APPLE TREAT (mid-1800s)—Follow the directions
given for Ham and Apple Treat (see above), but instead of molasses and
rum use brown sugar and sherry. Instead of Champagne Sauce use Peppery
Tomato Sauce (see Index).*

COOKED HAM AND MASHED POTATO CAKES (early 1800s)—Mix equal
amounts of minced or mashed ham and mashed potatoes; season lightly with
crushed rosemary and pepper, also salt, if needed. Dust with flour and fry
in butter or ham drippings.*

HAM BALLS (mid-1800s)—A good way for a small family to eat a large
ham without tiring of it is to chop cold, cooked ham, add an egg for each
person, beat together, add enough cooked rice or soft bread crumbs to bind
the mixture into balls, and fry until brown in hot butter.*

FRIED HAM WITH CREAM GRAVY (late 1800s)—Cut a nice slice of baked or boiled ham about 1½ inches thick and fry it slowly in your best beef drippings (or butter). When brown on both sides, pour 1½ gills (¾ cup) of heavy cream over the ham; when the cream bubbles up, remove the ham. Have ready the yolks of 2 or 3 eggs beaten up in a few tablespoons of whole milk; take the cream gravy off the fire and stir in the yolks; return to the fire to let the gravy thicken, but do not let it boil as that will make the eggs separate. Be sure to have the gravy absorb all the ham browning on the bottom of the pan. Pour over the ham and serve.*

BREAKFAST PORK CAKE (mid-1800s)—Take ½ pint (1 cup) of lean chopped cooked pork, ¼ pint (½ cup) of stoned and plumped raisins, ½ pint (1 cup) each of molasses and milk, 1 teaspoon each of salt and soda and 1 quart (4 cups) of flour. Make a dough in the usual manner; work in the pork and raisins; lastly add the soda. Bake in a cake tin in a moderate (350°F.) oven 35 to 40 minutes. Neither frosting nor sauce is called for with this cake, but housewives who like to go to the trouble make a Cream Sauce (see Index), which they season with finely chopped Piccalilli.*

APPLES AND BACON (mid-1800s)—Cut some nice, sweet bacon into thin slices and fry it almost to a crispness. Have prepared some Greenings, pared, cored and thickly sliced; fry them in the fat left by the bacon, which should be kept hot until the apples are ready, when the apples should be placed upon the slices of bacon.*

A CHEESE RELISH (early 1800s)—Take ½ pound of fresh cheese, cut it into thin slices and put it in a frying pan, turning over it a good ½ pint (1 cup) of sweet milk; add ¼ teaspoon of dry mustard, a pinch of salt and pepper and a piece of butter the size of a butternut (2 teaspoons); stir the mixture all the time. Roll 3 Boston crackers very fine, making ½ cup of crumbs, and sprinkle them gradually over the cheese; then turn it at once onto a warm serving platter.*

MILK TOAST—Toast the bread very quickly; dip each slice in milk which has been brought to nearly boiling heat; it is better to spread butter on the bread after it is dipped in hot milk than to melt the butter in the milk; thicken what milk is left with a little cornstarch and pour it over the toast when it is sent to the table.—Anon.

TONGUE TOAST—Take cold boiled tongue and mince it fine; mix it with cream or milk, and for every ½ pint (1 cup) of the mixture allow the well-beaten yolks of 2 eggs; place the mixture over the fire and let it simmer a minute or two; have ready some nicely toasted bread; butter it; place it on a hot dish and pour the mixture over; send to the table hot.—M. A. P.

LEMON TOAST—Take the yolks of 6 eggs; beat them well and add 3 cups of sweet milk; take baker's bread not too stale and cut into slices; dip the slices into the milk and eggs and lay them into a spider with sufficient hot melted butter to fry them to a nice delicate brown. Take the whites of the 6 eggs and beat them to a froth, adding a large cup of white suger; add the juice of 2 lemons, heating well; serve this over the toast as a sauce, and you will find it a very delicious dish.—E. A. Forsyth

CORNED BEEF HASH— One and a half pounds of nice lean corned beef, boiled tender and chopped fine; 1/3 more chopped boiled potatoes than meat; 3 large onions sliced fine and browned in butter; when the onions are tender, add the meat and potatoes, well seasoned with salt and pepper, and enough water to moisten. A small red pepper chopped fine helps. Spread the hash over a lightly greased pan and warm it through.—Anon.

BREAKFAST STEAK— A nice steak of beef or veal; pound it with a steak mallet, if tough; lay it in a baking tin; dredge it lightly with flour; season with salt and pepper, and if you like, a little chopped onions and parsley. Then put it in a hot (400°F.) oven and bake for 20 or 30 minutes, or until sufficiently well done; take it up, put it on a platter and spread it with butter. Dredge into the juices of the meat in the baking pan a little flour and season with butter; let this boil up and pour it over the steak.—Anon.

A NICE BREAKFAST DISH— Mince cold beef or lamb; if beef put in a pinch of pulverized cloves; if lamb, a pinch of summer savory to season it; add a very little pepper and some salt and put the meat in a baking dish; mash potatoes, mix them with cream and butter and a little salt and spread them over the meat; beat up an egg with a very little cream or milk and spread it over the potatoes; bake the dish a short time, sufficient to warm it through and brown the potatoes.—Harriet N. Jenks

MACARONI MEAT PIE (mid-1800s)—Cook ½ pound of macaroni in salted water until tender; drain it; cut ½ pound each of raw lean pork and raw lean veal into tiny squares; fry 1 tablespoon of minced onions a light yellow in 2 ounces (2 tablespoons) of butter; add 2 ounces (½ cup) of sharp, grated store cheese; season with salt, pepper and sage or savory; mix in the diced meat; cook briefly; add ¼ pint (½ cup) of hot water and blend the whole with the macaroni. Butter a deep pie-pan and dust fine bread crumbs over the bottom and sides; pour in the meat and macaroni and bake, covered, in a moderate (350°F.) oven about 1 hour; remove the cover during the last 15 minutes so that the pie will brown on top.*

SCOTCH RAW BEEF HASH (early 1800s)—Chop lean raw beef very fine; take—for 1 pound of beef—2 tablespoons of butter, 1 teaspoon of chopped parsley and 1 tablespoon of minced onions that have been cooked in a small amount of butter, 1 very small blade of mace or bay leaf. Blend all the ingredients together, cover with boiling water and stew, well covered, for 15 minutes. Drain. Shape into ½-pound cakes, place them on slices of toast and cover with gravy and fried eggs. A most satisfactory breakfast dish.*

BEEF SHORTCAKES (mid-1800s) — Cut 2 pounds of tender beef rump into small, thin slices. Simmer it in water 2 hours and skim as needed. Save whatever broth is left for making a Cream Gravy (see Index); season the meat with pepper, salt, ½ teaspoon of sage and 1 teaspoon of parsley. Meanwhile, have the Shortcakes (see Index) ready; blend the gravy into the beef, reheat briefly and serve on the buttered Shortcakes.*

MOCK MACARONI (early 1800s)—Use what you have of broken crackers—any kind will do; crumb them up rather fine and stir them into sweet milk, a little butter, pepper and salt; add 2 tablespoons of grated cheese. Put in enough milk to enable them to bake for ¾ hour without baking dry; let them be light brown on top.**

CREAMED OX-TONGUE BREAKFAST DISH (mid-1800s)—Take 1 teacup (1 cup) of cold boiled tongue, mince it fine, mix it with 1½ gills (¾ cup) of cream, and heat it gently. Add slowly the well-beaten yolks of 2 raw eggs; stir until the mixture thickens; do not boil. Season with pepper and salt and 1 teaspoon of minced parsley. Serve on toast with sweet gherkins.*

RAISED BEEF HASH PUDDING (mid-1800s)—Mix 1½ cups of finely minced cooked beef with 2 gills (1 cup) of cold mashed potatoes and 1 gill (½ cup) of cold mashed turnips, carrots or celery roots. Stir in 1½ gills (¾ cup) of good beef gravy or a like amount of soup into which 1 teaspoon of arrowroot has been blended; add 3 tablespoons of butter or drippings, melted, with pinches of thyme, salt and pepper and 1 teaspoon of curry powder; stir in 3 beaten egg yolks followed by 5 stiffly beaten egg whites. Pour this into a greased bread pan and bake in a moderate oven (350°F.) for 40 to 45 minutes.*

VEAL OR LAMB HASH (late 1800s)—Mince any kind of cooked veal, lamb or mutton very fine; to each cup of minced meat add ¼ cup of finely minced ham and ditto of bread crumbs soaked in milk and squeezed very dry; also 1 tablespoon of minced onion and ½ teaspoon of parsley. Finally, whisk in 1 whole beaten egg seasoned with pepper and salt to taste. This hash can be cooked on top of the stove, but it is much better if baked until hot in a moderate (350°F.) oven about ½ hour. Serve with a Brown Cream Sauce (see Index) seasoned with Tomato Catsup.*

MEAT AND POTATO PUFFS— Take cold roast meat (either beef, veal or mutton); clear it of gristle; chop it fine; season with pepper and salt. Boil and mash some potatoes, and make them into a paste with 1 or 2 eggs; roll out the paste with a little flour; cut it into a round with a saucer; put your seasoned meat on one half; fold it over like a puff; turn it neatly round and fry it a light brown.—Anon.

RED FLANNEL HASH (mid-1800s)—Heat 1 pint (2 cups) of chopped corned beef with ½ pint (1 cup) each of chopped boiled potatoes and chopped boiled, but not pickled, beets in 4 tablespoons of butter. In another skillet, fry a smallish onion a golden brown in butter. When the hash is hot and the onions are done, blend them together and moisten with cream or hot soup stock to induce the beets to color the hash a fine crimson. For this dish, many people use Meg Dods' Hash Gravy (see Index), which induces the same results.*

LAMB OR MUTTON HASH (late 1800s)—Mince 1 or 2 onions and fry them in 1 tablespoon of butter very slowly until they are yellow; mix 2 teaspoons of minced parsley with the onions. Make 1 cup of Cream Sauce (see

Index), flavor it with ½ teaspoon of Worcestershire sauce and stir this into the skillet mixture; lastly, add 1 cup of finely minced cooked lean lamb or mutton. Add a very small laurel (bay) leaf. Set the skillet, covered, in a moderate (350°F.) oven to bake for ½ hour; stir from time to time. Pile the hash in the center of a flat serving platter and surround it with Browned Potato Border (see Index).*

CREAMED CHICKEN HASH (late 1800s)—Make a medium Cream Sauce (see Index) but double the quantities given in this recipe and use one-half liquid and one-half left-over chicken gravy if you can. For 1 pint (2 cups) of cubed chicken or turkey, have ready 1/3 cup of chopped cooked celery, 1 cup of cooked potatoes chopped fine but not minced, 2 dessertspoons (4 teaspoons) of minced celery and 1 tablespoon of slivered blanched almonds. Have the Cream Sauce good and hot; stir in 3 tablespoons of sherry; let it heat; then add the other ingredients slowly and let the whole simmer gently as they warm. Season to taste with salt, white pepper and a dash of cayenne; serve with small triangles, or sippets, as they were called, of nicely browned toast.*

CHICKEN AND VEAL CROQUETTES— One plump chicken, 2 pounds of veal cut from the round. Boil the chicken and veal separately in just enough cold water to cover them; pick to pieces and chop the meat. Cut up 1/3 loaf of bread and soak it in the broth of the chicken while warm; put all in a chopping bowl; season with salt, pepper, mace and nutmeg; beat 3 eggs light and mix them with the above ingredients. Make the mixture up in oblong balls and fry them brown in equal parts of hot lard and butter.— Mrs. Chaffee

POTTED CHICKEN AND HAM (early 1800s)—Strip the meat from a cold roasted chicken or other fowl; when it is freed from gristle and skin, weigh the meat and to every pound add ¼ pound each of minced cooked lean ham and unsalted butter, ½ teaspoon of nutmeg and ¼ teaspoon of pounded sage leaf. Cut the meat fine and pound it well with the butter; add the spices slowly, plus salt and pepper as wanted, until you have a very smooth paste. Put this into clean stone or earthen jars and cover with Clarified Butter (see Index) about ¼ inch in thickness. Serve cold with potato salad or on sandwiches.*

HASHED POND DUCK (mid-1800s)—Cut the remains of a cold roast duck into nice small pieces; put the carcass and trimmings into 1 pint (2 cups) of water; add 1 large sliced onion that has been slightly fried in butter and let this boil away until the liquid has been reduced to ½ pint (1 cup); then strain, skim away the fat and make a Cream Sauce (see Index) with the liquid; season to taste and add just a touch of pulverized ginger. Put the duck into the Cream Sauce and let it heat slowly, without boiling, for about 15 minutes. Serve on toast.*

TO FRY HAM AND EGGS (early 1800s)—Cut thin slices of ham and take off the rind; if it is very salty, pour hot water upon the ham but do not parboil it as that toughens the ham, nor suffer the slices to lie too long in the water, as the juices of the meat will be lost. Wipe the slices in a cloth; have the spider greased and ready hot; lay in the pieces and turn them in a minute or 2. They will cook in a very short time. The secret of having good fried ham is in cooking it quickly, and not too much. Remove the ham from the spider and fry the eggs in the ham fat, adding a little butter if necessary.*

FRIZZLED SMOKED BEEF (mid-1800s)—With a sharp knife, shave slices of smoked beef as thin as the thinnest paper. Do not attempt to cut across the whole piece; it matters not how small the shavings be, if they are but thin. Put the slices in a small kettle or saucepan with ½ pint (1 cup) of milk; boil the milk a few minutes, then add a small bit of butter and an egg beaten with 1 teaspoon of flour, and stir well. Put a little more milk to it if needed. These proportions call for ¾ pint (1½ cups) of beef shavings.*

BACON, TO BAKE (late 1800s)—You avoid the danger of under- or overdoing bacon, as well as the risk of burning it in a frying pan, by placing bacon strips on a rack over a dripping pan and putting them into a hot (400°F. oven) for about 10 to 15 minutes.* (Incidentally, you never had nicer, whiter bacon drippings than the drippings from this method of cooking.)

BEEF OMELET BALLS (early 1800s)—Three pounds of round beef, uncooked, chopped fine, 6 eggs beaten together, 5 or 6 soda crackers rolled fine, a little butter and suet, pepper and salt, and sage, if you choose; mix, shape into cakes and fry in butter on both sides until done, or 10 to 15 minutes.*

MINCED BEEF COLLOPS (mid-1800s)—Take a rump steak; chop it; put it in a spider with hardly enough boiling water to cover it, 6 peppercorns and a piece of bay leaf. Add plenty of butter and cook just long enough for the meat to become tender and for the water to cook away. Season with pepper, salt and minced parsley. Serve with Creamed Potato Pancakes (see Index) for breakfast or supper.*

CHEESE SANDWICHES— One-half pound of grated fresh mild cheese, a tablespoon of butter, the yolks of 3 hard-boiled eggs and a teaspoon of Mayonnaise. Mash the yolks well; mix them with the other ingredients. Spread slices of bread with butter and then with the dressing.—Anon.

BREAKFAST VEAL STEW— Two pounds of veal steak cut in strips. Put it in cold water in a skillet or spider over the fire. The water should be just sufficient to cover the meat. Pare, wash and slice 1 small potato and put it in with the meat. Stew for 20 or 30 minutes gently, taking care that the water does not boil away. When the meat is tender add to the broth 1 cup of fresh milk and 1 heaping tablespoon of flour wet with milk; season all with butter, salt and pepper, and, if you like, a little parsley. Have ready 2 or 3 eggs boiled in the shell. Cut the hard-boiled eggs in slices and put them into the broth. Let all boil up once and serve with or without toast on the platter.—Anon.

FRIED EGGPLANT FOR BREAKFAST (mid-1800s)—In summer, when good meat is not always easy to get, eggplant is a good substitute for meat at breakfast. About 1 hour before breakfast, slice the eggplant about ½ inch thick, salt the slices on both sides and pile them up in two even stacks; put a board over the stacks and something heavy, such as a flatiron, on it, this to rid the eggplant of its copious stores of water and thereby reduce much of its naturally bitter flavor; season with pepper, salt and nutmeg. Fry each slice in hot fat until brown. Done this way it is not necessary either to egg-crumb the slices or to coat them with a batter.*

STEWED FISHCAKES (per-1800s)—Pick the meat from the bones of cooked fish; put the bones with the heads and fins into a stew-pan with 1 pint (2 cups) of water; add 1 sliced onion, 1 sprig of parsley, 1 chopped stalk of celery, also pepper and salt as needed. Let them stew slowly 1 hour or more. Chop the fish fine and mix it with equal portions of bread crumbs and cold boiled potatoes rubbed through a sieve; add the white of 1 egg; mix and shape into cakes. Brush the cakes with 1 whole beaten egg, cover with bread crumbs and brown them in a spider in fresh (salt-free) butter. Strain the liquor, pour it over the fishcakes and let them stew gently, covered, for 15 minutes, without turning them.*

SWEET-AND-SOUR FISH HASH (mid-1800s) — Take 1 pound of boiled or baked fish, any kind, and chop it fine. Make a dressing as follows: 2 raw eggs, 3 tablespoons of vinegar, 1 tablespoon of cream, 1 teaspoon of white sugar, ¼ teaspoon each of salt and dry mustard. Cook this over boiling water until it is thick as cream. Add it to the fish, heat and serve.*

FISH HASH FIT FOR KINGS (mid-1800s)—First you must have ready 1 dozen small, white, peeled and parboiled onions and an equal number of what are called small button-mushrooms. Lightly fry the onions whole in butter; cook the mushrooms also in butter in another skillet, with a tea-spoon of lemon juice, pepper and salt; add the mushrooms to the onions and allow these items to stew gently together. Now, skin and remove from the bones the raw meat of a mixed mess of lean and fat fish, cut it into small pieces and place in a stew-pan with just enough wine, red or white, to cover it; add a cheesecloth bag containing 1 bay leaf, 4 cloves, 6 peppercorns, 1 big pinch of rosemary; sprinkle with salt and pepper to taste. Bring this to a fast boil, skim well and add to it 1 tablespoon of flour kneaded into 1 tablespoon of butter; stir the sauce as it thickens. Next, add the onions and mushrooms and their liquor; let all simmer gently about 10 minutes or until the pieces of fish are done. Serve with Boiled Rice (see Index) and re-move the bag of spices before you do.*

KEDGEREE (early 1800s)—Use ½ pint (1 cup) of cooked fish picked from the bones; heat it in a pail set into boiling water (double boiler) with 1 large teacup (1 cup) of boiled rice, 1 ounce (2 tablespoons) of butter, 1 teaspoon of dry mustard and 2 eggs that have been boiled for 4 minutes and sliced; add seasonings to taste, mix well and serve with a plain sauce of melted butter.*

OLD COLONY FISH BALLS (pre-1800s)—Use ½ pound of cold cooked codfish with 3 ounces (¼ cup) of suet shredded fine, a small lump of butter, ½ pint (1 cup) of bread crumbs, pepper, salt, nutmeg and 3 mashed anchovies. Pound all together in a mortar, mix with an egg, divide into small balls and fry the balls a light brown.*

CODFISH HASH— One pint (2 cups) picked cooked salted codfish well freshened, 1 quart (4 cups) of chopped cold boiled potatoes mixed well together, 1½ slices of salt pork freshened, cut in very small pieces and fried brown. Add the fish and potatoes to the pork; let the mixture stand and steam 5 minutes without stirring it; be careful not to let it burn; then add 1/3 cup of hot milk and stir thoroughly. Put it on a hot spider, with melted butter and simmer it over a slow fire for ½ hour until a brown bottom crust is formed, then turn it over on a platter and serve.—Mrs. N. P. Wilder

CURRY DISHES OF COOKED FLESH, FISH AND FOWL (early 1800s)— Now that curry powder again comes from the Indies in good supply, thanks to the end of hostilities and peaceful Atlantic waters, it is no longer necessary for housewives to make their own curry powder. They can therefore turn out curry dishes with less effort—and, maybe, with better curry powders, also. Anyway, take cold chicken, turkey, lamb, veal or pork, cut it into small pieces and put it into a frying pan with about 1 pint (2 cups) or more of boiling water; let it stew a few minutes with 1 bay leaf and some parsley. Take the meat out and keep it hot; toss away the parsley and bay leaf; thicken the liquid with a little watered flour or cornstarch; use pepper and salt to taste; then add 1 heaping teaspoon of curry powder; let it boil up once. Have some rice boiled in the Italian mode (see Index). Pile the rice on a platter, scoop a hollow in the center and put the meat into it; pour the gravy over the meat—not over the rice—and serve.*

WELSH RAREBIT NIFTY-NINETIES (late 1800s)—Beat 2 eggs lightly; assemble 1 teaspoon each of made mustard and Worcestershire sauce, ½ teaspoon of salt and ¼ teaspoon of white pepper; also, slice thinly 1 pound of old and strong store cheese. Now heat, over a lively fire, ½ cup of ale or beer; when it boils, add the cheese and blend it into the beer; start your toast; when the cheese is melted, put in the seasonings and stir about steadily until all is absorbed. Then add a lightly beaten egg and go to it with the stirring spoon until you have a smooth and fragrant rarebit ready to serve.*

TOASTED CHEESE WITH COTTAGE CHEESE (mid-1800s)—This is just the thing for a chafing dish, but it will turn out equally well in a frying pan on the kitchen stove. Beat 1 heaping tablespoon of cottage cheese with three whole eggs and ¼ teaspoon of Worcestershire sauce in a cup of milk. Next, melt a piece of butter the size of a walnut (1 tablespoon) in a frying pan over a medium-hot fire; when the butter boils up, add ¼ pound of sliced and chopped rat-trap cheese; when that is bubbling, pour the egg mixture over it. Serve on buttered toast.*

IN PRAISE OF OATMEAL (mid-1800s)—Oatmeal is an ideal food for children; it is also quite as desirable for the student as the laborer, for the delicate lady as for the hard-working sister. It can be eaten with syrup and butter, like Hasty Pudding, or with cream and sugar, like rice. It is especially good for housewives upon whose nervous forces too great a demand has been made, when they lose the equilibrium of the system and become depressed and dispirited. Oatmeal requires to be cooked slowly, and the water should be boiling-hot when the oatmeal is stirred in.*

OATMEAL, TO PREPARE (mid-1800s)—Oatmeal is very nice prepared the following way. Put a piece of butter the size of a walnut (1 tablespoon) and 1 teaspoon of salt into 3 pints (6 cups) of boiling water; then add ½ pint (1 cup) of oatmeal; for 10 minutes let it boil fast, stirring frequently; then place it, covered, over a saucepan of boiling water, to continue cooking slowly for about 1½ hours. While over the water, the oatmeal will require stirring only occasionally. A better way is to start the oatmeal at night and let it cook itself over night in a hay cooker.*

OATMEAL GRUEL— Take 2 tablespoons of oatmeal, pour on it 1 pint (2 cups) of cold water; let it stand half a day; then pour it through a sieve and boil it well for 15 minutes, stirring all the time; season according to taste. Coarse meal is to be rejected. Good for invalids or children.—Anon.

MUSH— Indian meal or oatmeal mush is best made in the following manner. Put fresh water (4 cups) in a kettle over the fire to boil, and put in some (1½ teaspoons) salt; when the water boils, stir in 1½ gills (¾ cup) of cornmeal or oatmeal. In order to have excellent mush, the meal should be allowed to cook well and as long as possible while thin, before the final ½ gill (¼ cup) is added. When you desire to fry it for breakfast, turn it into an earthen dish and set it away to cool; then cut it in slices when you wish to fry it; dip each piece in beaten eggs and fry on a hot pan or griddle.—Mrs. George Munson

HULLED CORN (pre-1800s)—Use white corn, if you can get it, and none but plump corn; shell and boil it in a weak lye until the hulls are broken; then clean off the lye, and either refill the kettle or turn the corn into a dish-pan of water; take your hands and rub the corn well; wash it in several waters—the old way is 9 times, but 6 will do—then clean your kettle and return the corn to the stove; put plenty of water on the corn and boil until very tender, which usually takes the entire day, for which reason it is always best to start hulling corn at cock's first crow. As the water boils away, add more; it is better to add boiling water than cold.***

FRY LEFT-OVER CEREALS LIKE MUSH (late 1800s)—Pour any left-over cereal into a shallow baking pan and chill it. Next morning, remove the cereal from the pan and slice and fry it like mush; cover with syrup, molasses or brown sugar. A surprisingly welcome dish.*

RICE CAKES—One cup of soft boiled rice, the yolk of 1 egg, a pinch of salt and 2 tablespoons of sifted flour, beaten well together; add sweet milk until it is about of the consistency of sponge cake or thick cream. Just before baking in a quick (400°F.) oven, stir in lightly the beaten white of the egg. The less flour used, the better.—Mrs. A. M. Gibbs

THE BEAUTY OF POACHED EGGS (early 1800s)—Prime poachers always break the eggs into separate cups to ascertain their goodness; next, they take a pan of boiling salted water off the fire and, one by one, slip the eggs into it; the pan remains off the fire until all the eggs are set, that is, until the whites become snowy; only then is the pan moved over a very moderate fire where the water will come to a gentle simmer and no more. The beauty of a poached egg is perfect when the yolk is to be seen blushing through a thin window of white; as for the white around the eggs, it should be hardened only enough to make it firm, not tough and leathery. Send to the table, each egg resting on a bed of Herb-Mashed Potatoes (see Index). Serve with Browned Butter (see Index).*

A DISCOURSE ON FRENCH OMELETS (mid-1800s)—Never use more than 2 to 3 eggs in the making of a single omelet. Always beat the eggs lightly. Always pour the full contents of an omelet onto a hot, but not sizzling, buttered pan over a slow to medium fire. Always tilt the pan back and forth. Never give an omelet a chance to brown. Always lift the edges with a butter spreader so that the liquid egg will reach the surface of the metal. Never wait for the center of an omelet to dry, but turn one half over the other, like a hash, while the dew is still on the center.*

A PLAIN AMERICAN OMELET (late 1800s)—With 1/4 cup of cream beat 2 to 3 eggs with a fork just enough to mix the yolks and whites; season with 1 saltspoon (1/4 teaspoon) of salt and 1/4 saltspoon (a dash) of white pepper. Heat 4 teaspoons of butter in a 9-inch skillet; when the butter boils, pour the egg mixture into the pan and follow the directions given above under A Discourse on French Omelets.*

YOLKS IN SNOW NESTS (early 1800s)—Take each egg separately. Beat the white with a little salt; when it is stiff, push it into a small deep buttered saucer; make a nest in the middle and place in it a piece of butter the size of a hazelnut (1 rounded teaspoon); onto this pour a whole and unbroken egg yolk; season with salt, white pepper and a few grains of cayenne. Set the egg saucers in a small amount of boiling water in a saucepan or frying pan; cover the pan and let the eggs cook from 10 to 15 minutes or until done.*

EGG ROLLS (mid-1800s)—For 3 persons, separate 3 eggs; beat the yolks and mix them into 2 cups of cold milk; moisten 4 teaspoons of flour with 1 teaspoon of cold milk and add it to the yolks and milk; beat the whites stiff and stir them into the mixture. Season with salt and pepper, unless they are to be served wtih sugar, maple syrup or molasses. Put a very little of the mixture into a hot buttered frying pan; roll it over as you would an omelet and put it on a platter. Send in hot. For breakfast or tea.*

BAKED EGGS IN MEAT GRAVY (mid-1800s)—Heat left-over meat gravy in a greased and crumbed pie dish; break in the eggs; bake in a medium (350°F.) oven 15 minutes. (By "crumbing" is meant sprinkling the dish with fine bread or crumbs or cracker crumbs and shaking off all that does not adhere to the grease.)*

SCRAMBLED EGGS (early 1800s)—For each egg to be scrambled, put 2 tablespoons of milk in a saucepan; beat the eggs and milk together; place the dish in boiling water; stir constantly until the mixture thickens; remove and season with butter and salt. The eggs, when done, should be soft and creamy.*

BAKED PORK OMELET (mid-1800s)—For 4 persons, fry six ½-inch slices of parboiled pork. Meanwhile, heat ½ pint (1 cup) of milk with a dessertspoon (2 teaspoons) of butter in it. Beat 6 eggs together. Mix 1 tablespoon of flour with 1 teaspoon of salt and ¼ teaspoon of white pepper in a little cold milk until all is smooth; mix the eggs with the wetted flour; then add the hot milk, stirring very fast. Put the eggs into a greased round baking dish or pan just large enough to contain them; place the pork strips in it radiating out from the center like the spokes of a wheel. It will bake in a quick (400°F.) oven in about 20 minutes. Watch it. Besides being palatable, it is a beautiful-looking dish for the breakfast table and a very convenient addition to a family supper.*

BAKED EGGS— Break 6 or 7 eggs into a buttered dish, taking care that each is whole and does not encroach upon the others so much as to mix or disturb the yolks; sprinkle with pepper and salt and put a bit of butter upon each. Put the dish into an oven and bake until the whites are set. This is far superior to fried eggs, and very nice for breakfast, served on toast or alone.—Mrs. L. M. Angle

EGG BASKETS— Make these for breakfast or supper the day after you have had roast chicken, duck, or turkey for dinner. Boil 6 eggs hard, cut them neatly in half and extract the yolks; rub these to a paste with some melted butter, pepper and salt and set aside. Pound the minced meat of the cold fowl fine in the same manner and mix it with the egg paste, moistening with melted butter as you proceed, or with a little gravy if you have it to spare. Cut off a slice from the curved surface of the egg halves to make them stand securely; fill them with the paste; arrange them close together upon a flat dish and pour some left-over gravy over the eggs—Mrs. William Jenkins

WHAT TO DO WITH ORPHANED YOLKS AND WHITES OF EGGS (late 1800s)—For housewives who are given to avoiding dishes that shun the use of whole eggs because they hate to waste left-over whites or yolks, here are a few hints that may serve to widen culinary horizons.

What to do with whites: fishcakes, cake frostings, meringues, sherbert sauces, macaroons, white cakes, kisses, cake icings, marshmallows, angel cakes, fruit whips; sugaring cookies, clearing soup stock and coffee, glazing breads, rolls, cookies, pies, etc.*

What to do with yolks: mayonnaises, custards, crumb dippings, cakes, breadings, sauces, eggnogs, puddings, French toast dips, thickenings for cream sauces; also, it is claimed that 2 egg yolks serve as 1 whole egg in most bakings.*

The best way to keep orphaned egg yolks or widowed whites: place them in separate tight-lidded glass jars that have been cleaned, boiled and stood in a warm place to dry (do not use a cloth). Let them stand near the ice in the chest. Cover yolks with water; leave whites as they are. These egg left-overs seldom last more than 3 to 4 days.***

WHAT TO DO WITH WHITES OF EGGS (mid-1800s)—When you have 4 egg whites left over make a White of Eggs Pudding by beating the whites to a stiff snow; add 2 tablespoons of marmalade mixed with 1½ ounces (3½ tablespoons) of sugar; pour into a buttered baking dish and bake in a slow oven (300°F.) for about 30 minutes.*

TO PRESERVE EGGS (mid-1800s)—To 5 quarts of water in a large clean stone crock add 1 pound of quick or slow lime and stir well. After a few days, add ¼ pound of coarse kitchen salt. It is important to examine the eggs for cracks and to test for freshness. As to the latter, use a basin of cold water. Preserve only eggs that sink to the bottom and stay there; those that lift from the bottom are not fresh enough. Stand the eggs in the lime solution with rounded ends uppermost. In 2 or 3 weeks the lime will have sealed all the pores in the shells and the eggs can be removed, wrapped individually in newspaper and put to stand in cardboard boxes. Pack them with paper so that they stand solid and put the boxes in a cool, dry place; turn the boxes once a week to prevent the yolks from settling.***

CLARIFIED BUTTER (early 1800s)—Put freshly churned butter into a nice clean stew-pan over a very clear, slow fire; watch it; when it is melted, skim off the buttermilk, etc., which will swim on the top; let the butter stand for a moment or two to let the impurities sink to the bottom, then pour the butter through a hair-sieve or cheesecloth into a clean jar, leaving the sediments in the bottom of the stew-pan. Butter thus purified will be as sweet as marrow and a very useful covering for potted meats, sauces, etc., and for frying; it is equal to the finest Florence oil, for which purpose it is commonly used by those whose religious tenets will not allow them to eat viands fried in animal oil.*

TO SWEETEN SALTED BUTTER (mid-1800s)—Freshen only as much salted butter as you will use; for each ½ pound of butter you will need 1 pint of cold water. Pour the latter in a deep dish and add the butter cut into small chunks and fairly soft. With your hands, wash and squeeze the salt out of the butter. When it tastes fairly fresh, wash it in clean, cold water as many as 6 or 8 times more until all saltiness has disappeared. Freshened this way, butter is sweet but not very enduring.***

ROSE BUTTER FOR CAKES OR PUDDING SAUCES (early 1800s)—In the morning, gather full-blooming roses and put their petals in layers, alternating with thin layers of salt in a crock. The top layer must be of roses.

Put a platter on the top layer and place 1 pound of butter upon it. Lay a piece of thin muslin over the crock. In a short time, the fragrance of the roses will be absorbed by the butter.***

HOW TO SOFTEN BUTTER (early 1800s)—Because butter is inclined to become oily if softened near heat, the best way—especially in winter—is to soften it by kneading it with your hands; their warmth effects the change without danger of oiling. Of course, it is required that you wash your hands to rid them of other odors.*

TO SOFTEN BUTTER (mid-1800s)—Women who do not like to soften butter by taking it in the palms of their hands and kneading it like dough will welcome this new idea. Take 2 earthenware bowls, one larger than the other; heat each bowl by filling it with boiling water and letting it stand until each bowl is warm to the touch; empty them and wipe them bone dry. Put the butter to be softened in the smaller bowl and place the larger bowl bottom up over that. The warm bowls will do the work without oiling the butter.*

WHEN CREAM FAILS TO WHIP (early 1800s)—Chill it and, at the same time, chill the white of 1 egg; whip the two together with a large pinch of sugar and you will have highly satisfactory results.*

SOUR MILK, TO MAKE (mid-1800s)—Although it does not come up to the cooking mark of the real thing, it will do, as will any port in a storm. To make sour milk, add 1 tablespoon of cider vinegar to each pint (2 cups) of sweet milk; set it in the spring house or some other cool place for an hour or so. When it comes to sour cream, you must wait for Mother Nature to turn it out.***

TO LESSEN RISKS OF BURNING MILK (mid-1800s)—Pour some cold water into the cooking vessel before you pour the milk in; slosh the water around, drain it off, but do not dry the vessel; just pour the milk in while it is wet.*

COTTAGE CHEESE, TO MAKE (late 1800s)—Put a panful of sour milk in a cheesecloth over a bucket and let the whey drip away. Cover with a moist cloth to keep the cheese from drying out; let it stand over night. No harm is done by stirring the mixture occasionally before bedtime. Next morning, if the cheese is on the thin side, as some are, put it to steam very gently over a low but steady fire; stir occasionally and watch carefully lest it become dry and tough. The next step is to make the Cottage Cheese more palatable by the addition of cream or, as some prefer, melted butter that has not been salted.*

HOW TO MAKE COTTAGE CHEESE— Pour boiling water on thick sour milk in the pan in which it has turned, stirring while you pour; as soon as the milk separates from the whey and begins to appear cooked, let it settle; in a minute or 2 most of the water and whey can be poured off; if the milk is not sufficiently cooked, more hot water may be used; set the pan on its side, and with your spoon or hand draw the curd to the upper side of the pan pressing out as much water as possible; if desired, it can stand a few moments in cold water; when it is squeezed dry, work the curd fine, rolling it between the hands; add salt and cream to taste; in very warm weather, when the milk has turned quickly, it is very palatable without the addition of cream.—Mrs. A. M. Gibbs

TO KEEP CHEESE FRESH (mid-1800s)—Soak cheesecloth in white wine and wrap it, but not tightly, around the cheese. This not only preserves the cheese but keeps away mold and improves the flavor to boot.*

SAVE CHEESE BY GRATING IT (mid-1800s)—What with cheese costing 18 cents the pound, do not slice or cube it; grate the cheese; it goes by far longer that way. Try mixing minced parsley with grated cheese. It is good and also good for you.*

LIME WATER AND MILK (mid-1800s)—Place a piece of unslaked lime— size is immaterial, as the water will take up only a certain quantity—in a perfectly clean bottle or jug; fill it with cold water; keep it corked in a cellar or in some other cool, dark place. The lime water will be ready for use in a few minutes. When it is poured off, add more water; this may be done 3 to 4 times, after which new lime must be used. A teaspoon of lime water in a cup of milk is a remedy for children's summer complaint; also for acidity of the stomach for young and old; when added to milk, it has no unpleasant taste, and when put into milk that would otherwise curdle while heating, the milk will not curdle and can be used for puddings and pies. A small quantity of lime water will prevent cream and milk from turning. It also sweetens and purifies bottles, such as those of infants, that have been used for milk. Many housewives add a cupful to a sponge of bread to prevent it from souring during hot summer nights.***

SEA-GOING COFFEE CREAM (early 1800s)—To 1 pint (2 cups) of fresh cream put 1¼ pounds (3 scant cups) of pulverized loaf sugar; boil it and pour it into a jar to cool; then put it into vials and cork close. It will keep good for several weeks and is convenient to be carried aboard ships by seafarers.*

TO RAISE A THICK CREAM (mid-1800s)—Put new rich milk into an earthen pan and set it on a stove or over clear embers until hot. Set it aside until the next day and it will produce excellent cream for coffee or fruit, almost as thick as that made famous in Devonshire, England.*

7. Soups, Chowders and Garnishings

BROWN, WHITE AND CHICKEN STOCKS (early 1800s)—Stock should never be made of meat that has been kept too long. If meat or bones have become the least tainted, the defect is peculiarly offensive in soups and gravies.

To make Brown Stock: Use beef, vegetables and enough Browned or Caramelized Sugar (see Index) to get the desired shade of brown. For a rich stock, use about 3 pounds of meat for every pound of bones and 1 pint (2 cups) of water per pint of broth. Put the meat and bones in cold water, cook slowly, skim frequently until it boils up; then add ½ pint (1 cup) of cold water, which will make the remaining scum rise; skim again and again until no more scum rises and the stock is perfectly clear; put in a moderate-sized carrot, 2 turnips, 1 head of celery and 1 large onion. Do not add herbs, spices or salt. Now set the pan, covered, where the broth will simmer very slowly for 4 to 5 hours. Then strain it through a sieve into a stone pan or jar; do not skim off the fat, as that forms a good covering for the stock when it cools and hardens; keep the stock in an ice house, the spring house or some other cool place.*

To make White Stock: For white gravies and soups, use veal or chicken, alone or together; use also any trimmings you may have of giblets, such as gizzards, necks, livers and hearts. Follow the procedure given above for Brown Stock.*

To make Chicken Stock: Cut up an old 4-pound fowl and boil it slowly in 1 gallon of water for 2½ to 3½ hours, or until it feels tender. Then add 1 handful (½ cup) each of chopped carrot and celery and 1 small chopped onion. Cook it until the meat falls off the bones. The method to follow is that given above for Brown Stock.*

HOW TO CLARIFY CLEAR SOUPS (mid-1800s)—To remove the cloudiness from clear soups, you need the white of a raw egg and its shell. These are the steps you take. The white is beaten and the shell pounded into bits; these are mixed into the soup stock, which must be cold; place the kettle over a good fire and stir with a wooden spoon until the stock comes to a boil-up; stop stirring and let it boil just 3 minutes all by itself; then remove the kettle to a spot where the soup will merely simmer; this you let it do for 12 minutes; then strain it through cheesecloth in a fine hair-sieve; return it to the kettle for reheating.*

TO IMPROVE THIN SOUPS (mid-1800s)—Add 1 or more egg yolks while the soup is hot but not boiling; a good way to prevent the egg thickening from curdling is to beat up a yolk or a whole egg with 1 tablespoon of water, milk or cream in a large cup; then add several spoonfuls of hot soup to the egg, stirring as each spoonful is added; add the cupful of liquid to the soup when it is off the fire; the best results are obtained by using yolks only.*

ASPARAGUS SOUP— You'll need 3 to 4 pounds of veal cut fine, a little salt pork, 2 or 3 bunches of asparagus and 3 quarts (12 cups) of water. Boil half of the asparagus with the meat for 3 hours; add ½ pint (1 cup) of hot milk; thicken with a little flour and season. Start the rest of the asparagus cooking in water about 20 minutes before dinner; then chop and add it to the soup just before serving.—Mrs. D.

GREEN PEA SOUP— Four pounds of lean beef cut in small pieces, ½ peck (16 cups) of green peas, 1 gallon of water. Cook the empty pods of the peas in the water for 1 hour; strain them out; add the beef and cook slowly 1½ hours, skimming until clear. Half an hour before serving strain out the meat and add the peas; 20 minutes later add ½ cup of rice flour, salt and pepper to taste, and, if you choose, 1 teaspoon of sugar. Return the meat and cook it long enough to reheat it. Stir often to prevent burning.—Mrs. John B. Adams

CORN SOUP—One small beef bone, 2 quarts (8 cups) of water, 4 tomatoes, 8 ears of corn. Let the meat boil a short time in the water; cut the corn from the cob and put in the cobs with the cut corn and tomatoes; let them boil about ½ hour; remove the cobs just before serving; add milk to suit, which allow to boil for a few moments only; season with salt and pepper.—Mrs. W. P. Nixon

CLEAR CHICKEN SOUP WITH CHICKEN DUMPLINGS (mid-1800s)— Start a 4-pound fowl, unskinned but cut into fricassee pieces, cooking in 1½ quarts (6 cups) of cold water; cook the giblets, such as gizzard, heart, liver, with it and as long as it takes to make the meat fall from the bones, which should be from 4 to 5 hours, depending on the tenderness or otherwise of the bird. At that time, have ready a fragment of a blade of mace and a sprig of good curly parsley, 2 teaspoons of salt and 3 peppercorns; add these to the chicken with ½ gill (¼ cup) each of chopped onion, cabbage, celery, carrot and tomato. After these have cooked slowly for 1 hour, strain the soup through a sieve to remove the pieces of chicken and the parsley, mace and peppercorns. Many housewives leave out the vegetables and serve the soup perfectly clear; others put the vegetables back into the soup. In all cases, the fat should be skimmed off the soup. For Chicken Dumplings, see Index.***

OX-TAIL SOUP (early 1800s)—Have 2 ox-tails cut at the joints; wash and dry them; brown them in ½ gill (¼ cup) of suet fat with 1 smallish onion adorned with 4 cloves; when they are brown, add 2¼ quarts (10 cups) of cold water; let them simmer 4 hours, covered close, and then add 2 tablespoons each of chopped carrot and celery, ½ saltspoon (¼ teaspoon) of pepper, 2 teaspoons of salt and 2 sprigs of parsley; let these cook for 1 hour, strain through a cloth; set aside to cool; skim off fat. To 3 tablespoons of Brown Butter add 3 tablespoons of Browned Flour (see Index); thicken the soup with it and add Brown Stock (see Index) or plain water to obtain the desired consistency; remove the meat from the bones and add it to the soup; bring it to the proper heat; add ½ gill (¼ cup) of fine sherry or good Madeira.*

CELERY SOUP (early 1800s)—Scrape and cut into small pieces 2 bunches of celery, using the best parts only; add 2 quarts (8 cups) of good soup stock, with an onion cut into slices; stew gently until the celery is tender; rub through a colander; season with salt and pepper and a piece of butter the size of a small walnut (1 tablespoon). Return the soup to the fire; boil it up; add a coffee cup (1 cup) of very hot milk thickened with 1 dessertspoon (2 teaspoons) of cornstarch melted in cold water; stir soup well and turn it into a tureen. Now add 1 teaspoon of brown sugar or maple syrup, together with a few bits of fried bread, neatly cut.*

CREAMED CARROT SOUP (early 1800s)—Fill a 1-pint (2-cup) measure with chopped carrots, turn them into 1 pint (2 cups) of cold water and cook until they are tender; drain the carrots into a sieve and save the liquid; rub the carrots through the sieve and set aside. Set 1 pint of milk boiling in a pail set in a kettle of boiling water (a double boiler) and add ½ gill (¼ cup) of rice. In a skillet, let ½ small onion, thinly sliced, cook to softness in a piece of butter the size of an egg (4 tablespoons); when they are done, rub 3 tablespoons of flour into them and be sure they are smooth. When the rice is cooked, assemble the soup: add to the carrot liquid the carrots, and the rice, stir well and follow with the floured onions; stir again and let all cook in the pail in the boiling water for 20 minutes. Then strain the soup through a hair-sieve into a tureen. Whenever the soup is too thick, dilute with light cream.*

POTATO SOUP—Boil 5 or 6 potatoes with a small piece of salt pork and a little celery; pass these through a colander and add milk or cream (if milk, include a little butter) to make the consistency that of thick cream; chop a little parsley fine and throw it in; let the soup boil 5 minutes. Cut some dry bread in small dice and fry them brown in hot lard; drain them, place them in the bottom of soup tureen and pour the soup over them. Chop 2 onions and boil them with the soup, if this is liked.—M. A. T.

VEGETABLE SOUP (early 1800s)—Take 2 turnips, 2 carrots, 4 potatoes, 1 large onion, 1 parsnip, 4 stalks of celery and 1 sprig of parsley. Cut them all fine in a chopping tray; put them, with a heaping tablespoon of rice, into 3 quarts (12 cups) of water, and simmer the whole for 3 hours. Add a piece of butter the size of a walnut (1 tablespoon); stir the soup until the butter is melted; add ½ gill (¼ cup) of flour made smooth in cold water; let the liquid thicken and simmer for 10 minutes; after the soup is in the tureen, sprinkle 1 tablespoon of minced parsley over the surface.*

BAKED BEAN SOUP (early 1800s)—In 1 pint (2 cups) of water cook 1 pint (2 cups) of baked beans; allow them about 15 minutes. While the beans boil, bring an egg-sized piece of butter (4 tablespoons) to bubbling point in a frying pan and cook therein ½ gill (¼ cup) of minced onions; when they are done stir 3 dessertspoons (6 teaspoons) of flour into the butter and add 1 pint (2 cups) of chopped tomatoes; stir steadily as this cooks and thickens. Drain liquid from the beans and put them through a sieve; drain the liquid from the tomatoes and put them through a sieve; unite the two purees and the drained liquids and heat them. Season with salt and pepper; add hot soup stock if needed; add lemon juice, the amount of the latter governed by the sweetness of the beans. Some cooks overcome the sweetness by mixing chopped pickles into the soup.*

ROAST BEEF BONE SOUP (early 1800s)—Boil the bones at least 3 hours or until every particle of meat is loose; like all soups this needs a lot of skimming; then take the bones out, scrape off the meat and set aside the liquid. The next day, take all the fat from the liquid; cut up an onion, 2 or 3 potatoes, a stalk or 2 of celery and a small turnip; put these into the soup and let boil about 1 hour. Add, ½ hour before dinner, the remnants of boiled beef from the bones, also a touch of powdered marjoram and salt and pepper to taste. Bread Balls (see Index) go well with this soup.*

TURTLE BEAN SOUP FROM ROAST BEEF BONE STOCK (early 1800s)— If you have enough Roast Beef Bone Stock left for another meal, use it this way. Strain the stock and set it aside; soak ½ pint (1 cup) of turtle beans (black beans) in a little water over night. Add 2 quarts (8 cups) of cold water; let the beans simmer 3 to 4 hours or until they are soft; then strain them through a sieve. Add the Beef Bone Stock, 1 onion, 1 turnip and 1 carrot well chopped, also small pinches of sweet marjoram and thyme, 4 cloves, salt and pepper to taste. Let the soup cook an hour longer; if too thick add water or more stock. Take out the vegetables and cloves before serving.*

WHALEMAN'S PEA SOUP (early 1800s)—Take a pint (2 cups) of split peas, and, when carefully picked over and washed, put them into 1 pint (2 cups) of water to soak over night. Three hours before dinner, put them into a pot with 1 quart (4 cups) more water and about ½ pound of lean salted pork, or less if you do not want the sturdy soup that is whalemen's fare. Simmer it steadily and stir often to prevent scorching. It may need more water before dinner, and can be made to whatever thickness you prefer. The usual practice is to serve the salt pork in one piece and let each person cut his own slice.*

FARINA SOUP (late 1800s)—For 4 persons, allow 4 tablespoons (¼ cup) of the finest wheat farina and 1 quart (4 cups) of boiling water; pour the farina into the water, let it boil for 15 minutes and stir frequently with a wooden spoon—this saves housewifely fingers from being burned by hot iron utensils. Beat the yolks of 4 eggs into 4 tablespoons of cream; stir this into the soup just as you remove it from the fire; if done right, the soup should be of a creamy smoothness.*

This soup, without the egg yolks and cream, can be used as a base for making various sorts of cream soups, using such cooked and mashed ingredients as chicken, peas, celery, carrots, tomatoes, etc. A simple formula is to use 1 cup of one of these items to 1 quart (4 cups) of Farina Soup. If too thick, blend in milk to suit.*

TURKEY SOUP (early 1800s)—The remnants of a young turkey make good soup. Put all the bones and little bits left of a turkey dinner into about

3 quarts (12 cups) of water; add turkey gravy if you have it; let this cook about 2 hours. Skim out the meat and bones and set the soup aside in a cool place until next day. Then take all the fat from the top; take the skin and bones away and return the meat to the soup. If some dressing has been left, put that in also, and boil all together a few minutes. If more seasoning is needed, add to suit your taste. Noodle Balls (see Index) are good companions for this soup.*

SCOTCH MUTTON AND BARLEY BROTH (early 1800s)—To make this like it was made in Bonnie Scotland, take ½ teacup (½ cup) of barley and 4 quarts (16 cups) of cold water; bring this to the boil and skim; put in now a neck of mutton and boil for ½ hour; skim well on the surface and also the sides of the pot. Have ready 2 carrots, 1 large onion, 1 small head of cabbage, 1 stalk of parsley, 1 sprig of celery tops, all neatly and mannerly chopped. Add these to the broth; pepper and salt to taste; takes 2 hours to cook.*

MOCK TURTLE SOUP—One soup bone, 1 quart (4 cups) of turtle beans, 1 large teaspoon of powdered cloves, salt and pepper. Soak the beans over night, put them with the soup bone in nearly 6 quarts (24 cups) of water and cook 5 or 6 hours. When half done, add the cloves, salt and pepper. When done, strain through a colander, pressing the pulp of the beans through to make the soup the desired thickness, and serve with a few slices of hard-boiled egg and lemon sliced very thin. The turtle beans are black and can be obtained only from large grocers.—Mrs. C. H. Wheeler

EFFERVESCENT TOMATO SOUP WITHOUT MEAT—One quart (4 cups) of tomatoes, 1 quart of water, 1 quart of milk, and butter, salt and pepper to taste. Cook the tomatoes thoroughly in the water; have the milk scalding (over water to prevent scorching). When the tomatoes are done add a large teaspoon of salaratus, which will cause a violent effervescence. It is best to set the vessel in a pan before adding the salaratus, to prevent waste. When the commotion has ceased, add the milk and seasoning. When it is possible it is best to use more milk than water, and cream instead of butter. The soup is eaten with crackers and is by some preferred to Oyster Soup. This recipe is very valuable for those who keep abstinence days.—C. O. Van Cline

BEEF TOMATO SOUP—Get 3 to 4 pounds of beef from the round, cut it into small chunks and put it into 4 quarts (16 cups) of cold water; let it boil slowly for 3 to 4 hours; always skim and add fresh hot water as needed. Add 1½ quarts (6 cups) of fresh tomatoes and 2 cans of tomatoes; season with pepper and salt; add 3 whole cloves, 3 peppercorns and a large pinch of powdered mace. Simmer for 1 hour. Strain into an earthen dish, let it cool and skim off all the grease; return the liquid with the meat to the kettle. Mix 1 tablespoon of flour with a little milk until smooth and stir it into the soup when it simmers in the kettle. Dissolve ¼ teaspoon of soda in a little water and add it just before serving in large soup plates. When you set the table for this dish, put soup spoons at the places.—Mrs. T. H. Anderson

REGAL CREAM OF CHICKEN SOUP (late 1800s)—Boil a large hen, cut into quarters, in 2 quarts (8 cups) of water with a few stalks of celery, a carrot or 2, 6 white peppercorns, ½ teaspoon of salt and a small piece of bay leaf. At the same time, in another pot, boil 3 ounces (generous ½ cup) of Carolina rice until it is soft, but not mushy, and salt it well. Skim the chicken liquor as required. When the bird is done, remove it from the broth, together with all vegetables, etc. Next, remove all the white meat from the bones, throw away the skin and save the dark meat for another occasion. Be careful to skim the soup so that no fat remains. Pound the rice and white meat to a paste in a mortar and rub it into the soup through a sieve over a low fire. Stir as the soup simmers and thickens. Should the soup take on more than a velvety smooth consistency, add a little milk or very light cream. If thin, do not thicken with egg yolk, as this spoils the soup's pure white appearance; use instead a little cornstarch wetted with cold water.*

A FEW CLOVES (mid-1800s)—added to vegetable soup will give it a delicious flavor.*

A VERY STYLISH CHICKEN CREAM SOUP—Skim the fat from 1 quart (4 cups) of water in which a large, plump chicken has been boiled. Season with pepper, celery salt, and a little onion juice if desired; put the stock back and bring to a boil. Mash the yolks of 3 hard-boiled eggs fine and mix them with ½ cup of very fine bread or cracker crumbs soaked until soft in a little milk. Chop the white meat of the chicken until it is like fine meal; stir it into the egg and bread paste; add 1 pint (2 cups) of hot rich milk slowly; then rub all into the hot chicken liquor through a sieve. Simmer 5 minutes; add seasoning if needed; if too thick, add light cream; if too thin, add fine cracker dust.—Mrs. G. S. Weston

CREAM OF ONION SOUP (late 1800s)—Take 1½ cups of chopped onions; brown them very lightly in 2 tablespoons of butter; then cook them slowly in 1½ pints (3 cups) of cold water until ultra-soft, when you drain them— saving the liquid—and rub them through a sieve. Next make a Cream Sauce by blending 5 tablespoons of flour into ¼ cup of melted butter and adding 1 cup of the onion liquor and 1 pint (2 cups) of scalded milk—in that order. Season this with salt, white pepper, a pinch of powdered cloves, and keep the Cream Sauce simmering 12 minutes. In a larger pot, blend it in with the mashed onions; give the mixture time to reheat, but not boil, before you stir 1 or 2 egg yolks into the soup, according to the thickness wanted. Should the soup become too thick, correct this with milk as needed. Serve with grated Italian (Parmesan) or old Swiss cheese.*

FRENCH ONION SOUP (late 1800s)—This delightful dish has a grossly undeserved reputation among American housewives for trickiness in preparation; all that is needed are the right ingredients, patience and attention. First, slice rings of Bermuda onions gossamer thin until you have 1-1/3 cups; melt 2 dessertspoons (4 teaspoons) of fresh, not firkin (salted) butter in a skillet. Add the onions, stir steadily and the second they change from transparent lemon to golden tan, pour into the skillet 2 cups of hot brown stock; season to taste with pepper, salt and marjoram and let it simmer about 20 minutes or until the onions are done. Meanwhile, cut little circles out of 2 or 3 slices of baker's bread, dip them in melted butter, dredge both sides in grated sharp cheese and fry them a light brown. Place them in the soup plates; dish out the soup and serve. This is a small recipe but it can easily be expanded to meet large family or party requirements.*

CREAMED POTATO SOUP—Boil and chop 1 medium onion; boil and mash 6 run-of-the-bin potatoes; blend the vegetables and add 1 quart (4 cups) of boiling milk. Work the soup well with a potato masher over a low fire; strain it through a fine sieve into a saucepan; season with salt, pepper and 2 tablespoons of melted butter. If the soup is too thick stir in hot milk to suit. Serve piping hot with toasted and buttered bread.—Mrs. F. O. Sawyer

PLAIN CALF'S HEAD SOUP—Take a calf's head well cleaned and a knuckle of veal and put them both into a large kettle; tie 1 onion and a large tablespoon of sweet herbs into a cloth and put them into the kettle with the meat, over which you have poured about 4 quarts (16 cups) of water. If you wish the soup for a one o'clock dinner, put the meat over the fire to cook as early as eight o'clock in the morning; let it boil steadily and slowly and season well with salt and pepper. About 1 hour before serving, take off the soup and pour it through a colander; pick out all the meat carefully, chop it very fine and return it to the soup, putting it all again over the fire. Boil 4 eggs very hard, chop them fine, and slice 1 lemon very thin, adding these at the very last.—Mrs. F. D. J.

BEEF SOUP—Cut all the lean off the shank, and with a little beef suet in the bottom of the kettle, fry it to a nice brown; put in the bones and cover them with water; cover the kettle closely; let it cook slowly until the meat drops from the bones. Strain the soup through a colander and leave it in the dish during the night, which is the only way to get off all the fat. The day it is wanted for the table, fry as brown as possible a carrot, an onion and a very small turnip all sliced thin. Just before taking them up, put in ½ teaspoon of sugar, a blade of mace, 6 cloves, 12 kernels of allspice, a small teaspoon of celery seed. With the vegetables these must cook slowly in the soup an hour; then strain the soup again for the table. If you use vermicelli or pearl barley, soak it first in water.—Mrs. William H. Low

JULIENNE SOUP—Shred 2 onions and fry them brown in ½ tablespoon of butter; add a little mace, salt and pepper, then a tablespoon or so of cold stock; rub a tablespoon of flour smooth with a little butter and let it fry with the onions; strain all through a colander, then add more stock as desired. Cut 1 turnip, 1 carrot and 1 stalk of celery into fillets; add 1 gill (½ cup) of green peas and boil all the vegetables tender in a little water; add both water and vegetables to the soup. If wished, the flour can be left out, making a clear, light-colored soup. In that case, the onions should be cut into fillets and boiled with the vegetables.—M. A. T.

OYSTER SOUP—Pour 1 quart (4 cups) each of boiling water and scalded milk into a kettle; stir in ½ pint (1 cup) of rolled cracker crumbs; season with pepper and salt to taste. When all come to a boil, add 1 quart (4 cups) of good fresh oysters; stir well, so as to keep the soup from scorching; then add a piece of good sweet butter about the size of an egg (4 tablespoons); let it boil up once; then remove it from the fire immediately; dish it up and send to the table.—Mrs. T. V. Wadskier

CLAM SOUP—Cut ½ pound of salt pork into very small squares and fry them light brown; add 1 large or 2 small onions cut very fine and cook about 10 minutes; add 2 quarts (8 cups) of water and 1 quart (4 cups) of sliced raw potatoes; let it all boil; then add 1 quart of coarsely chopped clams (25 to 50 if large, 50 to 100 if small). Mix 1 tablespoon of flour with water, put it with 1 pint (2 cups) of light cream or milk and pour it into the soup; let it boil about 5 minutes. Butter, pepper, salt, Worcestershire sauce to taste.—Mrs. A. A. Carpenter

LOBSTER SOUP—One large lobster or 2 small ones; pick all the meat from the shell and chop it fine; scald 1 quart (4 cups) of milk and 1 pint (2 cups) of water; then add the lobster, 1 pound of butter rubbed into ½ gill (¼ cup) of flour, and salt and red pepper to taste. Boil 10 minutes and serve hot. —Mrs. Robert Harris

EEL, CLAM OR FISH CHOWDER—Five pounds of codfish cut in squares, or clams or eels, chopped; fry plenty of salt pork cut in thin slices. Put a layer of pork in your kettle, then 1 of fish, 1 of potatoes in thick slices, and 1 of onions in slices; plenty of pepper and salt; repeat as long as your materials last, and finish with a layer of Boston crackers or crusts of bread. Add water sufficient to cook with, or milk if you prefer. Cook ½ hour and turn the chowder over onto your platter, disturbing it as little as possible. —Mrs. Ayres

FISH CHOWDER—Four pounds of fresh fish skinned and cut in pieces; put in a pot some of the fish, then some crackers and sliced potatoes, salt and pepper; another layer of fish, crackers and potatoes; cover the whole with water; add a little onion, if liked, and some fried pork or butter; boil this until the potatoes are done, then add a quart (4 cups) of milk and let it boil again. When dishing for the table, take out all the large bones. Codfish or haddocks are the best; other fish will answer; use the head.— Mrs. R. A. Sibley

FALMOUTH CLAM CHOWDER (late 1800s)—Take 1 quart of clams (25 to 50 if large, 50 to 100 if small); cut 3 large slices of salt pork and fry them in the kettle the chowder will be made in; pare 6 medium potatoes and 2 large onions and slice them; separate the bodies of the clams from the necks and chop the necks. Put a layer of chopped necks in the kettle, a sprinkling of onions, a layer of potatoes, a little salt and pepper, then another layer of necks, and so on, until all the ingredients are in. Cover with boiling water and cook slowly for an hour; then add the coarsely chopped bodies of the clams, a piece of butter the size of an egg (4 tablespoons), 1 quart (4 cups) of cold milk; let the chowder come to a boil; serve with big, round Pilot Crackers.—Kate Burrill

TOMATO(!) CLAM CHOWDER (mid-1800s)—How this receipt ever found its way up from Rhode Island, where the practice of putting tomatoes in chowders is said to have started, a body would never know. Even so, this is a passable chowder, as housewives who try it will discover. Parboil 2 cups of potatoes cut into ½-inch cubes for about 8 minutes. Heat 3 tablespoons of pork fat over a light fire and cook ½ gill (¼ cup) of chopped onions in the fat until they are yellow but not brown; add 1½ pints (3 cups) of clams in their own juice and let all simmer very slowly for ½ hour; stir in 3 gills (1½ cups) of boiling water and the potatoes, with a small piece of bay leaf. In another pan, melt ½ gill (¼ cup) of butter; blend into it 2 tablespoons of flour and, when you have a paste, add 3 gills (1½ cups) of chopped and peeled tomatoes; cook them until tender, season to taste with salt, pepper and a pinch of red pepper and add them to the clams. To make a richer chowder, use half milk and half water or just milk, if so desired.*

CLAM CHOWDER (mid-1800s)—Have on hand a heaping soup-plateful of raw, thinly sliced potatoes. Next, brown and crisp ¼ pound of fat salt pork; put a small chopped onion into the fat until it turns golden. Pour the potatoes into a stew-pan and strain the pork fat over them; add the liquor from 1 quart of clams (25 to 50 if large, 50 to 100 if small); simmer until potatoes are done. Meanwhile parboil the clams for 3 minutes in 1 pint (2 cups) of water and 1 teaspoon of salt; drain the clams, but save the water; now cut away the hard portions of the clams; return them—with the soft portions— to the water they were cooked in; let them cook slowly another 15 minutes; then drain the clams again; sort out and throw away the hard parts. Add the clam water to the clam liquor and potatoes, also 1 gill (½ cup) of cream, 6 crushed water crackers and the pork and onions; season with powdered thyme and pepper; when all is sufficiently cooked, add the coarsely chopped soft parts of the clams; let the chowder cook slowly for 5 minutes and serve.***

LOBSTER CHOWDER THE OLD WAY (late 1800s)—For every pound of boiled lobster meat have ready 1 quart (4 cups) of milk, 3 Boston (big and round) crackers, ¼ cup of butter, a small teaspoon of salt, ½ saltspoonful (a pinch) of white pepper ground large and round, ¼ saltspoonful (a dash) of cayenne pepper. Heat the milk. Roll the crackers fine, mix them with the butter and the green fat of the lobster; season. Pour the simmering milk over this mixture; stir it well; put it into the top of a double boiler and add the diced lobster meat; let it come to boiling heat and serve in deep soup plates. This is a notorious second-, even third-, helping dish, so be sure to have plenty for all and sundry.*

COD CHOWDER (early 1800s)—For 4 persons, fry 3 pieces of salt pork, crisp, in a deep kettle; take them out and chop them up; fry lightly 1 large sliced onion in the fat and take it out, leaving the fat; have ready 1½ pints (3 cups) of raw potatoes cut into ¼-inch slices, floured and peppered; have also 4 pounds of boned, skinned and sliced cod similarly floured and peppered. Now place alternating layers of potatoes, chopped pork and fish, in that order, in the kettle until all is laid in. Pour over it almost enough boiling water to cover it; when it boils up, you may want to thicken the chowder by adding more flour made smooth with cold water. Dip a few Litchfield crackers, or Ship Bread (see Index), if preferred, lay them over the top and cover the kettle close. Simmer chowder ¾ hour. Many good cooks add a gill (½ cup) of fresh milk before it is served. Add part of a fresh lemon, if you like.**

COD'S HEAD FISH CHOWDER (early 1800s)—Two large cods' heads, 3 pounds of cod or haddock, 5 average potatoes, 1 medium onion, 5 Boston crackers, ½ cup of butter, 1 cup of milk, salt and pepper. Skin and bone the fish; cook the bones and the cods' heads 30 minutes; strain the fish and save the water. In a chowder kettle place the fish, potatoes and sliced onion in layers; season with salt and pepper; add a small blade of mace or bay leaf. Cover with the fish water and cook slowly until the potatoes are done; add the crackers, butter and milk; let the chowder boil up once and serve. Only cods' heads give Fish Chowder a really authentic taste.*

SALT COD CHOWDER (early 1800s)—Take 1 pint (2 cups) of finely shredded, cooked salted codfish; pick out all the bones and bits of skin the day that the fish is boiled, as this is most easily done while it is warm; have also on hand 1½ pints (3 cups) of cubed cooked potatoes; if they are left from the previous dinner, so much the better, because such potatoes are better for this purpose than those that are freshly boiled. Chop 2 onions fine and fry them in ½ gill (¼ cup) of pork fat and a little lard or beef fat; add the potatoes and fish when the onions become transparent, also ½ pint (1 cup) of lively boiling water; stir. Let this cook slowly while you make a thickening of 3 tablespoons of flour blended into 2 tablespoons of butter and diluted with 1 gill (½ cup) each of milk and cream. When this is thick, add it to the fish, mix well and serve on 1-inch-thick slices of buttered toast.*

CORNED BEEF AND CABBAGE CHOWDER(early 1800s)—Take a small, firm, head of green cabbage, discard the coarse outer leaves, cut away the core and mince the cabbage fine in a chopping trencher; put the cabbage into 1½ pints (3 cups) of cold water with 1 teaspoon of salt in it; let the cabbage cook to a pulp and drain. Meanwhile, melt a piece of butter the size of an egg (4 tablespoons) in a saucepan; when it melts, toss in a small onion that has been minced very fine and let it simmer slowly so that neither it nor the butter browns. Heat 1 pint (2 cups) of milk and have it near the scalding point when the onion is done. Now, into the onion, blend 4 table-spoons of flour; turn this into a cream sauce with the scalded milk; add the strained cabbage; season to taste with pepper and salt and cook for 10 minutes. By adding ¾ pint (1½ cups) of diced cold cooked corned beef with the seasoning, this cabbage soup becomes a first-rate chowder.*

CORN CHOWDER (early 1800s)—Fry 3 or 4 slices of salt pork, soak a dozen hard crackers, cut up 1 or 2 onions, slice ½ pint (1 cup) of corn kernels off the cobs, and cube ½ pint of cooked potatoes. When the pork is tried out, remove it and lay half the onions in the fat with one-half the crackers; mix well. Add the potatoes and the corn, also well mixed and seasoned with pepper and nutmeg. Place the remaining crackers and onions on top. Pour enough boiling water into the kettle to cover the whole and cook slowly for 1 hour.**

CREAMED CORN CHOWDER (early 1800s)—Grate 12 good-sized ears of corn. Boil the cobs for 30 minutes in enough water to cover them. Remove the cobs and add the corn, boil 10 minutes, then add 2 quarts (8 cups) of rich milk and ½ pound (1 cup) of butter; stir in 5 tablespoons of flour wetted in cold milk; season with salt and pepper. Boil 5 minutes and turn into a tureen onto the beaten yolks of 3 eggs. Stir and serve.*

IF SOUP IS TOO SALTY (early 1800s)—Add slices of raw potatoes, boil them a few minutes and remove them; if soup is still too salty, repeat the process. The potatoes can be used later in many ways.**

CAPE COD PEA CHOWDER (mid-1800s)—This is made in the manner of the Bravas (Portuguese fishermen) on the Cape. Put some dried peas into water and boil about 2 hours; strain the pea mush and put it over a low fire; add all kinds of cooked vegetables, except cabbage and turnips; fry an onion sliced into rings a crisp brown in butter and add this to the mixture; dice a small piece of cooked pork or ham and add this, too. Cut some buttered toast into small squares and stir them into the chowder just before serving.**

WORDS TO THE WISE ON MAKING SOUP BALLS (mid-1800s)—It is a good practice to try one ball first by cooking it before the rest. If it cooks to pieces, more solids are to be added; if it cooks too hard, more liquid should go into it.*

MARROW BALLS FOR SOUP (late 1800s)—Moisten the surface of a 9-inch frying pan with just enough melted butter to cover its bottom; when it bubbles, add ¼ cup of beef marrow. As this heats slowly, beat 1 egg in a bowl; add about ½ cup of soft white bread crumbs; strain the marrow into this egg-crumb mixture. Beat it with an egg beater and season to taste with nutmeg, white pepper and salt. Roll into balls the size of marbles and cook them in gently boiling water 15 to 20 minutes.*

NOODLE BALLS FOR SOUP (early 1800s)—Blend 2 saltspoons (½ teaspoon) of salt and 1 saltspoon (¼ teaspoon) of nutmeg with a pinch of cayenne into 1 well-beaten egg; work enough flour into this mixture to make a very stiff dough; knead it smooth on a flour board; roll it flat and shape it into balls about the size of hazelnuts; put the balls into heavily salted boiling water and let them boil at a lively clip for almost ½ hour.*

RICE BALLS FOR SOUP (late 1800s)—Blend 2 tablespoons of flour into ½ pint (1 cup) of cold boiled rice that has been rubbed through a sieve with 1 slightly beaten egg and 1 teaspoon each of grated orange rind and minced chives or parsley; season with a saltspoon (¼ teaspoon) of salt, ½ saltspoon (1 pinch) of white pepper and ditto of nutmeg. Shape into balls the size of hickory nuts; boil them briefly in the soup with which they are to be eaten.*

CHEESE STICKS FOR SOUP (late 1800s)—To 3 tablespoons of butter add ¾ cup of flour, ¼ cup of grated store (Cheddar) cheese, 4½ tablespoons (generous ¼ cup) of cracker crumbs, ½ teaspoon of salt and ⅛ teaspoon (a pinch) of pepper; blend well and stir into this 1 whole egg and 1 egg yolk beaten together. Make ready a very hot (450-75°F.) oven; on a floured board roll the dough into an ⅛-inch-thick square; cut the dough into strips ¼ inch wide and about 4 inches long. Bake 8 to 10 minutes. If your fingers are nimble you can add an extra touch by twisting the strips of dough before they go into the oven.*

CHICKEN DUMPLINGS FOR SOUP (late 1800s)—Chop 1½ cups of cooked white meat of chicken and rub through a sieve; follow the same course with ¼ cup of fine white bread crumbs soaked in milk and squeezed dry; blend the chicken and crumbs with 2 tablespoons of melted butter and 1 raw egg whipped with a fork. Season to taste with pepper, salt and sage or savory. Shape into ovals and cook them for about 10 minutes in the soup.*

CUSTARDS FOR CLEAR SOUPS (late 1800s)—Beat 2 whole eggs and 1 yolk with ¼ cup of cold soup liquor or water; add a dash of nutmeg and a little salt; pour this into a shallow pan; place the pan in hot but not boiling water; let it remain over a gentle fire until the eggs are set; remove the pan from the fire. When the custard is cool and firm, invert the pan on a platter and cut the custard into dice or strips.*

CHEESE CRUSTS FOR SOUPS (late 1800s)—Melt some sweet butter in a skillet; into it dip, one side only, thin slices of bread, decrusted and cut into squares; cover the buttered side with grated cheese, place on a baking tin and put into a hot oven (400°F.) until a deep yellow.*

BREAD BALLS FOR SOUP (late 1800s)—Melt 2 ounces (¼ cup) of butter and add 5 level tablespoons of coarse bread crumbs, a saltspoonful (¼ teaspoon) of salt, a little nutmeg or pepper; mix them, then add 1 whole egg and 1 yolk; stir until smooth and light. Shape into balls the size of hickory nuts and drop them either into boiling salted water or into boiling soup. Cover and allow to simmer for 10 to 15 minutes.*

SNOW BALLS FOR SOUP (early 1800s)—Beat the whites of 2 eggs and stir them into enough milk to make ½ pint (1 cup) of liquid; in a stew-pan blend 1 ounce (2 tablespoons) of butter into 1 cup of flour; then add the egg and milk and stir evenly and steadily until smooth; let the mixture cool and blend into it 2 egg yolks, a pinch of nutmeg and a little salt. Ten minutes before the soup is to be served, drop this dough by the teaspoonful into the boiling soup and let it cook for 8 minutes. Remove the soup from the fire and serve.*

FORCEMEAT BALLS FOR CHICKEN SOUP (early 1800s)—Use ½ pound of raw breast of chicken or a similar weight of lean veal; pound this into a paste in a mortar. Soak 2 ounces (2 cups) of pure white bread crumbs in milk; wring them dry in a cloth; pound the crumbs with 2 ounces (¼ cup) of butter and the yolks of 2 eggs, into the meat in the mortar and, finally, rub the whole through a colander; season with salt, nutmeg and pepper; shape teaspoonfuls into oblong pieces. Cook about 10 minutes in soup or soup stock.*

FOR A RICH, DARK SOUP— Use caramel, which is sugar browned in a frying pan until a golden brown and then dissolved in a little water (see below).*

BURNED SUGAR FOR SOUPS AND GRAVIES— Put 2 ounces (scant ¼ cup) of brown or white sugar in an old tin cup over a brisk fire; stir this until it is quite dark and gives forth a burned smell; then add ½ cup of cold water; let it boil gently a few minutes, stirring well all the while. Take it off the fire and, when cold, bottle for use. This keeps well, and may be used for flavoring soups, and gravies, too.—Jane Thomas

FORCEMEAT BALLS FOR BLACK BEAN SOUP—Take cold cooked meat; chop it very fine; add flour enough to make it stick together in balls about the size of a walnut; roll the balls in flour and fry them until brown; add them to the soup just before it is served.—Mrs. Baushar

NOODLES FOR SOUP—Rub into 2 beaten eggs as much sifted flour mixed with a saltspoon of salt as they will absorb: then roll out the paste until it is thin as a wafer; dust over it a little flour, and then roll it over and over into a roll; cut the roll into thin slices, starting from one edge, and shake them out into long strips; put them into the soup lightly and boil for 10 minutes.—Mrs. F. D. J.

8. Fin Fish and Shell Fish

HINTS REGARDING FISH PURCHASING (early 1800s)—Buy those which have just been caught, and you do well, in the end, to patronize just one good monger instead of flitting from stall to stall. To know that fish are fresh, you can judge by their being hard under the pressure of the finger, bright-eyed and red-gilled; fish lose their best flavor soon, and a few hours make a wide difference in the taste. Stiffness, generally, is a sign of freshness.

Cod are best in cold weather; mackerel are best in the early fall; halibut in May and June; oysters from September to April; lobsters are best at the time of year when oysters are not good.*

TO BROIL FISH (mid-1800s)—Rub the gridiron with lard or drippings to prevent the fish from sticking. To turn a fish, lay an old dish upon it, and hold it with one hand while you turn over the gridiron with the other. Lay the skin side down first.*

TO FRY FISH (mid-1800s)—Cut it into slices first, then lay it in a cloth that the moisture may be absorbed. The fish should then be dipped in a beaten egg and rolled in fine bread crumbs or Indian (corn) meal. Fry slowly in good drippings.*

BUTTERED BREAD IN BAKED FISH (early 1800s)—The simplest way of baking fish is very good. Spread little pieces of bread with butter; pepper and salt them and lay them inside the fish. Then take a needle and thread and sew the fish up. Put a small skewer through its lip and another through its tail, and fasten them together with a piece of twine. Lay the fish into a dish in which it may be served and dust it with flour; put 2 or 3 very thin slices of salt pork upon it. Bake in a fairly quick oven (375°F.) and baste frequently. A fish that weighs 5 pounds will bake in a short hour.*

MISS DODS' WAY OF BOILING FISH (mid-1800s)—Miss Dods, the lecturer, first plunged the fish (halibut) into boiling water, remarking that small fish should be plunged into cold water. She then put into the fish water a large pinch of salt and a tablespoon of vinegar. "In boiling the fish," said the lecturer, "it depends upon its thickness as to the time it should be boiled. The instant the fish slips from the bone, it is ready. While it is boiling, I make the sauce." To make the sauce, Miss Dods took the yolks of 2 hard-boiled eggs, a dessertspoon of dried parsley, 1 ounce (2 tablespoons) of butter, ½ gill (¼ cup) each of cream and milk, 1 teaspoon of dry mustard and a little pepper and salt. The parsley was then chopped; the yolks were mashed and made to blend with the mustard; the whites she chopped; then all the ingredients were added to the sauce. "Actually," concluded the lecturer, "the sauce is really Drawn Butter.***

STEAMED FISH (mid-1800s)—The best size is from 3 to 4 pounds. After the fish is washed, marinate it in milk for 1 hour; then rub it with lemon juice and a little salt. Wrap the fish in muslin cheesecloth, but do not skin it; simmer it, under cover, in salted water for ¾ to 1 hour.*

EASY FISH SCALING—This is accomplished if you first soak the fish in boiling water for 1 minute.

A SAVORY BED FOR BAKED FISH (late 1800s)—Butter the pan in which the fish is to be baked. Then spread for the fish a bed of the following finely minced vegetables: 1 carrot, 1 onion, 1 celery root—all large. Sprinkle this bed with 1 tablespoon of chopped parsley; place the fish upon the bed; baste it with melted butter and give it a light dusting of thyme. Bake in high moderate (375°F.) oven for 35 to 40 minutes. Add a little water from time to time to keep the pan moist; baste with the resulting liquid. The vegetables in the pan do not go to the table. Serve with Hollandaise Sauce (see Index).*

STUFFING FOR BAKED FISH (late 1800s)—Soak a stale breakfast roll in milk and press it dry in your hands; put it into a bowl and fork in 1 tablespoon of melted butter, 2 whole eggs, 1 teaspoon of savory, ½ teaspoon of salt and a pinch of pepper. If too soft, add crumbs; if too hard, blend in a little milk. This recipe is for a smallish fish. For larger catches, increase the proportions.*

RICH OYSTER FISH STUFFING (early 1800s)—Chop fine ½ gill (¼ cup) of fat ham; stir into this 1 large tablespoon of soft butter with pinches of minced parsley, marjoram and thyme, a little salt, nutmeg and pepper, together with 6 plump oysters chopped into bits. Beat 2 eggs and add them to the mixture, together with enough bread crumbs to compound ingredients. With this, stuff the fish, the interior of which should be well floured. Sew it up; fasten the head and tail together with thread and skewers. Bake slowly for 1 hour and baste with butter.*

CARP BAKED IN WINE (early 1800s)—Like all pond fish, the carp should be well soaked in cold, salted water; lime water is best. This removes the earthy taste common to them. Prepare the fish for cooking and make a stuffing (see Stuffing for Baked Fish, above); put in the stuffing and sew the carp up. Rub the fish with a beaten egg and cover it with bread crumbs; lay it in a deep earthen dish; drench it with melted butter and ½ pint (1 cup) of white wine; drop in 1 bay leaf, a faggot made of 1 stalk of celery, 1 sprig of parsley and 1 small carrot tied together, 6 chopped anchovies and 2 sliced onions. Bake it before a slow fire (300°F. oven) for 1 hour. Strain the liquor and melt 1 ounce (2 tablespoons) of butter in a stew-pan; dredge in sufficient flour to dry the butter up; pour the carp liquor into this and stir as it thickens; after it boils up, add the juice of ½ lemon.*

IN SELECTING COD (early 1800s)—Buy only those that are plump and round near the tail; make certain, also, that the hollow behind the head is deep.*

COD'S HEAD AND SHOULDERS (early 1800s)—What roast sirloin is to Beefeaters, this dish is to cod lovers. Cod may be boiled whole; but a large head and shoulders are quite sufficient for a dish. Also, by the time this, the thickest, part of the fish is done, the tail is insipid and overdone. The latter, cut into slices, makes very good material for frying. To cook head and shoulders alone, cover the fish with cold salted water at the rate of 1 ounce (about 2 teaspoons) of salt for each quart (4 cups) of water. Rub the fish, which should not be skinned, with salt and set it into a kettle; then add the cold salted water; pour it not over the fish but along its sides. If the cod stands for a few hours in this water before being put over the fire, its flesh will be firmer. Boil the fish 30 minutes or more or less, depending on its thickness. If water must be added, do not pour it over the fish, because the flesh may break. Serve with an Egg Sauce (see Index) and Buttered Parsnips (see Index); an Oyster Sauce (see Index) also makes a good accompaniment to this fine dish.*

COD SOUNDS (early 1800s)—Like boiled cod eyes and tongues, the air or swim bladders of the cod have always been highly prized by Boston epicures. They are served with a forcemeat in the following manner. Wash 4 sounds and boil them in milk and water for 30 minutes. Remove them and let them cool. Make a forcemeat by mixing 12 chopped oysters, 3 chopped anchovies, ¼ pound (1 cup) of bread crumbs, 1 ounce (2 tablespoons) of butter, 2 uncooked eggs and seasonings of salt, pepper, nutmeg and cayenne. Cover the sounds with spreads of this forcemeat; roll and tie them; rub them with lard, dredge in flour and cook slowly before the fire in a Dutch Oven or in a slow oven in a kitchen range (275°F.) until they are browned.*

BOILED SALT COD WITH PORK SCRAPS (early 1800s)—Lay a piece of salt fish into the cellar a day or 2 before it is to be cooked, that it may become softened by the dampness. The afternoon before the day on which it is to be boiled, wash it carefully in several waters. It is well to keep a brush on purpose to cleanse salt fish and to use it repeatedly while the fish is soaking. Leave the fish in water until morning, and then put it in a kettle; set it where it will be kept warm, and at length simmer but not boil it. Cut the fish into slices and serve it with beets and potatoes and Drawn Butter. When it is to be eaten with pork scraps, cut ¼ pound of sliced salt pork that has been parboiled into tiny squares; allow about ½ hour to fry these over a low fire to a state of perfect crispness; drain off all fat and sprinkle them upon the fish. Serve without butter.***

ROASTED CODFISH (early 1800s)—This can be done only before an open fire; a wooden board (preferably oak) is a prime requisite. You will need a smallish codfish or salmon or shad, about 3 to 4 pounds; split it and season with salt and a little cayenne pepper. Be sure that your board is just a little longer and wider than the fish is when it is spread open. Stand the board before a bright, hot fire until the whole piece is very hot to the touch, but take care that it does not catch fire. Tack the fish, skin down, to the hot board with 4 spiked nails, driven in so that they are easily drawn out again. Stand the plank on its end before the fire, setting a dish at the bottom to catch the drippings for basting. When you see that the cod is thoroughly done, withdraw the nails and send the fish to the table on the board, the ends of which may be rested on muffin rings or something of the sort to prevent injury to the cloth. Eat with a Parsley Butter Sauce, Pickled Beets and Creamed Potatoes (see Index).*

POTTED FISH (early 1800s)—This is a very convenient dish, and while this receipt is primarily for shad that weigh from 3 to 4 pounds, almost any fish of the same size may be done this way. Take 3 or 4 fish, and when they are nicely dressed, cut them down the middle and across into pieces about 3 inches wide; put them down into a jar in layers, with salt, whole cloves, peppercorns and allspice sprinkled between. When all is laid in, put in just enough sharp vinegar to cover the fish and bake it. The best way is to put the jar into a brick bake-oven (or any gas or electric oven) after the bread is drawn, if considerable heat still remains; let it stand 2 or 3 hours (at 200°F.). This will keep for several weeks, even in hot weather.***

CODFISH À LA CRÈME IN PUDDING—Take 4 pounds of codfish, let it come to a scald, pick it in pieces; mix the fish with 4 tablespoons of Worcestershire sauce, 2 tablespoons of Anchovy Sauce (see Index), ¼ pound (8 tablespoons) of butter, ½ pint (1 cup) of cream. Boil ½ dozen large potatoes and mash them; put the fish mixture into a pudding dish, then cover it with the potatoes; bake 15 or 20 minutes in a hot (400°F.) oven or until nicely browned.—Mrs. Baushar

BOILED SALTED CODFISH (early 1800s)—Soak 2 pounds of codfish in lukewarm water over night or for several hours; change the water several times. About ½ hour before dinner put this into fresh cold water and set it over the fire; let it come to a boil, or just simmer, for 15 minutes, but do not boil it hard; then take it out of the water, drain and serve with Drawn Butter for the family.*

EGG SAUCE FOR BOILED SALTED COD (early 1800s)—To 1 teacup (1 cup) of milk add 1 teacup of water; put this on the fire to scald, and when it is hot stir in a tablespoon of flour, previously wet with cold water; add 2 or 3 beaten eggs; season with salt and pepper, vinegar, a little celery and 3 tablespoons of butter. Boil 4 or 5 eggs hard, take off the shells, cut them in slices and lay the slices over the dish. Then pour the sauce over them and serve.*

CROQUETTES OF FISH—Take dressed fish of any kind; separate the fish from the bone and mince it with a little seasoning and an egg beaten with a teaspoon of flour and 1 of milk. Roll the mixture into balls, brush the balls with egg, dredge them well with bread and cracker crumbs, and fry them a nice color. The bones, head and tail, an onion, an anchovy and a pint (2 cups) of water will make the gravy.—Anon.

IN SELECTING EELS (early 1800s)—They should be smooth, dry and firm to the touch; they should also be springy when you bend them. Avoid red-eyed eels.*

TO SKIN AN EEL— Drive a long, sharp nail through a board 12 inches by 12 inches by 1 inch, about 2 inches below the top; turn the board so that the nail points up; hook the eel's head on the nail; cut the skin around the "neck" and pull it off like a stocking.

BROWNED EELS—Skin and parboil them; cleanse the backbone of all coagulations; cut them in pieces about 3 inches in length; dip in flour and cook in pork fat until brown.—Mrs. P. B. Ayer

FRIED EELS (early 1800s)—Skin and wash 4 small eels; cut them into 3-inch pieces, which you trim nicely and rub very dry; dip them into flour, then into a beaten egg, then into bread crumbs, and fry them a nice brown in very hot lard.*

IN SELECTING FLAT FISH (early 1800s)—If flounders and such are flabby and the skin is easily lifted from the meat, they are to be suspected.*

FRIED FILLETS OF FLOUNDER (late 1800s)—Have your fish dealer prepare 6 fillets of flounders or other flat fish and see to it that they are washed and dried. Rub them with a mixture of $\frac{1}{4}$ teaspoon of white pepper to 1 teaspoon of salt; spread them, on one side only, with a blend of 6 mashed anchovy fillets, 1 dessertspoon (2 teaspoons) of lemon juice, 1 ditto of melted butter and 1 saltspoonful ($\frac{1}{4}$ teaspoon) of dry mustard; roll the flounder fillets and tie them with a string; dredge them in fine cracker crumbs that have been rolled and sifted; dip them in a well-beaten egg and crumb them again. Fry them in deep fat moderately hot (365–75°F.) from 4 to 6 minutes and drain them on toweling before serving.*

BOILED FLOUNDER WITH CURRY SAUCE (early 1800s)—Clean the fish; do not skin it, but lay it in a kettle with 1 pint (2 cups) each of milk and water, 1 ounce (2 tablespoons) of butter, 1 teaspoon of lemon juice; season to taste with salt and pepper. Bring this to a gradual boil and let it simmer gently for 7 to 10 minutes. Remove, drain and serve covered with Curry Sauce (see Index).*

IN SELECTING HADDOCK (early 1800s)—Always select those that weigh from 2 to 3 pounds; when the fish is heavier than that, its flesh is coarse.*

CREAMED HADDOCK (late 1800s)—Simmer 4 to 6 pounds of skinned finnan haddock in 1 quart (4 cups) of water with 1 tablespoon of salt and 1 tablespoon of vinegar for 20 minutes; season with pepper and salt; flake the fish off on a platter. Meanwhile, have ready a cream sauce made from 3 tablespoons each of flour and butter blended with $\frac{1}{4}$ cup of strained fish water, 1 cup of rich milk and 1 teaspoon of onion juice and seasoned to taste with salt and white pepper. When this mixture is thick, stir in a lump of butter as big as an egg (4 tablespoons) and follow with the flaked fish. As a final touch, just before serving, add 1 teaspoon of minced parsley.*

BAKED FINNAN HADDOCK (early 1800s)—Do not buy fish that has stood in the fish market until it is of darkish color; really good finnan haddock should be honey-colored. To remove the skin, hold the fish before fire, slap it a few times on the skin side, and the skin comes right off. Cut the fish into 5-inch squares, place it in a spider with enough water to cover it and let it come to a boil; pour off all but a little of the water (just enough to cover the bottom of the spider) and put plenty of butter in lumps on top of the fish. Set it in a low medium oven (325°F.), bake 30 minutes and baste often. If you want to, you can serve this with a Cream Sauce (see Index) but if you do use all milk instead of an addition of fish water. Nothing goes better with this than firm waxy boiled potatoes (see Index).*

BAKED FINNAN HADDIE (late 1800s)—Put the washed fish, skin side up, in a baking pan just large enough to contain it; cover with cold water and add a little salt; let this stand for ¼ hour on the top of the range over a very slow fire. Drain the water out of the pan and rinse the fish with cold water under the kitchen tap. Now add enough milk to cover the fish and 2 tablespoons of butter; let it bake in a moderate (350°F.) oven for a short ½ hour.*

IN SELECTING HALIBUT (early 1800s)—When the skin is loose and flappy, buy some other kind of fish.*

TO BOIL HALIBUT (early 1800s)—Try to purchase the tail piece, because that is the richest. Wrap it in a floured cloth and lay it in cold water with salt in it. A piece that weighs 6 pounds should simmer for 30 minutes after the water begins to boil. It is eaten with Parsley Butter Sauce (see Index).*

BROILED HALIBUT (late 1800s)—Have the fish sliced about 1½ inches thick; wipe the pieces with a damp cloth, then with a dry one; rub a good coat of kitchen salt on both sides and let it stand an hour or so to harden. Have a nice bed of coals, not too hot (or a 400°F. broiler). Grease the griddle (or broiler) and give the pieces a nice browning on both sides, about 20 minutes all told. Have a platter hot; put the fish on it after removing the skin around the edges and breaking the salt coverings away; spread the fish generously with butter. Serve with Boiled New Potatoes and Parsley Butter Sauce (see Index).*

LEFT-OVER BOILED HALIBUT (mid-1800s)—When boiled halibut is left, lay it in a deep dish and sprinkle on it a little salt, throw over it 1 dozen or so of cloves, pour in some vinegar, add some catsup and chill it in an ice chest. It will, when cold, have much the flavor of lobster.**

IN SELECTING MACKEREL (early 1800s)—Be governed by the brightness of its appearance; a transparent silvery hue is good; redness about the head is bad.*

BROILED MACKEREL (mid-1800s)—When intended for broiling, mackerel should never be washed, but merely wiped clean and dry after gills, fins and insides have been removed. Open the front of the fish, wipe it inside and out with sweet oil and season with pepper and salt. Close the fish and broil it over a clear fire; turn it over with the aid of a platter; lastly, spread it open on its back. For a mackerel of average size, the broiling time is about 15 minutes, if the fire is right. Remove the bones and season with 1 table-spoon of parsley worked into 4 tablespoons of butter; spread this over the fish and give it a squeeze of lemon. Serve before the butter is quite melted.*

PERCH BOILED IN SHERRY (mid-1800s)—Scale the fish, remove the gills and fins and gut and clean them well. Let them simmer gently in equal parts of sherry and White Soup Stock (see Index) wherein has been placed 1 clove of garlic and 1 branch of parsley. Let the fish simmer gently for 10 minutes; keep them on a hot platter while you strain the liquor and make a gravy by thickening it with a butter ball of as much butter and flour, in equal portions, as you may need for the amount of liquor on hand (1 table-spoon each of flour and melted butter per cup of liquid).*

IN SELECTING SALMON (early 1800s)—The belly should feel thick and firm to the pressure of a forefinger. Many housewives put their faith in red gills, but do not follow their example; it could be that the gills have been artificially dyed to give a long-dead salmon a livelier look.*

COURT BOUILLON FOR BOILED SALMON (late 1800s)—This is the finest method by which one may prepare Boston's traditional Independence Day Salmon Dinner (see below). To 3 pints (6 cups) of water add ½ pint (1 cup) of cider vinegar, 1 large carrot quartered lengthwise, 2 quartered onions and 2 tablespoons of salt; add also 2 bay leaves, 12 peppercorns and 4 cloves, all wrapped together in cheesecloth. The marinade must taste salty; if it is not, add 1 more tablespoon of salt. Heat the marinade in a pan that fits your salmon—or cod or halibut—and bring it to a boil.*

INDEPENDENCE DAY SALMON DINNER—Cover a 4- to 5-pound salmon with boiling water and add 2 tablespoons each of diced carrots and onions, 1 branch of parsley, 1 tablespoon of salt, 1 bay leaf, 3 cloves and ½ cup of vinegar. The best method is to wrap the fish in cheesecloth and tie it loosely with a piece of trussing twine (see Index). When the water boils, remove the fish to a place where it will just simmer and let it cook thus for about 30 minutes.

Serve this with tiny green garden peas, cooked in butter with 1 tea-spoon of finely minced raw onion. Serve the fish with Egg Sauce, which is made by mincing 2 hard-boiled eggs into each cup of White Cream Sauce (see Index). Pour the sauce over the boiled salmon. Many use a Butter

Sauce (see Index), in which case, the peas are boiled in as little water as possible and without onions.—Mrs. Malcolm Truex

SALMON BAKED IN CREAM— Remove the scales from 3 to 4 pounds of salmon; wipe the fish with a cloth dipped in vinegar, rub it with salt and pepper, dredge it with flour, place it in a pan and douse it with 1 cup of hot water in which 2 ounces (4 tablespoons) of butter has been melted. Cook on top of the stove over gentle heat about 30 minutes. Transfer to a fairly hot (375°F.) oven and douse the salmon with 1½ cups of top cream. Bake until the fish is a good brown; baste every 5 minutes with the cream. When done, remove the fish; thicken the sauce, like meat gravy, with 1 tablespoon of flour dissolved in a little cold milk. Strain the gravy; pour it over and around the fish or serve in a separate dish.—Eda K. Smith

STEAMED SALMON WITH HOLLANDAISE SAUCE (late 1800s)—Clean the fish thoroughly but do not remove the skin. Rub it well with salt and lemon juice and place it in a steamer over boiling water. Allow 6 minutes per pound for a narrow piece of fish; allow more for a piece of a wider shape. Remove the skin while the fish is still hot. Serve with Hollandaise Sauce (see Index.)*

BOILED WHITEFISH— Lay the fish open; put it on its back in a dripping pan; nearly cover it with water; to 1 fish put 2 tablespoons of salt; cover tightly and simmer (not boil) it ½ hour; dress with gravy, butter and pepper; garnish with sliced eggs.

For the sauce use a piece of butter the size of an egg (4 tablespoons), 1 tablespoon of flour, ½ pint (1 cup) of boiling water; boil a few minutes and add 3 hard-boiled eggs, sliced.—Mrs. Andrews

FISH À LA CRÈME—Take any firm salt-water fish, rub it with salt and put it in a kettle with enough boiling water to cover it. As soon as it boils set it back where it will simmer and let it stand for ½ hour; then take it up and draw out all the bones. Put 1 ounce (¼ cup) of flour into a saucepan, to which add by degrees 1 quart (4 cups) of cream or new milk, mixing it very smoothly; then add the juice of 1 lemon, 1 onion chopped fine, a bunch of parsley, a little nutmeg, salt and pepper; put this on the fire, stirring it until it forms a thick sauce; stir in ½ pound of butter; strain the sauce through a sieve. Put a little on a dish, then lay the fish on it and turn the remainder of the sauce over it. Beat to a froth the whites of 6 eggs, spread them over the whole and bake until it is light brown in a moderate (375°F.) oven.—Mrs. J. A. Ellis

QUICK FISH PUDDING—Two gills (1 cup) of Drawn Butter (see Index) with an egg beaten in, 2 hard-boiled eggs, 2 gills (1 cup) of mashed potato, 1½ pints (3 cups) of cold cooked fish (cod, halibut or shad), the roe of a cod or shad, 1 teaspoon of butter, 1 teaspoon of minced parsley, pepper and salt to taste. Dry the roe, which has already been well boiled; mince the fish fine and season with the parsley, pepper and salt; mix the roe with the butter and the mashed yolks of the boiled eggs; cut the whites of the eggs into thin rings. Put a layer of mashed potatoes at the bottom of a deep buttered dish; then in, alternate layers, fish, drawn butter, rings of egg whites filled with roe, more potato above that and so on. Cover tightly and set in a quick (400°F.) oven until the pudding steams and bubbles; then brown it by removing the cover a few minutes. Send to the table in the baking dish, and pass pickles with it.—Marion Harland

FISH AND OYSTER PIE (early 1800s)—For this dish you will need 2 dozen oysters. Clear some cooked fish of bones and skin until you have 1 pint (2 cups) of fish and flake it coarsely; put a layer each of flakes and oysters in the bottom of a well-buttered pie pan; season with pepper and salt; follow with a layer of bread crumbs, on which you drop small pieces of butter; season with nutmeg and chopped parsley. Repeat this until the dish is quite full. Melt 2 ounces (4 tablespoons) of butter in ½ gill (¼ cup) of cream or rich milk and ditto of oyster liquor; pour this over the pie and cover with buttered bread crumbs made by cooking 1½ gills (¾ cup) of bread crumbs in ½ gill (¼ cup) of melted butter. Many people make a thick Cream Sauce (see Index) with the oyster liquor. But do not make too much, because oysters are in themselves very moist.*

CURRIED FISH (early 1800s)—Flake slices of any cold fish and fry the flakes in butter with thinly sliced onion until both are a golden brown. Make a medium White Sauce (see Index) of fish stock if you have it; if not, use water or milk. Add 1 teaspoon of East Indian curry powder to the liquid; taste for strength; if the curry is not strong enough add more curry powder; if the sauce becomes too thick, add cream to suit; season with salt, white pepper and cayenne. Pour this sauce into the pan with the fish flakes and onion; let all cook together 10 minutes over a very low fire. Curried lobsters and oysters are made the same way.*

BAKED BLACK BASS—For a large fish, take 8 good-sized onions chopped fine; measure and take half that quantity of dry bread crumbs and a piece of butter the size of hens' eggs (4 tablespoons); add plenty of pepper and salt and moisten thoroughly with Anchovy Sauce (see Index). Stuff your fish with this compound and pour any of the mixture that remains over the fish, previously sprinkling it with a little red pepper. Bake in a hot (400°F.) oven from ½ hour to 1 hour, depending on the fish being large or small. Shad, pickerel and trout are good the same way. Tomatoes can be used instead of anchovies, and are more economical. If you use them, take pork in place of butter and chop it fine.—Mrs. P. B. Ayer

BROILED WHITEFISH—Wash and drain the fish; sprinkle it with pepper and lay it with the inside down upon the gridiron; broil it over fresh bright coals. When it is a nice brown, turn it for a moment onto the other side, then take it up and spread it with butter. This is a very nice way of broiling all kinds of fish, fresh or salted. A little smoke under the fish adds to its flavor. This may be made by putting 2 or 3 cobs under the gridiron.—Mrs. G. E. P.

SALT MACKEREL—Soak the fish for a few hours in lukewarm water, changing the water several times; then put them into cold water loosely tied in cloths and let them come to a boil, turning off the water once and pouring over the fish hot water from the tea kettle; let this just come to a boil. Then take the fish out and drain them, lay them on a platter, butter and pepper them and place them for a few moments in the oven. Serve with sliced lemons, or with any nice fish sauce.—Mrs. F. D. J.

FRIED SMELTS (early 1800s)—Soak the smelts a little while in warm water; scrape them and cut through the heads so far that you can gently pull them off and thus draw out the dark vein that runs through the body; then rinse the smelts and lay them in a dry cloth while you fry 2 or 3 slices of salt pork to great crispness; remove the pork from the fat; dip the smelts into a plate of sifted Indian (corn) meal, and fry them brown. If you fry smelts in lard or drippings, do not sprinkle them with salt until they are nearly done, as they will not brown well if the salt is put on earlier.*

IN SELECTING OYSTERS (early 1800s)—Always pick them one by one and reject those whose shells do not remain tightly shut when you try to pry them open.*

TO KEEP OYSTERS (early 1800s)—In cool and cold months put them in a tub, covered with salted water. Leave them there for 12 hours, when they are taken out and allowed to stand for 12 hours without water. Repeat the process with fresh batches of salted water; never use the same water twice. In this manner, oysters keep better than if they were constantly kept in water.***

PREPARING OYSTERS FOR COOKING (early 1800s)—Oysters should be skimmed out of their liquor before being cooked, so that the latter may be strained, as there are often bits of shell in it.*

OPENING OYSTERS (pre-1800s)—In opening oysters, says an eighteenth-century culinary commentator, great care must be taken to remove the poisonous part. This lies in the head, all of which must be thrown away, as well as the vein which passes from it, through the body. All the other parts are good. Break the shells with a hammer. The liquor and the spawn should be saved.***

THE SIMPLEST WAY OF COOKING OYSTERS (early 1800s)—Take them, unopened, rinse the shells clean, and lay them on hot coals (or under a broiler going full blast) or on the top of a very hot cooking stove; be sure to put the deepest side of the shell downward, so that the liquor runs into it. When the shells begin to open a little, the oysters are done; the upper shell will be easily removed with a knife and the oysters will be eaten from the lower shell. The table should be supplied with coarse napkins, also a large dish to receive the shells.*

OYSTER PIE (mid-1800s)—Make a nice paste (see Index) and lay it into a deep pie dish; turn a small teacup upside down in the center; this will draw the liquor under it, and prevent the juices from boiling over; it also prevents the upper crust from falling in and becoming clammy. Lay in 1 quart of oysters (25 to 50 if large, 50 to 100 if small) to fill the shell, and dust with pepper, salt and flour as you proceed; make a wide cut in the upper crust so that you can pour in as much cream as will be needed at the proper time. Have the kitchen-range oven ready at a moderate heat (350°F.), because the pie should be put into the oven as soon as the upper crust is in place, else it will become clammy. Seal the edges of the crust by wetting the bottom shell with water and dusting it with flour, then pressing the upper crust's edge upon it. A warning: use but little of the oyster liquor, as oysters part with a good deal of moisture in cooking. Bake the pie about an hour and add the cream 15 minutes before the time is up.*

STEWED OYSTERS (early 1800s)—Boil the oysters up for 5 minutes in their juices; then set them off the fire, in order to remove the scum that rises. For 1 quart of oysters (25 to 50 large or 50 to 100 small) prepare 1 tablespoon of butter with as much flour rubbed into it as it will receive. Return the oysters to the fire, and when they begin to simmer, stir the butter in so that the liquid becomes a gravy.*

OYSTER STEW WITH MILK (early 1800s)—Boil 1 pint (2 cups) of milk; rub 1 heaping tablespoon of flour smooth in cold milk and strain this into the boiled milk; stir until the milk thickens. Strain into the milk the liquor from 1 quart of oysters (25 to 50 large or 50 to 100 small) and, when it boils up again, add 1 tablespoon of butter, a little pepper and salt and, lastly, the oysters; let the whole cook from 2 to 3 minutes.*

SHERRIED OYSTERS AND MACARONI (late 1800s)—Line a buttered, shallow pudding dish with fine bread crumbs; add a layer of cooked macaroni; add salt, pepper and pieces of butter; next make a thick layer of oysters. Build the layers in this way until the dish is full; then sprinkle it thickly with bread crumbs and dot the top with bits of butter. Make a medium Cream Sauce (see Index), but instead of using the full amount of the liquid that is called for in the recipe replace a quarter of it with a good dry sherry. Brown in a quick (400°F.) oven 15 to 20 minutes.**

FRITTER BATTER FOR OYSTERS (mid-1800s)—Beat the yolks of 2 eggs well; add 1 saltspoon (1/4 teaspoon) of salt, 1 gill (1/2 cup) of milk and 1 coffee cup (3/4 cup) of flour, or enough flour to make it almost a drop batter. When you are ready to use the batter, beat 2 egg whites stiff and mix them in. For about 40 middling-sized oysters the frying lard should be so hot that it browns a 1-inch cube of bread in about 50 seconds (355–60°F.)*

SCALLOPED OYSTERS (early 1800s)—This is best when the platter is of such size that there are only 2 layers of oysters. Start with cleaning 1 quart of drained oysters (25 to 50 large or 50 to 100 small), which you place in a baking dish that has been buttered and dusted with cracker crumbs; cover the oysters well with buttered and seasoned bread crumbs. These are made by boiling, quickly, 2 gills (1 cup) of bread crumbs in 1 gill (½ cup) of freshly made butter; when cool, add to it ½ gill (¼ cup) each of finely minced celery, cream and white wine. When this mixture has been spread over the first layer, put down another layer of oysters and cover that with the remaining crumb mixture. Bake in a slow moderate (325°F.) oven about ½ hour.*

OYSTER PATTIES (late 1800s)—The first step is to make and shape to size a Rich Puff Paste (see Index). Next, set the oysters on the stove in a saucepan, with liquid enough to cover them; as soon as they come to a boil, skim them; stir in a walnut-sized piece of butter (1 rounded tablespoon), some pepper and ½ gill (¼ cup) of rich cream. Grease small tins and line them with the puff paste; put 3 or 4 oysters in each, add a little of the liquor, then cover them with more paste. Bake in a very quick (425°F.) oven for 15 minutes, then for 9 minutes more in a cooler (350°F.) oven. Without allowing the patties to cool brush the tops with a beaten egg and set them in the oven again for a few minutes to glaze.*

ESCALLOPED OYSTERS (late 1800s)—Put a layer of rolled crackers in a buttered dish, then a layer of oysters, and dab them with small pieces of butter; season with salt and pepper. Continue like this until the dish is nearly full, then cover with cracker crumbs and butter and about 1 pint (2 cups) of milk for each quart of oysters (25 to 50 large, or 50 to 100 small). Bake in a rather quick (400-25°F.) oven for about ½ hour.*

FRIED OYSTERS (early 1800s)—Select the largest and finest oysters. Have ready a skillet of boiling lard. Dip your oysters, one at a time, in beaten egg yolks, then in fine bread crumbs, and lastly in sifted cornmeal. Drop the oysters into the lard, but only a few at a time; turn them, but allow them to become only slightly browned. Drain them upon a hair-sieve and serve with very hot catsup.*

PANNED OYSTERS (mid-1800s)—Have a moderate oven (350°F.) ready. For a dozen oysters, melt a piece of butter the size of an egg (4 tablespoons) in a baking dish. When it is hot, drop the oysters, dripping as they are removed from their liquor, into the butter, and put them into the oven, where they will remain until their edges begin to curl. Dust with a breath of salt and white pepper.*

ROASTED OYSTERS (early 1800s)—The best way to eat oysters is to eat them raw; the next best is to feast on them when they are roasted. This is done by placing the oysters, in their half-shells and in whatever juice they have, on a gridion over a hot fire (or in a 500°F. oven) just long enough to get them hot and plump. For this use the lower and more rounded shell.*

TRIED AND TRUE OYSTER STEW (early 1800s)—First, strain the liquor off the oysters, boil it up and skim it. Thicken this with cracker dust and add a lump of butter according to your means and your liking. In this cook the oysters and, when they roll their edges, add 1 teaspoon of heavy cream for each oyster in the pan. Serve with crisp Captain's or Cabin Biscuits (see Index).**

OYSTER FRICASSEE (late 1800s)—Take 1 pint (2 cups) of cream and a little more than 1 pint of oysters (25 to 50 if small, 12 to 25 if large). Let the cream come to a slow boil; have ready 1 tablespoon of flour mixed with a tablepsoon of creamed butter; stir this into the cream. Put the cream on the back of the stove while you bring the oysters to a quick boil in their own liquor. Drain off the liquor, pour the oysters into the cream and let it boil up; remove from the fire and stir in the yolks of 2 raw eggs, well beaten; reheat briefly, but do not let the cream boil while it thickens. Pour it over a platter of hot toasted and buttered crackers and serve with Browned Potato Border (see Index).*

STEWED OYSTERS (early 1800s)—Drain the liquor from 2 quarts of firm, plump oysters (50 to 100 if large, 100 to 200 if small); mix it with a small teacup (½ cup) of hot water, add a little salt and pepper and set it over the fire in a saucepan; when it bubbles, add a pint (2 cups) of rich milk. Meanwhile, cook ½ gill (¼ cup) of sifted cracker crumbs in 3 tablespoons of butter; add the oyster liquor and milk. Let the liquid boil up once; add the oysters; when they ruffle, add 2 tablespoons of butter; when the butter is melted and well stirred in take the saucepan off the fire.*

IN SELECTING LOBSTERS (early 1800s)—If you buy live lobsters, give preference to those that wave claws and legs briskly when you pick them up; when you buy boiled lobsters, they are fresh if their tails snap back under their bodies when you stretch them lightly. Live or boiled, lobsters should have a heavy feel; if not, they are watery. Medium-sized lobsters are best; the shells of old lobsters are apt to be encrusted. On no account should they be eaten later than 18 hours after being boiled; many housewives will not touch them after 12 hours.*

TO BOIL A LIVE LOBSTER (late 1800s)—Like many simple but delightful dishes, boiled lobster is a victim of over-simplification. To cook this dish right, fill a large kettle ¾ full and add 6 quartered medium onions, 24 peppercorns, 2 bay leaves, 1 tablespoon of salt for each quart (4 cups) of water and a small bunch of parsley. Bring this to a boil and let it cook for 15 minutes before you boil your lobster. While many believe that it is most humane to cut the lobster's spinal cord—by inserting a knife point between the tail shell and the body—the fact is that a lobster suffers painless and sudden death if it is plunged, head first, into briskly boiling water. The time of boiling, from 15 to 25 minutes, depends upon the size of the lobster. When it is done, take it out, twist off the claws and put the lobster on its back. Cut it into halves with a cleaver or heavy knife with a blow that reaches from head to tail. Remove the stringy vein called lady fingers, the liver and the stomach, but save the coral. From this point on, you can serve the lobster hot or cold, whole or cut into pieces. As for the claws, crack them on their lower sides so as not to disfigure them.*

OILING LOBSTERS (late 1800s)—Rub lobsters with sweet oil while they are still hot from the boiling pot and wipe it off after a few minutes. This gives the shells a rich crimson gloss.*

POTTED LOBSTER MEAT (early 1800s)—Remove the meat from 2 lobsters in their mature prime, but do not cut it up. Put some butter on the bottom of a pan; lay in the lobster meat as evenly as you can with 2 to 3 bay leaves and a seasoning of pounded mace, white pepper and salt. Cover it with ¼ pound (½ cup) of butter cut into pats and bake, covered, for ¾ hour in a gentle (250°F.) range oven. When this is done, drain the whole on a sieve, saving the liquor for a Lobster Sauce (see Index). When the lobster pieces are cool and dry, lay them in potting jars with a seasoning of pulverized ginger, mustard, cayenne, salt and mace. Cover with Clarified Butter (see Index) that stands well above the meat. If very highly seasoned and placed in a cool spot, this will keep some time.*

LOBSTERS IN GREEN PEPPERS (mid-1800s)—Cook as many green, or red, if you can get them, peppers as you need; have 1½ pints (3 cups) of cooked and minced lobster meat for a party of 4 to 6. Blend 3 tablespoons of flour and 1½ teaspoons of minced shallots or onions into 3 tablespoons of melted (unsalted) butter, and make a Cream Sauce with ½ pint (1 cup) of milk and ¼ cup of lobster liquor, or, in lieu of the latter, ¼ cup of cream. Cook this over a very slow fire 7 minutes; then add the mashed yolks of 3 hard-boiled eggs; cook it an additional 8 minutes; add the lobster and reheat; when it is ready, pour the mixture into the parboiled pepper shells, sprinkle bread crumbs on top, dot with butter and let them brown in a quick (400°F.) oven until they are a lush brown. (Crab meat and oysters can also be served in this manner.)*

LOBSTER NEWBURG (late 1800s)—The secret of this new dish is a deft touch combined with low heat and a really good double boiler. In the latter, melt 3 tablespoons of unsalted butter over boiling water, which must not touch the bottom of the top boiler; when the butter is hot, but not bubbling, put in 1 saltspoon (¼ teaspoon) of onion juice; season with salt, pepper and red pepper; after 5 minutes of ever so gentle cooking, add 1 sherry glass of sherry (1½ to 2 ounces) to the butter in the boiler. Break 2 egg yolks into 2/3 cup of very heavy cream and whip both together with an egg beater. Have the meat of 1 medium-sized boiled lobster cut into neat, small mouthfuls. Pour the lobster into the egg mixture; blend them in with a gentle hand, or the fragile lobster pieces will break. Now pour the lobster mixture into the top of the double boiler; do not mix it with any implement, but shake the cooker gently with a back and forth motion so that the ingredients blend and cook evenly. When the Newburg is properly cooked and thickened, remove it from the fire and give it a squeeze or 2 of lemon through a fine sieve; shake the top of the boiler to mix the lemon into the sauce. This dish should be served on crustless toast cut in slices ¾ inch thick and buttered on both sides. It is not desirable to sprinkle the servings with paprika or add any garnish; Lobster Newburg is *that* self-sufficient.*

LOBSTER CROQUETTES (mid-1800s)—Mix 2 cups of cooked and chopped lobster meat, 1 tablespoon each of minced parsley and lemon juice; 2 mashed hard-boiled egg yolks, ¼ teaspoon of nutmeg, a pinch of cayenne and pepper and salt to taste. For a very elegant meal, bind the ingredients with 1 cup of cold Lobster Sauce (see Index). Otherwise use a less stylish plain Croquette Sauce (see Index). Form the mixture into cakes. Dip them in crumbs, beaten egg, and crumbs again; fry them in deep fat at a heat in which a 1-inch bread cube browns in 40 seconds (375°F.).*

LOBSTER CUTLETS (late 1800s)—Pound the meat of 1 or 2 boiled hen lobsters to a paste with 1 or 2 ounces (2 or 4 tablespoons) of fresh (unsalted) butter and season with nutmeg, mace, pepper and salt as you like it. When it is all a smooth paste, blend in a little red spawn to color it; divide the mixture into equal portions and shape them into cutlets, but not too thick; dip them in beaten egg and sifted bread crumbs; fry them a nice brown in boiling lard; drain them on a sieve reversed and brown butcher's paper. Put them on a rather shallow serving dish and place a small piece of claw on the top of each; let them be surrounded by a Béchamel or Cream Sauce (see Index), which must surround but not cover the cutlets.*

LOBSTER PATTIES (mid-1800s)—Line patty shells with Puff Paste (see Index) and put into each shell a small piece of fresh bread to keep the top crust from falling on the bottom crust; cover with a top crust of paste, brush it over with beaten egg and bake a light brown in a hot (425°F.) oven. Take as much lobster meat as is required and mince it very fine. Make enough Cream Sauce (see Index)—seasoned with 1 teaspoon of anchovy paste and lemon juice, white pepper and salt to taste—to cream the meat; stir this mixture over the fire for 5 minutes. Remove the lids from the patty cases, take out the pieces of bread, fill the cases with the lobster mixture and replace the covers. Bake briefly in a moderate (350°F.) oven and serve.***

LOBSTER BISQUE (late 1800s)—Cook 1 pint (2 cups) each of cooked lobster meat and ditto of rice in 1 pint (2 cups) of Chicken Stock (see Index) or water until it is so soft that you can rub it through a colander; color this a rich red with lobster coral, which is also run through the colander. In another pan, thicken 3 tablespoons of flour in a like amount of melted butter and 1½ cups of rich milk; season this with pinches of salt, nutmeg and white pepper. Blend this Cream Sauce into the lobster and cook all in the top of a double boiler; adjust to the desired thickness by adding sherry or Madeira wine.*

SAUCED LOBSTER MEAT (early 1800s)—Boil a lobster. Pound the spawn and 2 anchovies; pour on this 2 tablespoons of any left-over gravy; sieve it into ½ gill (¼ cup) of melted butter; then put in the lobster meat, cut up; give it all one boil and add a squeeze of lemon.*

DEVILED LOBSTER (late 1800s)—Measure 1 pint (2 cups) of boiled and chopped lobster meat. Boil 1 red and 1 green pepper that have been cut into strips; drain them. Put together a thick Cream Sauce (see Index), but use lobster liquor for half of the liquid measure prescribed for the sauce. For a really strong "deviling" add, in addition to the red and green peppers, ½ teaspoon each of Worcestershire sauce and dry mustard and 1 teaspoon of onion juice. Those endowed with copper-lined throats also add ½ salt-spoon (⅛ teaspoon) of Tabasco sauce.*

LOBSTERS À LA MODE (late 1800s)—Dice the meat of a large freshly boiled lobster into small cubes. Heat ½ cup of White Soup Stock (see Index) or milk; add ½ cup of cream; season rather highly with a pinch of powdered bay leaf, cayenne and salt; take it from the fire and thicken with 2 egg yolks; return it to the stove; stir until it thickens. Add the lobster meat to this sauce; let it simmer slowly for 6 minutes. Place the mixture on thick slices of decrusted toast that have been heavily buttered; cover with bread crumbs, dot richly with small bits of butter and put them on a baking tin into a very hot (450°F.) oven for a quick browning.*

CRAB OR LOBSTER CROQUETTES—The same mixture as given for Stuffed Crabs or Lobster (see below) without the cream, made into pointed balls, dipped in egg, and then rolled in cracker crumbs and fried in very hot lard. Served dry and garnished with parsley.—M. A. T.

STUFFED CRABS OR LOBSTER—Boil crabs or lobsters and pick out the meat, carefully preserving the shell whole; rub the shell with salad oil. Add to the meat one-quarter as much fine bread crumbs and very little nutmeg, cayenne pepper, grated lemon rind, lemon juice and butter, and a little sweet cream (if lobster is used, rub the coral with the cream); replace the fish in the shells, dust lightly with bread crumbs and butter and brown in a quick (400°F.) oven. Garnish with parsley and lemon.—M. A. T.

CREAMED LOBSTER (late 1800s)—Take the meat from 1 or 2 large boiled hen lobsters and chop it into bite-sized pieces; mince all or part of the coral and soften it in 2 tablespoons of melted butter; combine meat and coral. Make a Creamed Lobster Sauce (see below) and blend it with the meat and coral.*

CREAMED LOBSTER SAUCE (late 1800s)—Mix ½ cup of finely minced lobster meat with a boiled and mashed lobster roe; make ¾ pint (1½ cups) of medium thick Cream Sauce (see Index) and blend in the lobster; if the sauce is too thick, thin it down with milk. A fancier lobster sauce can be made for parties by preparing the same quantity of lobster meat and roe and blending it into a similar amount of Hollandaise (see Index), but be sure of your ability to make Hollandaise before you, to quote Lawyer Marks, "go ahead."*

BUTTERED SHRIMP (mid-1800s)—Two pounds of raw shrimps are needed to make 1 pound of cooked and shelled shrimps. To cook, pour them, un-shelled, into just enough lightly salted boiling water to cover them. Let them simmer from 3 to 5 minutes, according to size, and put them to drain in a sieve at once. Shell and de-vein the shrimp and put them into a stew-pan. For each pound of cooked and shelled shrimp use ¾ pint (1½ cups) of White Soup Stock (see Index) or water; thicken this with a butter ball made of 4 tablespoons of flour worked into 1/3 pound (2/3 cup) of butter; season with salt, pepper and a pinch of curry powder; simmer for 3 minutes.*

CLAM BROTH (early 1800s)—This is made by washing the clams very clean and boiling the *shells* in very little water till they open; then take out the clams and put them into the water again; boil them a few minutes. Remove clams and thicken the broth with a little flour blended with butter; put toasted crackers in the tureen into which you put the broth. A very healthy dish for feeble persons.*

STEAMED CLAMS (mid-1800s)—Follow the method given for Clam Broth (see above), only watch for the clams to open; when they do, take the kettle from the fire at once as further cooking will make them leathery.*

CREAMED CLAMS (early 1800s)—Lay the clams on a gridiron over hot coals; take them out of the shells as soon as they open; save the juice, and add to it a gill (½ cup) of hot milk for every pint (2 cups) of clams; season with white pepper and very little salt; thicken with 1 dessertspoon (2 tea-spoons) of flour rubbed into as much butter for each gill (½ cup) of milk used, and simmer for 10 minutes. Add the clams; cook the Creamed Clams for 2 to 3 minutes and pour them over buttered toast dusted with nutmeg.*

CLAM STEW—Lay the clams on a gridiron over hot coals, taking them out of the shells as soon as they open and saving the juice; add a little hot water, pepper, a very little salt and butter rolled in flour, sufficient for seasoning; cook all for 5 minutes and pour it over toast.—Mrs. M. L. S.

TO DRESS CRAB—Two or 3 shallots and a little parsley chopped very fine; 1 ounce (2 tablespoons) of butter; a bunch of sweet herbs; a teacup of broth (or water). Boil a few minutes and take out the herbs; add the crumbs of a roll finely grated, 1 tablespoon of best sweet oil, 1 glass of sherry, the juice of ½ lemon, cayenne pepper and salt to taste. Remove the meat of 4 crabs from shells, cook in butter and stir into the above mixture; put all nicely into the shells, grate over some bread crumbs and put in a very hot (425°F.) oven a few moments to brown.—Mrs. Elia M. Walker

9. Beef, Veal, Lamb, Mutton and Pork

HOW TO SELECT MEATS (mid-1800s)—Ox (or Steer) Beef: Look for cuts in which the meat is red, smooth and firm, also well streaked with white fat. Meat poorly streaked is usually cow or bull beef. The outside fat should also be white; beware of yellow tinges; they denote age, ill health, or both.

Veal: If the animal was milk-fed, the meat should be a pinkish-brown and firm-fleshed and show little if any moisture. The bones are soft and show red in animals from 6 to 8 weeks old. Such fat as there is should be cream-colored.

Spring Lamb: To fall within this range, the lambs should be born about New Year and marketed by Easter.

Mutton: All lamb more than a year old is mutton. The fat of young lambs is white but can have touches of pink; the flesh is firm and pink. After the critter is 2 years old, mutton flesh turns to an increasingly darker red.

Pork: A suckling pig is perfect when 3 weeks old. Meat from corn-fed hogs should be a bright fireman's red, firm and dry; the bones should be soft, reddish and slender; the fat white, firm and dry. On hams, the skin should be thin, pliable, smooth and white.

TO TRUSS MEATS (mid-1800s)—A good general rule to follow is to truss all meats that are to be boiled, braised or pot-roasted, if for no other reason than appearance's sake. Trussed meat keeps its shape better. Always truss across the grain by tying single pieces of twine around the meat at 1½- to 2-inch intervals and two pieces of twine the long way, with the grain. Make the former very tight, the latter not so tight. Expert trussers tie their twine with bows for easy removal; others use strong knots and cut the strings away before serving.*

TO COOK MEATS (mid-1800s)—Except for meat to be used for soup, all fresh meat for boiling should be started in boiling water. Then the outer parts contract and the internal juices are preserved. Allow about 20 minutes to the pound.

For soup, it is just the opposite; place the meat in cold water so that its juices enter into the soup.

Salt meat should be put on in cold water, that the salt may be extracted in cooking.

In boiling all meats, it is necessary to keep the water at a constant and lively simmering, otherwise the meat will absorb the water. Be certain to add boiling water if more water is needed. The more constantly the water cooks at just below the boiling point, the more tender the meat will be.

Skimming is a constant and essential chore in boiling any kind of meat. Failure to do so will ruin the best cuts obtainable.

When you chop suet, cut it into small pieces and remove the membrane; sprinkle the suet lightly with flour and chop it in a cold place to prevent it from becoming sticky.

Roast meats require a brisk fire. Baste often. For each pound of fresh meat the roasting rule is generally 20 minutes. The variations in the meats that are roasted consist mainly in the method of preparing them before they go in the oven. Some are to be larded, some stuffed with bread dressing, and others plain, only seasoned with pepper and salt. However, before she undertakes to roast beef or meat of any sort, it is absolutely necessary that a woman must know how to build and maintain correct roasting fires in order to maintain even heats; she must also know how to overcome the vagaries of her cooking stove or kitchen range which make her oven run hot and cold but never even.

Broiling should be done on a greased hot gridiron over a fairly fierce, but not smoking, fire.

Pan-frying must never be done on a cold, dry pan. Like the gridiron, it must be greased and well heated before put to use. The chief benefits of pan-frying are the brownings left by the meat in the pan. They are good for gravies, but if the pan is too hot, the brownings will be scorched and useless. Avoid using butter alone in pan-frying. It burns too easily. Half lard and half butter is better, if butter *must* be used. Thrifty housewives usually rely on the good quality of their drippings.*

BRAISED BEEF HEARTS (early 1800s)—Cook 2 onions in beef drippings so that they become tender. Wash the heart and take care to cut away all veins. Stuff it with minced parsley, but loosely; truss so that the meat will keep its shape. Place the heart in a roasting pan, add the onions, and 2 carrots cut into cubes and a tablespoon of additional drippings; season generously with pepper and salt. Simmer this slowly, very tightly covered, for 2½ to 3½ hours. Test with a fork for tenderness. When done, strain the liquid from the heart; for each ½ pint (1 cup) of liquid blend 2 tablespoons of flour into 4 tablespoons (¼ cup) of cold water; pour this into the liquid and cook until thickened; stir continually.*

ROAST BEEF WITH YORKSHIRE PUDDING (mid-1800s)—Wipe the meat with a wet towel; dredge with salt and flour. Place in a pan in a very hot oven for a few minutes, then add enough water to cover the bottom of the pan. Baste every 15 minutes with liquid from the pan. A roast weighing 8 pounds should be cooked 50 minutes if desired rare; for medium, 1¼ hours. (The foregoing recipe is typical of the kind in use at the time when "roasting" beef with water was in vogue.)

For the Yorkshire Pudding, beat 3 eggs very light; add a scant teaspoon of salt and 1 pint (2 cups) of milk. Pour ½ cup of this liquid onto 2/3 cup of flour and stir; when this is perfectly smooth add the remaining liquid. Bake in a shallow pan for ¾ hour; serve hot with beef.***

YORKSHIRE PUDDING (mid-1800s)—When roasting a piece of beef, lay it on sticks in your baking pan, so that the juice from the meat will drop into the pan below. About 45 minutes before the beef is done, mix the following pudding and pour it into the pan under the meat, letting the drippings continue to fall upon it: 1 pint (2 cups) of milk, 4 eggs well beaten, ½ pint (1 cup) of flour, 1 teaspoon of salt.***

ROAST BEEF (late 1800s)—Place the trussed roast on the dripping pan's rack; dust it with salt, pepper and flour. (Note the departure from the old practice of not using salt until the roast is almost done; I still recommend it.) Put the roast into a hot (400°F.) oven for 15 minutes for a quick browning; then lower the heat to a good moderate (350-75°F.) oven. The cooking time is about 16 minutes for each pound for rare, 22 minutes for medium and 30 minutes for well done. (Here, too, procedures have been changed. In the old days, the browning or frothing came last.) Baste the beef often with the fat from the drippings. So as not to steam the meat, do not put water in the dripping pan. (A radical departure from the mid-1800s, when roasts were actually steamed.) Serve a Brown Gravy made by pouring all but ½ gill (¾ cup) of the fat from the pan, rubbing the same amount of Browned Flour (see Index) into the fat in the pan, adding 1 pint (2 cups) of water and cooking until all the brownings in the pan have been dissolved. Season with salt and pepper; strain through a sieve into a sauce boat.* Serve with Yorkshire Pudding (see below) and Marrow Dumplings (see Index).

YORKSHIRE PUDDING (late 1800s)—Beat 4 eggs, and when they are well started add, very gradually, 1 pint (2 cups) of milk; that done, add 1 pint (2 cups) of flour sifted with 2 saltspoons (¼ teaspoon) salt; beat for a total of 10 to 15 minutes. Put enough drippings into a baking pan to grease bottom and sides; make the pudding batter far enough ahead of time so that it may stand for an hour before it is put into the oven. It takes this pudding ½ hour to cook; at the proper time, pour it into the pan and place the latter on a rack under that on which the roast stands in place of the regular dripping pan, so that drippings will fall on the pudding; turn the pudding occasionally so that it bakes evenly. To serve, slice it into 2-inch squares.*

BRAISED BEEF (late 1800s)—Dice and try ½ cup of salt pork; put it into a large iron kettle, add ¼ pint (½ cup) of chopped onion and ditto of turnip, carrot and celery. While this cooks, truss your beef (see Index), rub it with pepper, paprika and flour. Put the meat atop the vegetables in the kettle and let it cook, turning it often to brown all sides. A piece weighing about 5 to 6 pounds will need 15 to 20 minutes. Now add 1 quart (4 cups) of boiling water and let it simmer slowly about 4 hours. If the water cooks away, add enough boiling water to maintain the level at about 1½ pints (3 cups). About ¼ hour before the meat is ready, stir into the juices ½ gill (¼ cup) of Browned Flour (see Index) blended into a similar amount of softened butter; mix this into the juices thoroughly to thicken them; season with salt and pepper, and put in 1 sprig of parsley, which is removed at serving time. Serve with Mashed Turnips and Baked Tomatoes (see Index).

STEWED BRISKET OF BEEF (early 1800s)—Put 3 to 4 pounds of brisket into 1 quart (4 cups) of boiling water in a kettle; let it cook in simmering water for 2 hours; take off the scum as it rises. Take the meat from the pot and brown it in a pan on every side in butter; return it to the pot and stew it gently 5 hours more. Add boiling water if the water cooks away. After 4½ hours put in a couple of carrots, turnips and onions; season to suit your taste. Serve with Boiled Potatoes and a Mustard Sauce (see Index).***

BRINES FOR CORNING (early 1800s)—Housewives are always told to make a brine strong enough to float an egg; but what does one do if an egg is not handy? Specifically, one can make brine by measuring 1 pint (2 cups) of salt for every 2½ quarts (10 cups) of water. To make the brine uniformly strong, many women boil it until the salt is completely absorbed by the water.*

TO BOIL CORNED BEEF (early 1800s)—Wash a 5- to 6-pound piece and put it into a pot that will hold plenty of water; the water should be cold and the same care should be exercised in skimming as for fresh meat (see Brown Soup Stock in Index). It is not too much to allow 40 minutes per pound after it has begun to boil and has been reduced to simmering. The goodness of Corned Beef depends much upon it having been boiled gently and long. When it is cooked, lay it into a flat earthen dish or pan and, over it, a piece of board the size of the meat. Upon this put a clean stone or some other heavy weight. Salt meat is very much improved by being pressed. Next day put the meat to boil in cold water with a shredded or quartered cabbage and peeled and halved large potatoes; serve when the potatoes are done and make a boatful of Drawn Butter (see Index).*

STUFFED CORNED BEEF (mid-1800s)—A nice way of making a change in this oft repeated dish is to take about 6 pounds of well-corned rump or round and, making several deep cuts in it, fill them with a stuffing of a handful of soaked bread squeezed dry, a little fat or butter, a good pinch of cloves, allspice and pepper, a little finely chopped onion and small pinches of marjoram or thyme; tie the meat up tightly in cheesecloth saturated in vinegar; let it simmer about 3 hours.* (Press and recook the beef following the directions under To Boil Corned Beef, above.)

MISS DODS' FAMOUS STEWED STEAK (mid-1800s)—To prepare this dish you will need sirloin steaks that weigh 1 pound each and measure 1 inch thick. First place equal amounts of butter and lard in a large skillet and brown the steaks on both sides. This done, put them into a proper stew-pan. Now measure the fat in the frying pan and for each tablespoon rub in 1 tablespoon of flour; let this bake a good brown before you gradually add enough hot water to make a smooth and fairly thick brown sauce. Season this with pepper, salt and just a smidgen of powdered ginger; pour this over the steak. Garnish the meat with fancy-cut pieces of carrots and turnip; then cook, tightly covered, as slowly as possible for 1½ hours. With Savory Baked Potatoes (see Index) this makes good eating.*

MARROW DUMPLINGS (early 1800s)—Beat 4 ounces (¼ pound) of beef marrow to a cream; whisk 4 eggs and add them to the marrow. Soak well ½ pint (1 cup) of bread crumbs in boiling milk, beat them up and add them to the other ingredients. Stir all well and form it into small dumplings. Drop one into boiling broth to see if it falls apart or boils stone hard. If the former, add more bread crumbs; if the latter, add part of a well-beaten egg. It always pays to experiment with dumplings and the like. Serve in soup or with roast beef.*

ROASTED MARROW BONES (mid-1800s)—Make a thick paste of flour and water and place disks of it at both ends of marrow bones that have been sawed into 2½-inch sections. Have a hot (450°F.) oven ready; place the bones on a baking sheet and let them roast in the oven from 7 to 10 minutes, as governed by their thickness.*

BROILED BEEFSTEAK—Lay a thick tender steak upon a gridiron over hot coals, having greased the bars with butter before the steak has been put upon it. A steel gridiron with slender bars is to be preferred; the broad flat iron bars of gridirons commonly used fry and scorch the meat, imparting a disagreeable flavor. When the steak is done on one side, have ready your platter warmed, with a little butter on it; lay the steak upon the platter with the cooked side down, that the juices which have gathered may run on the platter, but do not press the meat; then lay your beefsteak again upon the gridiron quickly and cook the other side. When it is done to your liking, put it again on the platter, spread it lightly with butter and place it where it will keep warm for a few moments, but do not let the butter become oily; to place it over boiling steam is best. Then serve the steak on hot plates. Beefsteak should never be seasoned with salt and pepper while cooking. If your meat is tough, pound *well* with a steak mallet on both sides.—Mrs. P. H. Smith

TRIPE WITH ONIONS (mid-1800s)—After 1 pound of tripe has been thoroughly washed, cut it into finger-sized pieces, which you cover with boiling water and suffer to cook until tender. Meanwhile, simmer, in ½ gill (¼ cup) of butter, 1 gill (½ cup) of chopped sweet onions until they are yellow; then stir in 2 tablespoons of flour until the flour has been absorbed by the butter; now add the tripe, making certain first that it has been well drained. Season with white pepper and salt and add milk if it seems too thick; let it cook 15 minutes in a pail (pot) over boiling water, and serve on freshly made Baking Powder Biscuits (see Index) or on slices of toast.*

HAMBURG STEAK (mid-1800s)—One pound of round steak, chopped with an onion; pepper and salt to taste. Make this stick together with an egg yolk or 2, shape into small cakes as you do fishballs, and fry in butter on both sides.* (This simple version of the now not so simple Hamburger seems to have appeared in New England kitchens when housewives had not as yet learned how to prepare and cook this *innovation*. For a more sophisticated version see Fried Beef Balls, below.)

FRIED BEEF BALLS (late 1800s)—Chop and mince a cheap cut of beef fine until you have 1½ pounds (or buy 1½ pounds of chopped beef). Mix with ½ pint (1 cup) of fine-rolled cracker crumbs, 1 lightly beaten egg, ½ cup of butter softened but not melted; add salt and pepper to taste. Shape into balls as large as apples, flatten, dust with flour and fry in 1 tablespoon each of lard and butter.*

GRILLED BEEF RUMP (mid-1800s)—Start with washing a small bunch of parsley, dry it and chop it on a board very fine; mix the parsley with 1 ounce (2 tablespoons) of softened butter, 6 drops of lemon juice and pepper and salt according to taste; make it all up into small pats. Now have at hand as many ½-pound rump steaks as you need, each of which should be ½ inch thick; pour about a teaspoon of salad oil on a plate; dip both sides of each steak to be grilled into this; add oil as necessary, but never drown the steaks in oil. Place the oiled steaks on brown butcher's paper. Be sure that your gridiron is hot and that your fire is bright and steady. Grill each steak for 10 minutes and turn it often. Since steaks wait for neither man nor gourmand, be sure that the rest of your dinner is ready when the steaks are done. Serve steaks with parsley-butter pats on top of each.*

BEEF (OR VEAL) LOAF—Three pounds of meat chopped fine with ¼ pound of parboiled salt pork, 6 Boston crackers powdered fine, 1 sheet of isinglass dissolved in a coffee cup of warm water (or 1 envelope of gelatin), 1 tablespoon of butter, 1 teaspoon of salt and 1 of pepper, and 1 of powdered cloves, or a nutmeg grated. Mix well together with 2 eggs; bake 1 hour. This will slice well when cold.—Anon.

SALT HORSE FOR THE CLIPPER—For preserving 100 pounds of beef: 6 pounds of salt, 2 ounces of salt-petre, 2 tablespoons of soda, 2 pounds of sugar, 4 gallons of water. Mix well together; sprinkle the bottom of the barrel with salt; put in the beef with very little salt between each layer; pour over the brine; put on top a weight to keep all well covered.—Mrs. Carter

TO CORN BEEF OLD WAY AND NEW— Old way: To each gallon of cold water, put 1 quart of rock salt, 1 ounce of salt-petre and 4 ounces of brown sugar (it need not be boiled). As long as any salt remains undissolved, the meat will be sweet. If any scum should rise, scald and skim well; add more salt, salt-petre and sugar; as you put each piece of meat into the brine, rub it over with salt. If the weather is hot, gash the meat to the bone, and put it in salt. Put a flat stone or some weight on the meat to keep it under the brine. (Early 1800s—next item 50 years later.)

New way: For every 4 gallons of water allow 2 pounds of brown sugar and 6 pounds of salt; boil about 20 minutes, taking off the scum; the next day turn it on the meat packed in the pickling tub; pour off this brine; boil and strain, every 2 months, adding 3 ounces of brown sugar and ½ pound of common salt. It will keep good a year. Sprinkle the meat with salt the next day; wipe dry before turning the pickle over it. Let it entirely cover the meat; add 4 ounces of salt-petre. Canvas lids are excellent for covering, as they admit the air and exclude flies. Mutton and beef may be kept sweet several weeks by simply rubbing well with dry salt and closely covering. Turn the pieces whenever the vessel is uncovered.***

BOILED TONGUE AND TOMATO SAUCE—Boil a pickled tongue until well done; then peel it. For the sauce, 1 can of tomatoes, boiled half down, then strained; rub together 1 tablespoon of butter, 1 teaspoon of flour and a little salt; put these into the tomato and let it come to a boil; then pour over the tongue and serve.—Mrs. A. L. Chetlain

STEWED TONGUE—Cut square fillets of bacon, which dredge with a mixture of chopped parsley, salt, pepper and a little allspice. Lard the tongue with the fillets. Put in a saucepan 2 ounces of bacon cut in slices, 4 sprigs of parsley, 2 of thyme, a little garlic, 2 cloves, 2 carrots cut in small pieces, 2 small onions, salt and pepper. Lay the tongue on the whole; wet with a glass (4 ounces) of white wine and a ditto of broth. Set it on a moderate fire and simmer about 3 hours, keeping it well covered. Put the tongue on a dish and strain the sauce over it.—Anon.

BREADED VEAL CUTLET (late 1800s)—Depending upon the appetites of your household, have the butcher cut you boneless servings of leg of veal that weigh from 3 to 6 ounces each, all ½ inch thick. Pound these to half their thickness with a rolling pin or meat mallet; season them with salt and pepper. Break 1 or 2 eggs into a bowl and for each egg add 1 tablespoon of milk; season lightly with pepper, salt and a little nutmeg and whip with a beater. Cover the meat pieces with flour on both sides; dip them in egg and then in cracker crumbs. Brown in deep hot fat (350°F.) 5 to 8 minutes; then put the cutlets into a baking pan with a good cover and let them bake, covered, in a slow (325°F.) oven for about 1 hour or until well done. Serve with Horse-Radish Sauce (see Index).*

JELLIED VEAL (late 1800s)—Cook 4 pounds of veal slowly in 2 quarts (8 cups) of *cold* water until you can pick the meat apart with a fork. Salt the meat shortly before it seems done. Be sure that there is a cupful of liquor left when the meat is ready. Pick the meat up in fine strings with a couple of forks, or use your fingers, and lay the strips in a small bread pan; have the meat's grain run the long way of the pan. Season the liquor, while still hot, with powdered marjoram, rosemary, savory and 1 tablespoon each of onion and lemon juice. Pour it over the meat. Press in pan for 18 hours.*

MARBLED VEAL (late 1800s)—Follow the same procedure as for Jellied Veal (see above) with respect to boiling the veal and seasoning the liquid. But instead of "stringing" the meat, pound it to a paste in a mortar. Cut the newly boiled tongue of an ox into pieces and mortarize it with a piece of butter the size of an egg (4 tablespoons). Put a layer of veal into a brick-shaped tin, then put down a layer of tongue, and so on, until the tin is full; then add the seasoned veal liquor and press the loaf beneath a stack of bricks. This, cold, is best when sliced very thin and served with a cold Potato Salad (see Index).*

ROAST VEAL—Prepare a leg of veal for the oven by washing it, drying it and larding it with strips of fat bacon or ham, dredging it well with flour and seasoning it with salt and pepper. Baste frequently in a moderate (350°F.) oven, roast ½ hour to the pound, and serve with the gravy thickened.—Mrs. D. S. F.

ROAST FILLET OF VEAL—The fillet should be prepared by stuffing it with bread crumbs seasoned with chopped ham, summer savory, pepper and salt. Dredge lightly with flour and bake in a brisk (400°F.) oven about 15 minutes; then reduce oven to slow moderate (325°F.) and roast it 25 minutes to the pound.—Mrs. D. S. F.

NECK PIECE OR SHOULDER OF VEAL—Put a piece of butter the size of an egg (4 tablespoons) into a kettle; put it on the stove; when it begins to fry, put in the veal, season it and let it fry until brown; then add water sufficient to cook it. When it is done take cream and flour well stirred, thicken as for fricasseed chicken, and you have a nice dinner, very like chicken and much cheaper—Mrs. C. C. Stratton

MOCK FRIED OYSTERS—Cut a ¼-inch-thick slice of veal in small pieces 3 or 4 inches square; dry them with a towel; season to taste; have ready a beaten egg and some crackers rolled fine, each on separate dishes; dip each piece of the cutlet in the egg, then in the rolled crackers. Have enough butter hot in your spider as will nearly cover the cutlets when you put them in. A rich gravy can be made after the meat is done by adding a little boiling water and enough moistened flour to thicken.—Anon.

VEAL LOAF—Three and one-half pounds of lean and fat raw veal, chopped fine, 1 slice of salt pork, 6 small crackers rolled fine, a piece of butter the size of an egg (4 tablespoons), 2 eggs, 1 tablespoon of salt, 1 tablespoon of pepper, 1 tablespoon of sage, 3 tablespoons of extract of celery; mix thoroughly. Pack tightly in a deep square tin; cover with bits of butter and sprinkle fine cracker crumbs over the top; cover with another tin. Bake 2 hours in a moderate (350°F.) oven; uncover and brown the top.—Mrs. Lamkin

FRICANDEAU—Three and one-half pounds of cold roast veal chopped fine, 1 tablespoon of salt and 1 of pepper, ½ nutmeg, 2 rolled crackers, 3 eggs. If the veal is lean, add a piece of butter half as large as an egg (2 tablespoons) and 1 tablespoon of cream. Form all this into a large roll and spot the roll over with bits of butter; then strew over it 3 pounded crackers. Put it in a low moderate (325°F.) oven, and from time to time add a little water; cook 2 hours. When it is cold slice it thin, and it makes an excellent relish.—Mrs. J. M. Brown

VEAL PIE (mid-1800s)—Boil and skim 3 pounds of veal 3 to 4 hours; when it is done pick out all bones and gristle. When it is cold chop it, but not very fine. Season to taste with salt and pepper as well as with powdered basil, marjoram, minced parsley, peppermint, thyme and 1 small bay leaf broken into bits. Put the meat in the dish you will bake it in and pour on it about 1 pint (2 cups) of the liquor it was boiled in, thickened with 2 tablespoons of flour; add bits of butter over the top. For the top crust, use 1 heaping coffee cup (1½ cups) of flour, sift in a small teaspoon of baking powder and a pinch of salt and mix with sweet milk (1/3 to 1/2 cup); it should be about as stiff as biscuit dough. Roll the dough out to the size of the dish; cut a slash in the top or stick a pie bird in the center of the crust. Bake in a moderate (350°F.) oven about 1 hour.* (A pie bird was a small tube of baked clay, usually made to look like an open-beaked bird. It was stuck into the center of a meat pie to allow steam to escape.)

SWEETBREADS, TO PREPARE (mid-1800s)—Soak the sweetbreads in cold water until you use them. Then drain them and cover them with 2 cups of cold water; add 4 cloves, 1½ teaspoons of salt, 2 tablespoons of lemon juice and 1 slice of onion; let them simmer for ½ hour; remove them from the fire and let them stand in cold water ½ hour; then remove the membranes, etc., and the sweetbreads are ready for broiling or salads.*

CROQUETTES OF VEAL OR SWEETBREAD— Put in a stew-pan a piece of butter the size of an egg (4 tablespoons), 1 tablespoon of flour, a little pepper, salt and nutmeg; let it melt and mix well. Chop the cooked meat, but not too fine; put it in the mixture and stir until well mixed. When it is cold add the yolks of 2 eggs to bind it; roll into oblong shapes, dip into egg beaten with cold water, pepper and salt; roll in crumbs of bread or powdered crackers; fry in boiling lard.—Mrs. T. J. Dana

TO FRY SWEETBREADS—Prepare the sweetbreads as directed above; season with salt and cayenne; dredge in flour, in a beaten egg and in bread or cracker crumbs; fry in 1½ tablespoons (4½ teaspoons) of butter and a like amount of lard or drippings until browned nicely.*

SWEETBREADS—Scald them in salt and water; take out the stringy parts; then put them in cold water a few minutes; dry in a towel; dip in egg and bread crumbs, and fry brown in butter. When they are done place them in a hot dish; pour into the pan a cup of sweet cream, a little pepper and salt and a little parsley chopped fine; add flour, and when it is boiling pour it over the sweetbreads; add a dash of sherry and some mushrooms, if desired. —Anon.

BREADED CALF'S BRAIN (early 1800s)—Boil the brain 20 to 25 minutes, tied up in a piece of muslin; to 1 quart (4 cups) of water for the boiling add ½ gill (¼ cup) of vinegar. After the brain has been drained and cooled, cut it into serving pieces and dredge it in flour; season with salt and pepper; roll in cracker crumbs, dip into beaten egg and roll again in crumbs. Fry in deep fat, heated to the temperature it takes for a 1-inch cube of bread to brown in 45 seconds (375°F.).*

HEAD CHEESE—With 1 calf's head use 1 heart, ½ a liver and 1 tongue. First clean the head very nicely, then put it in a brine for 24 hours; boil it with heart, liver and tongue until it is very soft; pick out the head bones and chop the meat very fine; then add salt, pepper, 4 small onions, and a little sage, if you wish; mix it very thoroughly. Put it in a colander and set it over a kettle of hot water, or in a fireless cooker, over night; in the morning put in the press and press it as cheese.—Mrs. C. Bradley

CALF'S LIVER MARINE—Lard the liver; add pepper and salt sufficient to season it, then roll and tie it. Cut 2 onions in thin slices and lay them in the bottom of an earthen crock; add 2 slices of salt pork cut thin, and lay the liver on that; add more pepper and salt, a little vinegar and enough salad oil to cover the liver, and set in a cool place for 24 hours. Cook over a slow fire from 2:30 until 6; a wineglass of claret added at 4:30 is excellent. This is arranged for dinner at night; of course the rule for time will do for noon dinner. Easily mistaken for canvasback duck.—Mrs. J. M. Ayer

CALF'S LIVER, STEWED—Boil the liver until partly done; take it out of the saucepan; chop in small pieces; put back in the saucepan; skim well; stew until tender; season with butter, pepper and salt; thicken with a little flour, and serve over slices of toasted bread.—Anon.

ROAST LAMB (mid-1800s)—If it is a hind quarter and very fat, take off the thickest fat from the kidneys; wipe the meat, dredge with flour, season with pepper and thyme and place in a moderate (350–75°F.) oven. Put diced salt pork in the dripping pan to provide basting juice, which will be needed if the lamb is lean. Some cooks put slices of juicy onions on top of the lamb, for flavor and moisture. Roasting time is generally about ½ hour to the pound. When you test for doneness, the liquid that oozes out should be colorless; never serve pink lamb. Serve with Mint Sauce (see Index).*

BOILED LEG OF LAMB (early 1800s)—Cut off the shank bone; have enough boiling water to cover the meat; if the pot is well skimmed, (see Brown Soup Stock in Index), the liquid will make fine broth for another day. A leg of lamb is only nice when it is well cooked, because lamb is neither good nor healthy unless well done. Allow 25 to 30 minutes per pound, depending on size of the leg. A Caper Sauce (see Index) with some minced mint and sage added is a favorite with this.*

BROILED MUTTON OR LAMB STEAKS (mid-1800s)—Cut a leg of mutton or lamb into steaks with a sharp knife and make the slices about as thick as your finger; separate them from the bone neatly. Broil them exactly as you would beef steaks (see Index) but, since both are leaner than beef, keep the steaks well greased with drippings or butter. The steaks are improved if a little powdered sage is sprinkled upon them during the broiling. Serve with Cranberry Sauce (see Index) and Creamed Boiled Onions (see Index).*

MUTTON À LA VENISON—Take a leg of mutton and lard it well with strips of salt pork inserted in deep slits in the meat, which has been previously rolled in pepper and cloves. Bake 2 hours, or according to the size of the roast, basting frequently in a moderate to hot (375°F.) oven. About an hour before serving, spread over it currant jelly, return to the oven and let it brown.—Mrs. J. B. L.

MUTTON CHOPS—Cut them nicely, clearing away all ragged ends and edges; fry for a few moments covered closely, and then dip each piece in cracker crumbs and beaten egg, or you may prepare them as for frying; then, lay them in a dripping pan, and put into a moderate (350°F.) oven to bake; baste frequently with a little melted butter and water and bake 35 minutes per pound—Anon.

SLASHED LAMB WITH DRESSING (late 1800s)—For a nice hind quarter of lamb, make the same dressing as for fowl (see Index). With a sharp knife, cut slashes in the lamb and fill them with the dressing. Roast the lamb in a moderate (350°F.) oven; 15 minutes per pound, "pink," 25 minutes per pound, well done. Serve with Currant Jelly Sauce (see Index).*

LAMB OR MUTTON CROQUETTES (late 1800s)—Mince enough cooked meat, free of all fat, until you have ½ pint (1 cup) of meat; season this with salt and pepper; cook 1 gill (½ cup) of finely chopped onions in 2 tablespoons of butter until they turn yellow and blend in 3 tablespoons of flour; thicken this paste into sauce by the slow stirring of ½ pint (1 cup) of gravy, soup stock or water into it; stir in 1 beaten egg and 4 tablespoons of sifted bread crumbs; if the mixture is too dry, add a little milk; knead the meat thoroughly into this mixture and place it in the ice chest to chill. Later, shape the meat into croquettes, roll them in flour, dip in beaten egg and roll in sifted bread crumbs. Fry them in hot fat (375°F.) from 4 to 5 minutes until brown on all sides. All meats may be used for this dish when free from fat.*

TO TRY LARD (mid-1800s)—The fat should not be suffered to stand too long without being tried, because, even in cold weather, some parts of it may soon become musty and useless. Remove all lean bits; they will adhere to the kettle and cause the fat to burn. Cut the fat into pieces little more than 1 inch square; take care to have them almost of a size. At the start, put about ¼ pint (½ cup) of water into the kettle with the fat; stir often and keep a good, steady fire, without much blaze. When the fat no longer bubbles but is still, it is done. Strain through a tow-cloth bag, without any pressure, into jars, and waste no time in adding salt, since salt serves no purpose. Stone jars are best, but pottery does very well. In warm weather, a fireplace with a closed board in a cool room keeps lard fine, firm and fresh.*

LARD SCRAPS (early 1800s)—When you try out lard, and you are almost done, add whatever you have of lean bits of pork that have been cut very fine; let them brown to a turn and remove; while they are still hot, season the scraps with salt, pepper and pulverized sage; stir them well and serve as an afternoon surprise to your menfolk.*

PORK CHOPS STEWED IN ONIONS (early 1800s)—Cut some good lean and meaty pork chops 1½ inches thick and trim the lard closely. Try it out. For each chop, slice 1 large onion and cut the slices into halves. Take a piece of butter the size of a large egg (5 tablespoons) and set it boiling with the onions over a slow fire in a saucepan so that neither butter nor onions brown. As the onions cook, dust the chops lightly with salt, pepper and flour and brown them quickly on both sides in another skillet in their own fat. When the onions are done, pour ½ pint (1 cup) of soup stock or water over them and bring to a boil; add the pork chops. There must be just enough boiling liquid in the saucepan to cover the pork chops. Cover the saucepan and let the chops simmer gently 55 to 65 minutes or until done. (In a 350°F. oven, about the same time will be required.) Serve them covered by onions. Do not thicken the sauce.*

PORK AND POTATOES (early 1800s)—Parboil some salted pork that is well streaked with lean; then dice it until you have a good 2 gills (1 cup). Brown it in a skillet with a piece of butter as large as a walnut (1 rounded tablespoon); drain, and set it away from the fire. In the fat fry ½ dozen halved potatoes of even, medium size; when they are brown, remove them from the fat and, of the latter, save all but ½ gill (¼ cup), which you will reheat; into it stir ½ gill (¼ cup) of flour; when this is smooth, add slowly ¾ pint (1½ cups) of hot milk. When that has been stirred into a cream sauce, add the pork and potatoes and let them cook very slowly, uncovered, until the potatoes are tender. As an afterthought, many cooks add, at the last minute, 6 tablespoons of chopped onions that have been browned in a bit or 2 of butter.*

EARS AND FEET SOUSE (early 1800s)—When the pig's feet and ears are well cleaned and scraped, put them in cold water and over the fire to boil; when they are tender, put them in a jar; prepare a pickle of ½ gallon of cider vinegar, whole black pepper, mace and cloves; boil the spices up with the vinegar and then pour it over the pig's feet and ears. Let them stand for 2 or 3 days, when they will be ready for use.*

HANDY ANNIE'S SAUSAGE—Take 1 pound of young pork, fat and lean, without skin or gristle, 1 pound of lean veal, 1 pound of beef suet, chopped very fine together. Put in ½ pound of bread crumbs, 6 sage leaves, a teaspoon of pepper and 2 of salt, some thyme, marjoram and savory shredded fine; mix well together. Pack this into a jar and pour hot lard over the top. The lard you remove and reheat as you use the sausage.—M. A. Sadler

OVEN-ROAST PIG—See that the pig has been well scalded; put in the body a stuffing of dry bread crumbs seasoned with sage, salt and pepper, and sew it up; skewer the legs back, or the underpart will not crisp; put in a hot (400–25°F.) oven after dredging well with flour, and baste it frequently with melted butter while roasting, or rub the pig at intervals with a cloth wet with melted butter. When the pig is done, serve it whole on a platter, and garnish with parsley and celery tops alternately. Take off some of the fat from the gravy, set the rest of the gravy on the top of the stove, thicken with a little flour, add ½ glass of sherry wine and the juice of ½ lemon and serve in a gravy boat.—Phoebe Jane Chapin

HAM AND BANANA ROLLS (late 1800s)—Slice boiled ham 1/16 inch thick; trim off the fat; spread over each slice a thin layer of mild made-mustard and a fine sprinkling of powdered ginger. Roll a whole, peeled banana into each slice and hold it in place by using toothpicks as skewers. Make a Cheese Sauce by melting 2/3 cup of diced American store cheese (Cheddar) in ½ pint (1 cup) of thick Cream Sauce (see Index); pour this sauce over the ham-banana rolls and bake in a slow (325°F.) oven for ½ to ¾ hour. Always test the bananas for doneness with a kitchen fork.*

SPARERIBS AND SAUERKRAUT (late 1800s)—Divide the ribs into sections of 3 to 4 ribs each. Put them, without seasoning, into a hot (400°F.) oven long enough to brown; give each section room enough for browning; then season with salt and pepper. Put the sauerkraut needed (to make, see Index) into a greased baking dish; season lightly with caraway seeds; some add an unpared quartered apple; place the browned ribs on the kraut. Meanwhile, let the oven drop down to slow (325°F.) and bake about 1¾ to 2 hours, when the ribs should be done. Half way through, the kraut might need additional moisture in the form of soup stock or water; it should be moist, not dry, when served with heated Chili Sauce (see Index).*

TO FRY SAUSAGES NEATLY (mid-1800s)—Prick them and lay them in a little water in a baking pan; place them in a hot (400°F.) oven until the water cooks away and they are moist though well done, also a splendid brown.*

PORK RIB ROAST (late 1800s)—Have a moderate (350°F.) oven ready. Put the rib roast in a baking pan with 2 halves of onion, each of which has a few cloves stuck into it. For a good crunchy crust, sprinkle the fat well with salt. Let the roast cook undisturbed 25 minutes per pound. When it is done, remove it from the oven and sprinkle the crust with a light coating of brown sugar, very fine bread crumbs and nutmeg. Lastly, baste carefully with melted butter. Return it to the oven long enough for the crust to become a golden brown.* The gravy for this is:

CUMBERLAND SAUCE (early 1800s)—After the fat has been poured out of the pan in which a roast of pork has been done, add ½ pint (1 cup) of soup stock to dissolve the brownings; do this over a low fire on top of the stove; add ½ cup of sherry and 1 tablespoon each of mild made-mustard and currant jelly; let it boil up; strain into a gravy boat.*

Apple goes with pork the way Juliet goes with Romeo. Therefore, serve Pork Rib Roast with:

FRIED APPLE RINGS (mid-1800s)—Use tart apples. Core but do not pare them, and cut into ½-inch slices; coat the slices by dipping them alternatingly into flour and powdered sugar; fry them in butter over a low fire till they are brown and tender.*

PORK CUTLETS IN BLANKETS (late 1800s)—Have the butcher slice on the bias as many ½-inch cutlets as can be obtained from 1 tenderloin of pork; beat them on both sides with a meat mallet; season with salt and pepper and savory or sage. Brown the cutlets slowly in a frying pan for 15 minutes and turn them almost constantly with meat tongs. If you use an all-iron skillet, transfer to a moderate (350°F.) oven for about 25 minutes and add 2 tablespoons of cold water. Sauté a good lump of butter; beat 4 eggs with 8 tablespoons of cold water. With this mixture, fry as many omelet blankets as you have cutlets; wrap the cutlets in the blankets and serve with a Bordelaise Sauce (see Index).*

HOW TO BOIL AND BAKE SALT PORK (early 1800s)—Salt pork, for boiling, should have lean streaks running through it. From such a piece cut 2 pounds, more or less, according to the size of your family; scrape the rind well, wash clean, then put the pork to boil in cold soft water (see Index); boil 1 hour, then pour the water away and fill up with fresh boiling water from the tea kettle; boil another hour, then take the pork from the water, lay it on a tin and set it in a well-heated oven (350°F.) to bake 1 hour. Let the tin in the oven be inclined so that the pork does not swim in its own grease (or put the meat on a rack). Turn the pork from side to side at intervals so that it may brown nicely; turn the grease from the tin as it fills up. Serve hot with Pickled Beets (see Index) and Boiled Potatoes.*

ROAST TENDERLOIN OF PORK (late 1800s)—See that it is well trimmed but not entirely free from fat. The first step is to boil for 5 minutes 1 cup of vinegar with 1 small sliced onion, 1 bay and 1 sage leaf, a blade of mace, 1 thin slice of lemon, 6 black peppers, 2 cloves, 1 good pinch of rosemary and a sprig of parsley. Remove from fire. Marinate the pork on all sides in the hot vinegar for 15 to 25 minutes. Meanwhile, heat 3 tablespoons of butter in a suitable dripping pan (not too large); next brown the meat all around quickly on top of the stove; bake in a moderate (350°F.) oven, allowing about 45 minutes for each pound, depending on the size of the tenderloin. Baste often with the vinegar mixture to keep the pan moist. Just before the loin is done, pour 1 cup of cream over the meat and baste with it to help make the gravy, which should be skimmed for fat before serving.*

PORK CHOPS, PAN-FRIED—They are best if well beaten on both sides with a meat mallet; dip in bread crumbs, next in beaten egg seasoned with salt and pepper; dip again in crumbs. Let them stand 5 to 10 minutes before you fry them in a butter-lard mixture. Watch out for scorching and cook them a good ½ hour.—Mrs. William Day

ROAST LEG OF PORK (mid-1800s)—First, weigh the leg; next remove all hide as well as most of the fat, so that only a thin, even layer of fat remains on the top or outside of the leg; make criss-cross knife slashes in this fat and rub into those slashes such seasonings as salt, pepper, sage and ginger, the last, sparingly. Sprinkle the pork evenly and lightly with flour by using a fine sifter. Let your oven become very hot (425–50°F.). Roast the leg at this temperature at the rate of a good ½ hour to the pound. The old way of basting a pork roast with beer is still the best. When the roast is done, keep it warm on top of the stove; pour off the pan juice, from which all fat must be skimmed. Of this fat, reheat 3 tablespoons in a skillet; when it is hot, rub 4 tablespoons of flour into it and, finally, add the skimmed juices. If these do not make 1 pint (2 cups), add more beer or water. Stir this pan gravy until it thickens; be sure that all the brownings in the pan are absorbed, as they are the best part of the gravy. Serve with Apple Sauce and Baked Potatoes or Mashed Potatoes.*

FRIED SALT PORK AND FRIED SOUR APPLES (early 1800s)—This makes a very satisfying summer dinner when served with Boiled New Potatoes (see Index). Cut the slices of pork; lay them in cold water in the spider; boil them up 2 or 3 minutes; then pour off the water and set the spider again on the coals; now dredge the slices in Indian (corn) meal seasoned with pepper and brown them on both sides in the spider. In another, fry ½-inch slices of good tart cored but unpeeled apples in butter or drippings after dredging them in a little flour mixed with a pinch of cinnamon or ginger. Serve the pork and apples together.*

STUFFED ROASTED SHOULDER OF PORK (mid-1800s)—With a sharp knife, score the skin into diamonds or in strips about an inch wide. Also make some deep incisions in the thickest part of the meat and fill these with a dressing made of fine soft bread crumbs, seasoned with pepper, salt, sage and 1 stalk of celery finely minced and moistened with milk to make a soft dough. Rub a little finely powdered sage where the meat is scored and smear the entire surface well with sweet oil to prevent the skin from blistering. Roast about 45 minutes to the pound in a moderate (350°F.) oven. Baste frequently with drippings. Warning: pork burns easily and it is much injured by being burnt.*

PORK STEAKS (early 1800s)—To fry pork steaks requires about 25 minutes. Cut slices, about 1/3 inch thick, from loin or neck, shoulder or leg. Turn them often. Pour all the fat off that has fried out when the steaks are half done. Season some bread crumbs with powdered sage or tarragon; dip the steaks in this and lay them back in the frying pan with plenty of not too hot fat. When they are done through, take them up; dredge 4 tablespoons of Browned Flour (see Index) into the pan gravy; add a little salt and pepper and ½ to ¾ pint (1–1½ cups) of boiling water, depending on the amount of flour used; turn it instantly, as it boils up, upon the dish of steaks.*

COOKED WHOLE HAM (early 1800s)—Remove a well-aged ham from brine or hook, according to whether it was only cured or cured and smoked. Jab an awl to the bone near the hock; if it comes out with a wholesome odor, the ham is good; if not, it isn't. Scrub the ham thoroughly with cold water and set it to soak for 10 hours; change the water and soak it another 10 hours, or over night. When ready, after giving it another scrubbing, weigh the ham and put it into your boiling pot with enough cold water to cover it by about 1 inch; do not allow the water to boil, but keep it at a steady but gentle simmering; allow ½ hour to the pound of the ham if it is to be served boiled; if the ham is to be baked, simmer only 20 minutes to the pound. When the cooking is ended, be the ham to be served boiled or baked, the skin is removed and unsightly fat is trimmed away. If the ham is to be sent to table cold, it is best to let it chill in the water it was cooked in, because it will keep and taste better that way. Serve boiled ham with Mustard Butter Sauce, Creamed Cabbage with Cheese, and Mashed Potatoes (for all of which, see Index).*

HOW TO BOIL A HAM— Take a smoked or cured ham weighing about 8 or 10 pounds; soak it over night in cold water; then cover it with boiling water, add 1 pint (2 cups) of vinegar, 2 or 3 bay leaves, a little bunch of thyme and parsley (the dried and sifted will do, or even the seeds of parsley may be used, if the fresh cannot be procured); boil very slowly 2½ hours. Take the ham out, skin it and remove all the fat, except a layer ½-inch thick; cut off with a sharp knife all the black-looking outside; put the ham into your dripping pan, fat side uppermost, grate bread crust over it and sprinkle a teaspoon of powdered sugar over it; put it in the oven for ½ hour, until it is a beautiful brown. Eat cold; cut the nicest portion in slices; the ragged parts and odds and ends can be chopped fine and used for sandwiches. Or, by adding 3 eggs to 1 pint (2 cups) of chopped ham and frying the mixture brown, you have a delicious omelet for breakfast or lunch. The bones should be put in a soup kettle; the rind and fat should be rendered and strained for frying potatoes and crullers. Ham cooked in this way will go much farther than when cooked in the ordinary manner.—Mrs. C. Waggoner

BAKED HAM (early 1800s)—The prettiest way to serve ham is to trim its blanket of fat neatly, after the ham has been properly cooked (see above) and the skin removed. Make cuts across and along the top of the ham and place it on pieces of sawed-off broomsticks in a large baking pan so that the ham does not touch the pan's bottom. Now dress the scored fat by sticking cloves and peppercorns into the squares, drenching it with a mixture of honey and rum or cider and dusting it with ginger and sage or nutmeg. Bake the ham before a fairly hot fire (375°F. oven) and baste liberally every 10 minutes over a period of about 1¾ hours. This recipe is based upon a small, 12-pound ham. Serve with Apple Fritters (see Index), Raisin Sauce (see Index) and Stuffed Baked Potatoes (see Index).*

CAKE ICING FOR BAKED HAM—Trim a boiled ham neatly, cover it with the white of a raw egg and sprinkle sugar or bread crumbs over it; put it in the oven and brown. It is delicious also covered with a regular Cake Icing (see Index) flavored with nutmeg instead of vanilla and browned. —Bella Lyon

SLICED BOILED HAM IN WINE SAUCE (late 1800s)—If the ham is on the salt side, soak a 1½-inch slice in milk for 1 hour before cooking time and trim off the fat. Make a Brown Cream Sauce by browning 3 tablespoons of flour in 3 tablespoons of butter and, when baked brown, blending in a cup of soup stock or water; cook over a gentle fire about 30 minutes with 1 small bit of bay leaf, 1 clove and 3 peppercorns; strain the gravy into a saucepan and add ½ cup of port or Burgundy. Put the ham into this sauce and keep the dish over boiling water 15 minutes or until the ham is heated through. Do not overcook.*

A VALUABLE (HAM) SUGGESTION—Soak ham or salt pork (cut in slices for broiling or frying) in a quart or 2 (4 to 8 cups) of milk and water; soak it over night if it is for breakfast, and for several hours before any other meal. The milk may be either fresh or sour, and it is diluted with an equal quantity of water. Before cooking the slices rinse them in water until it is clear. It will be found a very excellent method, and when once adopted will be invariably the choice of preparation.—Anon.

SALTING PORK—Cover the bottom of the barrel with salt an inch deep; put down 1 layer of pork and cover that with salt ½ inch thick; continue this until all your pork is disposed of; then cover the whole with strong brine; pack as tight as possible, the rind side down or next to the barrel; keep the pork always under the brine by using an inner cover and clean stones. Should any scum rise, pour off the brine, scald it, and add more salt. Old brine can be boiled down, well skimmed and used for a fresh supply. —A. M. G.

CURING HAMS—Hang up the hams a week or 10 days, the longer the tenderer and better, if kept perfectly sweet; mix for each good-sized ham ½ pint (1 cup) of salt, 1 tablespoon of molasses, 1 ounce of salt-petre; lay the hams in a clean dry tub; heat the mixture and rub it well into the hams, especially around the bones and recesses; repeat the process once or twice, or until all the mixture is used; then let the hams lie 2 or 3 days, when they must be put for 3 weeks in brine strong enough to bear an egg; then soak 8 hours in cold water; hang up to dry in the kitchen or some other more convenient place for a week or more; smoke them from 3 to 5 days, being careful not to heat them. Corn cobs and apple-tree wood are good for smoking. The juices are better retained if the hams are smoked with the hock down. Tie up carefully in bags for the summer. Housewives whose kitchens have big tall chimneys can use them for smoking if they hang the hams high above the fire and use only hickory wood.—Mrs. Mulford

10. Barnyard and Pond Fowl

HOW TO SELECT POULTRY (late 1800s)—Ages and Weights of Chickens: About 2½ pounds—about 3 months old, best for broiling; about 3½ pounds—about 5 months old, right for pan-frying; about 4½ pounds—about 9 months old, ready for roasting. Old fowls and roosters over 4½ pounds are only for stews, soups and salads. Capons, at their prime from 8 to 10 months, weight about 4½ pounds. Roasting is best for these.

In young, tender birds, the tip of the breastbone is easily bent. The skin is smooth, moist and thin. In old birds, the skin is coarse, dry and thick. Good birds have short claws, flexible feet, legs free from scales, and the breasts are well rounded.

Ducks: One can tell the age of a duck by spreading a wing open and locating the small triangular groove just beyond the longest of the 2 small, hard, sharp feathers near the beam feather. There you'll find a triangle for every year of the duck's life. In young ducks, windpipes break easily. Best is a yearling; ducklings are usually too small to be economical.

Geese: Geese are catalogued as light (8 pounds) or heavy (over 12 pounds); the best weight is 9 pounds, which serves 6. That is perfection; a more mature goose, even as a less mature one, falls short of that desirable mark.

Turkeys: Young toms and hens are tender-fleshed and their keels (breastbones) bend like whalebone. The longer and straighter the keel, the more white meat; look for smooth and soft skins. Young toms weigh up to 25 pounds, young hens up to 15 pounds. Old toms and hens are apt to be bluish in the region that goes last over the fence.

Pigeons: Squabs—use no other kind—are recognized by the lively red of their breast meat and their well-fleshed legs. Do not buy dark-breasted, scrawny-legged pigeons; they are old and apt to be tough. When a pigeon weighs more than a pound, it is no longer a squab.

(Giblets in the old days included not only the gizzard, but also the heart, liver and neck.)

THAT TROUBLESOME BREASTBONE (late 1800s)—The breastbone can be disposed of in this manner. When preparing poultry to be cooked, take a small sharp knife; passing it up through the body cavity, cut off the little slender bones which join the hug-me-close (i.e., the bones on each side of a fowl's neck, like the collarbone in the human frame) to the sides. Then push the breast down by pressing heavily upon it. A little practice will make it easy to do this. This method is better than beating the breast flat with a rolling pin or a stone jug.*

TO TRUSS POULTRY (mid-1800s)—Chickens and Turkeys: To keep their shape and to roast right, they should be well-trussed after the dressing has been stuffed into place. A highly desirable tool for this is a trussing needle.

You can make one by boring a hole, large enough for your trussing twine, near one end of a knitting needle. Just insert the threaded needle in the lower part of one leg opposite the center of the dressing slit. Run the needle through the carcass and the other leg; draw both ends of string across the bird tightly so that the legs close and cover the slit, and tie the ends firmly on the back of the bird.

Next, pull the neck skin down along the back of the body and fold the wings under the bird; run the needle through the second wing joint, through the neck skin and the second joint on the other wing. Pull fairly tight and tie over the back. Develop the knack of tying bow knots if you do not already have it; this facilitates the withdrawal of the trussing strings at serving time.

Ducks: Some over-particular cooks truss their ducks, but, actually, the best and easiest way to treat a duck is to cut the wings at the joints and to leave the stumpy legs alone. The dressing slit must be stitched with needle and strong thread.

Geese: The only way to handle their short legs is to loop them together with a piece of twine. Fold the wings and tie them close to the body by running a string around the body and the wings. The dressing slit must be stitched with needle and strong thread.

Pigeons: If stuffed, they should be stitched. As for trussing, handle them much the same as chickens.*

ROASTED CHICKEN (mid-1800s)—For Sunday Dinner, nothing beats a nice, plump roasting chicken. But the success of the meal does not lie as much in the roasting as in the preparations for it. First, remove all pin feathers; singe the bird over a bright fire. Second, draw the skin down the neck and chop the neck bones away as closely to the body as you can; remove the windpipe and crop through the opening thus made. Third, open the chicken below the breastbone; remove the entrails and oil bag carefully or the meat may become tainted. Wash the cavity with a rag dipped in cold water and wrung almost dry. Wipe and sprinkle the interior gently with fine salt, pepper and a touch of nutmeg. Cover the bird with the moist rag while you make the following dressing.

SAGE STUFFING FOR ROASTED CHICKEN—Chop 1 teaspoon of parsley, squeeze or grate ½ teaspoon of onion juice and mix them together with ¾ teaspoon of salt and ½ teaspoon of white pepper. Have ready ½ pint (1 cup) of soft white bread crumbs; melt ½ gill (¼ cup) of butter and add to the crumbs; mix in 1 dessertspoon (2 teaspoons) of powdered sage and ½ teaspoon of nutmeg and do it thoroughly; next, equally thoroughly, add the parsley mixture. This is, and should be, a dry stuffing. Some cooks, even good ones, add hot water to moisten it. This, however, is not recommended.

Stuff the chicken and close the opening; truss (see above); dust with salt and white pepper, rub with softened butter and, using a sieve, let fall a very light amount of flour upon it. Have ready a very fast (400°F.) oven and place the chicken in this for 15 minutes. Remove the chicken from the oven and leave the door open to reduce the oven to a medium moderate heat (325°F.); meanwhile dredge a dripping pan with flour; return the chicken to the oven; place the dripping pan beneath it; baste with butter every 10 minutes and let it roast 15 to 20 minutes to the pound. Make Pan Gravy from the drippings (see Index).*

TO LAY POULTRY ON THE DISH FOR THE TABLE (early 1800s)—
Fowls should lie on their backs with their legs toward the carver; a turkey,
duck or goose should lie on its back with the legs toward the left hand.
The appearance of any roasted or boiled bird when on the table depends
much on it having been handsomely trussed or skewered.

CHICKEN RURAL NEW ENGLAND STYLE (mid-1800s)—Take a young
chicken, disjoint it, wash the pieces in cold water and dry them in a cloth;
now dip them in a beaten egg and roll them in fine cracker crumbs; repeat. Fry the chicken slowly in fresh (unsalted) butter to which a little
freshly tried suet has been added to prevent the butter from burning. When
the chicken is almost done, turn 1 pint (2 cups) of cream onto it in the frying
pan; turn the chicken over after 5 minutes; stir the gravy quickly, and cook
slowly until the chicken is done. Thicken gravy with 5 tablespoons of flour
wetted in 3 tablespoons of cold water; simmer for several minutes. Serve
with Baked Potatoes (see Index).*

CHICKEN FRICASSEE (mid-1800s)—Singe the chickens and cut them at
the joints into pieces for serving. Cover with boiling water and cook until
tender, reducing the water to about 1 pint (2 cups); season well with pepper
and salt and a touch of powdered tarragon. Remove the chicken and let it
drain as you put about 1/3 cup of butter into a hot frying pan; fry the
chicken a delicate brown in this. Thicken the liquor in which the birds
were boiled with 4 tablespoons of flour well moistened with cold milk; pour
this over the chicken in the frying pan and let all simmer 10 to 15 minutes.
Stir as it thickens to prevent lumps from forming. Serve in a deep dish with
Mashed Herb Potatoes (see Index).*

CHICKEN AND OYSTER SURPRISE (late 1800s)—Prepare 1 quart of fine,
fat oysters (25 to 50 if large, 50 to 100 if small), and mince, as uniformly as
possible, enough cooked breast of chicken to fill a 1-pint (2-cup) measure.
Whip ½ pint (1 cup) of heavy cream and beat the yolks of 4 or 5 eggs until
lemon-colored. Melt ½ gill (¼ cup) of unsalted butter and in it sauté a
like amount of minced onion; blend 1 glass (2 ounces) of white wine into
the butter-onions and thin this out with 1 gill (½ cup) each of Chicken
Stock (see Index) or water and oyster liquor; let this simmer slowly about
10 minutes; then add the cream, eggs and minced chicken in that order.
Keep stirring until the mixture is thick and smooth; then set it in an ice
chest or near an open window or some other cool place to cool and harden.
When this has come to pass, give the oysters a quick boil up in freshly
salted water and put them to cool, drain and dry in a colander. The next
moves in preparing this unusual dish are to wrap each oyster in a blanket
of the chicken mixture, roll them in rather coarse crumbs, dip them into
beaten eggs, put them into the fry-basket and bring them to perfection in
fat as hot as that which croquettes are usually fried in (370-75°F.).*

OPEN-FACED CHICKEN PIE (early 1800s)—Boil 12 eggs until they are
hard and cook 1 pint (2 cups) of mushrooms in butter until they are tender;
put the eggs in cold water and remove shells; set the mushrooms aside to
cool. Joint 2 or 3 young chickens into serving-size pieces, cover them with

boiling water and let them simmer slowly; skim as called for. When the meat becomes tender, add ¼ teaspoon each of powdered marjoram and bay leaf, ½ teaspoon each of powdered thyme and chopped parsley, with 2/3 pound of lean parboiled bacon cut into small cubes. Simmer until the chicken is done. Save the bacon cubes.

Slice and chop the eggs and the mushrooms. Butter the bottom and sides of a fitting baking pan or large earthenware serving dish. Put a layer of chicken into it; cover with eggs and mushrooms; build the dish with alternating layers. Strain the chicken liquid, skim the fat off the surface and make a gravy by putting a butter ball—made by working ½ gill (¼ cup) of flour into 3 tablespoons of butter—into ¾ pint (1½ cup) of strained liquid. Pour this over the chicken very slowly and give it time to sink in; dust the top with bacon cubes and chopped parsley; set the dish in a not too hot (375°F.) oven to reheat. Some folks make Soup Dumplings for this dish (see Index); others cover the surface with slices of buttered bread, which will take on a golden brown, and still others cover it with pulped (mashed) potatoes.*

OVEN-BAKED FRIED CHICKEN (mid-1800s)—Chop nice young chickens, preferably pullets, into halves or quarters; have your oven going at a fair and steady heat (350°F.). Rub each piece with salt and pepper, roll it well in flour, cover with beaten egg and blanket it with finely crumbed stale bread. Butter a baking dish well and place each bird piece on a pat of butter as big as a hazelnut (1 rounded teaspoon) that has been flattened. Pour in just enough hot water to cover the bottom of the dish; the latter should be so large that the pieces of chicken do not touch each other. Let the chicken bake for about ¾ hour and baste frequently with the liquid in the dish. Add hot water if called for.*

BATTERED PULLETS (late 1800s)—Only chickens less than 1 year old can qualify for this dish. Cut each bird into 4 pieces so that you have twin sets of legs and breasts, and figure on ½ pullet per person. Skin the birds, but leave the meat on the bones; rub them with lemon juice and dip them into a Croquette Batter (see Index); put only a few pieces into your deep-frying basket at a time and have the fat in your kettle at a heat so low that it will take an inch cube of bread a good minute to brown (345–50°F.). The cooking time ranges from 8 to 12 minutes, depending on the size of the pieces. It is a good idea to do breast pieces together and leg pieces together. Drain on brown kitchen paper in a warm (225°F.) oven. Serve with Tartare Sauce (see Index).*

CHICKEN CUTLETS (early 1800s)—Remove the breastbones and legbones of 2 cooked chickens; cut the meat into small pieces and season it to taste with cayenne, salt and pepper, nutmeg and powdered sage; add 1 egg and enough white bread crumbs to firm the mixture, then shape it into cutlets, dredge lightly in flour and set aside. Put the bones and all the giblets (see Index) into 1 quart (4 cups) of water and boil with 2 chopped carrots, 1 ditto onion and 1 strip of lemon rind for 1½ hours, by which time, stewing gently, the quart of water should have boiled away to 1 pint (2 cups); strain the liquid; make a paste by rubbing ½ gill (¼ cup) of flour into a lump of butter, melted, as large as an egg (4 tablespoons); turn it into a Cream Sauce with the giblet juice and season to your liking; add 2 tablespoons of ketchup and stir in 1 egg, beaten; heat but do not boil the sauce. Now egg and bread-crumb the cutlets and fry them in equal quantities of butter and lard to get them well browned but not scorched. Pour the sauce over them just before they go to table.*

A NICE WAY TO COOK CHICKENS (mid-1800s)—Cut each chicken up into 6 pieces—breasts, thighs, drumsticks; put them into a pan, and cover with water; let the chicken stew, covered, until done. Make a thickening of cream and flour in a saucepan with some melted butter; season with pepper and salt; have ready and freshly baked a pair of Shortcakes (see Index). This is much better than Chicken Pie, and more simple to make.**

PRESSED CHICKEN WITH DRESSING (early 1800s)—Cut up the chicken and put it on to cook in boiling water with ½ small peeled onion; after boiling it ½ hour, season with pepper and salt; keep just enough water on the chicken to prevent burning, so that when the cooking is completed there is only ½ pint (1 cup) of liquid. Let the chicken cook until the meat drops from the bones. Take it from the fire, pick the meat from the bones and add a small piece of butter. Have ready some left-over poultry dressing. Put alternating layers of chicken and dressing in a square tin with layers of sliced hard-boiled eggs. When the tin is full, pour ½ pint (1 cup) of liquor over the contents and press it over night. A good supper dish; served cold.*

BARNYARD HEN DRESSED AS TERRAPIN (late 1800s)—Boil a large tender fine chicken; when done and while still warm, cut it from the bones into small pieces, as for chicken salad. Put this into a stew-pan with 1 gill (½ cup) of simmering water over a gentle fire. Stir together until smooth ¼ pound of butter, 3 tablespoons of flour and the yolk of 1 egg, which add to the chicken one half at a time, stirring all well together until it thickens; season with pepper and salt; if too thick, add more hot, but not boiling, water. After simmering for 10 minutes, add 1½ tablespoons of good dry sherry or, if that is against your convictions, use 1 teaspoon of vinegar instead.*

CHICKEN PUDDING (mid-1800s)—The fowl should be large and tender. Cut it up as for fricassee, divide it at every joint and parboil until tender. Lay the bird on a flat plate to cool; take the water in which the chicken was cooked and set it aside. Make a batter of 1 quart (4 cups) of milk, 3 cups of flour, 3 tablespoons of melted butter, ½ teaspoon of baking soda, 1 tablespoon of cream of tartar, 4 eggs well beaten and a little salt. Put a layer of chicken in the bottom of the dish and pour about ½ cup of batter over it, enough to conceal the meat; then another layer of chicken and more batter, until the dish is full. The batter must form the top crust. Bake 1 hour in a moderate oven (350°F.). Beat up an egg and stir it into ¼ pint (½ cup) of left-over chicken juice; thicken it with 2 tablespoons of flour rubbed into 2 tablespoons of butter and send to the table in a gravy dish, seasoned with salt, white pepper and powdered sage to taste.**

GIBLET AND STEAK PIE (early 1800s)—From 1 large bird, such as goose or turkey, or from several smaller birds, such as chicken, capon and duck, collect the giblets—namely, gizzards, hearts and livers; have handy 1 pound of rump steak cut thin and into many small pieces, which you roll richly in flour and set aside. Put the giblets ito a stew-pan with 1 sliced onion, 12 black peppercorns, 2 chopped celery stalks and 3 branches of parsley in 1¼ pints (2½ cups) of cold water; bring to a boil and let it simmer 1½ hours. Add water when necessary and skim often. Remove the giblets; when they are cool, chop them coarsely and mix them well together. Line the bottom of a large pie dish with pieces of beef; cover with a layer of giblets; dust with pepper and salt; lay down alternating layers until nothing is left. Strain the giblet juice into the dish; it must not reach above the top layer. Cover with a rather thick plain crust (see Index), slash it so that steam will escape, and bake the pie in a good (375°F.) oven for about 1½ hours, when the meat should be tender. It is best to cover the pie with a piece of oiled paper to prevent the crust from taking too much color.*

FOWL HASHED IN WINE (mid-1800s)—Cut a cooked fowl into small pieces; cook the inferior joints and trimmings in a stew-pan with 1¼ pints (2½ cups) of water to make the gravy; slice and fry 2 onions a very pale brown in 2 ounces (¼ cup) of butter and add that to the chicken liquid; let all cook slowly for 45 minutes, then skim and drain the liquor; thicken it with 1 dessertspoon (2 teaspoons) of flour wetted with a little cold water; flavor this gravy with ½ gill (¼ cup) of port wine, ¼ teaspoon of powdered ginger and a pinch of sage or curry powder; season with salt and cayenne. Place the meat pieces into this gravy to heat. If the sauce is too thin, add the yolk of 1 egg; stir as it heats; do not let it boil.*

CHICKEN CROQUETTES—The proportions that we give below are for half a good-sized (4 pounds) hen. Use the other half for salad. After boiling, chop the meat very fine; fry it with 1 ounce (2 tablespoons) of butter; then add 2 tablespoons of flour; stir for ½ minute. Add a good gill (½ cup) of meat broth, salt, pepper and a pinch of nutmeg; stir for 5 minutes; then take it from the fire and mix the yolks of 3 eggs with it; put it on the fire again for 1 minute, stirring the while. Lastly, you may or may not add 4 mushrooms, minced, or 2 ditto truffles, or both, according to taste. Turn the mixture into a dish and set it away to cool; when it is perfectly cold mix it well, as the upper part is apt to be drier than the rest. Put it in parts on the pasteboard, a rounded tablespoon for each part; make them into any form required; cover with bread crumbs and dip each croquette in beaten egg; roll in bread crumbs again and fry in hot fat (at 365-70°F. for 7 to 10 minutes).—Mrs. Harold G. Wallace

BOILED FOWL WITH OYSTERS (early 1800s)—Place 36 oysters that have been washed and cleaned in their own liquor in the body of a young fowl;

sew it up and truss it (see Index). Put the bird in a container, which you plunge into a saucepan of boiling water. Let it cook 1½ to 2 hours until the fowl is tender. Then take the gravy that has flowed into the container from the bird and the oysters, stir into it ¼ pint (½ cup) of heavy cream, 1 powdered blade of mace, and the yolks of 2 or 3 eggs, depending on the quantity of liquid; also add a few oysters scalded in their liquor if you have them; let the sauce heat to thicken over a low fire; it must not boil; season to taste.*

CHICKEN AND OYSTER PIE—Stew the chicken until tender; line the sides of a deep pie dish with nice pastry (see Index). Put in the chicken and the water in which it was boiled, which should be but ½ pint (1 cup); season with a large piece of butter, salt and pepper and then cover loosely with a crust. While this is baking for 45 minutes in a fast (375°F.) oven, make ready a quart of fine oysters (25 to 50 if large, 50 to 100 if small); put on the fire a pint (2 cups) of rich milk (or the liquor of the oysters will do); let it come to a boil; remove the liquid and thicken it with a little flour; season with butter, pepper and salt; pour this over the oysters boiling hot, and about 15 minutes before the pie is done, lift the crust and mix the oysters and all into the pie; then return the pie to the oven to finish.— Mrs. H. Webster

ROAST CAPON—This delicacy is prepared exactly like Roast Chicken with respect to dressing and trussing, but the roasting time should not be more than 12 minutes per pound. Use a high moderate (375°F.) oven and baste at 10-minute intervals. The following dressing is fine.—Mrs. Julian Edwards

DRESSING FOR ROASTED CAPON—With 2 cups of soft bread crumbs mix ¼ cup of melted butter, 1 teaspoon each of raw grated onion and chopped parsley and ½ teaspoon of powdered sage leaf. The onion flavor can be increased by using 1 tablespoon instead of 1 teaspoon. Since the dressing will seem dry, moisten it with a little boiling water. Season to taste with salt and pepper.—Mrs. J. F. Norton

PAN-FRIED FOWL CROQUETTES—Take the cooked meat of any kind of fowl with slices of ham, fat and lean; chop all together very fine; add half as much grated bread, and season with salt, pepper and nutmeg; moisten with tomato catsup, 1 teaspoon of made-mustard and 1 lump of butter, melted; mix all well together, make it up in little rolls or balls, dip them in beaten yolks of eggs, cover with grated bread crumbs, and fry brown in lard.—Mrs. I. N. Isham

MOCK CHICKEN FORCEMEAT—Mix with 1 pound of chopped raw veal 1 egg, a little butter or ½ pound of raw pork chopped fine and 1 cup or less of bread crumbs, the whole well moistened with warm water, or, what is better, the broth from stewed fowl; season with salt and red pepper. Do the forcemeat up in small balls; fry them brown and place them in a roasting chicken; sew the bird firmly.—Mrs. Hugh Waters

CHICKEN PILAU (early 1800s)—Place a full-grown chicken and about 1 pound of pickled pork with a pod of red pepper and bunch of thyme in a pot with enough water to cover them and cook. When perfectly tender, put the chicken and pork in a steamer which fits the pot; wash your rice carefully, and boil it 17 minutes in the pot in the water from which the meat was taken. Make a large gravy tureen full of Drawn Butter Sauce (see Index), to which you add 2 hard-boiled eggs, sliced, and capers or chopped pickle; use about a pint (2 cups) of the water in which the meat was boiled for the sauce, and if the food is very fat, skim the grease off the top and use instead of butter for the sauce; thicken with flour. When you serve, place the rice on a large flat dish, and the chicken on top.*

CHICKEN CHEESE—Two chickens boiled tender in as little water as possible; chop the meat, but not too fine; add salt and pepper; 3 or 4 eggs boiled and sliced; line dishes or moulds with the eggs; pour in the chicken and the liquor it was boiled in; when cold, slice.—Anon.

DRESSING FOR CHICKENS—Chop cracker crumbs quite fine; season well with pepper, salt and plenty of butter; moisten with a very little water; add a few oysters with a little of the liquor, if you please. The best authorities say the dressing is the finest when it crumbles as the fowl is cut.—Mrs. F. D.

THANKSGIVING TURKEY—When the bird is oven-ready, put in the stuffing (for which see Dressing for Turkey, below), but do not pack it too tightly, as the dressing expands in cooking. Truss it as suggested (see Index). Rub it well with lard or unsalted butter; let it stand 30 minutes and cover the breast and thighs with heavily oiled paper. Put it into a slow to moderate (325°F.) oven unseasoned; the bird should not receive salt and pepper until after 1 hour of roasting; then, remove the paper and season with salt and pepper; baste at frequent intervals with butter kept melted in a pot on top of the stove; put no water or other liquid into the roasting pan. One can usually figure on 15 to 18 minutes per pre-drawn pound of a young tom or hen. Older and larger birds take much longer. A turkey is done when a pinprick in the white meat produces a watery juice with no trace of pinkness.—Adele Livingston

DRESSING FOR TURKEY—Have ready 1½ pints (3 cups) of selected sweet green grapes, cut into half and seeded; pluck 6 quarts (24 cups) of soft white bread crumbs fine. Blend 4 dessertspoons (8 teaspoons) of sage, 2 teaspoons of salt and 1 teaspoon of white pepper into 1 cup of melted butter or turkey fat (if the latter, use a little more salt); in a large pan, mix these with the crumbs, 1 well-beaten egg, the grapes and ½ cup each of minced celery and sweet onion. If you have it, add 1½ cups of giblet juice; if not use White Soup Stock or water and knead thoroughly. This makes about 3 quarts (12 cups) of dressing. For a very dry, crumbly dressing, use 6 quarts (24 cups) of cracker crumbs instead of bread. Shape any left-over stuffing into apple-sized balls, bake them with the turkey and baste occasionally.—Adele Livingston

GIBLET GRAVY FOR TURKEY—Make a savory seasoning bag (of muslin) with 1 medium bay leaf or mace blade, 2 branches of parsley, 3 or 4 whole cloves, 1 quartered stalk of celery with leaves and 1 quartered medium-large onion. Put the giblets and neck with the seasoning bag into a saucepan and cover with cold water. Boil it up and let it simmer for 2 hours very gently; skim when needed. It is best to do this before you roast a small turkey, especially if the giblet juice is wanted for the dressing, in which case you must add 1½ cups of water; to offset this weakening, many cooks add the liver and remove it after ½ to ¾ hour of simmering. When the bird is done, remove it and pour off the drippings. Measure your giblet juice into a roasting pan, and for each ½ pint (1 cup) of juice, put 2 tablespoons of butter into a bowl with an equal amount of flour that has been wetted with a little cold water. Mix well and stir this on top of the stove over a good heat until it thickens and the brownings on the bottom of pan have colored the gravy a rich brown; season to taste and let it cook about 15 minutes. Worry not about the turkey; this rest between cooking and carving has a most salutary effect upon it. Since a very small turkey will cool faster than a large one and will also need less gravy, the cooking time for gravy can be cut by more than half by the use of 1 dessertspoon (2 teaspoons) of cornstarch per cup of giblet liquid.—Adele Livingston

BOILED TURKEY (early 1800s)—Hens, and not too large, are best for boiling. Stuff with Forcemeat Dressing (see below) and truss the bird as you would for roasting (see Index); break the breastbone to give the bird a rounded look. Have ready enough simmering water in your boiling kettle —hot but not boiling—to cover the turkey. Immerse the bird and let the water boil up, reduce it to simmering and skim for as long as it takes to cook. If this takes too much time, boil the bird in a floured pudding cloth. A large young hen will simmer about 1¾ hours; a small one about 1½ hours.*

FORCEMEAT DRESSING FOR BOILED TURKEY (early 1800s)—Mix in a bowl 1 good slice of boiled or baked ham and 4 slices of boiled ox-tongue, ¼ pound of white, crumbly beef suet, the rind of ½ lemon, 1 teaspoon of parsley, 1 pinch each of sage, rosemary and mace or nutmeg—all finely and carefully minced; add 1½ cups of bread crumbs (no crust); then stir into it 1 large or 2 small well-beaten eggs; blend well. Shape into small balls; fry in boiling lard until brown and well crusted. Let them cool and place them in the turkey. If oysters are to be used, omit the tongue and add ½ pint (1 cup) of minced raw oysters without their liquor. Do not use crackers in this dressing, as they make it too dry.*

GRAVY FOR BOILED TURKEY—Make a White Celery, Oyster or Mushroom Sauce (see Index). If Oyster Sauce is used—and it is good—then there should be oysters in the stuffing. A quick way of making the latter is to make a White Cream Sauce of 3 tablespoons of flour rubbed into 3 tablespoons of butter in a hot spider for each cup of turkey juice used. Cook about 10 minutes; then add 1 quart of oysters (25 to 50 if large, 50 to 100 if small) in their liquor; stir until blended; remove from the fire when the oysters begin to plump and curl at the edges. The right way to serve boiled turkey is with slices of boiled ham and tongue or corned beef. Before bringing the turkey to table, pretty it up with a good basting of Butter-Parsley Sauce (see Index).—Mrs. Herbert Howe

FRICASSEED TURKEY—Cut some nice slices of cooked turkey, dark and white meat both, and lay aside in a deep and large skillet, which should be warm but not hot. Put some bones and trimmings into a stew-pan with a small spiral of lemon peel and a savory seasoning bag (see Giblet Gravy in Index) with 1 pint (2 cups) of cold water; season to taste with salt and pepper and let stew gently 1 hour. Strain, and place the pot on the stove where the juice does not even simmer but remains very hot. Then stir in 4 tablespoons of heavy cream and 1 egg yolk with a slow but steady round-the-clock motion. If the sauce does not get thick enough add ½ egg yolk; if it is too thick, add 2 tablespoons of good milk. Pour this over the turkey meat and let the skillet stand a few minutes on a hot spot to give the meat an opportunity to become wedded to the sauce.—Mrs. Arnold Day

TURKEY HASH—For each pint (2 cups) of minced turkey, boil 1 quartered carrot, 1 sliced and peeled turnip, 1 quartered onion, 1 blade of mace, ¼ cup of quartered mushrooms (caps and stalks), 1 teaspoon of minced parsley, plus seasonings of salt and pepper to taste in 1⅛ pints (2¼ cups) of water with some turkey bones and trimmings for added flavor; let it simmer for 1 hour. Remove it from the fire and pound the turnip, onion, and mushroom into a paste. Run the juice that is left through a strainer and add to it the vegetable paste with a ball as big as a walnut of well-mixed half-and-half butter and flour (1½ teaspoons of each). When the liquid is thick, add the hash and let it warm gently for 20 to 30 minutes. Just before serving, add 1 tablespoon of brandy per pint (2 cups) of finished hash.—Mrs. Anthony Melrose

TURKEY CROQUETTES—Four and a half pounds of cooked turkey pounded very fine; moisten to a thick pulp with gravy. Mix with this 1½ pints (3 cups) of mashed potatoes beaten to a cream, 3 eggs, 1 teaspoon of mustard, sweet marjoram, salt and pepper to taste, a little celery chopped very fine; stir in 1 tablespoon of melted butter; soften with milk. Mold into forms, dip in egg and cracker dust, and fry in boiling lard.—Mrs. J. A. Ellis

STEWED TURKEY—(early 1800s)—An old turkey, if you are saddled with one, is more tender stewed than when cooked in any other way. Put into a large pot ½ pound of bacon cut in slices, ¼ pound of knuckle of veal, 3 sprigs of parsley, 2 of thyme, 6 small chopped onions, 1 carrot cut into small pieces, 3 cloves, salt and pepper as needed. When this is well blended, add the dressed and trussed turkey with 2 quarts (8 cups) of water. Cover as closely as possible and simmer gently about 2½ hours; then turn the turkey over and let it cook another 2½ hours. When it is done, dish the turkey, strain the sauce and spoon off the fat; put the sauce back on the fire and after reducing it to a glaze spread it over the turkey and serve. Some prefer stewed turkey when cold; some do not like it stewed in any form whatever.***

AN EAST INDIAN TURKEY DISH (mid-1800s)—Cut the cooked meat into serving pieces. Fry 4 large onions, coarsely chopped, in an adequate amount of butter for 5 to 6 minutes; keep the onions hot but do not let them color. Make an even mixture (1 teaspoon each) of salt and curry powder; sift this blend over the turkey through a fine sieve so as to cover the meat thoroughly but lightly; fry these pieces in butter for about 10 minutes or until brown; place the turkey on a platter and cover with the fried onions. Reheated turkey gravy goes well with this, as does reheated left-over dressing rolled into balls and fried or baked. Serve with Rice Pilau (see Index).*

LEFT-OVER TURKEY SCALLOP (late 1800s)—Chop cold turkey meat, white, dark or both, very fine; put a layer of bread crumbs or turkey dressing on the bottom of a buttered tin; moisten this with left-over gravy or plain milk; now lay down some turkey, more crumbs or dressing and more moistening until the pan is almost full. Thin out what gravy you have left and pour a cupful or 2 over the turkey. Take 2 eggs, 2 tablespoons of milk, 1 tablespoon of melted butter, a little salt and mix them; add cracker crumbs, as much as will make the mixture thick enough to spread over the top of the Turkey Scallop with a knife; put bits of butter over it. Cover with a plate to avoid too early browning. Bake in a moderate (350°F.) oven about 35 to 50 minutes. After the first 25 to 40 minutes remove the platter to let the topping brown.*

RAGOUT OF TURKEY (mid-1800s)—Cut cold left-over turkey into bits about an inch long; put it in a saucepan with gravy left from the roast, adding a little water if the quantity is small; add a tablespoon of butter, 1/2 teaspoon of Worcestershire sauce, 1/4 teaspoon of powdered cloves, a little nutmeg grated and a bit of salt; stew very gently for 10 to 15 minutes and then stir in 1 tablespoon of Cranberry Jelly (see Index) and a teaspoon of Browned Flour (see Index); sprinkle it with a little cold water and a wineglassful (1/2 cup) of white wine and 1 teaspoon of lemon juice as it leaves the fire; serve in a covered dish. A ragout without spice, jelly or wine is often preferred.**

PIGEONS, TO BE GOOD—Must be eaten fresh and drawn right after they are killed; also, no bird requires more careful washing. Squabs should not be more than 1 month old; after that, their pink flesh begins to darken.

STEWED PIGEONS (late 1800s)—Mince the livers of 6 pigeons and blend them into 3 ounces (6 tablespoons) of butter with 2 tablespoons of minced parsley. Divide into 6 and place a portion in each of the pigeons, which should thereupon be trussed. Put the pigeons in a stew-pan with a slice of bacon under and over each bird; add stock or water to cover and stew, rather gently, for about 90 minutes. Dish the pigeons, strain the gravy and skim it free from bacon fat; blend in enough wetted flour to thicken; add 1 tablespoon of port wine and 1 saltspoon (1/4 teaspoon) of Worcestershire sauce. Reheat the birds in the gravy and serve.*

PIGEON PIE (early 1800s)—Cut 1½ pounds of rump steak into 3-inch squares, roll them in flour, season with pepper and a little powdered marjoram and put them in the bottom of a deep pie dish. Rub the cleaned pigeons inside and out with butter, salt and pepper; place 3/4 ounce (4½ teaspoons) of butter into each bird; lay them on the beef and cover each with a slice of lean cooked ham. Fill the dish half way with soup stock or water; cover with a slashed Puff Paste (see Index) and bake before the fire in a Dutch Oven (see Index) or in the brisk oven of a kitchen range (375-400°F.) for 1½ to 2 hours. Many deem it best to cover the pie with oiled paper lest the crust get too brown.*

ROASTED PIGEONS (mid-1800s)—After cleaning the pigeons thoroughly, wipe the insides with pepper and salt and put a piece of butter as big as a chestnut (1 tablespoon) or a similar sized piece of salt pork inside each bird. Put them down to a bright fire and baste them well while they cook. Before an open blaze, this may take from 60 to 75 minutes; in a kitchen range, with a slow heat (300°F.) the time will run to about 2 hours.*

BROILED SQUABS (late 1800s)—Split the backs of freshly killed and cleaned squabs; rub inside and out with butter, salt, cayenne and broil them for 15 to 20 minutes on each side, depending on the size of the birds. Baste constantly with a mixture of lard and butter.*

DRESSING AND ROASTING SQUABS (mid-1800s)—First, remove heads and innards. Next, prepare the stuffing (see Index) and make room for it by loosening the skin from the inside along the entire breastbone; fill this space from the neck in small portions at a time; wind a thread around the top of this passage; skewer the legs close to the body; rub the birds with salt and pepper; give them a rich greasing of butter; place them in a fairly hot (375°F.) oven and baste frequently for 3/4 hour while they bake.*

BOUGHTEN POND DUCKS (mid-1800s)—To be any good they should have plump bellies and thick, yellowish feet. Never cook a duck the day it was killed; let it hang 2 to 3 days if the weather is right.*

STEWED POND DUCK AND PEAS (mid-1800s)—Put 2 ounces (1/4 cup) of butter in a stew-pan and reduce what is left of a roasted duck into joints; cut 2 thin slices of lean ham into 2-inch squares and brown them, with the duck, in the butter; then dredge 5 tablespoons of flour into the pan and work it into the meat; add 1 pint (2 cups) of thin gravy or soup stock or water, 3 stalks of minced celery, 1 chopped onion (fried in butter), 1 table-spoon of minced parsley, a pinch of powdered cloves, 1 teaspoon of pounded loaf sugar and 1 pint (2 cups) of green peas. Cook slowly 3/4 hour; season to taste with salt and pepper.*

ROAST DUCK WITH HARD CIDER—First, weigh the bird before you draw it; next, when oven-ready, stuff it with peeled and quartered tart (Northern Spy) apples mixed with 1 diced orange and ½ diced lime or lemon. Place in a roasting pan and add 1 quart (4 cups) of hot hard cider; if unavailable, sweet cider will do. Build a quick, hot faggot (see Index) fire that will blaze for 15 to 20 minutes and provide a very hot (500°F.) oven for the duck. Before the end of that time, kindle a hardwood fire for a moderate (350°F.) oven. In that heat continue to roast the duck. If young, allow 25 minutes per pound (undrawn); older ducks will require from 30 to 35 minutes per pound, depending on age and size. Ladle cider over the duck at frequent intervals. Numerous housewives add a big glob of butter to the cider to aid browning; but for really spry skin, trickle a spoonful or 2 of ice water over the bird 15 minutes or so before it is taken out of the oven. —Mrs. Herbert Howe

CIDER GRAVY FOR ROAST DUCK—Remove the duck from the roasting pan and put it on a plate in the oven; pour cider into a bowl; skim off the fat and save it in a jar. Have ready, cooked and chopped, the duck giblet and liver. For each ½ pint (1 cup) of gravy needed add the juice of 1 orange to ½ pint (1 cup) of the roasting cider; put this into the roasting pan—to brown and to gain flavor—on top of the stove. For each ½ pint blend 3 table-spoons of the butter-duck fat into 1½ teaspoons of cornstarch; stir this into the cider-orange mixture; heat until it thickens; let it boil up briefly and serve in a gravy boat with the duck.—Mrs. Herbert Howe

ROAST XMAS GOOSE (mid-1800s)—Be sure that your goose—if not "green" (which means less than 4 months old)—has a plump breast, yellow feet and pure white skin, all of which indicate health and youth. Truss as directed (see Index) and beat the breastbone flat with a rolling pin after the Onion-Sage Dressing (see below) has been stuffed rather loosely into the goose. Roast in a not too quick oven (375°F.); if the bird is large, the time is about 4¾ to 5 hours; a smaller one takes 2¼ to 3½ hours. Serve with Cranberry Sauce and Apple Sauce or with Cranberry-Apple Sauce (see Index).

ONION-SAGE DRESSING FOR XMAS GOOSE (mid-1800s)—Put 4 large peeled onions into boiling water and let them simmer for 5 to 7 minutes; add 10 sage leaves and let them simmer for 1 minute; remove the onions and sage from the water; this treatment moderates their flavor. Mince both very fine and add 2½ to 3 cups of bread; when well blended stir in 2 rounded tablespoons of butter, 1 well-beaten egg and season with salt and pepper to taste. It is better to season the dressing too highly than not enough when it is used for goose since the bird absorbs a great deal of flavoring.—Mrs. Ralph Fitch

SAUCE FOR THE GOOSE— Make a gravy by pouring the fat out of the roasting pan and pour onto the brownings in the pan ½ cup of boiling water for each person to be served. Thicken with 2¼ teaspoons of corn-starch wetted in a little cold water for each cup of gravy and season to your liking with salt, pepper, a small pinch each of ginger and cayenne pepper and 1 large pinch of sage. Do not pour the gravy on the goose, but serve it in a sauce tureen.—Mrs. Sarah Adams

TO CHOOSE A DOMESTIC GOOSE (late 1800s)—Select one with clean, white skin, plump breast and yellow feet. If the latter are red, the bird is old. Weather permitting, let it hang a few days to improve its flavor. At the proper time, you can round its breast by beating it flat with a rolling pin or a stone jug.*

GREEN GEESE (late 1800s)—Geese are called green until they are about 4 months old; after that, maturity and surplus fat set in rapidly. It is not unusual for housewives to sweat an adult goose—any bird over 10 pounds— by placing it, dressed but not stuffed, in a fairly hot (375°F.) oven for some 40 minutes. This drives out a lot of excess fat that can be put to good use by thrifty housewives.*

STUFFINGS FOR VARIOUS KINDS OF POULTRY (mid-1800s)—
Bread: Take light bread enough to make 3 gills (¾ cup) of fine crumbs; cut off the crust and lay it in just enough boiling water to cover it. Rub the soft crumbs fine between your fingers; put in 1 teaspoon of salt and ditto of powdered sweet marjoram or sage, a little pepper and a piece of butter half as large as an egg (2 tablespoons); add the softened crust and mingle thoroughly. Season to taste; if too thick, add a little milk.
Crackers: If made of pounded crackers, the seasoning is the same as for Bread Stuffing (see above), but crackers swell so much that ¼ pint (½ cup) will be plenty for a middling-large turkey. Milk will be necessary to mix it and 1 well-beaten egg to make it cohere. Some people prefer stuffing made of crackers, but it is hard and not nearly as healthy as that which is made of good bread, without an egg.
Stuffing for Ducks: This is made the same way but with a little onion in it.
For a goose, sage should be used, not marjoram.*

CHESTNUT STUFFING FOR DUCKS OR TURKEYS   (late 1800s)—Boil, peel and mash 12 large chestnuts. Mince the cooked livers of the birds very fine; add ¼ cup of minced ham and 1½ teaspoons each of minced onion, shredded lemon peel and salt; blend all this into the mashed chestnuts and add a binding mixture made up of 2 beaten egg yolks, 3 ounces (6 table-spoons) of melted butter and ¼ cup of bread crumbs. Season to taste with pepper and salt.*

OYSTER DRESSING FOR POND AND BARNYARD FOWL (early 1800s)—
This stuffing, measured for roast chickens, can be used for ducks; but it must be increased for geese and turkeys according to their size. Rub a large earthenware basin with a cut garlic clove; into the basin, drop the following items and stir them in as you go: 1 pint (2 cups) of oysters scalded in their own liquor, ¼ cup of chopped green peppers; 1 teaspoon of salt and 1 heap-ing saltspoon (¼ teaspoon) of peppers; mix 1 dessertspoon (2 teaspoons) of lemon juice into 1 gill (½ cup) of melted fresh butter; stir this into 1 quart (4 cups) of crumbs from fresh wheat bread—use no crusts; lastly blend the bread crumbs with the oysters and strive to obtain equal distribution. Be not afraid of making too much stuffing, because it can always be served with left-overs or it can be rolled into balls and baked in the oven with the bird.*

POTATO STUFFING FOR ALL DOMESTIC FOWL (late 1800s)—Fry 1/3 cup of parboiled and diced salt pork; when the pork is nice and brown, add ½ gill (¼ cup) of sliced and chopped onions; let them simmer in fat until they show color. Meanwhile, fry ¼ pint (½ cup) of broken-up sausage meat in another skillet until brown and done. Have ready 1 pint (2 cups) of Mashed Herb Potatoes (see Index); blend them with the other ingredients; let the mixture cool and stuff the bird. Use any surplus as fried cakes with other meals.*

STUFFING FOR POND DUCKS (early 1800s)—Take 4 each of apples, cored and peeled, onions, leaves of sage and thyme (or use ¼ teaspoon of each in powdered form); boil them in a saucepan with sufficient water or soup stock to cover them. When done, remove sage and thyme and pulp the remainder through a sieve; add sufficient Mashed Potatoes (see Index) to cause it to be so dry that the stuffing does not stick to the hands; season with pepper, salt and a little nutmeg, and stuff the bird forthwith.***

SAUSAGE MEAT BREAST STUFFING FOR TURKEY (late 1800s)—To make this breast stuffing, chop enough raw lean pork and sweet beef suet to obtain 6 ounces (¾ cup) of each. Mix this with 2 ounces (2 cups) of bread crumbs, 1 small teaspoon of powdered sage, 1 blade of pounded mace and 1 whole egg. Season with salt and pepper, as required, together with 1 small grated nutmeg. This stuffing goes into the breast cavity, which is reached through the neck; it bears no relation to the stuffing that goes into the interior of the turkey.*

GIBLET STUFFING FOR SQUABS (early 1800s)—Cook the gizzards, liver and heart in salted water; then mince all and mix well into 1 or 2 well-beaten eggs, depending on the number of squabs to be roasted. Heat the amount of white soft bread crumbs you will need in melted butter. Stir all together. Season with pepper, salt and a little grated nutmeg.*

11. Sauces for Flesh, Fish and Fowl

GENUINE FRENCH BÉCHAMEL SAUCE (early 1800s)—Cut into square pieces ½ inch thick 1 pound of lean veal and ½ pound of lean ham and melt 2 ounces (¼ cup) of butter in a stew-pan. Add the meat and let the whole simmer until it is ready to catch at the bottom. This requires great attention, because any touch of brown will spoil the sauce. Now work 1 gill (½ cup) of flour into the meat; when well mixed, add to it 1½ pints (3 cups) of White Broth or water; pour a little at a time so that the thickening will be smooth; stir until the sauce boils, then put the stew-pan near enough to the fire to simmer slowly for 2 hours; season it with 4 cloves, 1 small onion cut in half, 12 white peppercorns, a blade of mace, a few mushrooms and a faggot made of parsley, a sprig of thyme and a bay leaf. Let the sauce reduce to a very thick consistency, skim the fat off and strain through a hair-sieve. To serve, add sufficient cream to the sauce base so as to obtain adequate thinning in keeping with the occasion for which the sauce is to be used. The above was given by a French artist. (For less complicated White Cream sauces see Index.)*

DRAWN BUTTER—Drawn Butter forms the basis of many sauces. From this a great variety may be made, by adding to it different flavors—anchovies, ochra, onions, celery, parsley, mint or relishes—using those flavors which are suitable for the meat, game or fish with which the sauces are to be served. A good standard receipt for Drawn Butter is as follows:

Rub 1 tablespoon of flour with ¼ pound (½ cup) of butter; when well mixed, put in a saucepan with a tablespoon of milk; set it in a dish of boiling water, shaking it well until the butter melts and is near boiling. It should not be set directly on the stove or over the coals, as the heat will make the butter oily and spoil it—Janice Gilbert

MINT SAUCE (late 1800s)—For 1 cup of good wine vinegar, have ½ cup of finely minced leaves of fresh mint; add them with 2 dessertspoons (4 teaspoons) of sugar and 1 ditto of lemon juice to the vinegar; this can be served hot or cold, but should stand ½ to ¾ hour to mature before serving.*

BORDELAISE SAUCE (late 1800s)—Set 1 cup of dry red wine over a slow fire and let it simmer about 10 minutes with a bouquet of 1 sprig each of parsley and thyme and a blade of mace. Remove the herbs. Add 1 teaspoon of onion well minced and ½ cup of soup stock, meat or fowl. Boil it up. Add ¼ cup of butter, 1½ teaspoons of lemon juice, a dash of pepper and salt to taste. Remove from the fire. Stir 1 or 2 egg yolks into the sauce, but do it quickly. Return the sauce to the fire to thicken, but do not allow it to boil.*

BROWNED FLOUR FOR SAUCES (mid-1800s)—When not browned with butter in a skillet at the time a meal is prepared, flour can be browned in good quantity ahead of time. Spread the flour in an ungreased baking pan and place it in a moderate (350°F.) oven until it starts to brown; stir during this process to get the color even; beware of the flour getting too dark.*

BURNT OR BROWNED BUTTER (early 1800s)—This sauce, good for boiled fish or poached eggs, should, to be at its best, be made of fresh Clarified Butter (see Index). Put 2 ounces (¼ cup) of such butter into a small frying pan; cook it slowly until it becomes dark brown, when you add 1 teaspoon of good vinegar and a little pepper and salt.*

BUTTER SAUCE (early 1800s)—Cut 2 ounces (¼ cup) of butter into bits, that it may melt more easily and mix more readily. Put it into a saucepan with 2 tablespoons of flour absorbed into 2 tablespoons of cold milk. When this has been mixed with the melted butter, add 6 tablespoons of water; the sauce should be the thickness of good cream. Observe that milk alone blends better with butter than does water, even better than milk and water mixed. In making Butter Sauce *do not stir the sauce* after the water has been added, but hold the saucepan over the fire and shake it round every minute, all the while the same way, until it just begins to simmer, then let it stand quietly and boil up. This is the secret of a superior Butter Sauce. If the butter should "oil" (separate) put a teaspoon of cold water to it and stir; if it is very much oiled it must be poured backwards and forwards from the saucepan to the sauce boat until it is right again.*

BUTTER SAUCES, VARIATIONS OF (early 1800s)—The basic recipe is that of Butter Sauce (see above).

Parsley: Wash parsley; pick it leaf by leaf; put a teaspoon of salt into ½ pint (1 cup) of boiling water; boil the parsley about 10 minutes; drain it on a sieve, mince it fine and then bruise to a pulp in a mortar. Put it in a sauce boat and mix by degrees with ½ pint (1 cup) of Butter Sauce. For this sauce, use only 1 tablespoon of flour in making the Butter Sauce, as the parsley will thicken it.*

Gooseberry: Top and tail close with scissors and scald ½ gill (¼ cup) of green gooseberries; drain them on a sieve; put them into ½ pint (1 cup) of Butter Sauce. Many add ginger and lemon peel to this.*

Anchovy: Pound 6 boned anchovies in a mortar and rub them through a sieve with a wooden spoon. Blend this into ½ cup of Butter Sauce and season with ½ teaspoon of lemon juice and a fleck of cayenne.*

Lemon: Pare a lemon; cut it into slices ⅛ inch thick; divide these into dice and put them into ¼ pint (½ cup) of Butter Sauce. Many cooks favor adding a bit (¼ teaspoon) of finely peeled and well-minced lemon skin to the sauce.*

Curry: Blend a sufficient quantity of curry powder into 2 tablespoons of cream; the composition of curry powders and the palates of those who eat them vary so much that any specific quantity cannot be recommended. The curry powder and cream must be added to the Butter Sauce by degrees, and the good housewife should take care that she does not add too much of the fiery stuff.*

CREAM SAUCES, THICKENING FOR (early 1800s)—Clarified Butter (see Index) is best for many sauces, but absolutely necessary for Butter Sauces. For ½ pint (1 cup) of sauce as thick as cream use 2 tablespoons of flour and a scant ounce (2 tablespoons) of butter—the more flour and the less butter you use in proportion, the better your sauce will be. Make the thickening over a slow, clear fire and stir the butter and the flour well together with a wooden spoon for 15 to 20 minutes; if you put it over too fierce a fire to hurry it, the paste will become bitter and empyreumatic (burnt). This, in French kitchens, is called a *roux*. It can be either white for white sauces or browned for brown sauces. If made in large quantities, it will keep good for a week or more in summer and longer in winter. To make sure that all fats have been absorbed completely into the *roux,* add to it a small amount of hot water—about 2 tablespoons to a pint (2 cups) of *roux*—and set it by the side of the fire; this will raise any free fats, which you must remove as they appear. When you make sauce with a prepared *roux,* use about 2 table-spoons of *roux* to thicken ½ pint (1 cup) of liquid.*

THICKENINGS FOR CREAM SAUCES (mid-1800s)—There are 4 ways to thicken a Cream Sauce. They are:

Flour: Flour has a tendency to impregnate the sauce with its own flavor unless thoroughly cooked (see Three Cream Sauces, below). Use 2 table-spoons of flour to 2 tablespoons of butter.

Cornstarch: Cornstarch makes a clearer and finer sauce than flour; also, it is less likely to lump than flour if it is thoroughly dissolved in cold liquid before being added to the gravy. In thickening, use 3 teaspoons of corn-starch to ½ pint (1 cup) of liquid. Flour is not sensitive to being beaten; cornstarch is apt to turn watery. Like flour, it must be cooked to kill its flavor.

Arrowroot: Arrowroot has advantages and disadvantages. It helps to make delicious dishes and is free from flavor; therefore, it does not require protracted cooking. On the other hand, gravies held together by arrowroot must be served shortly after they are made, as arrowroot has little staying power; also, gravies thickened by it cannot be used for left-overs as they reheat badly. Arrowroot should not be boiled; 2 rounded teaspoons will thicken ½ pint (1 cup) of liquid.

Yolks of Eggs: Many recipes which call for the use of egg yolks for thickening fail to mention that it is good practice to break the yolk into 1 tablespoon of cold liquid and blend it in, next to add a spoonful or 2 from the hot sauce or liquid to which it is to be added—and never let that liquid boil when or after the yolk goes into it.*

THREE CREAM SAUCES (mid-1800s)—The basic ingredients of the Thin, Medium and Thick Cream Sauces that follow are ½ pint (1 cup) of water, soup stock, milk or other prescribed liquids in various receipts; 2 saltspoons (½ teaspoon) of salt and 1 saltspoon (¼ teaspoon) of pepper; all are seasoned with pinches of sage for birds, ditto of thyme or marjoram for meats and ditto of parsley for fish. To thicken with flour, these are the methods:

For Thin Sauce: Blend 1 tablespoon of flour into 1 tablespoon of melted butter in a saucepan over a low fire. Used usually for creamed soups.

For Medium Sauce: Blend 2 tablespoons of flour into 2 tablespoons of melted butter over a low fire. Used usually for sauces and vegetables.

For Thick Sauce: Blend 3 tablespoons of flour into 2½ tablespoons (7½ teaspoons) of melted butter over a low fire. Used usually for croquettes.

Mix the flour into the melted butter until you have a smooth dough. Add the liquid; it can be cold, but it is best to have it heated. Cook and stir incessantly until it is thickened and then stir the seasoning into it. To kill the taste of the flour, the sauce should cook at least 10 minutes—15 minutes is better—over a low fire without letup in stirring.*

CORNSTARCH CREAM SAUCE (late 1800s)—Cornstarch makes a clearer, tastier and finer sauce than flour. For 1 cup of Cream or White Sauce, heat 1 tablespoon of butter over boiling water; from 1 cup of cold milk take 2 tablespoons to moisten 1 tablespoon of cornstarch and make it smooth; add ¼ teaspoon of salt and a pinch of white pepper. Heat the remainder of the 1 cup of milk in the butter; when hot, stir in the cornstarch and keep stirring until velvety and thick.*

CHAMPAGNE SAUCE (mid-1800s)—Have 1 tablespoon of whole raisins plumped by standing them 10 minutes in a pan of very hot water; drain; then stone them by rubbing each raisin through your fingers. In a saucepan put 2 tablespoons of flour to 2 tablespoons of freshly churned butter which has been melted. Mix very carefully, making sure that neither the butter nor flour browns. When you have a smooth white blend, add ¼ pint (½ cup) of light cream and make a thick cream gravy. Season to taste with salt and ginger, but omit pepper and cook 15 minutes. Stir in ¼ pint (½ cup) of champagne and add the raisins.*

CURRANT JELLY MEAT SAUCE (late 1800s)—Blend and brown 4 tablespoons of flour in 3 tablespoons of butter; thin it out with ½ pint (1 cup) of warm milk; season with salt, pepper and a touch of ginger; let it cook over a low fire about 15 minutes and stir continually; then add ¼ pint (½ cup) of currant jelly, 1 teaspoon of lemon juice and a few drops of juice squeezed from an onion. Let the sauce come to a slow boil, and it is ready. It goes well with any roast of meat, game or domestic.*

EAST INDIAN CURRY SAUCE (early 1800s)—Mince 1 cup of onions and simmer them tender and golden in ¼ cup of sweet butter and 2 teaspoons of white bacon grease; when done, put them on the back of the stove and blend in 4 tablespoons of brown sugar with 2½ teaspoons each of curry powder and powdered ginger. Now heat and add 1¾ pints (3¼ cups) of hot chicken stock slowly; bring to an easy boil and stir steadily; run through a sieve and correct the flavor to taste with salt and pepper. Beat 3 egg yolks in 7 tablespoons of cold cream. Reheat the Curry Sauce; when it is hot and almost boiling, add the egg mixture. Instead of pouring this sauce over meats that have cooled while standing, why not add the meats to the sauce at this point and let them reheat over boiling water for whatever time it takes?* Serve with East Indian Pilau (see Index).

EGG SAUCES (late 1800s)—The easiest way is to make a medium Cream Sauce (see Index) and go on from there in one of two different directions. You may add 2 minced hard-boiled eggs and (for fish especially) 1 or 2 pounded anchovies, or you may pound a small slice of onion very fine and stir the sauce into it, with 1 or 2 raw egg yolks to give it color.*

GINGER SNAPS GRAVY (mid-1800s)—This sauce goes well with any kind of a roast that calls for a Brown Meat Gravy. Prepare the sauce the usual way by removing the fat from the roasting pan and dissolving the brownings with boiling water. However, instead of adding the thickening for a medium Cream Sauce, stir in 2/3 cup of ginger snap cookies rolled into fine crumbs. This amount of crumbs will thicken a good ½ pint (1 cup) of Cream Sauce liquid.*

HASH GRAVY (early 1800s)—Cook slowly 1 tablespoon of minced onions in 1 tablespoon of butter for 10 minutes. Place 5 teaspoons of flour in another pan; turn it into a paste with a little cold water; add 6 tablespoons of hot broth gradually, stir the while and place the pan over a low fire until the flour, etc., thickens; add 1 teaspoon of finely minced parsley, 1 tablespoon of currant or other red jelly and the onions; stir, but keep your fire low because the gravy must not boil. When all has been blended, add 1 glass (¼ cup) of port wine; when all is well heated, pour the gravy over the hash while it is still in the pan, but do not stir them together if the hash has a browned bottom.*

HERB SAUCE FOR COLD MEATS (mid-1800s)—Chop ½ teaspoon each of chervil, tarragon, pimpernel, chives and parsley; mix and blend them into the mashed yolks of 2 hard-cooked eggs; add 1 teaspoon each of made-mustard, melted butter and vinegar with a dash of salt and white pepper. Stir thoroughly for 5 minutes; add cream or milk, but only 1 tablespoonful at a time, until it is thick as cream.*

HORSE-RADISH SAUCE FOR ROASTS (early 1800s)—Grate horse-radish into a basin until you have 1 gill (½ cup); add 2 tablespoons of thick cream, with a pinch each of dry mustard and salt; mix well and add 3 to 4 tablespoons of the best and clearest vinegar; blend all thoroughly. If it is too strong, add more cream; if not strong enough, add more horse-radish.*

PARTY HORSE-RADISH CREAM SAUCE (mid-1800s)—Grate enough horse-radish until you have ¼ cup; set it aside. Whip ½ pint (1 cup) of heavy cream; by easy stages add the grated horse-radish, 2 tablespoons each of lemon juice and vinegar, 1 teaspoon of salt, ½ teaspoon of mustard.*

FAMILY HORSE-RADISH SAUCE (late 1800s)—Whip ½ cup of cream until it peaks and stir in 5 tablespoons of freshly grated horse-radish; season with salt, paprika and cayenne to suit your taste; lastly, add 1½ tablespoons of lemon juice. This is for family dinners; for parties add ½ teaspoon of Worcestershire sauce and ½ teaspoon of dry mustard. Also, increase the cream from ¼ cup to ¾ cup.*

MUSHROOM SAUCE FOR BEEFSTEAK (mid-1800s)—Put in a saucepan 1 ounce (2 tablespoons) of butter, a small onion chopped fine, a little ground sage and a little thyme, and put it over the fire. When the butter is hot, shake in 2 tablespoons of flour, and when it becomes brown, put in 1 gill (½ cup) of water; let it cook slowly for ¼ hour. Then add 3 tablespoons of Beef Stock, a little salt, a little nutmeg and 1 wineglass (¼ cup) of sherry wine. Slice and fry lightly 1 gill (½ cup) of mushrooms; add to the sauce and let it simmer for 10 minutes. Pour this over a nicely broiled beefsteak.*

MUSHROOM CREAM SAUCE (late 1800s)—In a saucepan, melt ¼ pound (½ cup) of butter and, over a slow fire, cook therein 1 pound of washed and thinly sliced mushroom caps with the juice of 1 lemon. Bind this mixture with 4 tablespoons of flour and let it cook until the mushrooms are tender. Heat ¾ pint (1½ cups) of heavy cream in the top of a double boiler; when it is hot, mash the mushrooms and rub them into the cream through a sieve. If the mixture is too thick, add cream or milk; if too thin, mix a small amount (1 teaspoon) of arrowroot into a little cold milk; let it dissolve and stir it into the Mushroom Sauce.*

MUSTARD BUTTER SAUCE (early 1800s)—Make a basic Butter Sauce by blending 1 tablespoon of butter with 1½ tablespoons (4½ teaspoons) of flour; dilute with 2 tablespoons of cold milk, after which add 6 tablespoons of water; let it cook slowly for 10 minutes. Add 2 dessertspoons (4 teaspoons) of mustard made in this manner: take 2 tablespoons each of dry mustard and vinegar; blend with 1 dessertspoon (2 teaspoons) each of good Florence oil (salad oil) and sugar, plus a pinch of salt; stir well. Add this preparation to the Butter Sauce, heat and serve.*

MUSTARD SAUCE (mid-1800s)—Rub 2 tablespoons of flour into 2 tablespoons of melted butter in a spider; add 2 dessertspoons (4 teaspoons) of mild made-mustard and a small teaspoon of white sugar. Dissolve into a sauce with ½ pint (1 cup) of soup stock or, for boiled fish, ½ pint (1 cup) of fish broth. Season with salt and a pinch of cayenne. After it has slowly simmered about 15 minutes add 1 tablespoon of lemon juice and remove from the top of the stove.*

OYSTER SAUCE— Take 1 dozen oysters out of their liquor, remove their beards and throw them into cold water; put the liquor over the fire with the beards of the oysters and boil them with a bit of mace and lemon peel; then strain the liquor; take the oysters out of the water; drain them and put them with the strained liquor into a saucepan, with sufficient butter and milk for your sauce; dust into this some flour; let it boil up; add a squeeze of lemon juice, and serve *hot.*—Mrs. L. Tinkham

RAISIN SAUCE FOR BAKED HAM (early 1800s)—When the ham is done, empty the baking pan of basting juices and skim off 2 dessertspoons (4 teaspoons) of drippings; in the skillet, blend these with 2 dessertspoons (5 teaspoons) of moistened cornstarch and thin it out with ¾ pint (1½ cups) of hot cider in which ½ pint (1 cup) of stoned raisins have been plumped; make a smooth gravy; if it chances to be too thick, add as much champagne or sherry as may be needed.*

POULTRY CELERY SAUCE—Mix 2 tablespoons of flour with ½ teacup of butter; have ready a pint (2 cups) of boiling milk; stir the flour and butter into the milk. Take 3 heads of celery, cut into small bits, and boil them for a few minutes in water, which strain off; put the celery into the melted butter and keep it stirred over the fire for 5 or 10 minutes. This is very nice with boiled fowl or turkey.—Mrs. J. B. L.

GRANDMOTHER LYON'S ONION SAUCE (mid-1800s)—Slice and chop 2 large onions; cook them until yellow in 3 tablespoons of butter over a low fire; dust occasionally with the contents of 3 tablespoons of sifted flour and stir during the flourings; otherwise, keep the spider well covered. When the flour has disappeared, add ½ pint (1 cup) of hot milk and season with ¾ teaspoon of salt and ¼ teaspoon of pepper. Stir slowly as the onions thicken. This sauce, good with all sorts of steaks and chops, is improved by being poured into the pan in which the meat was fried in order to absorb the brownings.*

A SIMPLE OYSTER SAUCE (early 1800s)—Blend 2½ tablespoons (7½ teaspoons) of flour into 2 tablespoons of melted butter in a frying pan; when done, add ½ pint (1 cup) of oyster juice. The latter may be stretched with water if need be. Season with a little powdered mace and white pepper. Oysters that have been scalded may be served in this sauce, but it is intended mainly for roasts and steaks.*

PEPPER SAUCE FOR BOILED MEATS (early 1800s)—Pulverize 18 black peppercorns in a mortar (or use ¾ teaspoon of freshly ground black pepper). Make a Cream Sauce by blending 3 tablespoons of Browned Flour (see Index) into 3 tablespoons of Browned Butter (see Index); add ½ pint (1 cup) of soup stock or water; let it simmer slowly and stir often for 15 minutes. During this time, put ½ gill (¼ cup) of fine vinegar into another saucepan with 6 tablespoons of minced onions and 3 tablespoons of minced celery; let this simmer uncovered with the pepper until the vinegar has nearly boiled away, then add it to the Cream Sauce. If the sauce seems too thick, add soup stock or water.*

A PEPPERY TOMATO SAUCE (late 1800s)—Take ½ pint (1 cup) of canned, drained tomatoes and boil them in a saucepan with 1 cup of water, 2 cloves, 2 allspice berries, 2 peppercorns, a small finely minced onion, ½ teaspoon each of table salt and celery salt. When this mixture boils, melt 1 tablespoon of butter in a small skillet and add 1 heaping teaspoon of flour; stir this into the tomato mixture and let it simmer 10 minutes; run through a sieve and beat smooth with an egg beater.*

SAUCE FOR BOILED TRIPE (pre-1800s)—Of vinegar, 1 tablespoon; of dry mustard and brown sugar, 1 teaspoon each; of minced garlic and black pepper, 1 saltspoonful (¼ teaspoon) each; stir all into ¼ pint (½ cup) of melted butter.*

SOUR CREAM SAUCE FOR VEGETABLES (late 1800s)—Apply the beater to 2 egg yolks until they are thick; stir in ¾ cup of sour cream; when well blended, add 1 dessertspoon (2 teaspoons) of wine vinegar; season with salt, pepper and powdered marjoram or nutmeg. Put this mixture into a small saucepan and place it over simmering water; stir until it thickens and serve hot with or over boiled vegetables. If too thick, thin with cream and a dash of vinegar; if too thin, add the yolk of 1 egg blended with a little milk or cream.*

LOBSTER SAUCE (late 1800s)—With 2 nice anchovies chop the coral, or roe, of a boiled lobster and moisten it with broth or water. Rub it through a hair-sieve into a bowl that contains a piece of hand-softened butter the size of a walnut (1 rounded tablespoon). Now, with 3 tablespoons of flour, make a butter ball of this mixture and set is aside. Next, fry lightly in a small amount of butter 1 teaspoon each of finely minced onion, and carrot; put these, with a minute piece of bay leaf, ½ teaspoon of salt and ¼ teaspoon of white pepper, into a cupful of simmering white stock, such as chicken soup (or use a cube of chicken extract); let it cook about 5 minutes, then add the butter ball; stir steadily as it dissolves and thickens the liquid. Simmer 8 minutes; add ½ cup of cream; simmer 2 minutes. Serve as a sauce or use it as a cream base for Creamed Lobster (see Index) by adding pieces of boiled lobster meat.*

MUSTARD SAUCE FOR FISH (late 1800s)—Beat the yolk of 1 egg into ½ pint (1 cup) of milk and, while continually beating, add 1 tablespoon of dry mustard, 1 teaspoon of brown sugar and a pinch of salt; cook in the top of a double boiler until smooth and thick; add 1 dessertspoon (2 teaspoons) of lemon juice just before serving.*

OYSTER SAUCE (mid-1800s)—Make sure that you have ½ to ¾ (1–1½ cups) of oyster liquor and ½ pint (1 cup) of scalded oysters. Make a medium Cream Sauce (see Index), but use the oyster liquor for making the sauce. If the oysters are large, chop them coarsely before they are added to the Cream Sauce; small oysters go into the sauce as they are. Season the sauce to taste before serving it.*

TARTARE SAUCE (mid-1800s)—Mince, as finely as you can, 1 dessertspoon (2 teaspoons) of sweet or sour pickles and ½ tablespoon (1½ teaspoons) each of sweet onions, olives and parsley, plus ¼ teaspoon of lemon pulp. Blend this well into ½ cup of Mayonnaise (see Index).*

CREAM SAUCE FOR BOILED FISH—Cream together a large tablespoon of butter with 1½ tablespoons (4½ teaspoons) of flour, and put over a gentle heat; add a little chopped parsley, a little grated onion, pepper, salt and nutmeg; when these ingredients are well mixed, add ½ pint (1 cup) of cream or milk and let it boil for 15 minutes. If used with fresh fish, a little horse-radish, shredded, may be added.—Miss Hattie Bucks

FISH SAUCE—One-quarter pound (½ cup) of fresh butter, 1 tablespoon of finely chopped parsley, a little salt and pepper and the juice of 2 lemons. Cream the butter; mix all well together, adding at least a teaspoon of Mayonnaise. Less lemon juice may be used if preferred.—Anon.

12. *The Vegetable Kingdom*

VEGETABLES, PREPARATION OF (mid-1800s)—The way some people pare and skin vegetables is a sinful waste. Vegetables should be scraped and not peeled. Parings take away the rich, nourishing and full-tasting foods that lie close to the skins of such vegetables as potatoes, carrots, turnips, squash, yams, and so on. Better yet, instead of skinning vegetables raw, cook them in their skins and remove those thin outer layers with the back of a knife before they go to the table.*

ARTICHOKES (early 1800s)—Potatoes came into our world by way of Peru; artichokes, on the other hand, began their journey to our kitchens from down Gloucester way. There are as many ways of treating artichokes as there are ways of skinning cats, but the easiest, best and oldest is this. Allow 1 artichoke per person; remove the stem; wash and scrub the artichoke. Cook in boiling salted—1 tablespoon of salt to the quart (4 cups)—water 45 to 50 minutes until the thick meat on the large leaves is tender; test with a fork; drain upside down in a colander and serve with melted butter.*

A SMALL PINCH OF BAKING SODA (early 1800s)—Accelerates the cooking of green vegetables and preserves the freshness of their color.*

ASPARAGUS—Cut off the green ends and discard the remainder of the stalks; scale them; boil until tender, and season with salt and pepper. Have ready some toasted bread in a deep dish. Mix together equal parts of flour and butter to a cream; add to this slowly enough of the asparagus water or clear hot water to make a sauce; boil this up once; put the asparagus on the toast, and pour all the sauce over it.—J. F. W.

TO KEEP STRING BEANS GREEN—Cover them with rapidly boiling water; have a red-hot poker on the fire and jab it into the water so that it continues to boil. A pinch of baking soda also keeps beans green—J. F. W.

GREEN BEANS IN MUSTARD SAUCE (late 1800s)—While the chopped beans cook, uncovered, in boiling salted water, make a blend of 2 beaten egg yolks, ¾ teaspoon of dry mustard, 1 teaspoon of flour, ½ teaspoon of salt and a pinch of white pepper. Cream this with a piece of softened butter as big as ½ walnut (1½ teaspoons); stir this preparation into 1 cup of hot, scalded milk and cook slowly in a double boiler as it thickens. Remove from the fire and add 1½ teaspoons of lemon juice. Put the cooked beans into a serving dish and cover with the Mustard Sauce.*

158

BEETS— Clean these nicely, but do not pare them, leaving on a short piece of the stalk. Then put them over the fire to boil in hot water. Young beets will cook tender in an hour; old beets require much longer boiling. When done, skin them quickly while hot; slice them thinly into your vegetable dish; put on salt, pepper and a little butter; put over them a little vinegar and serve hot or cold.—J. F. W.

TO KEEP VEGETABLES FRESH (mid-1800s)—Put vegetables in a pan with about 3 inches of cold water and cover them with a cloth large enough to cover not only the vegetables, but also the pan. Let the edges of the cloth hang in the water and put the pan in a cool place. In this manner, nearly all vegetables will keep fresh and green.*

RED CABBAGE IN WINE (late 1800s)—Shred a large head of red cabbage as fine as you can with a knife or slaw-cutter. Heat 1 tablespoon each of lard and butter in a kettle, stir the cabbage into this to get it thoroughly coated. Cover the kettle and let it cook over an easy fire 15 minutes. Since it is not good to lift the lid for stirring, shake the kettle at 5-minute intervals to prevent sticking. While this cooks, heat, but do not boil, 1 gill (½ cup) of any kind of soup stock; add this when the ¼ hour is up. Continue cooking and shaking the kettle for another ¼ hour, at which time you add 1 gill (½ cup) of good vinegar—cider vinegar if you have it—and 1 cored, pared and quartered apple; cook covered another ½ hour; then add 1 gill (½ cup) of heated sweet red wine into which have been placed 1 teaspoon each of Parsley Salt (see Index) and fine white sugar. Stir this well, let it cook 5 more minutes and serve without delay. This goes wonderfully well with roast duck or goose, nearly all game, and roasted pork of any kind.*

NEW WAY OF COOKING CABBAGE (mid-1800s)—Trim and cut in half 1 medium-sized head of cabbage; put it to cook in cold water; let it boil 15 minutes, then pour off the water and refill the cabbage pot with boiling water from the tea kettle; boil 20 minutes longer; drain the cabbage dry; chop it fine; season with salt, pepper and butter to taste. Beat together 2 fresh eggs and 4 tablespoons of sweet cream; stir this into the seasoned cabbage. Butter a pudding dish; put the cabbage into it and bake in a well-heated (375°F.) oven 20 minutes or until it is browned over the top.*

CREAMED CABBAGE WITH CHEESE (early 1800s)—For this a small, young head of cabbage is needed; slice it into thin sections and cut out the core; boil it in salted water until tender (about 10 minutes); drain. Make a genuine Béchamel Sauce (see Index); chop the cabbage; put it into the sauce with 1 gill (½ cup) of chopped cheese. Heat slowly until the cheese melts.*

FRIED CABBAGE (mid-1800s)—Cut the cabbage very fine, on a slaw-cutter, if possible; sprinkle with salt and pepper; stir well and let it stand 5 minutes. Have an iron kettle smoking hot, drop 1 tablespoon of lard into it, then the cabbage, stirring briskly until the cabbage is quite tender (about 10 minutes). Then add ½ cup of good new cream and remove it from the fire; only then stir in 3 tablespoons of vinegar, preferably cider.*

CANDIED SPRING CARROTS (late 1800s)—In the spring, when carrots are short and sweet, collect as many as you need and boil them just short of tender; remove them from the fire, drain them and wipe them dry. Melt ¼ cup of butter and ½ cup of maple sugar in a skillet; when they bubble, add the carrots and let them simmer until completely candied. Serve hot with Butter Sauce (see Index). This will candy about 12 very young and plump carrots.*

SIMPLE BUT DELIGHTFUL CARROTS FOR DINNER (mid-1800s)—Wash the carrots, and, after scraping them, let them lie in cold water for 1 hour or more; then boil them until tender; drain them, mash them and season with salt, pepper and a good lump of butter. Keep them over boiling water and serve very hot. If you have a cup or so of left-over mashed potatoes, this is an elegant way of using them; just stir the potatoes into the mashed carrots.*

CORN ON THE COB (early 1800s)—If the corn is really in the milk, that is, young and just off the stalks, strip away the husks and silk; drop the ears slowly into lively boiling water to which 1 teaspoon of maple syrup has been added for every quart (4 cups) of water. Let the corn boil until you smell it, which should be in 4 to 5 minutes. Eat the ears as soon as they are cool enough to handle, seasoned and with a Parsley Butter Sauce (see Index).*

CORN OYSTERS—To grate corn, run a sharp knife through the kernels down along the ears and scrape them with a dull knife. This produces a nice pure pulp. Take 1 dozen ears of corn, 2 eggs, salt, pepper and a dredging of flour. Grate the raw corn, over which dredge a little flour; season well; add the beaten eggs. Drop the mixture by the tablespoonful on a hot skillet and fry quickly in butter.—Mrs. W. P. Nixon

ROASTED EARS OF CORN (mid-1800s)—Keep the ears in their husks; dip them quickly in cold water and place them, dripping wet, in a fairly hot (375°F.) oven. After ½ hour, dress the ears, and eat them hot, with cold, cold butter. Let those who want to, season with pepper and salt.*

CUCUMBERS (early 1800s)—These vegetables should be sliced and put into salt water at least 1 hour before using; then dress with vinegar, mustard, pepper and salt. They are more wholesome if served with sliced onions. A sour-sweet cucumber is obtained if a cucumber is sliced thinly and submerged in a bath of cold vinegar that has been cooked with sugar and chilled —to ½ pint (1 cup) of vinegar allow 1 tablespoon of white sugar. This is excellent. A large cucumber, just about to turn white, can be fried like a tomato (see Index) and is quite as good.*

THE MANAGEMENT OF CUCUMBERS (late 1800s)—Housewives are getting away from the old idea of getting the juice out of cucumbers by salting the slices, which—when the truth is told—is like saving the skin and throwing the eel away. Peel and slice cucumbers from the stem down to the ends, which usually are bitter and should be discarded.***

FRIED EGGPLANT— Slice the unpeeled eggplant at least ½ inch thick; pare each piece carefully; lay them in salt and water, putting a plate upon the topmost to keep it under the brine, and let them remain for 1 hour or more. Wipe each slice, dip it in beaten egg, then in cracker crumbs, and fry in hot lard until well done and nicely browned.—Mrs. F. M. Cragin

BRAISED LETTUCE (mid-1800s)—Set 1 quart (4 cups) of water to boil with 1 tablespoon of salt. Mince an onion and a stalk of celery fine, including the top greens; blend them; season with salt and pepper. Wash 2 good heads of Boston lettuce and let them cook 30 minutes in salted water; drain; cut the lettuces in half the long way, place them in a baking dish, sprinkle with onion and celery and add ½ pint (1 cup) of soup stock. Bake uncovered in a moderate (325°F.) oven about ½ hour. Move the lettuce to a serving platter. Thicken the soup that is left into a cream gravy with a butter-flour ball, made by mixing 1 tablespoon each of flour and butter; pour this over the lettuce.*

TO COOK MUSHROOMS (early 1800s)—Fresh mushrooms demand but little attention, but that little is important. After they have been cleaned, peeled and quartered or sliced put them in a saucepan with enough melted butter to cover the bottom of the pan generously; add ½ teaspoon of vinegar; cut an onion into halves and place each half, cut side downward, in the pan; add a sprinkling of freshly mortared pepper and a good pinch of salt. Let the mushrooms stew with a lively bubble for about 5 minutes and stir frequently. Serve without the onions, but use the sauce.*

COOKING ONIONS WITHOUT TEARS (early 1800s)—In taking the skins off, stand by an open window or door, and there will be no cause for tears to flow, as the current of air in passing takes the pungent odor of the onion with it, thus giving relief to the eyes. Put the onions to boil for about 1 hour in soft water (see Index). When cooked, have on hand 1 teacup (1 cup) of very hot rich cream seasoned with butter, pepper and salt; using a small sieve, dip the onions directly from the boiling water into the heated cream, taking care that they are drained quite free of water. Onions cooked and served this way will not flavor the breath so fully as those served the usual way and are not as liable to rise on the stomach.*

BAKED ONIONS (late1800s)—Onions, when baked in a quick (400°F.) oven, are delicious and sweet; they are so easily prepared that they can be added to any dinner without extra labor. Select smooth, evenly sized onions, place them on a baking sheet and bake for 30 to 45 minutes, according to size. Now, pare away the burnt skins, season well with pepper and salt and bring to the table with Parsley Butter Sauce (see Index).*

TINY BOILED ONIONS (early 1800s)—Boil ¾ pound of small young onions in well-salted water about 10 minutes. Drain them and cover them with soup stock, which must stand at least ½ inch above the onions. Bring to a quick boil, reduce to simmering and cook, slowly and well covered, until soft but not soggy, or about 15 minutes. Remove the onions and reduce the liquid to 1 gill (¼ cup) by boiling it; pour this over the onions with a little melted butter and serve.*

CHINESE WAY OF COOKING PEAS (early 1800s)—Wash the pods before you strip the peas out; instead of throwing the pods into the slop pail for the pigs, cut them in halves and put them into a saucepan with the peas; both take the same length of time to cook; when done, the pods will be floating but the peas will not; serve separately and season the pods with butter melted with a mere touch of salt, sugar and vinegar.*

PARSNIP AND POTATO PIE (mid-1800s)—Take 12 parsnips, 3 onions and 6 potatoes, already boiled; slice everything fine and add ½ pound each of butter and diced cooked salt pork; season with pepper, mix in a little water and bring to an easy boil over a slow fire. Take up the vegetables and bake them in a deep dish between two rich crusts (see Index). There is no better pie for autumn or winter time.**

BUTTERED PARSNIPS (late 1800s)—Clean and pare the parsnips; slice them the long way only once, dry them and roll them well in melted butter; put them into a well-buttered baking dish with a good cover; season them with salt and pepper; add 1 gill (½ cup) of stock or water; let them bake in a moderate oven (350°F.) just a little less than an hour.*

NEW POTATOES, TO BOIL (late 1800s)—These treasured jewels of the soil must first be soaked in cold water, then washed with gentle care and, lastly, just in time for cooking, placed in their skins in simmering water that is not allowed to boil. Test for doneness with a toothpick. When they are tender, drain, dry and serve them with their skins on. The proper way to send them to the table is on separate platters with saucers of cold but softened butter. The proper way to eat them is this: At the table, each person cuts his portion into bite-sized slices and places upon each bite a bit of cold butter, pepper and salt.*

BOILED POTATOES (late 1800s)—Of all the foods that are treated disrespectfully by housewives, the potato easily heads the list as the greatest sufferer. Anybody can boil a potato, but few housewives take the trouble of finding out how to do it right. When you buy potatoes for boiling, pick them of uniform size; soak them in cold salted water and brush, but do not break, their skins. In boiling potatoes, use a kettle with a fairly large, flat bottom and straight sides. Start the potatoes in cold water, but do not drown them; for ½ dozen of middling size, 1 cup of salted water is adequate. Cook them tightly covered—the steam does the work; use the tines of a kitchen fork to determine when they are done. Pour the water off and let them stand, uncovered, for a spell, to dry out in the kettle. Never peel a potato the way you pare an apple; remove the skin as you do that of a peach or a tomato, by lifting it off.*—An Indignant Skowhegan Housewife

MASHED POTATOES (late 1800s)—Like good boiled potatoes, good mashed potatoes do not grow on trees. Many housewives produce a soggy and dull product because they add too many good things to make a good thing better, and thereby spoil it. To 1 quart (4 cups) of hot mashed potatoes, add no more than ½ cup of hot milk or cream and 1 tablespoon of butter. If heavy cream is used, omit the butter, because too much butter makes mashed potatoes soggy. Season the milk that is meant for the potatoes with salt and pepper.*

MASHED POTATOES WITH HERBS (late 1800s)—Mash the hot potatoes with a small lump of butter. Have ready, carefully drained, a small amount of parboiled mixed herbs, such as powdered tarragon, thyme, minced parsley, celery tops, chervil and basil; use all or just a few of this assortment. Blend the seasonings with the mashed potatoes and serve after they have been allowed to stand a few minutes to absorb the various flavors.*

PLAIN BAKED POTATOES (mid-1800s)—Soak largish potatoes in cold salted water for 1 hour. Brush their skins clean, dry them and stick them 2 or 3 times with the point of a small knife. Give the potatoes a light coating of melted drippings, butter or lard before they are placed in a quick (400°F.) oven to bake about 75 minutes, according to size. When a baked potato is done, its insides should feel soft to the touch and its skin should be shiny and crisp. The knife sticking is done to let steam escape, so that potatoes do not blow up in the oven. Always roll baked potatoes on a board with gloved hands to make the insides soft and mealy, before you slice them open with a sharp knife. Cut lengthwise first, then across the center; press the potato from both ends to open slits and insert a lump of softened butter.*

SAVORY STUFFED BAKED POTATOES (late 1800s)—Bake the potatoes in the usual manner (see above); when they are cooked, slash the tops and scoop out the mealy parts. Prepare them as you would for Mashed Potatoes with Herbs (see above) or beat them well with the yolk of 1 egg, a little butter and a tablespoon (for 4 potatoes) cream or milk, together with 1 teaspoon of minced chives, scallions or onions. Rather than keep the egg white, whip it white and stir it into the potato; it does not add much, but it is one way of using it. Season with salt and pepper; return the mixture to the potato skins; dust with nutmeg and bake until brown.*

BAKED POTATOES STUFFED WITH HAM (mid-1800s)—Take 4 large newly baked potatoes (see above) and have ready a mixture of 1 tablespoon of minced ham, 2 pounded anchovies, 1 tablespoon of minced onion and 1 minced hard-boiled egg, white and yolk both; whisk this together with the beaten white of 1 egg. Slice the top of each potato lengthwise; remove the contents. Mash the potato centers with 2 tablespoons each of butter and cream; stir this in the egg-ham-anchovy mixture. Heap the potato shells with this stuffing and return them to the oven to brown.*

STEWED POTATOES (mid-1800s)—Melt a piece of butter the size of an egg (4 tablespoons) in a saucepan; blend in a heaping tablespoon of flour and cook a few moments, but do not let the mixture brown; stir in ½ pint (1 cup) of hot milk to which ½ teaspoon of salt and 1 saltspoon (¼ teaspoon) of white pepper have been added. When the mixture thickens and boils, add 1 pint (2 cups) of neatly sliced cold boiled potatoes, and simmer slowly, uncovered.*

LYONNAISE POTATOES (late 1800s)—Dice 1 quart (4 cups) of cold boiled potatoes and chop 3 large onions. Fry the onions in 2 tablespoons of butter and 1 tablespoon of lard until they are brown; spoon the onions out and put the potatoes in their place. Stir with a spatula to brown the potatoes on all sides, but do not break them. When brown, add 1 tablespoon of minced parsley and cook for 2 minutes; then return the onions to the pan; blend in with the potatoes and serve when hot.*

TOP-OF-STOVE ROASTED POTATOES (early 1800s)—Use medium potatoes, raw, of an even size; peel them; pour boiling water over them in a basin, and let stand covered for 10 minutes; drain them, place in colander and put them over a warm spot till they are dry. Put some butter in a pan —about 2 ounces (¼ cup) for 1 quart (4 cups) of potatoes. When the butter is hot, place the potatoes in the pan and sprinkle a little salt over them. Cover them during the first 45 minutes; shake the pan frequently so that they will brown on all sides. The heat over which they stand must be moderate. Remove the cover and let them brown uncovered another 45 minutes or until done. To speed browning, add more butter and sprinkle the potatoes with a little white sugar after the first 45 minutes. This is the most elegant way of dressing potatoes for any roast meat course.*

BAKED POTATO BALLS (mid-1800s)—Day-old Mashed Potatoes (see Index) that have stood uncovered lend themselves best to this, because they will dry over night. Take 2 cups of them, season with 1 tablespoon of onion juice and ditto of light cream. Beat a small egg very light; add half of it to the Mashed Potatoes; whip it in with a whisk. Form the potatoes into balls, and dip them into the remainder of the egg, using another egg for this purpose if necessary. Place the balls in a buttered pan and brown in a quick (400°F.) oven. Care should be taken not to get the potatoes too moist, as they should have a rather mealy quality.—Mrs. Nicholas Braden

POTATO BALLOONS (late 1800s)—The night before you wish to eat them, boil 6 potatoes in their skins; peel and grate them before they cool. Keep them covered in a bowl over night in a cool place, under a cheesecloth cover, so that they will have air. Before meal-time the next day, mix the yolks of 3 eggs, ½ pint (1 cup) of flour, ½ pint (1 cup) of milk and ½ teaspoon of salt; whip this well and stir it into the cold potatoes; after that, stir in the egg whites, stiffly beaten. Have ready a kettleful of boiling (380–90°F.) lard and use a tablespoon to drop the potatoes into it. Serve the balloons before they descend.*

BROWNED POTATO BORDER (late 1800s)—Pare, boil and mash 6 potatoes with ½ cup of boiling milk. When fine and light, add 1 tablespoon of butter, 1 teaspoon of salt, ¼ teaspoon of pepper and 2 well-beaten eggs. Arrange around a large flat serving platter. Fill the center with Stewed Oysters or any fricassee. Brown in a 400°F. oven.*

SWEET POTATO AND CARROT PUDDING (mid-1880s)—Prepare 6 each of grated carrots and small grated sweet potatoes; ½ pound of finely chopped beef suet, of raisins, of currants, seeded and chopped fine, and 4 cups of bread crumbs; mix the foregoing items with ¼ pound of sugar, 1 small teaspoon of salt, ½ grated lemon peel and spice to taste, with ginger or nutmeg. Boil in a can, pudding mold or floured pudding bag 4 hours. Serve hot with a Cream Sauce. This is a winter dish, and a nice, inexpensive one at that.**

FRIED SWEET POTATOES (mid-1800s)—What to do with left-over baked or boiled sweet potatoes? Try this! Slice the potatoes thin; have in a frying pan a large tablespoon of hot butter, or mixed lard and butter; put the potatoes in; sprinkle them evenly with brown sugar mixed with a small amount of ginger. Never take salt or pepper to sweet potatoes when you dress them this way.*

YANKEE YAMS (late 1800s)—Peel 1 medium-sized yam or sweet potato per person; rub each with a blend of warm maple syrup and butter; sprinkle with brown sugar and a pinch of salt. Place the yams in a baking pan and cover each with a slice of orange on which a slice of lemon has been placed. Bake in a very slow (275°F.) oven until tender and baste with butter every ¼ hour. Governed by the size of the potatoes, the baking time averages about 2½ hours.*

SAUERKRAUT, TO MAKE AND PRESERVE (mid-1800s)—The new quart glass jars with airtight tops make it possible to make good Sauerkraut with little preparation and effort. First, scald the washed jars as required and stand them, bottoms up, on a clean towel to drain. Wash, drain and shred enough cabbage to fill the jars almost to the top, but do not pack them too tightly; place 1 teaspoon each of white sugar, table salt, chopped onions and dill on the cabbage in each jar; fill the jars to the brim with boiling water. Screw on the tops tightly and turn the jars upside down to make sure that no air bubbles are present. Let the Sauerkraut stand 6 weeks before using it.*

HOT SAUERKRAUT, TO SERVE (mid-1800s)—Home-pickled Sauerkraut can be given an extra flavor without much trouble. Remove the dill from the jar; drain the Sauerkraut. While it drains, mince 1 raw potato and ¼ pound of parboiled pork into tiny bits and cook all slowly in a large spider with 2 tablespoons of butter; when the potatoes soften, stir in 2 teaspoons of mild made-mustard; strain away the fat and add the solids to the Sauerkraut; let it cook slowly for 10 minutes and serve when hot.*

SICKQUATASH OR SUCCOTASH (early 1800s)—Here is a rich and succulent sample on how the Colonists added touches of magic to a simple Indian dish called Sickquatash. Actually, it was seldom more than hulled corn; they named it Succotash. Cut the kernels off 12 ears of Indian corn; string a quart (4 cups) or more of green beans, cut them in inch lengths, wash them and put them to the corn in a stew-pan; add ½ pint (1 cup) of boiling milk, cover it close and let cook gently for ¾ hour. Then add 1 small teacup (½ cup) of butter, 1 teaspoon of salt, 1 saltspoon (¼ teaspoon) of pepper; stir well, cover and cook for 10 minutes; take the beans and corn into a dish, with more or less of the liquid as may be liked. Some people use ½ pound of nicely corned, parboiled and thinly sliced fat pork instead of butter. Lima beans and corn make a very fine and acceptable succotash.***

STEAMED SPINACH (late 1800s)—Pick and wash, but do not dry, the spinach; remove the roots, but let the leaves remain on the stems; pack, but not too tightly, into a baking dish; add no water; cover and steam in a moderate (350°F.) oven for 30 minutes or until tender. Before serving, cut cross-wise through the spinach down through the stems; cover with Egg Sauce (see Index) and serve.*

ESCALLOPED TOMATOES—Put in an earthen baking dish a layer of cracker crumbs and small bits of butter, then a layer of sliced tomatoes with a very little sugar sprinkled over them, then another layer of cracker crumbs seasoned with butter and another layer of tomatoes, until your dish is full, with a layer of cracker crumbs at the top; pour over all this a little water to moisten it, and bake ½ hour in a moderate (350°F.) oven.—Mrs. A. A. Carpenter

STEWED TOMATOES—Put some ripe tomatoes into hot water and skin them; then throw them into an *earthen* stew-pan (a new tin will do, but it is not so good); cut up the tomatoes and let them cook gently a few minutes; season with butter, pepper and salt and serve. Or, you may add bread crumbs and sugar to the tomatoes if preferred. Some cooks stew tomatoes for a long time, but the flavor is finer if they are allowed to simmer but a few moments, just sufficient time to heat them well through.—Anon.

FRIED TOMATOES—Cut some large Feejee tomatoes in half; flour the cut side; have a pan very hot, and put in the tomatoes, floured side down; when they are brown on one side, turn them; when done, pour over a teacup (1 cup) of hot cream or rich milk.—Anon.

ROASTED TOMATOES (mid-1800s)—Remove the core and peel the tomatoes; put in the core's place a bit of butter, salt and pepper; cork with a piece of bread; put in a quick (400°F.) oven for ½ to ¾ hour and baste the while with melted butter.*

CURRIED TOMATOES (early 1800s)—Cut up 8 large tomatoes; put them in a china-lined kettle with 4 ounces (generous 2/3 cup) of rice which is about 2/3 done (cooked 10 minutes); let them cook, stirring *frequently* until the rice is well done; add 1 large tablespoon of butter, a dessertspoon (2 teaspoons) of sugar, a little salt and pepper; depending on its strength, add 1 teaspoon or more or less of curry powder and ½ teaspoon of dry mustard. Stir for 5 minutes and serve. The consistency should be that of well-boiled rice. This is a delicious dish.*

BREADED BAKED TOMATOES (late 1800s)—Cut unpeeled tomatoes in two and squeeze each half, very lightly, to press out some of the water and seeds; place the tomatoes, cut side up, in a buttered baking dish; sprinkle with salt and pepper; cover with a layer of bread crumbs and put on each a piece of butter the size of a large lima bean (½ teaspoon). Bake in a fast moderate (375°F.) oven about 35 to 40 minutes.*

CREAMED TURNIPS—It is about time to take turnips out of the Ugly Duckling class of menu-making and here is a long step in that direction. Peel and cut 2 medium-sized yellow turnips into small dice and cook. Serve them in this white sauce: Heat ½ pint (1 cup) of milk to boiling point; melt 2 tablespoons of butter in a saucepan; when it bubbles add 2 heaping tablespoons of flour with ½ teaspoon of salt and ¼ teaspoon of white pepper; stir these into the butter quickly until well mixed; now add the hot milk very slowly and in a thin stream as you stir to prevent lumps from forming. Drain the turnips, turn them into this sauce and, just before serving, stir in 1 teaspoon of lemon juice.—Mrs. Henrietta Gable

EAST INDIAN PILAU FOR LAMB (early 1800s)—Hang a heavy iron pot well above the fire and in it put a piece of butter as large as a duck's egg; if it is fresh butter, add 1 teaspoon of salt. When the butter foams, add 1 gill (½ cup) of onions chopped fine. Let them become almost tar-brown; then add 1 gill (½ cup) of butter, together with ½ pint (1 cup) of raw, well-picked rice that has been washed and rubbed. Let it cook slowly so that, in time, the butter will be absorbed by the rice, which will turn from white to wheat-yellow. When that point is reached, have ready a small handful (2 tablespoons) of raisins that have been softened in hot water and seeded as well; add them, together with 4 dessertspoons (8 teaspoons) of sweet slivered almonds, a blade of mace, a snip or 2 of cinnamon bark and a few cardamon seeds. Stir for 5 minutes and pour boiling water into the pot until the water stands exactly at an even level with the rice. Taste to see if the seasoning is correct; add more salt and a little white pepper if needed. Let the rice cook, well covered, until tender; then place it, uncovered, near the fire (or in a 275–300°F. oven) so that the rice will become fluffy and dry.*

RICE BOILED IN MILK (early 1800s)—This is a very good dish for women who have milch cows, as it is a nice substitute for a pudding. Put 1 pint (2 cups) of rice into nearly 2 quarts (4 cups) of new milk an hour before dinner; add 2 teaspoons of salt. Boil the rice slowly on the back part of the stove; stir often to prevent burning. Let it boil until the kernels lose their distinct form; then take it up in a mold, or bowl, wet in cold water, and let it stand until you unmold it at dinner time.***

RICE IN THE ITALIAN MODE (late 1800s)—In a heavy saucepan, heat ½ pound (1 cup) of butter and sauté 2/3 cup of finely minced onions. When tender, add 1 cup of raw rice. Stir as it cooks for about 15 minutes; then add 1½ pints (3 cups) of boiling soup stock. Let it cook slowly, covered, until all moisture is absorbed; make sure of this by tilting the pot from side to side until no water appears. Put the pot away from the fire. A large cup of shredded Italian cheese (Parmesan) goes into this, but for the best results, do not stir it into the hot rice until serving time.*

WHEN BOILING RICE (early 1800s)—Pick over the rice, rinse it in cold water until perfectly clean, then put it in a pot of boiling water, allowing a quart (4 cups) of water to 1½ gills (¾ cup) of rice; boil it hard for 17 minutes; drain off the water very close and let it steam 15 minutes with the lid off. When carefully done in this way, each kernel of rice stands out by itself, while it is perfectly tender. Water in which rice has been boiled makes, it is said, good starch for muslin, if boiled a few minutes by itself.***

RICE CROQUETTES (mid-1800s)—Boil 1 cup of rice in 1 quart (4 cups) of milk or water, until tender; while it is still warm add a piece of butter the size of an egg (4 tablespoons), 1 egg yolk, 2 whole eggs; make the mixture into rolls; dip them in cracker crumbs and fry them in a pan in equal measures of lard and butter.*

13. *Salads and Hot and Cold Dressings*

SYDNEY SMITH'S SALAD SONG (early 1800s)—

To make this condiment, your poet begs
The pounded yellow of two hard-boil'd eggs;
Two boil'd potatoes, pass'd through kitchen sieve,
Smoothness and softness to the salad give.
Let onion atoms lurk within the bowl,
And, half-suspected, animate the whole.
Of mordant mustard add a single spoon,
Distrust the condiment that bites so soon;
But deem it not, thou man of herbs, a fault,
To add a double quantity of salt.
And, lastly, o'er the flavor'd compound toss
A magic soupçon of anchovy sauce.
Oh, green and glorious! Oh, herbaceous treat!
'Twould tempt the dying anchorite to eat:
Back to the world he'd turn his fleeting soul,
And plunge his fingers in the salad bowl!
Serenely full, the epicure would say,
Fate can not harm me, I have dined to-day.

BEET SALAD (late 1800s)—Dice 6 cooked but not pickled beets and marinate them with French Dressing (see Index); let them stand 1 hour. Meanwhile, cook 4 eggs until they are hard-boiled (12 minutes is best). Separate the yolks from the whites. Press the yolks through a sieve; chop the whites fine as snowflakes. Place the beets on a serving dish and season them slightly with cider vinegar. Over the beets put a flurry of mashed egg yolks and chopped whites. You can pretty this very attractive dish up by covering it with a fine sprinkling of minced parsley.*

BUTTER BEAN SALAD (late 1800s)—Cover 2 cups of cold (cooked) butter beans with a Fancy French Dressing (see Index) and let them stand 45 minutes. Drain the beans, sprinkle with juice squeezed from ½ onion and mix them into a Cream Dressing (see Index).*

CABBAGE SALAD (late 1800s)—For a simple, yet very satisfactory Cabbage Salad, mix 1½ cups each of cabbage and celery; to this add 1 tablespoon of chopped onion and 1 cup of Boiled Dressing (see Index).*

SHARP AND SOUR CABBAGE SALAD (mid-1800s)—Cut 4 pounds of cabbage into small pieces; slice and mince 2 large Bermuda onions; mix them and add the following salad cream. Beat together 3 whole eggs, 2 raw egg yolks, 1 tablespoon of mixed mustard, 1 gill (½ cup) of soft as cream butter, 1 pinch of red pepper, salt and nutmeg to taste; add 1 gill (½ cup) of vinegar and stir the whole in a saucepan over boiling water until of the consistency of cream. If too thick, add a little milk.*

CHESTNUT SALAD (late 1800s)—Blend 2 cups of minced chestnuts that have been boiled tender with 2 cups of minced oranges; stir this into 1 cup of Family Dressing Mayonnaise (see Index) and 1 tablespoon of lemon juice. Serve when very cold on lettuce leaves and sprinkle with grated orange rind.*

THE MANAGEMENT OF CHICKEN SALADS (late 1800s)—It is a rare hen who knows her own white meat of chicken salad after pieces of cooked veal, pork or rabbit have been added to increase the bulk at small expense. The fact is that these non-chicken meats give extra zest and flavor to the salad without detracting from its traditionally pure appearance. Dice boiled breasts of chicken with identical amounts of any of the other meats mentioned. Blend the meat in a bowl with thinly sliced celery stalks, boiled or peeled and sliced celery roots, or both; season with the juice of 1 lemon, white pepper, salt and a pinch of powdered sage. Mix in as much Mayonnaise as needed. If it is yellow because of the egg yolks in it, you can bleach the dressing by adding a little whipped heavy cream. If the salad is served on a platter, place it on a bed of lettuce leaves and coat it with pickled beets, sweet and sour gherkins, sliced stoned olives, half-moons of hard-cooked egg whites and disks of sliced hard-cooked yolks.*

SUGGESTIONS FOR SALAD DAYS—Chicken for salad should boil until it parts from the bone easily. It is also better to shred it than to cut or chop. Equal parts of melted butter and salad oil are by many preferred to the entire quantity of either. The addition of the liquor the fowl is boiled in, to moisten the salad with, is a great improvement. Crisp celery and cabbage in ice-cold water for an hour or 2 before using for salads.—Miss M. A. Ayer

MOCK CHICKEN SALAD—Cut the cooked white meat of veal or pork (lean) into small bits the size of peas (no dark meat, if you please); chop the whole parts of celery nearly as small. Prepare a dressing thus: Rub the yolks of hard-boiled eggs smooth; for each yolk put in ½ teaspoon of mustard, the same quantity of salt, a tablespoon of oil and a 2-ounce wineglass of vinegar. Mix the meat and celery in a large bowl and pour over it this dressing with a little cream added. The dressing must not be put on until just before it is served.—Mrs. Morgan

WHITE MEAT CHICKEN SALAD—Take the breasts of 4 large well-boiled chickens; cut them in small pieces, but not too fine; mix with the chicken 8 teacups (6 ounces) of celery cut also in small pieces and the chopped whites of 12 hard-boiled eggs. For the dressing, take the yolks of 4 raw eggs; beat into them half of an ordinary-sized bottle of olive oil, beginning with a teaspoonful and adding no more than that at a time, until it is all thoroughly mixed; then add the well-mashed and pounded yolks of 12 eggs, salt and pepper, 3 tablespoons of mustard, a pinch of cayenne pepper and a gill (½ cup) of vinegar; then stir this dressing thoroughly into the mixed chicken, celery and whites of eggs.—Mary Norton

CHICKEN-POTATO SALAD (late 1800s)—Mix the salad on the basis of 1 cup of chicken for every ¾ cup of potatoes and every ½ cup of chopped onions. When these have been put together in a bowl, add ½ cup of Mayonnaise (see Index) that has been seasoned with 1 hard-boiled chopped egg, 1 teaspoon of minced parsley and 1 teaspoon of mild made-mustard, some salt and white pepper. Stir this into the chicken salad. If too dry, add more Mayonnaise. In many homes, the chopped white parts of celery stalks are added in the same quantity as onions. (The potatoes should, of course, be boiled and cold.)*

CREAM CHEESE SALAD (late 1800s)—Mix 2 Philadelphia (3-ounce) cream cheeses with 1 cup (chopped) of walnut meats; moisten with cream if needed and fashion into balls; chill. In French Dressing (see Index) marinate 2 heads of Boston lettuce. At serving time, arrange the lettuce in nests according to the number of servings and put from 4 to 5 nutballs into each serving. Drench with a shower of yolks of hard-boiled eggs rubbed through a sieve and color with paprika.*

CUCUMBER AND SWEETBREADS SALAD (late 1800s)—Cut 4 cucumbers in strips lengthwise, then into ½-inch pieces. Add 1 cup of sweetbreads, cooked (see Index). Blend with Cream Dressing (see Index). Chill and serve on toast or crisp lettuce.*

FRESH CUCUMBER "PICKLE" (early 1800s)—Peel the cucumbers and slice them without cutting through to the bottom. Make a mixture of 3 tablespoons of vinegar, an equal amount of pounded white sugar, 1 teaspoon of salt and ¼ teaspoon of white pepper; drip this dressing over the cucumbers so that it falls between the slices. This salad should be served as cold as possible.*

KOHL SLAW WITH BOILED DRESSING (late 1800s)—The secret of good Kohl Slaw, like good hired hands, is not to let 'em hang around the kitchen longer than necessary. Have your cabbage cleaned and ready but do not slice and chop it—thin slices and finely chopped—until table time. You can, however, sliver green pepper, and red, too, if you have it; cut paper-thin onion rings and ditto slices of carrots in the afternoon; let them soak in cold water in the ice chest. At the proper time, assemble the Kohl Slaw as quickly as possible and have your Cooked Salad Dressing (see Index) chilled in the ice chest.*

TO STRETCH FRUIT SALAD FOR COMPANY (mid-1800s)—Use cubes of fruit gelatine instead of all fruit. Drain the juice from canned fruit and use it in making the jelly; the liquid, when ready, is poured into a shallow pan that must be wet with cold water. When it has jelled, cut it with a small cookie cutter. To make the jelly extra firm, use slightly less liquid than the gelatine directions call for.*

BANANA, GRAPEFRUIT AND ORANGE SALAD (late 1800s)—To 1 pint (2 cups) of orange sections and 3/4 pint (1½ cups) of grapefruit sections add ½ pint (1 cup) of sliced bananas and ¼ pint (½ cup) of thinly sliced celery. Toss these ingredients together with due consideration for the frail bananas. Add ½ pint (1 cup) of Family Dressing Mayonnaise (see Index) just before the salad goes to the table.*

CHEESE AND PINEAPPLE SALAD (late 1800s)—Cut a head of lettuce into sections and chop it small; have 1 cup of chopped pineapple ready and ½ cup of sharp cheese (Cheddar) grated on the coarse side of the grater. Blend with ¾ cup of Mayonnaise (see Index) at serving time and dust it with shredded coconut.*

TO FRESHEN SHREDDED COCOANUT (late 1800s)—Cover it with cold milk; let it stand 40 minutes in the milk and 10 minutes in a sieve to drain; it will look and taste as if it came fresh from its native palm.*

MIXED-UP FRUIT SALAD (late 1800s)—Wash and core, but do not peel, ½ pint (1 cup) of sweet apples; cut them into small cubes; dice sliced pineapple and oranges to provide ½ pint (1 cup) of each; slice and chop a small head of lettuce coarsely, as you would cabbage for Cole Slaw; mix these ingredients in a bowl with enough French Dressing (see Index) to provide a rich coating.*

FISH SALAD (mid-1800s)—Break cooked fish that has been boned and skinned into 1 pint (2 cups) of large pieces; in a basin mix it lightly, so as not to break the pieces, with 1½ gills (¾ cup) of finely chopped white ends of celery stalks and 6 tablespoons of chopped sweet pickles; season with salt and white pepper. Make a Sharp Dressing Mayonnaise (see Index) and stir it into the salad gently. Decorate with half-moons of quartered hard-cooked eggs. Salmon, cod, halibut, any form of cooked white firm fish, as well as boiled crab, lobster and scallops, may be utilized.*

LOBSTER SALAD (early 1800s)—The simplest way of serving lobster is very good and most healthful. Take the cold boiled lobsters from their shells and eat them as they are with vinegar and mustard. But, if simplicity does not serve, try this dressing: To the yolks of 4 eggs, boiled hard, add a little sweet oil, ditto dry mustard, salt, pepper and 1 gill (½ cup) of the best vinegar you have. Stir these all together a long time. Cut up some celery or lettuce, or both, very, very fine; sprinkle this on the lobster meat in the dish in which it is to be served and pour the dressing over it.*

A STYLISH LOBSTER SALAD (late 1800s)—To make this salad really impressive, cut boiled female lobsters—one can tell them apart from males by their narrower tails—into large chunks; roll them in a bowl as you dust them with salt and white pepper; moisten them with fine vinegar in which some tarragon has been steeped; this should be done about 1 hour before serving time and the lobster kept in a chill place. To complete the salad, mash the corals and add as much olive oil as they can absorb; next mash the yolks of 2 hard-cooked eggs and add 3 tablespoons of olive oil, 1 table-spoon of lemon juice, 1 ditto of mild made-mustard, 1 tablespoon of finely minced onions and a touch of basil. Chill the dressing and blend it into the lobster meat as the last moment. Serve on lettuce leaves and decorate with slices of hard-boiled eggs topped by fillets of anchovy.*

MEAT SALAD (mid-1800s)—Any and all cooked meats can be used in this salad; the meat should be chopped very, very fine. For ½ pint (1 cup) of meat, take 6 or 8 cold hard-cooked eggs and cut them into slices about ¼ inch thick; remove the yolks and mash them with enough Mayonnaise (see Index) to get them quite moist; add the meat and season with pepper and salt, a little powdered thyme and 1 teaspoon of mild made-mustard; shape into balls; if more moisture is needed for this, add more Mayonnaise. Mince the whites of the eggs exceedingly fine; roll the balls in them; place the balls on slices of pickled beets set upon lettuce leaves; serve the salad cold in individual portions.*

SWEETBREAD SALAD--Four hard-boiled eggs, 1 raw egg, 3 tablespoons of salad oil, 1 teaspoon of salt, ½ teaspoon of pepper, 2 teaspoons of sugar, 2 of mixed mustard, ½ teacup (½ cup) of vinegar, 1 cooked calf's sweetbread and 2 heads of lettuce. For the dressing, mash the yolks and mix the oil thoroughly in them; then add the raw egg well beaten; mix in the other ingredients for the dressing slowly and thoroughly, adding the vinegar last. Break the sweetbread up in small pieces, break the lettuce also in small pieces, and then put in a dish alternate layers of lettuce, sweetbread and dressing. Use the whites of the eggs sliced over the top.—Mrs. D. C. B.

FOR SALMON SALAD—Use the same dressing as for Sweetbread Salad (above). Put the salmon on a platter, pour over it the dressing and garnish with celery leaves.—Mrs. D. C. B.

OYSTER SALAD (mid-1800s)—Heat 1 quart of oysters (25 to 50 if large, 50 to 100 if small) to the boiling point in their own juices. Strain well and drain. Season them with a mixture of 2 tablespoons of melted butter, ½ teaspoon of salt, ⅛ teaspoon of pepper and 1 tablespoon of lemon juice. Put this into the ice chest to chill for at least 2 hours. Wash and scrape the nicest parts of stalks of celery and mince them till you have 1 pint (2 cups). Put this in a bowl with a large lump of ice and set it with the oysters in the ice chest. When ready to serve, mix the oysters and celery with 1 gill (½ cup) of Mayonnaise Dressing (see Index) and place on the table.**

COLE SLAW—Half head of cabbage chopped fine. Rub to a paste the yolks of 3 hard-boiled eggs; add 1 tablespoon each of melted butter and sugar, 1 teaspoon of dry mustard, 1 gill (½ cup) of vinegar. Mix this into the cabbage. Garnish with sliced egg whites.—Bella Lyon

DRESSED CABBAGE—One small (4-ounce) teacup of vinegar, 1 egg, 2 tablespoons of sugar, 1 teaspoon of salt, and a piece of butter ½ the size of

an egg (2 tablespoons). Beat the egg before mixing it with the other ingredients, which should be simmering over a low fire; then put in the egg; stir the dressing until it thickens; cool and pour over chopped or shaved cabbage.
—Mrs. B. J. Seward

HOT POTATO SALAD (mid-1800s)—For each pint (2 cups) of cubed raw potatoes, have 4 thin slices of parboiled bacon cut into small squares; fry the bacon a light brown. Slice 1 onion into rings; cut the rings into quarters and part them; combine the onion, bacon and potato; add 1 teaspoon of caraway seeds and 1 dessertspoon (2 teaspoons) of sugar; cover with cold water and stir in 1 teaspoon of dry mustard, 1 teaspoon of salt and ¼ teaspoon of white pepper. Cover, heat to boiling point and let this simmer about 15 to 20 minutes or until the potatoes are almost done, but not quite. Stir in ½ gill (¼ cup) of vinegar, being careful not to mash the potatoes. Cook until tender. This salad is served without a dressing but it is usual to sprinkle freshly minced parsley leaves over it just before serving. Some cooks drain off the liquor and use Mayonnaise or French Dressing instead.*

COLD POTATO SALAD (late 1800s)—Marinate over night in a cool place as many boiled and sliced potatoes as you may need with one-quarter of that amount of thinly sliced onions, as well as 1 small drained and sliced cucumber, plus 1 tablespoon of minced parsley in a plain French Dressing (see Index). In the morning, drain off such dressing liquids as remain; at mealtime make a Mayonnaise (see below) and stir it into the salad with a fork— and use a light hand. Spread a thin layer of Mayonnaise over the entire salad and decorate it with anchovies, sliced olives and quartered hard-boiled eggs. It is best if the potatoes are boiled and peeled the day before they are marinated.*

OLD YANKEE POTATO SALAD WITH COOKED DRESSING (mid-1800s) —Peel and slice enough cold potatoes to fill a quart (4 cup) measure; salt and pepper to taste; slice and mince 2 onions very fine and mix with the potatoes. Put 1 gill (½ cup) of vinegar into a saucepan with 1 tablespoon of fresh butter and let it heat slowly. Beat the yolks of 2 eggs thoroughly, pour them into a ½-pint (1-cup) measure and fill it with thick, sweet cream; beat the eggs and cream together; pour them into the butter-vinegar mixture and continue cooking it. Season with salt, white pepper and a pinch of cayenne. Stir constantly until the dressing reaches the boiling point, then pour it over the potatoes and mix; serve cold. If, at the time of cooking, the dressing is too thin, add egg yolk; if too thick, add cream.*

POTATO, BEET AND TURNIP SALAD (mid-1800s)—Dice and blend ½ pint (1 cup) each of cooked beets, potatoes and turnips; season with a Mayonnaise (see Index); pepper and salt to taste. Pile individual servings on separate plates on leaves of lettuce and decorate with sliced hard-boiled eggs and minced parsley.*

PICNIC POTATO SALAD—Sliced cold boiled potatoes mixed with a very small quantity of chopped onions, almonds blanched and quartered, and hickory nuts, also, if liked (the nuts may be omitted). Mix a nice salad dressing of 1 teaspoon of salt, a little pepper, 2 tablespoons of finely cut crisped parsley; about 2 teaspoons of grated onion and 4 tablespoons of salad oil or butter; to this add 8 tablespoons of vinegar. This receipt is for 2 quarts (4 cups) of cold boiled potatoes; pour the dressing over them and let them stand ½ hour before serving.—M. A. T.

TOMATO SALAD—Twelve tomatoes peeled, sliced and drained on a cloth under pressure, 4 eggs boiled hard and sliced, 1 egg (raw) well beaten, 1 dessertspoon (2 teaspoons) of salt, ¼ teaspoon of cayenne pepper, 1 tablespoon of sugar, 1 teacup (4 ounces) of vinegar. Blend the dry ingredients in the vinegar and beat in the raw egg; build the salad in layers by placing slices of egg on each slice of tomato and moisten each slice with the dressing; set it on ice so that it becomes perfectly cold.—Miss Spruance

SPRING GARDEN SALAD (late 1800s)—Assemble ¼ head each of chicory and lettuce, 1 stalk of endive, 2/3 cup each of chopped cucumber, celery and radishes, also 1 large tomato scalded, peeled and cut into small chunks. Tear the lettuce, chicory and endive into small pieces and blend them with all the other ingredients in a bowl. Serve chilled with French Dressing (see Index).*

LETTUCE, CELERY, RADISHES AND ONIONS (late 1800s)—When served raw, these should be soaked for 2 hours in salted water with ice in it, if possible, before coming to table.*

SALAD ASPIC JELLY (mid-1800s)—Put a pair of neatly trimmed calf's feet in 3 pints (6 cups) of cold water and 1 teaspoon of salt. Let it simmer 3 hours; skim when called for. Now add 1 small onion, small carrot and small celery root, 3 sprigs of parsley and 6 whole white peppers. Cook 75 minutes longer, at which time the meat should be ready to drop off the bones; strain the liquid through a hair-sieve and let it stand until the next morning, when you will remove the fat that has collected on the surface. If the aspic is too soft, boil to reduce its volume; if too hard, heat and add a requisite measure of boiling water. To clear the jelly, beat 2 egg whites to a foam and add this, with the egg shells, to the jelly, when it is reaching the simmering point; stir constantly until you take it away from fire. Now is the time to season the aspic with vinegar, white wine, salt and powdered spices. The next and last step is to run the aspic through several thicknesses of cheesecloth in a colander into a granite crock where, stood in a cool place, it will keep for a week. More difficult to make than gelatine but also much more worthwhile.***

BREAST OF TURKEY SALAD (late 1800s)—This is good made according to the directions given under The Management of Chicken Salads (see Index).*

UNCOOKED VEGETABLE SALAD (late 1800s)—Chop equal amounts of raw cabbage, tomatoes, green peppers, carrots, celery stalks and red peppers; season with salt and pepper; mix them well and place them in a cool spot

until serving time, when French Dressing (see Index) is worked into the
salad to moisten it; but do not make it so moist that the salad drips; place
on lettuce leaves. This is a good salad for left-overs, such as ham and tongue.
A nice way to do it is to chop these meats and add them to the salad when
the French Dressing goes into it.*

A VENERABLE SALAD DRESSING (early 1800s)—Boil 3 eggs quite hard
for about 15 minutes, put them in cold water, strip off the shells and mash
the yolks in a mortar; when smooth, add very gradually, with much in-
between stirring, 1 dessertspoon (2 teaspoons) of made-mustard and 1 tablespoon of vinegar; season to taste with salt and cayenne; now add 3 tablespoons of fine Florence (olive) oil; drip it, drop by single drop, from a
saltspoon (1/4 teaspoon) and keep rubbing continuously with the back of a
wooden spoon; lastly, mix in the yolk of a raw egg; stir well. At this point
one may add the finely chopped whites of the 3 eggs, but it is not a common
practice, as it makes the dressing seem rather heavy and thick. For boiled
vegetables that is acceptable, but not for salads of greens and herbs.*

BOILED SALAD DRESSING (late 1800s)—Beat 3 egg yolks and cream 1/4
cup of butter with 1 teaspoon each of salt and mustard and 1/2 teaspoon of
paprika; add 1 cup of heated milk; stir well and beat into the egg yolks;
beat fast as you add it; put the mixture into a double boiler and cook until
thick; at the last moment add 4 tablespoons of hot vinegar; beat and serve.*

CREAM DRESSING (NOT BOILED) (mid-1800s)—Mash the yolks of 3
hard-boiled eggs; add 2 tablespoons of vinegar and 1 teaspoon each of salt
and mustard; beat the mixture until it is firm; add 1 1/2 cups of whipped
cream, but only 1 tablespoon at a time. When you have almost done whipping, dust in a good pinch of cayenne.*

SOUR CREAM DRESSING (late 1800s)—For 1 cup, array on the kitchen
table 1/2 cup each of sour cream and salad oil, 2 tablespoons each of strained
lemon juice and cider vinegar, 1 teaspoon of dry mustard and 2 of white
sugar. Rub the bottom and sides of a bowl with 1/2 clove of garlic; whip the
cream and, starting with the oil, blend in the remaining items, as you rotate
the egg beater, in this order: vinegar, lemon juice, mustard and sugar.
Season with salt and color with 1/2 teaspoon of paprika.*

FANCY FRENCH DRESSING (late 1800s)—Mix 1/2 teaspoon of finely
minced onions with a like amount of dry mustard; add 3/4 teaspoon of salt,
a dash of paprika and a pinch of cayenne; mash this mixture in a mortar,
and, when it is a mush, take your egg beater and whip in, in alternate spoonfuls, 6 tablespoons of Italian (olive) oil and 6 dessertspoons (4 tablespoons)
of vinegar. This dressing takes a lot of beating to be good.*

POOR MAN'S SAUCE (early 1800s)—Pick a branch of parsley leaves from
the stalk, mince them very fine and strew a little salt over them; shred fine
6 green young onions (scallions); add these to the parsley and put all into
a sauce boat, with 3 tablespoons of oil and 5 of vinegar; add some ground
black pepper and salt, also some minced gherkins or a little grated horse-

radish; stir this well and use at once. (This is actually a primitive French Dressing.)*

FRENCH DRESSING (late 1800s)—The following recipe is so simple and good that it really does pay to put up French Dressing in large quantities. Blend 2 tablespoons of vinegar and 1 of lemon juice with 1/3 cup of olive oil, using an egg beater. This done, beat in salt, paprika and pepper to taste. Pour this into a large bottle so that you can give it a good shake-up when you want it, because it separates while standing.*

FRENCH DRESSING FOR FRUIT SALADS (late 1800s)—Have a quart canning jar scalded, cool and ready. Into it pour 1 cup of olive oil, 1/4 cup of honey, 1/3 cup of tarragon vinegar—or you may use ordinary vinegar plus a small pinch of powdered tarragon, 1 halved clove of garlic, 1/2 teaspoon each of dry mustard, salt, paprika and white sugar. Cover with a screw top and shake vigorously; place in the ice chest near the ice until it is time to use it, then shake it again.*

HOT MAYONNAISE OR HOLLANDAISE SAUCE (late 1800s)—First of all, place a saucepan in a pot of simmering, not boiling, water; make sure that the water in the pot does not reach the saucepan's bottom; this sauce is made by steam and not by direct heat. Put 2 tablespoons (slightly rounded) of Clarified Butter (see Index) into the pan; when it is liquid, add a tablespoon of dry sherry, 1/2 teaspoon of freshly squeezed and well-sieved lemon juice, a touch of cayenne pepper. Stir the bottom and sides with a wooden spoon and, as you stir, blend in 2 raw egg yolks, which must be free of whites and white spots. As this begins to thicken, remove the pot and saucepan from the heat, but do not lift the saucepan from its perch above the pot unless the eggs thicken too quickly; in that event, lift the pan from the pot for a count of 3 and then return it. Blend in 2 tablespoons of softened butter; when this is absorbed, add 2 more and again 2, always stirring; blend well and you are done. If the sauce falls apart, rush to the rescue with a third egg yolk.*

HOLLANDAISE SAUCE (late 1800s)—Much mystery has been thrown around the making of this sauce, but it is really quite simple if done this way. Cream 1/2 cup of sweet butter and add 1 tablespoon of lemon juice; when this has been stirred in, put in 4 egg yolks—devoid of all whites—one by one; do this blending thoroughly and gently, then add 1/2 teaspoon of salt, 1/4 teaspoon of white pepper and a few grains of cayenne. It is best to assemble this mixture in a saucepan which can then be set over simmering, but not boiling, water. Cook just long enough to heat it thoroughly. If the sauce is overcooked, remove it from the hot water, add 2 teaspoons of cold water and whisk well. That done, finish heating the sauce over simmering water.*

BOILED KOHL SLAW DRESSING (mid-1800s)—Some women make a big batch at a time and keep it stored, but this dressing does not stand too well; so, for one meal, follow this suggestion: In a saucepan, blend together 1 teaspoon of arrowroot, a small teaspoon each of salt and mustard powder, 3 tablespoons of sugar and a touch of peppermint; beat the yolk of an egg with 2 tablespoons of cold milk and stir it into the saucepan. Take your time doing this. Warm 1½ gills (¾ cup) of milk and pour this into the dish; heat it, but do not let the milk boil; when all is well blended, add, spoon by spoon, 4 tablespoons of vinegar, very slowly to prevent curdling. Let the mixture simmer for 5 minutes; set aside to chill and beat with an egg beater before adding it to the salad.*

SECRET OF GOOD MAYONNAISE (late 1800s)—Women who know their way about salad-making discovered long ago that one of the great secrets of turning out good Mayonnaise is that all the ingredients must be of identical temperature. For that reason, always assemble all the ingredients on your kitchen table 1 hour before it is time to make it.*

FAMILY MAYONNAISE (late 1800s)—Take the yolks from 2 hard-boiled eggs, mash them and beat them up with the yolk of 1 raw egg; add 1 teaspoon each of salt and mustard and a large pinch each of paprika and cayenne. In a tumbler, mix 1 tablespoon each of kitchen vinegar and lemon juice. Using an egg beater, whip into the egg, by the saltspoonful (¼ teaspoon), 8 tablespoons (½ cup) of olive oil; keep it workable by adding a few drops of the lemon-vinegar when necessary. When this is well blended, add 1 cup of olive oil by the teaspoonful. She who hurries in this enterprise is lost— and so is the Mayonnaise.*

There are nineteenth-century salad and meat dressings to suit almost every taste and occasion; most of them are quite simple; all are delightful.

ICE DRESSING——So called because one will need a bowl of ice in order to make it, as well as an ice chest to keep it in. Place a deep bowl over a basin of ice. Drain 2 egg yolks of all their whites and place them on the basin; next, teaspoonful by teaspoonful, stir 1 gill (½ cup) of salad oil into the yolks. One does this by letting the oil fall drop by drop as one holds the oil spoon with one hand and the stirring spoon with the other. After the first 3 teaspoonsful, add, drop by drop, 6 drops of lemon juice after each spoonful of oil. This somewhat tedious method prevents curdling and insures a smooth dressing. When the oil is completely absorbed season with a vinegar which has been flavored with tarragon or basil; add this also drop by drop, to taste; lastly, season with a little salt and white pepper. This dressing keeps fairly well, but only if well protected from air and completely chilled on ice.—Mrs. Jane Brumager

A MILD DRESSING—Mash the yolks of 3 hard-cooked eggs and give them, gradually, 2 tablespoons each of salad oil and vinegar, in that order; add 1 tablespoon of minced capers or parsley or chives, a pinch of finely powdered marjoram or basil; blend in 6 tablespoons of cream; season with pepper and salt.—Miss Lucile Prescott

A SHARP DRESSING—Rub the yolks of 2 hard-boiled eggs through a sieve; put in 4 tablespoons of oil, slowly and one at a time; follow with 4 tablespoons of vinegar, also one at a time; add 1 teaspoon of sharp made-mustard, a little pepper and salt.—Mrs. Walter G. Baker

AN EASY DRESSING—Roll a lemon so as to free all its juices, then squeeze the latter into the yolks of 2 raw eggs; stir; when thick add, 1 teaspoon at a time, 1/3 cup of salad oil; follow with 1/3 cup of good wine or cider vinegar; season with pepper and salt.—Mrs. Charles Hart

A STYLISH DRESSING—Soften 4 ounces (½ cup) of unsalted butter and cream it; in a leisurely way, stir in the mashed yolks of 8 hard-boiled eggs; when well mixed, add, one by one, the raw yolks of 5 eggs (which must be at room temperature). If the mixture separates meet the emergency with 1 more egg yolk. Season with lemon juice to your liking; add also salt, pepper and a little cayenne. Since egg yolks differ in size, the dressing may be too stiff, in which case you will need to add some more oil; mix another boiled egg yolk into the dressing if it is too runny.—Miss Blanche Lorimer

AN HERB DRESSING (mid-1800s)—For this you will need powdered tarragon, basil, spearmint, parsley and celery leaves in the quantity of 1 saltspoon (¼ teaspoon) of each; blend them well. Mince and mash 1 anchovy and rub it into 1 teaspoon of mustard (French); now add the yolk of a 10-minute egg; stir; add the yolk of an uncooked egg; stir; drip in, as you stir, ¼ cup of olive oil, 1 tablespoon of sweet cider, 1 ditto of lemon juice. When this is ready, blend in the herbs and let the dressing stand to steep in a cool place before you use it. Very good for a party dressing, but it becomes too savory if kept too long.*

"CREAM" DRESSING FOR VEGETABLE SALADS—Two raw eggs, 1 tablespoon of butter, 8 tablespoons of vinegar, ½ teaspoon of mustard; put these in a bowl over boiling water and stir until the mixture becomes like cream; pepper and salt to your taste. Serve hot. Nice with hot sliced potatoes.—Mrs. Hoge

ONE FOR ALL SALAD DRESSING—Take the yolks of 2 raw eggs; beat with them 1 teaspoon of made-mustard; this mustard should be mixed with water, not vinegar; then add to this, drop by drop, olive oil, stirring constantly until the mixture becomes very thick; then add 2 teaspoons of powdered sugar and a scant one of salt; mix thoroughly; squeeze in the juice of 1 lemon; beat well, and if too thick, thin with a little sweet cream. If preferred, omit the lemon and cream and use vinegar. This dressing fits any purpose and all salad occasions. If it is needed for chicken salad, the yolks of hard-boiled eggs added make it richer. Garnish lettuce salad with nasturtium blossoms and sliced lemon. Garnish potato salad with cold boiled beets, chopped parsley and sliced lemon.—Mrs. Oliver Perry

14. *Game from Soil, Stream and Sky*

POT ROAST OF BEAR (early 1800s)—Have ready, peeled and chopped, 1 large potato, 1 large onion, 1 medium turnip, 2 carrots, 2 roots of celery and a kettle of boiling soup stock or water. Place the bear joint—haunch is best—well floured in a large pot which contains 1 gill (½ cup) of hot salt pork drippings from which the meat has been removed; after the bear has been browned on all sides, add boiling soup or water so that it stands about one third the way up the roast; add the vegetables, as well as 1 medium bay leaf, a few whole juniper berries and 1 saltspoon (¼ teaspoon) of mortared (powdered) marjoram. If you have some left-over meat gravy, add ½ pint (1 cup) of that. Let the meat cook, well covered, for 3 to 4 hours until done, always simmering, never boiling; by the time the meat is cooked the vegetable mush should have thickened the pot-gravy so that no other thickening is necessary. During cooking, add boiling water as required. Thick slices of toast help to scoop this up and down.*

TO TENDERIZE TOUGH GAME MEAT (mid-1800s)—Even the toughest cuts of the game meat will respond to a carbonate of soda treatment. Cut the meat, the day before using, into slices; rub them over with a small quantity of soda, wash it off next morning and cook the meat to notion. This same process will answer for tough fowl, leg of mutton, beef, etc.***

TO ROAST VENISON THE VERMONT WAY—Wash a saddle of venison thoroughly in several waters, then rub it over with vinegar, red pepper and a little salt; lard with strips of salt pork rolled in seasoned bread crumbs; season, if you like, with sweet marjoram and sweet basil, 1 teaspoon of each, also pepper; then rub the whole over with currant jelly and pour over it 1 bottle of claret wine. Let it stand over night, and next morning cover the venison with a paste made of flour and water ½ inch thick; then cover with soft paper and secure well with strings; place it in the dripping pan with some claret, butter and water and baste very often; ½ hour before you take it up, remove the paste and paper, baste it with butter and dredge it with flour to make it brown.

For the sauce take 1½ pounds of scraps of venison, with 3 pints (6 cups) of water, a few cloves, a few blades of mace, ½ nutmeg, and salt and cayenne pepper to taste; boil it down to a pint (2 cups); skim off the fat and strain; add ½ pint (1 cup) of currant jelly, 1 pint of claret and ¼ pound (½ cup) of butter divided into bits and rolled in ¼ pound (1 cup) of flour. —Mrs. Porter

CORNED VENISON HASHES (mid-1800s)—These may be prepared in the same manner as Beef Hashes (see Index); however, because of the dryness of the meat it is well to add ½ gill (¼ cup) of minced salt pork for each 2 gills (1 cup) of chopped venison.*

BROILED VENISON CHOPS WITH OYSTERS (late 1800s)—Place unseasoned venison chops, cut about 1½ inches thick and rubbed with sweet oil, about 3 inches beneath a hot broiler flame and broil 8 to 12 minutes or until brown. Season with a small sprinkling of cayenne and caraway seeds and rub with ½ juicy onion. Turn, broil the other side and repeat the seasoning. Scald as many oysters as you may need in their own liquor; shift the chops to a suitable baking pan, pour the oysters over them and distribute small pieces of butter evenly over the surface; let the pan stand in the oven just long enough to allow the oysters to curl around the edges; remove from the oven. Serve with a Caper Butter Sauce (see Index).*

VENISON STEAKS AND CHOPS— To fry them, follow the procedure set for Lamb and Mutton Steaks (see Index).

CURRIED SALMI OF VENISON (mid-1800s)—Cook enough rice (see Index) to suit your needs. Strip the meat from the remains of roasted venison; break the bones, cover them with cold water and bring it to a slow boil. As this cooks, brown ½ gill (¼ cup) of chopped onions slowly in 3 tablespoons of butter in a large saucepan; trim the meat and cut enough of it into small pieces until they fill a pint (2-cup) measure; cook the meat with the onions 15 minutes very, very slowly and stir often; run 1½ pints (3 cups) of the bone broth through a hair-sieve and stir it into the meat; season with salt, pepper and minced stalks of celery; thicken slightly with ½ gill (¼ cup) of flour made smooth in a similar amount of cold water; stir into this gravy 2 to 3 teaspoons of curry powder, depending on your taste; cook 30 minutes; serve in a ring of rice.*

BOILED VENISON LIVER (early 1800s)—Pour boiling water over sliced liver twice within a few minutes. The thinner the slices, the better the dish. Sprinkle them with flour, salt and pepper; fry quickly in drippings to a nice brown on each side; cover with hot milk and let them cook slowly 45 minutes, closely covered. Meanwhile, slice 1 gill (½ cup) of onions for each serving and fry them in butter; when they brown add the liver, season with a pinch of marjoram, cover and cook 15 to 20 minutes. Make a Cream Sauce by melting a butter ball of 2 tablespoons each of butter and flour, well blended, and use it to thicken ½ pint (1 cup) of the milk in which the liver was cooked; this milk should be put through a hair-sieve first. Pour the sauce over the liver; let all cook slowly for 10 to 15 minutes. Remove from the fire, add 1 teaspoon of lemon juice, correct the seasoning to taste and serve.*

CORNED VENISON (early 1800s)—Bone a 4-pound shoulder of venison; do not truss it, but remove what fat there may be. Boil 1 gallon (16 cups) of water and with it 1½ gills (¾ cup) of brown sugar, 1 quart (4 cups) of rock salt, 2 tablespoons each of baking soda and cream of tartar, 1 teaspoon each of allspice and caraway seeds. Let this cool in a stone crock; immerse the meat, which should be well covered by the liquid; place a scoured board atop the meat to keep it down; to insure that, put a scrubbed brick or stone upon the board; cover the jar with a piece of muslin. After a fortnight, the venison should be well corned. Truss the meat neatly (see Index) and place it in cold water to cover, after washing it carefully in cold water; add 2 coarsely chopped onions and 1 laurel (bay) leaf, 4 peppercorns, 4 cloves and 1 gill (½ cup) of cider vinegar or other good vinegar. For a 4-pound shoulder figure the cooking time at about 1½ hours; allow an extra ½ hour of cooling time, in the liquid, after the meat is removed from the fire. It is quite common to add corned beef vegetables, such as carrots, potatoes, turnips and cabbage, during the last ½ hour of cooking.*

RABBIT POT ROAST (mid-1800s)—Skin, gut, wash and disjoint the rabbit; rub the pieces with pepper and dredge heavily in flour; have ½ gill (¼ cup) of freshly tried salt pork fat hot in a kettle or pot with a close-fitting lid; let the meat pieces brown in this, then add 1½ gills (¾ cup) of boiling soup stock or water, which should be replenished as it steams away during 1½ hours of very slow cooking. Pour what liquid remains into a ½-pint measure and add enough milk to fill the measure. Heat this, and stir in 2 tablespoons of flour rubbed into a paste in ½ gill (¼ cup) of cold milk or water. Put the rabbit into this and let the dish cook slowly for 15 minutes, stirring frequently.*

BRUNSWICK STEW (late 1800s)—After 2 or 3 squirrels have been made kitchen-ready, cut them into sections; drop the meat into a stew-pot with ½ pint (1 cup) each of beans—lima are best—kernels of corn, chopped onions and quartered carrots; cover with soup stock or boiling water; skim as it comes to a boil; reduce to simmering and skim as long as needed. After 1 hour of this add 3 quartered potatoes and 3 skinned and chopped tomatoes; season as required with salt, pepper, a touch of rosemary and 3 juniper berries. Let it simmer 30 to 45 minutes longer. It is usual to thicken this stew with bread crumbs that have been sautéed in butter; figure on about 1½ gills (¾ cup) of soft white crust-free crumbs and 1 gill (½ cup) of fresh (unsalted) butter. Use a few more crumbs if, at the last minute, you wish to add 1 gill (½ cup) of heated sherry.*

TO PRESERVE DEAD GAME FOWL (mid-1800s)—Remove the feathers and intestines, fill the insides with unground wheat and place the fowl in a cask or heap of the same grain in such a manner as to be completely covered. Another method is to rub the interior with powdered charcoal and a little salt. Any kind of game will keep better in hot weather if the meat is laid in an earthen jar, sprinkled with charcoal and covered with netting to admit air and keep out flies.**

PIE OF GAME BIRDS (mid-1800s)—Remove the skin, bone and gristle from disjointed land birds and measure the quantity. For each pint (2 cups) of meat, have ½ pint (1 cup) each chopped carrots, mushrooms and onions cooked but not fried in butter; make a thick Cream Sauce (see Index) and pour this, with all other ingredients, into a large greased pie pan; cover this with a top crust of plain paste (see Index), which should be perforated for escaping vapors; bake in a moderate (350°F.) oven for 1½ hours.*

CORNED GAME BIRDS (early 1800s)—All land fowls will do for this dish; in fact, a mixed bag of fairly large birds strikes a welcome note. Disjoint the birds; make a brine of 1 pint (2 cups) each of cold water, vinegar, salt; add ½ pint (1 cup) each of brown sugar and chopped onions, 6 black peppercorns, 6 cloves and 1 small grated nutmeg. If this brine does not cover the birds after you lay them in a clean crock, make more in the same proportions. Cover with a platter turned upside down and let it stand 10 to 12 days in a cool cellar; cover the crock with a piece of muslin. When the corning is done, wash the pieces thoroughly in cold water and make a Pie of Game Birds (see above).***

ROASTED REDHEAD (mid-1800s)—Take cleaned and gutted redheads; rub them with salt, pepper and butter inside and out; truss the wings and legs close to the body and cut off the head at the base of the neck. If the ducks are suspected of being feeders on fish, the placing of a piece of apple or part of an onion in the body cavity is recommended. Roast in a very hot (425–50°F.) oven from 15 to 20 minutes and baste with hot unsalted water at 5-minute intervals.*

TO ROAST BLUEBILLS, MALLARDS, BUTTERBILLS AND OTHER MEMBERS OF DUCK FAMILY—Follow the procedure set for Roasted Redhead (see above).

SALMI OF WILD DUCK— (early 1800s)—First, partly roast the duck; cut it into joints and slices. Put the refuse bits of fat, bone and skin into a saucepan with ¾ pint (1½ cups) of gravy; add 2 onions fried in butter, pepper and salt to taste, a pinch of cloves and nutmeg and parsley, marjoram and sage chopped fine. Boil 1 hour; skim when cool, strain and return to the fire with a piece of butter the size of a walnut (1½ teaspoons); thicken with Browned Flour (see Index); let it boil a few minutes; add the pieces of duck, after which the saucepan should be placed over a pan of boiling water. Fry some bread in some of the duck fat; cut it into squares; lay the toast on a hot dish; lay the duck neatly upon them and pour the gravy over all.*

WHAT TO DO WITH PARTRIDGE (early 1800s)—If the birds seem to be young and tender, split them open at the back and broil them whole; but if not young, use only the breasts for broiling and reserve the remainder for stew or to help toward making that best of all hash dishes, a Game Pie (see Index). Use as little water as possible in cleansing game; many use none at all, thinking that by the use of water the blood—and consequently the flavor —is washed away and the meat is left dry and tasteless. Dip the portions to be broiled in melted butter and broil over a steady fire of live coals, turning and basting with hot butter twice during the cooking. Be careful not to cook them overdone. Place the birds on a hot platter; sprinkle a little pepper and salt and pour melted butter over each; then strew them lightly with chopped parsley and place a slice of lemon on each breast. Serve with toast and Currant Jelly (see Index). For breakfast, Fried Mush (see Index) may take the place of toast.*

BOILED PARTRIDGES (early 1800s)—Put the birds in a floured pudding cloth into boiling water but, of course, clean and gut them first; simmer them for 45 minutes or a little longer. For sauce, rub a small piece of butter into a little flour and boil in a teacup (¾ cup) of cream. Add cut parsley if so desired.**

PHEASANTS BAKED WITH HAM (late 1800s)—In a skillet with as much boiling butter as needed sauté breasts of pheasants that have been coated with whipping cream and seasoned with salt, white pepper and powdered sage; next, place the breasts in a greased baking dish to bake for 45 minutes in a moderate (350°F.) oven; baste with melted butter at brief intervals. When the birds are ready, broil as many thin slices of ham as you have servings; place the breasts on these slices and have ready, in a double boiler, Sauce for Baked Game Birds (see Index).*

PIGEONS, WILD OR DOMESTIC—These can be cooked in identical ways as there is, from the cook's point of view, little if any difference between the two kinds.

WILD PIGEONS, TO PREPARE (early 1800s)—Skin the birds to avoid the troublesome pinfeathers. Examine the inside very carefully, especially the liver, to make sure the birds were healthy. Soak them 30 minutes in a good deal of water to take out the blood. Truss and boil them with a little salt for another ½ hour and take off the scum as it rises. Take them out, season and flour them well; lay them into a dripping pan; strain the water in which they were boiled and put part of it into the pan; stir in a little piece of butter and baste the pigeons often; add sweet marjoram to the basting juice if you prefer. Let the birds roast in a not too hot oven (350°F.) for about 1½ hours. Check for doneness; pigeons need to be cooked a long time.*

WILD PIGEON PIE (mid-1800s)—Pick, soak and truss pigeons with the same care as that directed in the receipt for roasting them (see Wild Pigeons, To Prepare, above) and let them simmer in clean water for 30 minutes. Make a crust just as for Chicken or Meat Pie (see Index). Season the birds by rubbing them with pepper, salt, shavings of butter and sweet marjoram; flour them thickly; strain in the water in which they were boiled and fill the dish two-thirds with it. Lay the top crust over, close the edges well and make many pricks in it with the prongs of a kitchen fork; bake in a more than moderate (375°F.) oven for 1½ to 2 hours.*

STUFFED ROASTED WILD PIGEONS (mid-1800s)—Boil and mince the livers and hearts of 6 pigeons. In the boiling liquid soak 2 cups of bread crumbs; mince a small onion and 1 teaspoon of tender white celery; beat 2 eggs; season them highly with pepper and salt; melt ¼ pound (½ cup) of butter. Squeeze the crumbs dry with your hands and fluff them into the bowl with a fork; add the melted butter and beat; mix the remaining ingredients into the eggs and stir the whole into the bread-butter mixture; knead thoroughly. Before you stuff the birds, rub the inside with salt and slices of lemon. After stuffing, close the aperture with needle and thread; truss (see Index). Wrap the birds in slices of bacon that have been parboiled to reduce the salty bacon taste. Roast about 90 minutes in a slow (300–25°F.) oven. Baste with bacon drippings.*

WHAT TO DO WITH QUAIL (early 1800s)—First of all, pluck them carefully so as not to break the skin; split each one down the back and rub well with melted or soft butter; then broil over a bed of live coals (charcoal will do) and baste twice with butter while cooking. As soon as they are done, lay each bird on a slice of buttered toast, sprinkle with pepper and salt, put 1 tablespoon of melted butter and 1 teaspoon of currant jelly on each bird and serve immediately.*

TO BROIL WOODCOCK AND OTHER SMALL BIRDS (early 1800s)—Pull off the skin, split them down the back, pepper the breasts and lay them, insides down, upon the greased gridiron with a small bit of pork skewered upon each one with a pin or needle. Turn them 3 times at 7-minute intervals. The total broiling time is about 20 minutes.*

PIES OF WOODCOCK, QUAIL AND OTHER SMALL BIRDS (early 1800s)—Follow the directions for Barn Pigeon Pie (see Index).

PARTRIDGES AND QUAIL— Clean the birds nicely, using a little soda in the water in which they are washed; rinse and dry them, and then fill them with Cape Cod Stuffing for Game Birds (see below), sewing them up nicely and binding down the legs and wings with cords. Put them in a steamer over hot water and let them cook until just done. Then place them in a pan with a little butter; set them in a very hot (450°F.) oven and baste them frequently with melted butter until of a nice brown. They ought to brown nicely in about 15 minutes. Serve them on a platter, with sprigs of parsley alternating with currant jelly.—Miss Sarah Page

QUAIL ON TOAST—After the birds are nicely cleaned, cut them open down the back; salt and pepper them, and dredge with flour. Break down the breastbones and backbones, so that they will lie flat, and place them in a pan with a very little water and butter in a hot (400°F.) oven, covering them up tightly until nearly done. Then place them in a spider in hot butter and fry them a moment to a nice brown. Have ready slices of baker's bread toasted and slightly buttered upon a platter. The toast should be broken down with a carving knife, so that it will be tender. On this place the quails; make a sauce of the gravy in the pan, thicken lightly with Browned Flour (see Index), and pour it over each quail and the toast.—Anon.

CAPE COD STUFFING FOR GAME BIRDS (mid-1800s)—Chop enough cranberries in a bowl to make 1 pint (2 cups); add 1 gill (½ cup) of minced celery stalks, including the tops, and ½ gill (¼ cup) each of chopped onions and parsley leaves. In a saucepan heat ½ gill (¼ cup) of nice drippings and add the items just listed; cover and, when they are half way done, add ½ gill (¼ cup) of light-brown sugar, maple syrup or molasses; stir well and allow it to cook slowly under a cover. Meanwhile, cut the crusts from enough bread slices to measure 1½ pints (3 cups) of coarse crumbs; soak the crusts in hot water; when they are soft, wring them dry in a cloth, stir them with a fork and add them to the crumbs; stir ½ gill (¼ cup) of minced sour and sweet pickle into the crumbs; add all to the stuff in the saucepan, stir thoroughly and season to taste.*

GAME BIRD DRESSING (mid-1800s)—Make 1½-inch cubes of salt pork and dredge them in powdered sage for roast pheasant, partridge and other land-birds, oregano for ducks and other waterfowl. Stuff into cavities. Remove and discard the dressing before serving.*

STEWED TROUT (early 1800s)—Take 2 middling-large trout, clean and dry them. Lay them in a stew-pan with 1 pint (2 cups) of soup stock—Brown or White or Chicken—(see Index) and 1 glass (½ cup) of port wine, ½ small onion sliced thin, a little pounded thyme and pounded dried parsley, 2 cloves, 1 blade of mace, 1 laurel (bay) leaf, ½ teaspoon of salt and ¼ teaspoon of pepper. Let this simmer gently for ½ hour, or rather a little longer until done. Take the fish out, strain the gravy and thicken it with 2½ tablespoons of butter. When it is done, pour the gravy over the trout and take them to table.*

BROOK TROUT (early 1800s)—If they are small, dip them in (corn) meal and fry them with salt pork; if they are large, stew them and serve with Drawn Butter (see Index).*

TROUT FRIED IN DEEP FAT (mid-1800s)—Make the fish ready for the range but leave their heads on. Rub each fish with lemon inside and with salt and pepper outside; dip it into Onion Deep Fry Batter (see Index) and have the fat at a heat that will tan a 1-inch bread cube in 60 seconds (365–70°F.); the frying-time is usually about 8 minutes, take or leave 60 seconds.*

BOILED TROUT (early 1800s)—Trout too large and old for frying are very appetizing when cooked in the following style. Put 2 tablespoons of vinegar into enough boiling water to cover the fish; add 1 teaspoon of salt and boil the fish gently for 20 minutes or until it is tender. It helps to lay 1 or 2 sprigs of parsley with 1 or 2 very thin slices of lemon inside the fish to improve the flavor and texture while it is cooking. Serve with a Caper Sauce (see Index).*

BROILED BASS FILLETS (late 1800s)—Cut the fish into serving pieces and marinate them in warm melted butter seasoned with pepper, salt and lemon juice for 5 minutes; place them, dripping with butter, under a broiler; broil a side for 5 minutes; turn with a spatula; baste with butter and broil the other side for 5 minutes. Serve with Wine Fish Sauce (see Index).*

BAKED SALMON (late 1800s)—Clean the salmon and dip it briefly in very hot water to aid the removal of scales with the back of a knife; set the fish aside in a cool place while you make the following:

FISH STUFFING—Wet ½ pint (1 cup) of soft bread crumbs with ½ gill (¼ cup) of milk or soup stock; sauté 3 slices of bacon; when it is done, re- move the bacon and break it into bits; sauté 1 thinly sliced and minced onion in 2 dessertspoons (4 teaspoons) of butter; chop 1 hard-cooked egg; mince 1 dessertspoon (2 teaspoons) each of minced celery and parsley; blend all of these ingredients into a dough; season it with salt, pepper and 1 table- spoon of lemon juice. Place into the fish and skewer or sew it carefully.

Rub the fish with oil or butter, season with salt and pepper and place it in a hot (400°F.) oven, allowing 8 minutes per pound up to 3 pounds and 5 minutes per pound beyond that. Serve with Hollandaise Sauce (see Index).*

BROILED SALMON STEAKS (late 1800s)—Cut uncooked salmon into 1½-inch slices and place them in a marinade of ½ gill (¼ cup) each of vinegar and salad oil seasoned with a large pinch of rosemary and 2 teaspoons of minced parsley; stir the marinade frequently and spoon it over the salmon steaks almost constantly for 5 to 10 minutes. Place the fish within a few inches of the broiler flame; baste with marinade; turn it after 7 minutes and repeat the basting for 7 minutes. Serve with Parsley Butter Sauce (see Index).*

FROGS' LEGS, STEWED OR FRIED (late 1800s)—The gaslight era was drawing to a close before such foreign ideas as eating frogs' legs took hold in New England, this despite the fact that the ponds of Yankeeland had heavy populations of fat and sassy croakers which would seem to invite culi- nary attention. Actually, it was not until continental cookery gained a firm footing in cities along our North Atlantic coast that frogs' legs leaped upon local menus.

Stewed: Skin the legs, cut off the toes and place the legs in salted cold water. For 6 legs, make a sauce of 2 tablespoons each of butter and flour thickened with 1 cup of water which has been seasoned with the juice of ½ lemon, the grated peel thereof and a little nutmeg. Let the legs stew in this until tender. Then add ½ cup of cream, stir and serve.*

Fried: Scald the skinned and trimmed legs in boiling milk quite briefly; dry them; soak them in a bath of lemon juice seasoned with salt and pepper for 30 minutes. Prepare beaten egg and bread crumbs; dip each leg twice in these mixtures and fry to a golden brown in butter over a slow fire.*

SWEET SAUCE FOR VENISON (pre-1800s)—Open a tumbler of currant jelly into a saucepan; fill the now empty tumbler with port wine; add this to the jelly and heat slowly with a small piece of cinnamon bark (1 stick). Heat it; do not boil it.*

BREAD SAUCE FOR GAME (mid-1800s)—Heat 1 quart (4 cups) of milk over a low fire and cook therein 6 cloves, 2 peppercorns, ½ teaspoon of nutmeg, 1 saltspoon (¼ teaspoon) of salt and a small peeled onion cut into halves. When the milk is scalded, remove it from fire and place over steam to continue cooking. At serving time, strain the milk and thicken it with white bread crumbs from freshly made bread until the sauce has the consistency of thin porridge. Blend in ¼ cup of butter and season lightly with 1 teaspoon of minced parsley.*

SAUCE FOR BAKED GAME BIRDS (late 1800s)—Make a soup by boiling crushed bird bones and giblets (gizzards, hearts, livers) plus trimmings in 1 pint (2 cups) of cold water. When the soup is good and strong, let it boil down to ½ pint (1 cup) and pour it through a strainer. In the top of a double boiler blend 2 tablespoons of wheat flour into the same amount of melted butter; when this is done, stir the soup into it; when it is thick, add 4 tablespoons of cream and stir until hot; then add 6 tablespoons of heavy cream whipped to a froth; season with white pepper, a saltspoon (¼ teaspoon) of pounded and sifted bay leaf, 1 of powdered basil or marjoram and 1 of onion juice. Stir until smooth and thick; if not thick enough, stir the yolk of 1 egg into the sauce.*

VENISON JELLY AND WINE SAUCE (late 1800s)—Make a thick Cream Sauce (see Index); cook 4 tablespoons of minced mushroom caps in 2 tablespoons of butter; when it is done, add the Cream Sauce, a wineglass (¼ cup) each of currant jelly and port wine and 1 gill (½ cup) of pitted grapes, preferably Concord. Season lightly with salt; use no pepper; if desired, a pinch of ginger or nutmeg will make the sauce more piquant.*

VENISON SAUCE (early 1800s)—This fits all roasted, fried or broiled venison dishes. Mix equal amounts of melted butter, parsley and Apple Sauce and heat slowly on the stove; season with pepper and salt and pulverized cinnamon. Pour 1 tablespoon of lemon juice into a sauce boat and stir well as you pour the sauce in.*

CURRANT JELLY GAME SAUCE (mid-1800s)—Make a Brown Sauce by browning 3 tablespoons of flour in 2 tablespoons of butter. Thin this batter with ½ pint (1 cup) of soup stock; add 1 saltspoon (¼ teaspoon) of onion juice, 1 dessertspoon (2 teaspoons) of lemon juice and 1 gill (½ cup) of currant jelly. Let it simmer 10 minutes and serve very hot.*

15. Breads, Quick Breads and Others

TO BUILD AND OPERATE BAKE-OVEN (mid-1800s)—For a family of medium size, an oven holding 10 to 12 plates is large enough. After the first tier of bricks, which form the arch (see Index), is laid, 3 bushels of ashes with dead coals in them should be laid over the bricks. Then the usual brickwork should be laid over these ashes. The advantage of this is, when the oven is heated, these ashes and coals are heated also, and, being so thick, they retain the heat a long time. Five successive bakings have been done in such an oven with one heating; the bread first, then the puddings, afterward pies and other pastry, then cake and gingerbread and, lastly, custards, which, if made with boiled milk and put into the hot oven and allowed to stand a considerable time, will bake sufficiently with a very slight heat.***

WHAT LADIES SHOULD KNOW ABOUT STARTING NEW OVENS (early 1800s)—The first time an oven is heated, a large fire should be kept burning in it 6 to 8 hours. Unless this is done, it will never bake well. The sizes and structures of ovens are so different that no precise rules for heating can be given. A lady should attend to this herself until she perfectly understands what is necessary. It is easy to find out how many sticks of a given size are necessary for baking articles that require a strong heat, and also for those which are baked with less heat. To bake brown bread, beans, apples and other things, all at one time, the oven should be heated with hardwood, and if the fire is rather large, so as to be 2 hours in burning out, so much the better. To make thin cakes and most kinds of puddings, pine wood, split small, answers very well.***

TENDING THE BAKE-OVEN FIRE (early 1800s)—After the wood is half burnt, stir the fire equally to all parts of the oven to get an equal diffusion of the heat. Do it several times before the oven is cleared. If the oven is to be very full, put in a brick or two at the half-way mark, so that they will be hot enough to set pans or plates upon, if there is not room on the oven floor itself. When you empty the oven of the remnants of the fire, be sure no windows or doors are open near it to reduce the oven's heat. Let the coals remain in it until they are no longer red; however, they should not look dead on removal, but like hot embers. When you take them out, leave a few in the oven's back part so that things like beans and Indian Pudding, which require the most heat, can be placed near them.***

TESTING THE OVEN WITH FLOUR (mid-1800s)—Women no longer actually need to scorch their hands by sticking them into their ovens to determine the heat. The new way is just as good and less painful. Before putting in the things to be baked, throw in a little flour. If it browns instantly, the oven is too hot; let it stand open 3 to 4 minutes. If the flour browns without burning in the course of 30 seconds, it will be safe to set in the articles immediately.*

THE SUREST WAY TO GOOD BREAD (early 1800s)—Bread is the one thing on which a family depends for health and strength. With good bread, the coarsest fare is tolerable; without it, the most luxurious table has nothing to offer. For good bread, one must first of all avoid bad flour; to do this buy wheat in the grain so that you can wash and dry it—2 or 3 bushels at a time. Use several pails of cold well water till the water is clear; work quickly and never let the grain stand in the water, because that causes it to swell; spread it on a large cloth in the sun, or where it will have warmth and fresh air; stir it often; in a day or two it will be dry and can be taken to the mill for grinding. The flour is much improved by this process.***

HOW TO MAKE BREAD SPONGE (mid-1800s)—Making bread without a proper sponge is much like shaping bricks without straws. It is the sponge that makes the bread rise, light and fluffy. When you assemble the ingredients for your bread, set aside the yeast and one-half each of the liquid and flour to be used. Put these together and set the resulting dough or sponge in a bowl under a cloth in a comfortably warm place in cool weather, in a cool place in warm seasons. No matter what anybody says, it is best to set the sponge at night; then the bread will be ready for baking in the morning; this prevents bread-making from becoming a burden that hangs over a housewife's head the entire day like a dark and unwelcome cloud.**

HOME-MADE SIX-DAY YEAST (early 1800s)—Monday: Boil 2 ounces of hops in 4 quarts of water for 30 minutes. Strain it into an earthen bowl and let the liquor cool down to the warmth of new milk; then put in a small handful of salt, ½ pound of brown sugar; beat up 1 pound of flour with some of the liquor, and then mix it all well together. Set it aside in a warm place and let it stand, but stir frequently, until Wednesday, at which time you add 3 pounds of boiled and well-mashed potatoes; keep it in a warm place and stir often. On Thursday strain, bottle and cork. On Saturday the yeast can be used. Before using, always shake the bottle well. This yeast will keep in a cool place for many weeks and is better for keeping.***

THE ART OF KNEADING BREAD (early 1800s)—No bread is better than it is kneaded and no dough can be kneaded too much. In order to knead properly, flour the hands and, folding the fingers over the thumb, make a fist; beat and pummel the dough on every side; work until it ceases to stick to your hands. In cold weather, bread should be kneaded in a warm room; nor should the dough be allowed to become cold or chilled while rising. If dough does not rise well, set the pan over a bucket of boiling water. Two major steps in bread baking are: make it up in loaves when dough is honeycombed all through, and the loaves should go into the oven when the impression of a finger upon the dough leaves no permanent trace.*

BAKING BREAD IN FLOWER POTS (mid-1800s)—The best oven for bak-baking bread is the old brick bake-oven with its saturation heat, but good bread can be made in iron ovens if care be taken in the operation. Here ladies may take a leaf out of the books of Italian peasants, who bake their loaves in rough earthen bowls made of material identical with that we use for flower pots. Now, if the dough be placed in a larded flower pot, instead of a bread pan, of the size preferred, and the bread baked in an iron oven, it will bake quite as well as in a brick oven, because the heat will be graduated in the same way. The right heat of an oven for bread-baking can be ascertained thus: the oven is not too hot (400°F.) if the hand can be held in it whilst counting to 20.***

ON REMOVING BREAD FROM OVEN (mid-1800s)—Scrape off burnt or brown spots with a nutmeg grater; place the bread on its side to cool; to preserve freshness, wrap loaves in clean brown paper, but never use cloth —it imparts a musty taste.**

HOW TO HAVE FRESH BREAD DAILY (mid-1800s)—In the winter, dough for bread and rolls may be kept sweet many days in a cool place where it will not freeze. It should be raised light and kneaded a little, then covered with a damp cloth, so that a dry crust will not form. Fresh bread can thus be served every day without extra work. The dough should be made at least in part with milk when used for this purpose.*

COUNTRY BREAD—Take 4 quarts (16 cups) of sifted flour, 1 cake of yeast, a pinch of salt, and wet this with warm milk and water until stiff enough to knead. Work it on the board until it requires no more flour. If made at night the bread will be light enough to work over and put in pans early in the morning. This quantity will make 3 large loaves. One-third of the lump may be taken for rolls, which can be made by working in a piece of butter the size of an egg (4 tablespoons) and setting it aside to rise again. When the dough is light the second time make it out in oblong shapes; cover them with a cloth and let them rise again. As soon as they break apart bake in a quick oven; they will not fail to be nice if they are baked as soon as they seam; this is the great secret of white, flaky rolls. Two or 3 potatoes will improve the bread. Good housekeepers always have flour sifted in readiness for use, and never use it in any other way.—Mrs. E. S. Chesebrough

EXCELLENT BREAD—Four potatoes mashed fine, 4 teaspoons of salt, 2 quarts (8 cups) of lukewarm milk, ½ cake of compressed yeast dissolved in ½ cup of warm water, flour enough to make a pliable dough. Knead well and mold it with hands well greased with lard; place in pans; and when sufficiently light it is ready for baking from 45 to 60 minutes in a moderate (375°F.) oven.—Mrs. George W. Pitkin

WHEAT BREAD—Take a pan of flour and put in a small handful of salt and a bowl of soft yeast and 1 pint (2 cups) of lukewarm milk; mix it stiff with flour and let it rise. Then knead it into pans and let it rise; if wanted very white, knead it down 2 or 3 times. Warning: while this makes the bread whiter, it also makes it lose its sweet taste. Bake 45 minutes in a good moderate (350–75°F.) oven.—Mrs. D. W. Thatcher

MILK BREAD (late 1800s)—Place 1 tablespoon each of lard, sugar and butter with 1½ teaspoons of salt in a bowl and add 1 pint (2 cups) of scalded milk; dissolve 1 gill (½ cup) of yeast (or use ½ yeast cake dissolved in ¼ cup of tepid water). Hold the yeast separate until the milk has cooled to lukewarm; then add it and combine with 1½ quarts (6 cups) of flour very gradually; knead thoroughly and let it rise in a warm corner of the kitchen until it has risen to twice its size; knead again; form loaves; set aside in bread pans until the loaves have risen to twice their size. Bake in a hot (400°F.) oven for 1 hour. This dough keeps very well (see Index for How to Have Fresh Bread Daily). If used for biscuits, use only 1¼ quarts (5 cups) of flour and beat the dough for ¼ hour without kneading it. Let it rise, shape biscuits and bake them for about ½ hour or less in a hot (400°F.) oven.*

MILK AND WATER BREAD (late 1800s)—Made in the same proportions as Milk Bread (see above), except instead of using 1 pint (2 cups) of scalded milk, use ½ pint (1 cup) each of scalded milk and hot water. Bake as you would Milk Bread. This dough keeps especially well for daily use.*

SALT-RISING BREAD (mid-1800s)—Scald ½ pint (1 cup) of good milk and add 1½ teaspoons each of sugar and salt; incorporate in this ½ pint (1 cup) of flour; beat it with an egg beater for 10 or 15 minutes. Set aside covered with cheesecloth in warm spot. Do this at night after the dishes are done. Early the next morning, beat this dough again and add 1 pint (2 cups) of flour, very gradually to prevent lumps from forming, and ½ pint (1 cup) of scalded milk that has cooled; set aside, again covered, to rise. When the dough is light, add just enough whole wheat flour to enable you to give it a good kneading; make loaves to fit your well-greased pans, in which you place them; let them rise until light, but not too much, since the dough sours easily; bake in a more than moderate (375°F.) oven for 40 to 45 minutes.*

RICE BREAD—Boil ½ pint (1 cup) of rice quite soft; while hot, add a piece of butter the size of an egg (4 tablespoons), 1½ pints (3 cups) of milk and rather more than ½ pint (1 cup) of bolted cornmeal; add 2 tablespoons of flour, 2 beaten eggs and a little salt. Bake just 1 hour in a moderate (350°F.) oven. The bread should be about 2 inches thick.—Mrs. E. S. Chesebrough

CORN AND RYE BREAD (mid-1800s)—Take a pint (2 cups) of rye meal, and the same of fine Indian (corn) meal. If the latter is bitter, scald it before mixing with the rye. Mix with ½ pint (1 cup) each of molasses and warm water, a teaspoon of saleratus (baking soda) melted in a little boiling water, 1 ditto of salt and 2 tablespoons of yeast; add 1 gill (½ cup) of boiled pumpkin or winter squash. The dough, though stiff, should be easily stirred. Grease a deep, brown pan thickly and put the bread in it; dip your hand in water to smooth over the top. This will rise faster than other bread and should not be made over night in the summer. If put into an oven when it is moderately hot (350°F.) the bread will bake in about 1 hour.*

STEAMED BROWN BREAD—Scald 2 quarts (8 cups) of Indian meal;

when sufficiently cool add 2 quarts (8 cups) of rye meal, ½ cup each of yeast and molasses; add warm water, and stir as hard as you can with a spoon; set it down to rise; when it is light, stir well; put in pans to rise a second time. Steam it 1 hour and let it bake from ½ hour to 1 hour in a slow (300°F.) oven.—Mrs. J. M. Durand (For a description of how to steam bread, see Steamed Brown Bread below.)

BAKED BROWN BREAD—Two cups of Graham flour, 1 of wheat flour, 2 large tablespoons of molasses, a little salt, 1 yeast cake or ½ cup of yeast, warm water enough to make a very stiff batter. Put the batter in the bake-tin, and, when it is light enough, bake it in a fast moderate (375°F.) oven ¾ hour.—Mrs. Banks

BOSTON BROWN BREAD—One and one-half cups of Graham flour, 2 cups of cornmeal, ½ cup of molasses, 1 pint (2 cups) of sweet milk and ½ teaspoon of soda; steam 3 hours and put it in a moderate over (350°F.) for 15 minutes. —Mrs. F. E. Sterns (For a description of how to steam bread, see Steamed Brown Bread, below.)

BROWN BREAD TOAST—Cut the bread in slices and toast it. Put it in the dish for the table; take a bowl of thick cream, add a little salt, then pour the cream over the toast; put it in the oven until it heats through.—Anon.

STEAMED BROWN BREAD (early 1800s)—For a very small family, take ½ pint (1 cup) of rye meal, not sifted, and 1 pint (2 cups) of sifted Indian (corn) meal, a pint (2 cups) of sour milk, ½ gill (¼ cup) of dark molasses and 1 teaspoon of salt; mix. Dissolve 1 teaspoon of saleratus (baking soda) in 1 tablespoon of boiling water; add this to the other ingredients and stir. Grease a container having a close lid; having put the bread into it, let it stand, uncovered, for 2 to 3 hours; then cover the container and set it in boiling water. The bread should not quite fill the container; it must have room to swell. See that the water neither boils to the top of the container nor boils away during the 4 hours of cooking. To serve, remove the lid and set the container for a few minutes in the range or Dutch Oven to dry the top; then it will turn out in perfect shape.*

SOUR CREAM SAUCE FOR BROWN BREAD (mid-1800s)—Freshly baked or steamed brown bread can be used as a pudding by those who have sour cream; stir in brown sugar and grated nutmeg to taste.*

CORN MUFFIN LOAF (late 1800s)—Have ready ½ pint (1 cup) each of Indian (corn) meal, cooled scalded milk and flour. Cream ½ gill (¼ cup) of fresh (unsalted) butter; add ½ gill (¼ cup) of sugar and 2 egg yolks that are well whipped; sift the meal and the flour with 2 dessertspoons (4 teaspoons of baking powder and ¾ teaspoon of salt; add these to the butter as well as the milk; follow with the 2 whites of egg, beaten white and stiff. Bake in a buttered loaf tin in a moderate (350°F.) oven for 35 to 40 minutes.

STIR-ABOUT OR HASTY PUDDING (early 1800s)—Real Hasty Pudding experts will give this dish a wide berth unless it is made from water-ground flint corn. To make it takes 1½ gills (¾ cup) of meal and 1 pint (2 cups) of boiling water, well salted. Let the meal flow into the water in a slow and steady stream as you stir, and always stir in a clockwise direction; do not stop stirring for the next ½ hour while the pudding boils and bubbles; it takes a right strong arm to be a real Stir-About Pudding cook. As a breakfast porridge, serve with maple syrup or brown sugar and milk; as a supper dish, serve with a Brown Sugar Sauce (see Index) or Easy Hard Sauce (see Index).***

TO WARM OVER QUICK BREADS (early 1800s)—Place rolls, biscuits, muffins, etc., in a pan after rubbing them lightly with water; place the pan in hot water and put both pans into the oven until the breads are crisp.*

APPLE BREAKFAST ROLLS (late 1800s)—Make a batter of 2 cups of flour mixed with 1 teaspoon of cream of tartar and ½ teaspoon of soda, 1 cup of sweet milk, ½ cup of sugar. Put in 1½ cups of apples, diced small, the last thing. Grease gem pans with lard; place a dab of lard in the bottom of each pan; get the pans sizzling hot on top of the stove; fill them with batter and let them stand a good minute; then put the tins into a hot (400–25°F.) oven and bake quickly about 10 minutes, depending on the oven's heat.*

FRIED RICE ROLLS—Boil 1 cup of rice in 1 quart (4 cups) of milk or water until tender; while warm add a piece of butter the size of an egg (4 tablespoons), 1 yolk and 2 whole eggs; make the mixture into rolls, dip them in cracker crumbs and fry them in lard or butter.—Mrs. C. T. C.

ASTOR HOUSE ROLLS (mid-1800s)—Into 2 quarts (8 cups) of flour cut a piece of butter the size of an egg (4 tablespoons), a little salt, 1 tablespoon of white sugar, 1 pint (2 cups) of scalded milk and add, while still warm, ½ cup or 1 small cake of yeast. When the sponge is light, mold it for 15 minutes; let it rise again; roll out; cut into round cakes; when they are light, flatten them with the hand or rolling pin; place a piece of butter on top of each and fold it over itself; when they are light again, bake in a quick (400°F.) oven about 18 minutes.*

PARKER HOUSE ROLLS—Boil 1 pint (2 cups) of sweet milk and when partly cooled melt in it ½ cup of white sugar and 1 tablespoon of lard or butter; when lukewarm, add 1 yeast cake; make a hole in 2 quarts (8 cups) of flour and pour this mixture in. If the rolls are for tea, set the dough to rise over night; in the morning mix well and knead for ½ hour, then set it to rise again; about 4 o'clock knead again for 10 or 15 minutes; roll out thinner than for biscuit, rub melted butter upon half the surface and fold it upon the other; set to rise once more in pans, and when light slice it and bake 15 minutes in a hot (400°F.) oven—Mrs. L. J. Tilton

ROLLS—Put 1 pint (2 cups) of warm milk in the middle of 2 quarts (8 cups) of flour, beat up a thick batter, a little stiffer than pancakes, and add ½ cake of compressed yeast (½ cup). When this is light knead it up like bread, kneading the dough out in a long roll and folding it over like pie crust; do this 6 or 7 times. When it is again light, add a piece of butter the size of a large egg (5 tablespoons), pulling it through the dough, then work in 2 eggs and 1 tablespoon of sugar that have been beaten together very lightly. Knead again as before. Roll the dough out on your bread board with a rolling pin, cut it with small round or oval cutters, dipping the cutter occasionally in a cup of melted lard or drippings instead of flour, and put in pans to rise. When the dough is creamy light, bake 20 minutes in a moderately quick (375°F.) oven. It expedites the rising to set the pans over hot water.—A. M. G.

BROWN ROLLS—One quart (4 cups) of Graham flour, milk enough to make a stiff batter, 1/3 cake of yeast; mix and let it stand over night; in the morning add 2 eggs, 1 large tablespoon of sugar, ¼ teaspoon of soda, a piece of butter half the size of an egg (2 tablespoons) and a little salt; put in cups and let them stand 20 minutes before baking in a medium (375°F.) oven. —Mrs. Melancthon Starr

CORNMEAL ROLLS—To 1 quart (4 cups) of mush add, when hot, ½ cup of unmelted lard; salt it well; when lukewarm, add ½ cake of yeast; make this at noon, and at night add a small teaspoon of soda and knead in wheat flour as for biscuit. In the morning mold into biscuits and let them rise in the pan before baking. Bake in a quick (400°F) oven for 15 minutes.— Mrs. A. H. Dashiel

TREMONT BISCUITS—One and a half pints (3 cups) of warm milk, 1 tablespoon of lard, 2 tablespoons of white sugar, a little salt, ½ cake of compressed yeast (½ cup), 2 quarts (8 cups) of sifted flour. Make a hole in the flour and mix in all the ingredients except 7 cups of the flour to make a sponge; set in a warm place to rise; when it is quite light, work in the remaining flour and set the dough once more to rise; when well risen, work it a little more, roll out about 1/3 inch thick and cut with the biscuit cutter.

Moisten one edge with melted butter, then fold the biscuits together in the middle like rolls. Place them in a bread pan about 1 inch apart; set to rise for about ½ hour in a warm place, and, when light, bake in a very quick (425°F.) oven, allowing from 10 to 15 minutes if the oven is just right.

Make them up about 10 o'clock in the morning if wanted for tea. If wanted for breakfast, make them up about 9 o'clock in the evening and work in all the flour at the first fixing; then add—as soon as you are up in the morning—½ teaspoon of soda, mold your biscuits and they will be ready for baking when the oven is hot. With compressed yeast, about 6 hours rising is required. These are very delicate and delicious when properly made. —Mrs. O. B. Wilson

GREEN MOUNTAIN BISCUITS—Three cups of milk, 2 cups of sugar, 1 cup of butter; make a stiff batter at night with 2 tablespoons of yeast, ½ the sugar and ½ the butter melted; in the morning add the other half of sugar and butter, and make it not quite as stiff as yeast bread; 2 hours before tea make up the biscuits and set them to rise.—Anon.

RAISED BISCUITS—Take 1½ pints (3 cups) of milk, 1 tablespoon of lard, 2 of white sugar, 1 yeast cake (1 cup) and 2 quarts (8 cups) of flour; make a hole in the flour and put in all the ingredients; set it in a warm place to rise until morning, then mix all together and set to rise again; when it is well risen, roll the dough out rather thin; cut out the biscuits; wet one edge with melted butter and fold the biscuit together like a roll; when well risen, bake in a quick (400°F.) oven about 20 minutes.—Hannah Johnson

BAKING POWDER AND SODA BISCUITS—Sift with 1 quart (4 cups) of flour ½ teaspoon of salt and 3½ heaping teaspoons of baking powder; mix thoroughly through the flour, then add 1 tablespoon of softened shortening and milk as required; stir but do not knead, and bake quickly in a (450°F.) oven for 15 minutes. To use cream of tartar and soda, take the same proportions without the baking powder, using instead 2 heaping teaspoons of cream of tartar and 1 of soda. If good, the latter will bake in 5 minutes.—W. W.

BAKING POWDER BISCUITS (late 1800s)—These can be made twice as toothsome as they usually are by placing small dollops of honey in their centers.*

BAKING POWDER BISCUITS (late 1800s)—Put ½ pint (1 cup) of flour into a sifter with 4 teaspoons of baking powder and 1 ditto of salt; sift into a bowl twice; cut 1 tablespoon each of lard and butter into this mixture; add, slowly, just enough milk, from 1½ to 2 gills (¾ to 1 cup) to make a soft light dough; skimmed milk is best; half and half milk and water also does very well. This dough needs light handling. Have a floured board ready; pour the dough upon it; turn the mixture with a spatula until well floured; roll it to ½-inch thickness very lightly with a rolling pin; cut into rounds, place on a well-buttered baking tin and hurry the biscuits into a quick (400–25°F.) oven to bake from 10 to 15 minutes. Keep an eye on them.*

MILK BISCUITS (late 1800s)—For directions, follow the recipe for Milk Bread (see Index).

RAISED BREAD DOUGH BISCUITS (mid-1800s)—Take a pint (2-cup) bowl full of light bread dough; break into it a fresh egg and a piece of butter the size of an egg (4 tablespoons); incorporate these with the dough by strong kneading for 10 minutes. Roll the dough out about 1 inch thick, cut it into biscuits, lay them on a tin sheet and let them rise in a moderately warm place. They should become very light and are baked in a quick (425°F.) oven. Warning: they are injured by slow baking and should be done in 12 to 15 minutes. Eat fresh, but not hot; they are not so good the next day as are biscuits made without an egg. This makes about 24 biscuits.*

CREAM BISCUITS (late 1800s)—Dissolve 1 teaspoon of baking soda in a very little hot water; sift ¾ teaspoon of salt with ½ pint (1 cup) of wheat flour; unite ½ pint (1 cup) each of sweet or sour cream with the flour; stir in the baking soda. Sprinkle a flour board with just enough flour to hold the mixture smooth; roll and cut it; bake in a hot (450°F.) oven for ¼ hour or rather less.*

WHEN USING SALERATUS (BAKING SODA)— Always dissolve it in a little very hot or boiling water; never add it until the dough is mixed, as the foaming process caused by combining the liquid and the alkali raises the entire mass; this effervescence is lost if the saleratus is stirred into the liquid prior to it being added to the flour.*

SHORTCAKE DOUGH (mid-1800s)—Sift 2 teaspoons of baking powder and a little salt with 1 pint (2 cups) of flour. Rub a piece of butter one-half the size of an egg (2 tablespoons) thoroughly into the flour and mix it into a soft dough with sweet milk, about 1 coffee cup (1 cup).) Divide the dough into 2 equal parts; take 1 of these to a floured board and roll it into a sheet, handling as little as possible. Lay it into a medium-sized dripping pan and brush the surface very lightly with melted butter; then roll out the balance of the dough and lay it over the first piece. Bake in a hot (400°F.) oven 10 to 12 minutes, when it should be done. Divide the cake, which will separate without cutting where it was buttered. Try it with Apple Topping and Filling (see Index).*

APPLE SHORTCAKE (mid-1800s)—Stew juicy apples very slowly in their own juice if possible; if not, use only a little water or apple cider; when they are smooth and thick, season with a little sugar, cinnamon and salt. Butter the lower half of the Shortcake (see above) and spread it with a generous layer of warm apple sauce. Put the top of the cake, crust down, on the filling; butter the top and spread with apple sauce; serve warm with sweet cream or whipped cream seasoned with a small amount of cinnamon.*

BERRIES FOR SHORTCAKES (mid-1800s)—Pick or buy the amount of blackberries, raspberries or strawberries you may need; be sure they are fully ripe but firm; chop them, place them in a bowl, sweeten with white sugar as needed and flavor with a few tablespoons of sherry. Hold out a small amount of whole berries wherewith to decorate the tops to the Shortcakes. They always look nice when nestling on spoonfuls of whipped cream.**

STRAWBERRY BISCUIT SHORTCAKE (late 1800s)—Mix 1 cup of flour with 1 teaspoon of baking powder and ¼ teaspoon of salt and cut into it ⅛ cup (2 tablespoons) of butter; add 1 beaten egg and ¼ cup of milk. Do not knead or stir, but chop it with a knife to obtain a soft dough. Roll ½ inch thick on a floured board; brush half the dough with melted butter and cover it with the remaining half. Cut the dough to suit the size of the pans to be used. Bake in a good quick (425°F.) oven 13 to 16 minutes. Split and spread with creamed butter. There is a trick in fixing berries for Shortcake. An hour before dinner time, and after they have been washed and hulled,

put them in a bowl and sprinkle them richly with powdered sugar and douse
with sherry. At serving time take one-half the berries and mash them into
a sauce. Cut the remainder into quarters, mix them with the sauce and pile
them upon the baked Shortcakes with whipped cream.*

STRAWBERRY SHORTCAKE— Make a fine Soda Biscuit Crust (see Index);
separate it into 3 pieces; roll them out about ½ inch thick to the size of
your pan, which should be round (this is best baked in a jelly cake pan).
As you place the first crust in your pan, spread over it melted butter; then
roll out the second crust and place it on the first; butter this well and then
roll out and put on your third and last crust. Place in a hot (450°F.) oven
and bake for 15 to 20 minutes. As you take them out, the separate crusts
must be lifted carefully; butter each crust again and place the sliced and
sugared berries on, making alternate layers of crust and layers of berries
heaped quite thick. Serve with clear or whipped cream and sugar.—Bella
Lyon

ORANGE SHORTCAKE—Prepare the crust as you would for Strawberry
Shortcake (see above). Slice peeled oranges very fine and put them down in
sugar. When you separate the crusts, butter them nicely and then add the
oranges. For a sauce, boil the juice of 3 lemons with 2 teacups (2 cups) of
water, ¾ cup of sugar, ½ teaspoon of salt. Mix 3 tablespoons of cornstarch
with 1/3 cup of cold water and thicken the sauce. Remove from the fire and
stir in a piece of butter twice the size of 1 egg (8 tablespoons). Chill.—Mrs.
A. A. Carpenter

ELLEN'S TEA CAKE—Two eggs and 2 tablespoons of sugar, beaten together, 3 cups of flour, 1 cup of milk, 1 teaspoon of soda, 2 of cream of tartar;
add last 2 tablespoons of melted butter. Bake in a quickish (400°F.) oven
½ hour and use a square or round tin. To be eaten like Sally Lunn, hot, with
butter.—Anon.

POP OVERS—One cup of flour, 1 cup of milk, 2 eggs, a piece of butter the
size of a walnut (1 rounded tablespoon), a little salt; to be baked in cups in
a very quick (425°F.) oven for ½ hour. This rule makes 12 Pop Overs based
on 2 tablespoons per cup; the cups should be buttered and very hot.—Mrs.
Anthony Finch

TOP OVERS (mid-1800s)—Take ½ pint (1 cup) of sweet milk, ½ pint (1
cup) of flour a little heaped, a bit of butter the size of a small walnut (1
tablespoon), 2 whole eggs barely beaten with a fork, 2 teaspoons of sugar,
a dash of nutmeg and a pinch of salt. Melt the butter; add the milk slowly
to the flour, to prevent lumps from forming; stir in the eggs, butter and
other ingredients. Bake in heated and greased cups or iron drop-cake pans
in a quick (400°F.) oven for about 25 to 30 minutes. Do not open the oven
door until the time is up.*

CORN POP OVERS—One pint (2 cups) of sweet milk scalded; stir into the
hot milk a coffee cup (¾ cup) of cornmeal, a piece of butter one-half the

size of an egg (2 tablespoons), a little salt and 3 eggs well beaten and stirred in the last thing. No soda. Bake in a very quick (425–50°F.) oven 20 to 30 minutes in thick custard cups.—Mrs. A. T. Hall

TO MAKE STALE BREAD OR ROLLS FRESH—Plunge the loaf one instant in cold water; lay it upon a tin in a middling-hot (350°F.) oven 10 to 15 minutes. Rolls, similarly, may be made almost as nice as if just baked, but must be eaten immediately.—Mrs. M. G. Adams

BUNS—Take 1 large coffee cup (1 cup) of warm milk, ¼ cake of yeast (¼ cup) and salt; make a sponge; let it rise; when it is light work into a dough, adding ½ small teacup (¼ cup) of sugar, 1 egg, a piece of butter twice the size of an egg (8 tablespoons); let it rise; roll into a sheet; butter it; cut into strips 3 inches wide and 6 inches long; fold, not quite in the middle; let it rise again and bake in a hot (425°F.) oven ½ hour. If, when in preparation, it rises before you are ready, push it down.***

RUSKS—To 1 tumbler (1 cup) of warm milk add ½ gill (¼ cake) of yeast, 3 eggs and a coffee cup (¾ cup) of sugar beaten together, 2 ounces (4 tablespoons) of butter rubbed into flour, of which use only enough to enable you to mold it; let it rise over night; when it is very light, roll it and put it on tins to rise again, after which bake in a quick (400°F.) oven 20 minutes.
—P. B. A.

LITCHFIELD CRACKERS (early 1800s)—Only women with time and fortitude can make these good crackers. Rub a piece of butter the size of an egg (4 tablespoons) into 1 quart (4 cups) of flour; whip a well-beaten egg into 1 pint (2 cups) of cold milk with 3 saltspoons (¾ teaspoon) of fine salt; combine these ingredients. More flour is kneaded into the dough until it is as stiff as it can possibly be made; pound it with an iron pestle or the broad end of a flatiron for at least 1 hour. Then roll it very thin, cut it into rounds, prick the crackers and bake them in a highly hot brick oven (450°F.) about 10 minutes or a little longer until done.***

BASIC PROPORTIONS OF MUFFINS—Of flour and liquids, including eggs, about 1 gill (½ cup) of the latter to every ½ pint (1 cup) of the former. This rule, however, is elastic in that the flour must be adequate to make a rather thick batter. To bake well in rings, have the griddle of a moderate heat, grease it and also the rings; lay them on and fill them only half full of batter; increase the heat a little. In about 8 minutes turn the muffins and let them lie 2 or 3 minutes more. To turn them without spilling requires some practice.***

RAISED MUFFINS (mid-1800s)—Melt 1 tablespoon of butter in ½ pint (1 cup) of scalded milk; add a little salt and let it cool; add 2 unbeaten eggs and a ½ gill (¼ cup) of yeast; mix and stir enough flour (2 cups) into this to make a thick batter. Bake in rings (See Basic Proportions of Muffins, above.)***

OATMEAL MUFFINS (late 1800s)—At night, scald ½ pint (1 cup) of milk and add a similar amount of cold cooked oatmeal with 4 tablespoons of brown sugar and 3 saltspoons (¾ teaspoon) of salt. Melt ½ yeast cake (½ cup) in a little warm water; add this to the milk when it is lukewarm. Work about 1¼ pints (2½ cups) of white flour into this; you will want a stiff batter; beat with vigor for 4 to 6 minutes; set the dough aside to rise until morning, when it is beaten again for 4 to 6 minutes; fill greased tins two-thirds full; await their rising once more and bake 40 minutes in a moderate oven (350°F.).*

BLUEBERRY MUFFINS (late 1800s)—To 1 gill (½ cup) of creamed butter add an equal quantity of sugar and the well-beaten yolk of 1 egg; combine and sift 4 teaspoons of baking powder and 1½ saltspoons (2/3 teaspoon) of salt with ½ pint (1 cup) of white flour; stir this into the butter mixture; now add 1 gill (½ cup) each of milk and fresh washed and drained blueberries, and, lastly, the stiffly beaten white of egg seasoned with very little nutmeg. Put the dough into well-buttered gem or muffin pans, or bake whole in a cake pan; place in a brisk (400°F.) oven and bake 25 to 30 minutes.*

CREAM OF TARTAR MUFFINS (mid-1800s)—Mix ½ teaspoon of salt, 1 tablespoon of sugar and 2 teaspoons of cream of tartar with 1 quart (4 cups) of flour; add 2 eggs without beating them in; work this into a dough with 1 pint (2 cups) of light cream or rich milk; do this swiftly or the dough may become stringy; stir 1 teaspoon of saleratus (baking soda) dissolved in 2 teaspoons of boiling water into these ingredients with quick strokes. Half fill the buttered muffin tins and bake in a hot (450°F.) oven for a short ¼ hour.*

GRAHAM MUFFINS—One egg, a piece of butter one-half the size of an egg (2 tablespoons), 3 cups of Graham flour, 3 teaspoons of baking powder, a pinch of salt, ½ pint (1 cup) of milk or milk and water; to be of the thickness of ordinary cake batter. Corn Cake may be made same way, only use 2 cups of flour and 1 of meal instead of the Graham flour. Bake about 1/3 hour in a fast (400–50°F.) oven.—Mrs. L. Cornell

CORNMEAL MUFFINS—Soak a pint (2 cups) of meal over night in sweet milk, just enough to wet it; in the morning dissolve in a cup ½ teaspoon of soda in a tablespoon of boiling water, then fill the cup with buttermilk or sour milk; add this, with the yolks of 2 eggs and a tablespoon of thick cream or melted butter, to the meal, also ½ teaspoon of salt. Have your rings or muffin frames hot and bake 20 minutes in a lively (450°F.) oven. If preferred, a shallow pan can be used.—Mrs. A. M. Gibbs

FRITTER BATTERS FOR FRUITS (mid-1800s)—Into 1 cup of flour stir 2 teaspoons of baking powder, ¼ cup of brown sugar and a good pinch of salt; sift. Beat 2 eggs and add them to the flour with ½ gill (¼ cup) of milk and 1 dessertspoon (2 teaspoons) of lemon juice. Beat, strain and let it stand, over night if the batter is for breakfast, all day if it is for supper. (See Index for Raspberry Sauce to go with fruit fritters.)*

BANANA FRITTERS (late 1800s)—Skin and quarter the bananas; put them into a flat dish for 45 minutes with a marinade consisting of ½ gill (¼ cup) each of brown sugar and a tart wine; spoon this over the bananas at intervals. Drain the pieces and dip them into fruit fritter batter (see Fritter Batter for Fruits, above) and cook in deep hot fat (370°F.) from 2 to 3 minutes. (Quartered peaches, pears, oranges and apples may be handled in the same manner.)*

BREAD FRITTERS (early 1800s)—Measure 1 pint (2 cups) of light bread dough ready for the oven; roll it ½ inch thick on a floured board; sprinkle with cinnamon, nutmeg or ginger, cut into 2-inch squares and fry like fritters. Hot buttered maple syrup goes well with this.*

HARVEST TIME CORN FRITTERS (mid-1800s)—Cut 12 ears of corn down the center of each row of kernels; then, with the back of the knife, press out the pulp; to this add 1 pint (2 cups) of milk, the raw yolks of 2 eggs, salt, pepper to taste and 1 cup of flour; beat well. Whip the whites of the 2 eggs to a stiff froth and blend this into the mixture; lastly, stir in 1 teaspoon of baking powder. Put some lard in a frying pan and, when it is hot, drop the fritters by spoonfuls into it. When the fritters are brown on one side, turn them and brown the other; take them out with a skimmer, dry on brown paper and serve searing hot.*

LEMON FRITTERS—Beat up the whipped and strained yolks of 5 eggs with ½ cup of powdered sugar; add the grated peel of ½ lemon, 1 teaspoon of mingled nutmeg and cinnamon, a little salt and ½ cup of cream, then the beaten whites of the eggs and then 2 heaping cups of prepared flour; work all together quickly and lightly into a soft paste, just stiff enough to roll out; pass the rolling pin over it until it is about ¾ inch thick; cut into small circular cakes with a tumbler or cake cutter and fry in hot lard. The fritters ought to puff up like crullers. Drain on clean hot paper and eat warm with a sauce made of the juice of 2 lemons and the grated peel of 1, 1 cup of powdered sugar, 1 glass (¼ cup) of wine and the whites of 2 eggs beaten stiff.—Marion Harland

PARSNIP FRITTERS—Boil 5 or 6 medium-sized parsnips until tender; mash them very fine; add ½ cup of milk and a tablespoon of butter, 2 eggs, 3 tablespoons of flour and a little salt; fry a delicate brown in hot drippings. Serve on a hot dish or a napkin—Anon.

SPICED SUGAR FOR FRITTERS (mid-1800s)—One teaspoon each of powdered and mixed nutmeg, cinnamon and ginger (sifted), 3 tablespoons of powdered sugar. Mix the sugar with the spices.*

FRENCH FRITTERS—Beat the yolks of 4 eggs very light; add to them 1 pint (2 cups) of milk; cut some slices of baker's bread about an inch thick, cutting off all the crust, and lay them in the egg-milk about 15 minutes. Have your griddle hot and fry the slices a nice brown, using fresh lard for the purpose. Beat the whites of the eggs very light, stir into them 1 cup of powdered sugar and flavor with lemon, this to be used as sauce with the fritters.—Anon.

SNOW FRITTERS (early 1800s)—If it snows during the night or early morning hours, stir together, in the morning, 1 pint (2 cups) of milk, 1½ pints (3 cups) of flour and a little salt, to make a rather thick batter. Add 1½ gills (¾ cup) of newly fallen snow. Be sure to have the fat ready hot at the time you stir in the snow; drop the batter into it with a spoon. These fritters are even preferred by some to those made with eggs. (The ammonia in the fresh snow acts as the rising agent.)*

CROQUETTE BATTER FOR DEEP-FRYING (late 1800s)—The night before the batter is needed, mix ¼ pint (½ cup) of flour with a big pinch of salt and 2 teaspoons of baking powder; run it through a sieve a time or 2; beat separately 2 whole eggs with 4 tablespoons of milk and 1 dessertspoon (2 teaspoons) of lemon juice; strain the egg threads out of it; mix it with the flour and beat it thoroughly with an egg beater; run this batter through a sieve and set it in a cool place. Many women dip the croquettes—fruits, vegetables or meats—for which this batter is used, twice, though it is not at all necessary; essential, however, is to let the batter dry a little before the food is put into the deep-frying kettle, piece by piece or in a basket.*

ONION DEEP-FRY BATTER FOR FISH (mid-1800s)—Skin and cut the fish fillets into thumb-sized pieces and dip them into a batter made this way: Sift 1 tablespoon of baking powder and 1 teaspoon of salt with 1½ pints (3 cups) of wheat flour; beat 2 eggs and grate enough onion to make 1 gill (½ cup); add ½ pint (1 cup) of milk to the beaten egg, beat and add the onions; stir this into the flour slowly and work it free from lumps with a kitchen fork. Have the fat in your deep-fry kettle so hot that a 1-inch cube of bread will brown in 50 seconds (370–75°F.) and cook each piece 3 to 5 minutes, but avoid overloading the fry-basket.*

STEW DUMPLINGS (late 1800s)—Sift 2 teaspoons of baking powder and a large pinch of salt into ½ pint (1 cup) of flour and then into a bowl; stir in 1 gill (½ cup) of milk and make a batter. Drop this by the spoonful into the stew and let the dumplings cook 5 to 8 minutes, closely covered.*

ON FRYING CAKES (mid-1800s)—To have fried cakes good, it is necessary that the fat should be of the right heat. When it is hot enough, fat will cease to bubble and become perfectly still; when it is too hot, it will smoke. It is best to try it with a bit of the cake to be fried.

    If the heat is right, the dough will rise in a few minutes to the top and occasion a bubbling in the fat; the dough will swell, and the underside quickly become brown. The cake should then be turned over.

    Cakes should be turned over 2 or 3 times. The time necessary to fry them depends upon their thickness; if about as thick as the little finger, they should be done less than 5 minutes. It is best to break the first one open, in order to judge. If the fat is too hot, the outside will be burned before the inside is cooked at all; if too cool, they will become fat-soaked. The use of many eggs prevents cakes from absorbing too much fat.

It lightens fried cakes, and especially doughnuts, if they are allowed to stand ½ hour after being shaped or cut, before they are fried. When done, drain them well with a skimmer and put them on brown kitchen paper to dry; turn them at least twice.*

THE FIRE MUST BE CAREFULLY REGULATED (mid-1800s)—A person who fries cakes must attend to nothing else; the cakes, the fat, the fire, will occupy every minute. Yeast doughnuts or cakes fry in fairly hot (385°F.) fat; others at lower heat (375°F.)

Fat tried from suet or beef drippings heats better and lasts longer than lard. To use it repeatedly, use no more fat than you need; never overheat it, strain it carefully after using and always give your frying kettle a good cleaning. Many good cooks freshen the fat by cooking 2 sliced raw potatoes in the fat after the frying is done; this takes any and all flavors out of it.

It is a good idea, when making fried cakes, to melt the sugar in the liquid that goes into the cake dough; this lessens the chances of the cakes soaking in lard in the kettle.*

WORKADAY CRULLERS (mid-1800s)—To 1 pint (2 cups) of warm milk put 2 tablespoons of lard and 3 of butter cut into bits. Beat 4 eggs and 5 heaping tablespoons of white sugar together and stir them into the milk; grate in ½ small nutmeg; mix in enough flour to make a dough that can be rolled out; moisten 1 heaping teaspoon of saleratus (baking soda) in 1 tablespoon of boiling water; stir this into the dough; knead it. Roll it out ¼ inch thick; make strips that are 2 inches wide and 4 inches long and slash 2 cuts down the sides of each, ¾ inch from top and bottom; give each strip a twist; let them rest about 20 minutes before frying them.*

ROSE-FLAVORED CRULLERS (mid-1800s)—A day or 2 before you intend to fry the crullers, wrap ½ pound (1 cup) of butter in rose leaves; when you make the dough, remove the leaves; sift ¾ pound (1½ generous cups) of white sugar with 2 pounds (4 cups) of wheat flour; work in the butter; beat 9 whole eggs, add them and season with mace and salt to taste. Shape into crullers and fry (for directions, see Workaday Crullers, above).*

FRIED BISCUITS (early 1800s)—Work a piece of butter the size of an egg (4 tablespoons) into a large pint (2½ cups) of light bread dough (see Index). When it has risen again, roll it very thin, cut it into circles or squares, and fry them for breakfast. Eat them with salt or cider or sugar.***

CREAM OF TARTAR DOUGHNUTS (late 1800s)—Right after supper, beat 2 whole eggs and 1 yolk with 1½ cups of sugar; add 4½ cups of flour, 2 teaspoons of cream of tartar, ¾ teaspoon of salt, 1 teaspoon of baking soda, 1 saltspoon (¼ teaspoon) of grated nutmeg, all the dry ingredients first sifted twice together; incorporate 1 cup of milk slowly into the mixture. Beat this thoroughly before enough flour is added to make a pliant dough. Let this stand in a cool, even chilly, place during the night. This dough should be rolled to the thickness of 1 inch in the morning and made into doughnuts, allowed to rest 15 minutes and fried in very hot, almost smoking, fat (385°F.). Turn them frequently and drain on white blotting paper.*

RAISED DOUGHNUTS (early 1800s)—Before retiring, scald 1 quart (4 cups) of milk; rub smooth, in a little cold milk, a large gill (2/3 cup) of ground rice; when the milk boils up, stir the rice in with a big pinch of salt; let it boil until it thickens; stir 2 or 3 times. Pour this, hot, upon 1 quart (4 cups) of flour; when it is cool enough, add 1 gill (½ cup) of yeast and flour enough to make it stiff as bread dough. Knead it a great deal. Let it rise over night. When it is very light, in the morning, work in ¾ pound (1½ cups) of butter, 1½ pounds (3½ generous cups) of sugar beaten into 5 eggs, also ½ teaspoon of nutmeg, the juice and grated rind of 1 lemon; let it rise again and then roll out again. To flavor this receipt with oranges, leave out the nutmeg and lemon and use instead 3 tablespoons of orange juice and 1 teaspoon of grated orange rind. Fry in hot (375°F.) fat.***

MAPLE SUGAR ICING FOR DOUGHNUTS (mid-1800s)—Cook, slowly and for only 5 minutes, 3 teaspoons of cream, 1 dessertspoon (2 teaspoons) of butter, ½ pint (1 cup) each of white and maple sugar. Stir constantly until it is thick; dip the doughnuts into this icing and set them aside to dry.*

CRUMB GRIDDLE CAKES (late 1800s)—This nice addition to the supper table should be started soon after the noon meal, when 1 pint (2 cups) of scalded milk should be poured on a like amount of soft white bread crumbs free from crusts. At supper time, sift, twice, ½ pint (1 cup) of wheat flour, 2 teaspoons of baking powder and 1 of salt; blend this into the crumbs; beat the yolks and whites of 2 eggs separately; add the yolks first, then the whites. Best when baked on a buttered griddle.*

BUCKWHEAT CAKES (mid-1800s)—For a small family, take and sift 1 pint (2 cups) of buckwheat, 1 gill (½ cup) of Indian (corn) meal and 1 teaspoon of salt into a dough basin; add ½ gill (¼ cup) of yeast and ½ gill (¼ cup) each of tepid water and black molasses; work this well with a wooden spoon and let it stand to rise over night. Next morning, work it again with the wooden spoon; then add 1 teaspoon of saleratus (baking soda). Work again, briefly but vigorously. Add the saleratus whether the cakes are sour or not; they cannot be made to perfection without it; but never put the saleratus in until just before they are baked.

The commonest reasons why Buckwheat Cakes often fail is because they are made too thick and fried with too much fat. They should be as thin as can be and easily turned with a griddle shovel; no more fat should be used than needed to prevent them from sticking. If a gill (½ cup) of batter is left, it will raise the next parcel.*

BUTTERMILK CAKES (mid-1800s)—That which is sold in cities as butter-milk is often adulterated; therefore, be sure that you see yellow flecks of butter in the milk you have to buy. Into a bowl, sift 2 cups of flour, 3 table-spoons of sugar (white), 1 teaspoon each of baking soda and salt; and 1 pint (2 cups) of buttermilk and, lastly, 2 beaten eggs. Let this stand 20 minutes.

Allow 1 large tablespoonful for each cake, which should be dropped on a hot griddle well greased with a piece of salt pork. Turn only once. Have hot maple syrup and softened butter handy to go with the cakes.*

HOMINY GRIDDLE CAKES (late 1800s)—Take ½ pint (1 cup) each of cooked hominy and scalded milk when supper is done. Stir them together and set aside. Next morning, beat the mixture; also beat 2 eggs. Mix ¾ pint (1½ cups) of flour with 1½ tablespoons of sugar and 1¼ teaspoons of salt and 1 dessertspoon (2 teaspoons) of baking powder; stir these into the hominy batter; also the 2 eggs, 1 tablespoon of melted butter and ½ pint (1 cup) of milk, separately and in that order. Give this a good beating with your egg beater before browning it on a greased skillet.*

INDIAN MEAL FLANNEL CAKES (mid-1800s)—Take 1½ pints (3 cups) of sifted Indian (corn) meal at night and scald it with 1½ pints (3 cups) of hot milk; melt ½ gill (¼ cup) of butter in the mixture; let it stand until it is barely warm, then add ½ gill (¼ cup) of yeast, 2 tablespoons of brown sugar and 3 saltspoons (¾ teaspoon) of salt. After rising through the night, the batter is ready in the morning to be poured onto a greased skillet and browned.*

OATMEAL GRIDDLE CAKES—Take 1 cup of cooked oatmeal and thin it down to gruel with cold milk or water. Blend 1 cup of flour with 1 teaspoon of sugar, 2 teaspoons of baking powder and ½ teaspoon of salt. With the oatmeal form a batter of the consistency of Buckwheat Cakes; beat very well together and bake on the griddle at once. Serve with hot apple sauce and melted butter.—Mrs. J. M. Wetherill

GREEN CORN GRIDDLE CAKES—Grade 12 ears of corn and make a batter with them and 4 eggs, 1 cup of flour, 1 teaspoon of baking powder and 1 cup of sweet milk, (cream is better); if you use milk, add ½ gill (¼ cup) of melted butter, none if you use cream; a little salt and sugar to taste. Serve with hot maple syrup or boiled molasses.—Mrs. C. M. Dickerman

CORNMEAL GRIDDLE CAKES—Soak ¾ pint (1½ cups) of cornmeal over night in ¾ pint (1½ cups) of sour milk and ½ pint (1 cup) of sour cream; in the morning, add 1 pint (2 cups) of flour; stir in 2 beaten eggs, ½ teaspoon of baking soda and a pinch of salt.—Mrs. Laurence Forest

WHITE FLOUR GRIDDLE CAKES (early 1800s)—If made in the morning, the following batter will be light by supper time. Melt a small gill (1/3 cake) of yeast and 1 large tablespoon of butter in 1 quart (4 cups) of lukewarm scalded milk; beat 4 eggs with 2 saltspoons (½ teaspoon) of salt and stir them into the milk; use enough flour to make a batter as thick as for Buckwheat Cakes (about 4 cups), which is browned on a greased skillet. Some persons eat them with a sauce made of equal portions of butter and sugar, seasoned with nutmeg and thinned by a small amount of boiling water.*

PANCAKES IN THE FRENCH MANNER (late 1800s)—The new fad for French pancakes, stuffed with meat, seems to be taking kitchens by storm.

For housewives who have not been able to try this novelty, here is the way
to do it. Mince meat left-overs, after they have been neatly trimmed, with
finely minced onion, chopped chives and minced parsley. Heat this mixture
in a little butter in a skillet but do not brown. Bind it together by sprinkling
it with a little flour; stir and add a few tablespoonfuls of gravy if you have
it; if not use soup stock or light cream. Let it cook over a very low fire about
10 to 15 minutes. Put into the ice chest to chill. Make a batter of 3 whole
eggs, 2 tablespoons of salad oil, 1 tablespoon of French brandy, 1 saltspoon
(¼ teaspoon) of salt and 3 cups of flour; reduce this to the consistency
of heavy cream by thinning with equal amounts of milk and water.
Beat until the point of exhaustion with an egg beater and give the
batter, if not yourself, a rest for a couple of hours. At serving time,
make the pancakes on a lightly buttered skillet and stack them, one on top
of the other; this done, spread hash on one side of each pancake, roll it up
and skewer it with a toothpick; place the pancakes in rows in a buttered
baking pan, douse them with melted butter and place them in a moderate
(350°F.) oven about 20 minutes to heat and brown. Serve with a Currant
Jelly Sauce (see Index).*

POTATO PANCAKES (late 1800s)—Boil, peel and mash 6 fairly large potatoes; blend in 1 beaten egg, ½ teaspoon of salt, ½ teaspoon of minced
parsley, 1 teaspoon of minced chives (or onion) and 2 tablespoons of flour.
Knead into a dough on a floured bread board, flatten it into a rectangle with
a rolling pin and roll it tightly the long way into a sausage about 1½ inches
through. Put into a cool place to chill. When mealtime comes, cut the dough-
roll into 1-inch slices which you flatten into ½-inch-thick disks with your
hands; brown the pancakes in butter or lard, first on one side, next on the
other. Turn only once.*

WAFFLE OR GRIDDLE CAKE BATTER (mid-1800s)—To 1 quart (4 cups)
of milk put 6 eggs, ¼ pound (½ cup) of butter, a large gill (2/3 cake) of
yeast, a little salt and flour enough to make a batter the thickness of that
of griddle cakes. Be sure that your waffle iron is heavily greased; it takes
about twice as long to make them this way as it would to bake them on a
griddle, and they are really no better as waffles than they are as griddle
cakes, only more inviting.*

WAFFLE BATTER (mid-1800s)—Stir 1 teaspoon of salt and 2 ditto of baking powder into 1 pint (2 cups) of flour; beat the yolks of 3 eggs; add them
to the flour with 2½ gills (1¼ cups) of milk; beat the whites of 3 eggs into
stiff peaks and work them into the batter. For this, the waffle iron should
be very hot and greased with bacon fat.*

WAFFLES, THICK AND THIN— Thin: The yolks of 3 eggs, 1 quart (4
cups) of milk, ½ cup of melted butter, 1 heaping teaspoon of baking powder.
Afterwards add the whites of the eggs and flour enough to make a thin
batter.

Thick: One pint (2 cups) of sour milk, 3 tablespoons of melted butter,
3 beaten eggs, 1 teaspoon of soda, a little salt, flour enough to make a thick
batter.—Mrs. Harry Pennyman

16. Large and Small Cakes—Icings and Fillings

SHAVING BRUSH FOR BAKING (mid-1800s)—An old but not too worn shaving brush of good quality is really the best kind to use while baking. In dusting off flour, it is soft and pliable but, above all, the hairs do not fall out and it can be cleaned without injury in very hot water.***

TO PREPARE CAKE TINS FOR BAKING (mid-1800s)—Grease them cold with butter or lard; sprinkle flour on the bottoms and sides; then shake them to remove superfluous flour.*

WHEN CAKE IS DONE (mid-1800s)—Have a cooling rack handy and touch the cake, lightly, for safety's sake, with the tips of your fingers; if they leave no imprint and the cake springs back, it is done. Let the cake cool at least 10 minutes in the baking tin before you remove it to cool on the rack; on the rack let it remain about ½ hour if you plan to slice the cake into 2 layers. For slicing, instead of a knife, use a tautly held piece of strong thread.*

SOME DOS AND DON'TS IN CAKE-MAKING (mid-1800s)—First, it is very desirable that the materials be of the finest quality. Sweet, fresh butter, eggs and good flour are the first essentials. The process of putting together is also quite an important feature, and where other methods are not given it would be well for the young housekeeper to observe the following directions.

Never allow the butter to oil, but soften it by putting it in a moderately warm place before you commence other preparations for your cake; then put it into an earthen dish (tin, if not new, will discolor your cake as you stir it). Now add your sugar; beat the butter and sugar to a cream; add the yolks of the eggs, then the milk, the flour and lastly the beaten whites of the eggs.

Spices and liquors may be added after the yolks of the eggs are put in. Fruit should be put in with the flour.

The oven should generally be pretty hot (375°F.) for small cakes, and moderate (350°F.) for larger.

To ascertain if a cake is sufficiently baked, pierce it with a broom straw through the center; if the cake is done, the straw will come out free from dough; if not done, dough will adhere to the straw.

All cakes should be well stirred before the whipped whites of eggs are added to the batter.*

TO COLOR ICING (early 1800s)—It may be shaded a pretty pink with strawberry juice or cranberry syrup, or colored yellow by putting the juice and rind of a lemon in a thick muslin bag and squeezing it hard into the egg and sugar.

If the cake is well dredged with flour after baking and then carefully wiped before the icing is put on, the icing will not run and can be spread more smoothly.

Put frosting onto the cake in large spoonfuls, commencing over the center; then spread it over the cake, using a large knife and dipping it occasionally in cold water.

Dry the frosting on the cake in a cool, dry place.*

WHITE FROSTING—One pint (2 cups) of granulated sugar, moistened thoroughly with water sufficient to dissolve it when heated; let it boil, stirring often, until it threads from the spoon. While the sugar is boiling, beat the whites of 2 eggs until they are firm; then when thoroughly beaten, turn them into a deep dish, and when the sugar is boiled, turn it over the whites, beating all together rapidly until of the right consistency to spread over the cake. Flavor and color as preferred. This is sufficient for 2 loaves.—Mrs. Louise Dewey

ICE CREAM ICING FOR WHITE CAKE—Two cups of pulverized sugar boiled to a thick syrup; add 3 teaspoons of vanilla extract; when cool, add the whites of 2 eggs well beaten and flavored with 2 teaspoons of citric acid. —Mrs. P. B. Ayer

CHOCOLATE FROSTING—The whites of 2 eggs, 1½ cups of fine sugar, 6 rounded tablespoons of grated chocolate, 2 teaspoons of vanilla extract; spread rather thickly between layers and on top of cake. Best when freshly made. It should be made like any frosting.—Mrs. C. H. Wheeler

LEMON ICING (late 1800s)—While you boil a syrup with ½ pint (1 cup) of white sugar and 6 tablespoons of water, beat the whites of 2 eggs in a bowl and measure out 1 tablespoon of lemon juice and 1 teaspoon of vanilla extract. When it is ready, pour the hot syrup over the egg whites slowly and beat continually as you do so; next beat in the lemon juice and vanilla. An old trick to keep icing soft is to add a pinch of baking soda to the whites before beating them. This keeps the icing from getting hard.*

TO KEEP FROSTING FROM DRIPPING (late 1800s)—To keep icing from the sides of a cake, make a cake collar of a thick sheet of paper; fasten it with pins so that it sits tightly around the cake and rises a short inch above it; do this before you apply the frosting and let the paper remain until the frosting is firm.*

BROWN SUGAR ICING (mid-1800s)—In a container over boiling water heat ½ gill (¼ cup) of water and in it melt ½ pint (1 cup) of brown sugar; squeeze and strain the juice of 1 lemon and mix it with 1 tablespoon of rum. Whip the whites of 2 eggs; when they are stiff pour the hot sugar into them slowly and beat all the while; beat also as you add the lemon and the rum.*

SHERRY CHOCOLATE ICING (late 1800s)—Melt 2 dessertspoons (4 teaspoons) of butter in the top of a double boiler with 2 squares of chocolate

(½ cup of grated chocolate) and 1 gill (½ cup) of sugar; stir occasionally; when all is liquid, add ½ gill (¼ cup) of light cream and 1 dessertspoon (2 teaspoons) of sherry. The icing is done when small drops dripped from the tip of a spoon become soft balls as they fall into cold water.*

CREAM FILLING FOR LAYER CAKE (mid-1800s)—Sift ½ pint (1 cup) of sugar with 4 tablespoons (¼ cup) of cornstarch, ½ teaspoon of ginger, ¼ teaspoon of nutmeg; mix this well and add 2 beaten eggs; stir; add 1 tablespoon of melted butter and ¾ pint (1½ cups) of cold milk; cook in a pail put into boiling water (double boiler) and stir as it cooks and thickens for about 18 to 20 minutes.*

MARSHMALLOW FILLING (late 1800s)—This goes well with a two-tier Silver Cake (see Index). Melt ½ pound of marshmallows in a saucepan over boiling water; whip 1 egg white stiff; add this to the melted marshmallow and, with an eggbeater, whip the mixture until it peaks.*

APPLE CRUMB CAKE (mid-1800s)—Use about ½ pound each of sweet and tart apples and make an apple sauce by steaming them over boiling water with a tablespoon or 2 of cider or butter until they become a pulp; rub them through a sieve and stir 1 gill (½ cup) of light brown sugar and ½ teaspoon each of freshly grated nutmeg and cinnamon into them; melt a lump of butter as big as a duck's egg (½ cup) and add to it a similar amount of coarse dry bread crumbs with 1 gill (¼ cup) of sugar; fry this over a gentle fire until the crumbs are a golden brown. Butter a cake tin and fill it with alternating layers of crumbs and apples. To make the mixture firm, press it down with the flat bottom of a tumbler. Bake for ½ hour in a moderate (350°F.) oven. Tradition demands that this cake should be served lukewarm and that each helping should be topped with whipped cream dusted with cinnamon. Many housewives do not even bother to bake the cake. They simply put it together in a serving dish and let it stand to get warm on the back of the stove.*

BRANDY POUND CAKE (mid-1800s)—Cream 1 pound (2 cups) of unsalted butter with 1 pound (4 cups) of flour and spare no effort; beat the yolks of 10 eggs lemon-colored and add them to the butter-flour. Beat the whites of 10 eggs until firm with 1 pound (2¼ cups) of sugar and ½ saltspoon (a dash) of nutmeg. Stir ½ cup of brandy into the butter-sugar-yolks; when it is well absorbed, add the whites of eggs gently. Bake in pound cake tins greased with butter in a slow oven (290–315°F.) for 75 to 90 minutes.*

DOUGH CAKE—One pint (2 cups) of Bread Dough (see Index) ready to be molded into loaves, 4 eggs (whites and yolks beaten separately), 1 cup of butter, 2 cups of white sugar, 1 tablespoon of cinnamon, 1 grated nutmeg, ½ teaspoon of soda, 1 pint (2 cups) of stoned raisins; mix by hand. Put the dough in a large bowl; first work in the butter well, then the sugar and spice, next the yolks, then the whites of the eggs, then the saleratus (baking soda), first dissolved in a little warm water, lastly, the raisins. Let it stand to rise after putting it into the pans. Bake about as you would bread (45 minutes in a 350°F. oven). This quantity makes 2 loaves.—Mrs. W. P. Nixon

POUND CAKE—One pound (4 cups) of flour, 1 pound (4 cups) of sugar, 10 eggs. Beat the yolks and sugar together; add 1 pound (2 cups) of butter; work in the flour; add the whites, beaten to a froth, last. Very nice baked in small patty pans and frosted.—Mrs. W. H. Ovington

MOUNTAIN POUND CAKE— One pound (4 cups) of sugar, 1 of flour, ½ pound (1 cup) of butter, 6 eggs (the whites and yolks beaten separately), ¾ cup sweet milk, 1 teaspoon of soda, 2 of cream of tartar. Sift the soda and cream of tartar together into the flour, after sifting the flour; then rub the butter and sugar to a cream and add one-quarter of the whites and yolks of the eggs, next the flour, and then the milk; beat in the remaining yolks and mix in the remaining whites in that order. Have a not too easy (325°F.) oven ready and bake 1¼ hours.—Mrs. C. M. Dickerman

JELLY CAKE MADE WITH THE YOLKS OF EGGS— One and one-half cups of sugar, ½ cup of butter, ½ cup of milk, 1 egg and the yolks of 4. Stir well, then sift in 2 cups of flour and 2 teaspoons of baking powder; bake in 5 cakes for 15 to 20 minutes in a quick (400°F.) oven. Spread jelly on top of the cake and between the layers. This makes a delicious cocoanut cake if you spread between and on top of the cake, instead of jelly, a soft frosting thickly strewn with desiccated cocoanut which has been soaked ½ hour in warm milk.—Mrs. Brown

ALMOND CAKE— Two cups of sugar, ½ cup of butter, 1 cup of sweet milk, 2½ cups of flour, the whites of 8 eggs, 1 teaspoon of cream of tartar, ½ teaspoon of soda. Mix the butter and sugar to a cream; mix in the other ingredients, putting in the soda last; bake in layers like Jelly Cake (see above); make a cream frosting and spread almonds about an inch apart on each layer.—Mrs. Henry Stevens

GENTLEMAN'S FAVORITE—Seven eggs (whites and yolks beaten separately), ½ cup of butter, 2 cups of white sugar, 2 cups of flour, 2 tablespoons of baking powder, 2 tablespoons of water, ½ teaspoon of salt; bake in jelly cake pans. The jelly for the cake: 1 egg, a cup of sugar, 3 grated apples and 1 lemon; stir until the mixture boils and becomes thick; let it cool before putting it between the layers.—Miss Anna M. Whitman

IMPROMPTU JELLY CAKE— One cup of butter, 2 cups of sugar, 3 cups of flour, 4 eggs. Stir the sugar and butter to a cream, then add the yolks of the eggs and lastly the beaten whites and flour. Have ready the jelly, made as follows: 1 grated apple, the grated rind and juice of 1 lemon, 1 cup of sugar and 1 egg; boil until it jells, stirring constantly; cool before using. Bake your cake in jelly cake pans, or in thin layers, putting the jelly between the layers, as in ordinary Jelly Cake.—Mrs. P. B. Brown

BLACK FRUIT CAKE—Three-quarters of a pound (1½ cups) of butter, 1 pound (2¼ cups) of brown sugar, 1 pound (4 cups) of flour, 2 pounds of currants, 3 pounds of raisins (seeded), ½ pound of citron, ¼ pound of almonds, 8 eggs, 1 nutmeg, cloves and cinnamon, 1 wineglass (¼ cup) of brandy. The raisins are better if soaked in brandy over night. Bake 1½ hours in a slow (300°F.) oven.—Mrs. C. H. Wheeler

24 EGGS WEDDING CAKE—Two pounds (8 cups) of flour, 2 pounds (4½ cups) of sugar, 2 pounds (4 cups) of butter, 8 pounds of raisins, 4 pounds of currants, 1 pint (2 cups) of brandy, 2 pounds of citron, 24 eggs, 2 ounces (7 tablespoons) of ground nutmeg, 2 teaspoons of powdered cloves; add a little molasses to make it more moist and black. This makes 2 very large loaves, baked in tin pans or hoops. There is no use trying this for doneness with a broom straw until 4 hours of baking in a very slow (275°F.) oven. —Mrs. G. F. DeForrest

CHEAP FRUIT CAKE—Three cups of flour, 1 cup of sugar, ¾ cup of butter, ¾ cup of milk, 3 eggs, 1½ cups each of raisins and citron, 1 teaspoon of baking powder. This takes a slow oven (275–300°F.) and requires 2½ to 3 hours of baking.—Mrs. Earle

FARMER'S FRUIT CAKE—Take 3 cups of dried apples; wash them and soak them over night in water; in the morning drain off the water and chop them; add 2 cups of molasses and let them simmer 2 hours or until the molasses is all absorbed; let them cool before adding them to the other ingredients. Then take 1 cup of brown sugar, ¾ cup of butter, 2 eggs, 1 cup of milk, 1 small teaspoon of soda, 1½ teaspoons of cream of tartar, 1 large tablespoon of cloves, 1 of allspice, 2 of cinnamon, 1 nutmeg (all the spices powdered), the grated rind of 2 lemons and the juice of 1, ¼ pound of citron, 1 cup of raisins, flour enough to make it the consistency of cup cake. Bake in a moderate (325–50°F.) oven. Test after the first hour. —Mrs. W. P. Cragin

NEW ENGLAND ELECTION CAKE—Take 3 pounds (12 cups) of sifted flour, leaving out a pint (2 cups) to put in with the fruit, and mix it in warm milk until it is a stiff batter; weigh 1½ pounds (3½ generous cups) of sugar and 1 pound (2 cups) of butter; mix them to a cream, then mix half of this with the batter of milk and flour and ½ pint (1 cup) of good home-made yeast or ½ cake of compressed yeast dissolved in a little water. Beat very thoroughly together; set aside and when light, which will take several hours (in winter, better to mix at night and stand in a warm place till next morning), add the remainder of the butter and sugar with 6 eggs and 1 pound of raisins, 1 glass of brandy (¼ cup), cinnamon, mace or nutmeg, as to taste, and a little soda; if there is a season of scarcity of eggs, it is very good without any; the cake should be left to rise the second time before being poured in pans for baking. The more such cake is beaten the finer and lighter it will be. This cake calls for a moderately hot (375°F.) oven and is usually ready in just less than 1 hour.—Mrs. John King, Jr.

STALE CAKE CRUMBS CAN BE USED (early 1800s)—They make quick breads and small cakes; rolled and sifted they can be used with good effect instead of flour.***

MOIST CHOCOLATE CAKE (late 1800s)—A monument should be built to commemorate the woman who conceived the idea of incorporating mashed potatoes into a chocolate cake. This addition halts the tendency of chocolate cakes to dry out. You will need ½ cup of freshly cooked hot mashed potatoes —no cream, butter or seasoning should be added to them. Cream 1/3 cup of butter with 1 cup of white sugar; add 2 egg yolks that have been slightly beaten; when this mixture is well blended, beat the hot mashed potatoes into it. Heat ¼ cup of rich milk and melt 3 squares of unsweetened chocolate (¾ cup of grated chocolate) in the milk while it is hot. As this goes on, sift 1 cup of flour with 1½ teaspoon each of baking powder and cinnamon and ¼ teaspoon each of powdered nutmeg and clove; add a pinch of salt. Mix this with the milk and chocolate and beat it all into the potato batter; whip the whites of 2 eggs with ¾ teaspoon of vanilla extract and blend it into the main mixture. Pour into buttered layer cake pans and bake in a moderate (350°F.) oven about ½ hour.

MASHED POTATO DEVIL'S FOOD CAKE (late 1800s) —The important ingredient in this unusual and unusually good chocolate cake is 1 cup of mashed potatoes hot from the stove and fresh from the masher. To this add 3 ounces (¾ cup) of grated chocolate that has been melted in 2/3 cups of heated whole milk. Have 1 cup of butter, softened in your hands, ready for creaming with 2 cups of sugar and 1 teaspoon of vanilla extract; when blended, mix this with the potato. Separate 4 eggs; beat the yolks and add, as you do, 2 cups of flour with which ½ teaspoon of salt and 3 teaspoons of baking powder have been sifted. Lastly, whip the 4 whites of egg with 4 tablespoons of white powdered sugar and blend them into the main batter. Bake as you would any 3-tier layer cake in a moderate (325–50°F.) oven for about 30 minutes. Test with a straw for doneness. Cover with chocolate icing (see Chocolate Frosting, below) .*

CHOCOLATE FROSTING (mid-1800s)—In a pot, over boiling water, melt 3 or 4 ounces of chocolate (1 cup of grated chocolate), 1¼ gill (2/3 cup) of white sugar, 1 tablespoon of butter, 1 dessertspoon (2 teaspoons) of brandy and 5 tablespoons of strong coffee. Drip drops into cold water till a soft ball takes shape, when the frosting is ready for spreading.*

BOSTON CREAM PIE (mid-1800s)—Scrub, rinse and dry a 9-inch cast-iron frying pan and butter it well. See to it that you have a good, though not too hot, oven (375°F.) ready; also have a short gill (scant ½ cup) of softened butter (see Index) at hand. Into the latter cream a scant ½ gill (¼ cup) of white sugar followed by the beaten yolks of 2 eggs. Sift 3½ gills (1¾ cups) of flour with 2 teaspoons of baking powder and 2 saltspoons (½ teaspoon) of salt; add 2 saltspoons (½ teaspoon) of vanilla essence to ¼ pint (½ cup) of milk; alternately beat the flour and egg, a little of each at a time, into the sugar-butter with an egg beater. Do not stir. When done, beat the whites of 3 eggs to a firm froth; add this gently to the batter, which you pour into your frying pan; set it into the oven for about 30 minutes. When the cake is cool, split it and put the following Custard Filling between the top and bottom layers.*

BOSTON CREAM PIE CUSTARD FILLING (mid-1800s)—This is started by beating 3 egg yolks thick and lemon-colored; next, scald ¾ pint (1½ cups) of milk in one pan and put 11 tablespoons of sugar, 5 teaspoons of cornstarch moistened with a little cold water and 1 saltspoon (¼ teaspoon) of salt into another. When the milk is scalding, add it to the sugar, etc., and stir steadily over a low fire until velvety and thick. Pour the egg yolks into a pail that can be set in boiling water (a double boiler) and add the milk-sugar as you stir with a wooden spoon; continue stirring as the custard is steamed; when it is done, it will adhere to the spoon. Let the custard cool and add 1 teaspoon of vanilla essence; when ready, place the filling in the center of the pie and dust the top layer heavily with powdered sugar. Use left-over custard, if any, for Boston Cream Cakes (see below).*

WHIPPED CREAM FILLING (early 1800s)—Easy to make, this filling for Boston Cream Cakes (see below) only requires that you beat ½ pint (1 cup) of heavy cream with 2 tablespoons of pounded loaf sugar and season with lemon juice to taste. For other cakes, some wives color it with fruit juices (see Index).*

WASHINGTON CREAM PIE (mid-1800s)—Make and bake a batter as prescribed for Boston Cream Pie (see above). The difference is that, instead of custard, any kind of red jam, but preferably raspberry, is used as a filling. The top of the cake is sprinkled with powdered sugar.*

WASHINGTON PIE—One and a half cups of sugar, ½ cup of butter, ½ cup of sweet milk, 3 eggs, 2½ cups of flour, 2 teaspoons of baking powder; bake in 3 layers in jelly cake tins. Pare and grate 2 large apples; add 1 cup of sugar, and the grated rind and juice of 1 lemon; put this on the stove and let it steam until it forms a jelly; then take it off and stir in the yolk of 1 egg. When the cake and jelly are both cold put them together.—Mrs. A. L. Chetlain

BOSTON CREAM CAKES—One pint (2 cups) of water, ½ pound (1 cup) of butter, ¾ pound (3 cups) of flour, 10 eggs. Boil the butter and water together; stir in the flour when boiling; when cool, add the eggs and a quantity of soda the size of a pea; drop by the spoonful on a buttered baking pan, leaving spaces so that the cakes will not touch when risen. Bake in a very quick (400°F.) oven about 10 minutes. When cold, make an incision at the side of each and fill with the following cream: 6 gills (3 cups) of milk; 1½ cups of flour, 2 cups of sugar, 6 eggs; beat the flour, sugar and eggs together and stir them into the milk while boiling. Flavor with the rind of a lemon.—Bella Lyon

CREAM PUFFS (late 1800s)—Boil up ½ pint (1 cup) of water; add quickly 1 gill (½ cup) of sweet (unsalted) butter and 1 heaping tablespoon of sugar; let these boil together just 60 seconds; add 1 teaspoon of almond extract; next, pour into the mixture 3½ gills (1¼ cups) of sifted flour and a pinch of salt from a bowl so that all goes in at once; beat until this dough becomes a solid mass that does not stick to the sides of the pan; remove from the fire and, beating constantly, add 5 whole eggs one at a time. These eggs must not be cold. Have ready a fast (400°F.) oven. In this put the puffs, which you drip from a tablespoon onto a buttered baking sheet and let bake for 25 to 35 minutes. Always open the sides of the puffs to let steam escape, otherwise they will drop; also remove the moist dough from their interiors and fill with whipped cream.*

GOLD AND SILVER CAKES (mid-1800s)—Unless a housewife wants to be left with either 8 yolks or 8 whites of eggs if she makes only 1 Gold Cake or 1 Silver Cake, the best solution is to make both cakes at the same time by using the whites for the Silver and the yolks for the Gold.

For the Silver Cake: Beat ¾ pint (1½ cups) of white sugar into 1½ gills (¾ cup) of creamed butter; flavor with the juice of 1 lemon and ½ teaspoon of the grated rind; in a basin, mix 1 pint (2 cups) of flour with 4 teaspoons of baking powder and 1 saltspoon (¼ teaspoon) of salt; add the flour mixture, with an occasional dash from 1 gill (½ cup) of cold milk, to the butter-sugar until all, including the milk, is well mixed; whip 8 whites of eggs stiff and put them into the batter with thorough care; pour the batter into 2 greased tins (many women line the tin bottoms with buttered paper); bake in a fairly hot (375°F.) oven for about ½ hour or in a slow (300°F.) oven for 45 to 50 minutes.

For the Gold Cake: Beat 3 gills (1½ cups) of white sugar into 1½ gills (¾ cup) of creamed butter flavored with 3 saltspoons (¾ teaspoon) each of powdered cinnamon, nutmeg, clove and ginger; in another vessel, unite 1 pint and ½ gill (2¼ cups) of flour with 4 teaspoons of baking powder and 1 saltspoon (¼ teaspoon) of salt; beat 1 whole egg well and blend it into 3 gills (1½ cups) of milk; beat the yolks of 8 eggs until they are thick, then add them to the butter-sugar mixture; now—as with the Silver Cake —the milk and the flour mixture are worked together and then slowly into the butter-sugar-yolk mixture. The batter is poured into a well-buttered (loaf) baking tin and put to bake about ¾ hour in a somewhat slow (325°F.) oven, or in a hotter (375°F.) oven for 30 to 35 minutes. Of the two cakes, the Gold keeps better for the long run.

Bake the cakes in square flat pans, ice them thickly with Lemon Icing (see Index) and, when serving, cut them into squares.*

PUMPKIN CAKE (mid-1800s)—Rub 1 pound (2 cups) of boiled and mashed pumpkin meat and a large tart apple, which has been boiled mushy in its own juice, through a sieve and wring them dry through a cloth. Put them in a saucepan over boiling water and give them a good stirring with a fork as you add 7 tablespoons of butter and 8 tablespoons (½ cup) of brown sugar with a large pinch of nutmeg or ginger or smaller pinches of both; stir 1 pint (2 cups) of milk into the mixture and let it cook. When it starts steaming blend 1½ teaspoons of arrowroot into 1 tablespoon of cold milk; add this to the batter; let it cook for ½ hour, but beat every 10 minutes. Between while, break (separate) 3 eggs. Beat the yolks with 1 teaspoon of vanilla extract and a pinch of mace and add to the batter at the end of the cooking period; take it out of the saucepan to cool; whip the egg whites stiff and hard, put them into the batter and pour it into a greased cake mold. Bake for ¾ hour in a fairly slow (300°F.) oven.*

JELLY ROLL (mid-1800s)—Take 3 egg yolks and whip them thick and yellow; beat into them 3 gills (1½ cups) of sugar; after that, stir in 1 pint

(2 cups) of flour sifted with 3 teaspoons of baking powder and a large pinch of salt. Beat 3 egg whites until firm. Have ready a buttered baking pan of a size that will let the batter stand about ½ inch thick; put it into a moderate (350°F.) oven for a quick baking, seldom more than 12 minutes, often only 10 minutes. Have a moist but well-wrung piece of muslin spread on your kitchen table and sprinkled with sifted sugar; place the cake, top side down, on this, cover the cake with heated jelly, trim it and roll. Some cooks let the cake acquire firmness while rolled by wrapping it in a piece of sugared dry muslin.*

LIGHTKEEPER'S CAKE (mid-1800s)—This cake was so named because of its ability to keep fresh and tasty for long periods. It is unusual in that it employs cornstarch instead of flour. The main ingredients are ½ pound each of butter (1 cup), sugar (1 generous cup) and cornstarch (1½ cups) and 5 eggs. Have the butter so soft that it can be beaten smooth; separate the eggs in such a manner that you have 5 yolks in one cup, 3 whites in another cup and 2 whites in a third, these 2 to be used for some other dish. Beat the yolks lightly and work them into the sugar; next add this mixture to the butter and mix thoroughly; this will take time, fully 30 minutes. When done, blend in the cornstarch, the peel of a lemon carefully grated, a 4-ounce measure (¼ cup) of good Medford rum. There is still no rest for the work-worn keeper's wife. Now take the cup with the 3 egg whites, beat them to a firm foam, blend this into the batter, pour it into a buttered cake tin and bake in moderate (350°F.) oven from 35 to 50 minutes. It is best to test for doneness with a broom straw. Comes the straw out clean, the cake is ready. Do not leave it at the lighthouse until it is 2 days old, and then pull for shore.*

TO BEAT WHITES OF EGGS QUICKLY (mid-1800s)—In cake baking, use the very simple expedient of adding just a dash of salt for each egg white in the bowl.*

COCHINEAL MARBLE CAKE— One cup of butter, 3 cups of pulverized sugar, 5 cups of flour, 3 teaspoons of yeast powder sifted with the flour, 1 cup of water, 10 eggs (whites only). Cream the butter and sugar by stirring them together; beat the whites of the eggs to a froth, and gradually mix all together. Before beginning the cake, put a small teaspoon of cochineal to soak in 2 tablespoons of hot water; bruise it with a spoon and strain the water through a piece of Swiss muslin into ¾ teacup (¾ cup) of the cake batter. As you pour the batter into the cake tin, marble it with the red dough. A little practice will produce very satisfactory results. Bake 45 minutes in a 350–75°F. oven.—Mrs. Anna Yocum

HICKORY NUT CAKE—Two cups of pulverized sugar, 1 cup of butter, 1 cup of new milk, 4 cups of sifted flour (winter wheat flour), the whites of 8 eggs, 1½ cups of hickory nut meats, 1 tablespoon of vanilla extract, 3 heaping teaspoons of baking powder; put the baking powder into the flour and stir well before using; beat and add the eggs the last; bake slowly 1 hour in a moderate (350°F.) oven.—Mrs. C. C. Stratton

CHILDREN'S PLAIN CAKE— One cup of Indian meal sifted, 1 of flour, 1 of sugar, 1 teaspoon of soda, about a pint (2 cups) of sour milk, 1 teaspoon of salt, 1 egg, a piece of butter the size of a common egg (4 tablespoons). Bake 20 minutes or so in a fast (425–50°F.) oven.—Harriet N. Jenks

TIPSY CAKE— Take a Sponge Cake (see Index) and stick it full of almonds which have been blanched; turn over it as much white wine as it will absorb; put it in a deep dish or glass bowl and let it stand 1 hour, then pour over it as much soft custard as the dish will hold. Let it stand 2 or 3 hours. Very simple and very nice.—Mrs. N. J. T. Dana

RUNAWAY CAKE—One egg, 1 teaspoon of sugar, 2 tablespoons of butter, 1 cup of milk, 2 teaspoons of cream of tartar, 1 teaspoon of soda, enough flour to make the batter a little thicker than that for griddle cakes. This is very nice eaten hot with butter for breakfast and tea. Bake 12 to 15 minutes in a 375°F. oven.—Mattie Winslow

TUMBLER CAKE—Four eggs, 1 tumbler (1 cup) of sugar, 1 tumbler of butter, ½ tumbler (½ cup) of molasses, 1/3 tumbler (1/3 cup) of milk, 1 teaspoon of saleratus (baking soda); spices to taste; ½ pound of raisins, ¼ pound of currants, flour to make it the usual consistency. Bake 1¼ hours in a slow (300°F.) oven.—Mrs. Lamkin

TWO-FOUR-EIGHT SAND CAKE (mid-1800s)—Take 2 each of eggs and tablespoons of potato flour; take 4 tablespoons each of raw powdered rice and wheat flour; 8 tablespoons (½ cup) each of sweet butter and white sugar. Whip the yolks of the eggs; cream the butter and sugar together; add to the butter and sugar the yolks as well as the wheat flour, powdered rice, potato flour and a smidgen of salt. Work this well; when done, whip the whites of eggs and stir them in with an easy touch. If the dough seems dry, wet it with a little milk, but only if you feel an urgent need. True to its name, the Sand Cake is very dry. Bake in buttered pound cake tins in a fairly hot (375–95°F.) oven about ¾ hour.*

A CAKE WILL KEEP FRESH (mid-1800s)—if, while it is still hot, you will give it a slight icing and set it quickly in your cake box with a tumbler of cold water.***

WHITE THREE-DECKER CAKE (late 1800s)—To start this big, fluffy cake, grease three 9-inch tins and get a good moderate heat (350°F.) in your oven. Next, sift 3 cups of cake flour with 2 cups of white sugar, 3 teaspoons of baking powder and ½ teaspoon of salt. Do this 3 times. Turn this into a bowl, make a dent in the center and pour into it 1 cup of fresh milk and 1 teaspoon of vanilla extract; blend these into the flour mixture and let it stand. Cream 2/3 cup of softened butter until it is fluffy and work it into the flour; next beat 5 egg whites stiff and dry; fold the whites into the batter carefully and pour it into the 3 pans. Bake about 30 minutes.* Use the following frosting.

THREE-DECKER FROSTING (late 1800s)—Cream 1/3 cup of butter and beat into it 1 cup of powdered sugar, 1½ teaspoons of vanilla extract and ½ teaspoon of salt; when all is mixed add 3 cups of white sugar and a small ½ cup of scalded cream. Beat, beat and beat until the frosting is ready to spread. If it is too thin, add sugar; if too thick, add scalded cream. If you seek a praise-winning effect, divide this frosting into three-quarter and one-quarter portions. Spread the former over the cake, after the layers have cooled, in the usual manner. To the remaining fourth add 1½ squares of chocolate (1/3 cup) of grated chocolate that has been melted in scalded cream; let this much thinner frosting cool; after the white frosting has set over the top and sides of the cake, pour the dark frosting over it so that it runs like lava over white snow.*

As for the 5 orphaned yolks, you might use 3 in making a batch of Chicken Croquettes (see Index) and 2 in concocting a Fish à la Crème (see Index).*

SNOW CAKE—Three-quarters of a cup of butter, 2 cups of sugar, 1 cup of milk, 1 cup of cornstarch, 2 cups of flour, 1½ teaspoons of baking powder. Mix the cornstarch, flour and baking powder together; add this to the butter and sugar alternately with the milk; lastly, add the whites of 7 eggs; flavor to taste with vanilla or almond. Bake in a moderate (350°F.) oven and test after 45 minutes.—Mrs. Lamkin

DELICATE CAKE—One and a half cups of confectioners' sugar, ½ cup of butter; 1½ cups of flour, ½ cup of cornstarch, sifted with the flour, ½ cup of milk, the whites of 6 eggs beaten to a froth, 1 small teaspoon of cream of tartar, ½ teaspoon of soda; flavor with almond or vanilla. Bake in a moderate (350°F.) oven ¾ to 1 hour.—Mrs. J. A. Ellis

FEATHER CAKE—One cup of sugar, 3 eggs beaten well together, a piece of butter the size of an egg (4 tablespoons), 1 cup of flour mixed with 1 teaspoon of cream of tartar, ½ teaspoon of soda dissolved in 8 teaspoons of water. Bake in a buttered tin for 30 minutes in a moderate (350°F.) oven. —Mrs. W. H. Ovington

CREAM CAKE—Beat 5 eggs thoroughly; add 2 cups of sugar, 2 tablespoons of cream, 2 cups of flour in which has been mixed 1½ teaspoons of baking powder, and a little salt. Bake in 5 jelly tins in a moderate (375°F.) oven 15 minutes, leaving about 1/6 of the batter out. To this add 1 cup of milk, also lemon or vanilla; boil until it thickens, stirring constantly; then spread it over the cakes as they are laid together.—Mrs. James Wadsworth

CORNSTARCH CAKE— One cup of white sugar and ½ cup of butter beaten together, ½ cup of cornstarch, the whites of 3 eggs beaten to a stiff froth, 1 cup of milk, 1 cup of flour, 1 teaspoon of cream of tartar, ½ teaspoon of soda. Flavor with lemon. Bake in a moderate (350°F.) oven about 25 minutes. —Lucy D. Fake

BRIDE'S CAKE—One pound (2¼ cups) of sugar, ½ pound (1 cup) of butter,

1 pound (4 cups) of flour, the whites of 16 eggs, 1½ teaspoons of soda, 1½ teaspoons of cream of tartar. Rub the butter and sugar together, then stir the whites of eggs into them. Sift the flour 3 times with the cream of tartar and soda in it and add it last. Flavor with bitter almond and cover. When the cake has cooled after baking 1¼ hours in a low moderate (325°F.) oven, cover it with vanilla icing.—Mrs. Ervin

LEMON CAKE—Three cups of sugar, 1 cup of butter, 1 cup of milk, 5 eggs, 4 cups of flour. Stir the butter and sugar to a cream; beat the yolks and whites of the eggs separately, the whites to a stiff froth; dissolve a little soda in the milk; mix all these together. Sift the flour and put it in by degrees and add the juice and grated rind of 2 fresh lemons. This cake is delicious. The baking lasts about 45 minutes in a good (350°F.) oven. But always test first with a broom straw.—L. Forest

SPICE CAKE—Two cups of sugar, 2 cups of butter, 6 cups of flour, 1 cup of molasses, 1 cup of milk, 6 eggs, 1 glass of brandy, 2 teaspoons of cream of tartar, 1 teaspoon of soda, 2 teaspoons of ground cloves, 1 teaspoon of ground nutmeg, 2 pounds of raisins. Let the cake stand in a moderate (350°F.) oven 45 to 55 minutes.—Mrs. H. H. Hurd

COFFEE CAKE—One cup of butter, 1 of sugar, 1 of molasses, 1 of strong coffee, 5 of flour, 1 pound of raisins, 1 teaspoon of soda, 1 of powdered cinnamon, 1 of powdered allspice, ½ ground nutmeg, 3 eggs (it can be made with 1 or 2). Sift the soda into the molasses. Bake 45 minutes in a hot (400°F.) oven.—Mrs. E. S. Chesebrough

NOAH WEBSTER'S CAKE—One cup of butter, 2½ cups of sugar, 1 cup of sweet milk, 4 cups of flour, the yolks of 5 eggs and the whites of 7, 2 teaspoons of cream of tartar, 1 teaspoon of soda, 1 teaspoon of extract of lemon; stir the butter and sugar until they look like cream; beat the yolks separately and well; whip the whites to a stiff froth; add the whites and flour last; add the remaining ingredients and beat all very thoroughly. This will make 2 cakes. If you lack time, and wish variety, by changing the flavoring and adding fruit to 1, you will have 2 cakes entirely unlike, and very good. Bake 45 minutes in a moderate (350°F.) oven.—Mrs. Ada Sturtevant

WHITE SPONGE CAKE—One tumbler (1 cup) of sifted flour, 1½ (1½ cups) of powdered sugar, 1 heaping teaspoon of cream of tartar and a little salt. Sift all together into a dish; beat the whites of 10 fresh eggs and stir them (not beat) very carefully into the flour and sugar until well mixed. Flavor with extract of lemon, and put it in with the whites of the eggs. Bake with great care in a moderate (350°F.) oven about 1 hour or less. This is an excellent cake.—Mrs. L. H. Smith

ORANGE CAKE—Sift together 2 cups of flour, 1 of cornstarch, 1 tablespoon of baking powder. Cream 1 teaspoon of extract of lemon and 1 teaspoon of vanilla extract with 1 cup of butter and 2 cups of sugar; add 1 cup of milk to half the above ingredients; stir well and add the whites of 7 eggs well beaten and then the rest of the flour mixture. Bake in jelly tins in a quick (400°F.) oven for 30 to 35 minutes.

The Jelly: The whites of 2 eggs, 1 cup of pulverized sugar, the juice and grated pulp of 2 oranges. A meringue top adds to its appearance when piled on quite high.—Mrs. A. M. Gibbs

LEMON-HONEY CAKE (mid-1800s)—Two cups of sugar, 2/3 cup of butter, 1 cup of milk, 1 cup of cornstarch, 3 cups of flour, 3 teaspoons of baking powder. Rub the butter and sugar to a cream; then add the milk; add the whites of 8 eggs beaten to a stiff froth, then the cornstarch and flour, to which has been added the baking powder. Bake for about 1 hour in a fast (400–25°F.) oven.* Use the following filling.

LEMON-HONEY FILLING (mid-1800s)—One pound of loaf sugar, the yolks of 8 eggs with 2 whole ones, the juice of 6 lemons and the grated rind of 2, ¼ pound (½ cup) of butter. Put the sugar, lemon and butter into a saucepan; melt them over a gentle fire; when all is dissolved, stir in the eggs, which have been well beaten; stir rapidly until it is as thick as honey. Spread this between the layers of cake; set aside the remainder in a closely covered vessel for future use.*

CUSTARD CAKE—Three eggs, 1 cup of sugar, 2 cups of flour, 2 teaspoons of melted butter, 1 teaspoon of cream of tartar, ½ teaspoon of soda dissolved in 2 teaspoons of milk. This recipe is enough for two cakes. They can be baked in layers, or split into layers when they are cold. Spread between the halves the following custard.

Cream 1 egg with ½ cup of sugar and flavor them with lemon; beat in 1/3 cup of flour and put this mixture into ½ pint (1 cup) of milk. Cook the custard in a pail or pitcher set in boiling water (double boiler) until it thickens.—Mrs. F. M. Cragin

LEMON CAKE—Beat the whites of 3 and the yolks of 5 eggs separately; stir them to a cream. Cream 2 cups of sugar with ½ cup of butter; add ½ cup of cold water, 2½ cups of flour with 2 teaspoons of baking powder mixed into it, the grated rind of 2 lemons and all the juice except about 1 tablespoon; stir the eggs into the cake. Bake in two square tins.

Frosting: The whites of 2 eggs, 2 small cups of sugar, with the tablespoon of lemon juice saved from the cake. When the cake is cold, join the halves with this frosting and frost the top.—Anon.

LEMON SPONGE CAKE—Eight eggs, 10 ounces (1½ scant cups) of sugar, ½ pound (2 cups) of flour, the juice and grating of 1 lemon. Separate the eggs; beat the yolks, sugar and lemon until thick and light; whisk the whites until dry, which add to the yolks with the flour, half of each at a time; mix all together, but avoid beating. Butter your sponge tin well and bake in a moderate (350°F.) oven about 50 to 55 minutes.—Mrs. James Wadsworth

SOFT GINGERBREAD—One cup of molasses, 1 of sugar, 1 of milk, ½ of butter, 5 of sifted flour, 1 tablespoon of ginger, ½ teaspoon or rather more of soda; a little ground cloves can be added if liked. Melt the butter in the molasses and sugar, allowing the mixture to become hot, then add the spices and milk, with the soda and flour. Persons measure flour so differently, if you would be quite sure to have it right, try a small cake first. If it falls add a little more flour. Bake about 40 minutes at a moderate (350°F.) heat. —Anon.

HARD GINGERBREAD (mid-1800s)—Soften ¾ pint (1½ cups) of butter; beat 6 whole eggs with 4 tablespoons (¼ cup) of milk; mix 3 teaspoons of ginger with 1 ditto of soda and sift these with 2 quarts (8 cups) of flour. Cream the butter and add the remaining items in the order given. Pour the mixture onto a large buttered baking tin or on the well-greased turned-up bottom of a baking pan. Roll it with a pin to even thickness; put in lines or waves with the tines of a dinner fork. Have ready a quick (400°F.) oven and bake about ¾ hour or until a broom straw comes out clean. Cut into 2-inch squares while hot; after they cool, keep them in a good cake tin.*

TO IMPROVE APPEARANCE AND FLAVOR OF GINGERBREAD OR MOLASSES COOKIES (mid-1800s)—Melt and add 1 dessertspoon (2 teaspoons) of grated chocolate for each gill (½ cup) of molasses used. This method not only takes the harshness out of molasses but it also gives a good color to the bakings.*

CREAM CAKES (mid-1800s)—Boil 1 pint (2 cups) of water, melt ½ pound (1 cup) of butter in it and stir in ¾ pound (3 cups) of flour while it boils; when it is cool, add 1 teaspoon of saleratus (baking soda) dissolved in 1 tablespoon of hot water; beat 10 eggs good and proper and stir them into the batter. Drop the cakes on buttered tins and bake 20 minutes in a low moderate (325°F.) oven.***

CREAM CAKE FILLINGS (mid-1800s)—These are made by beating ½ pint (1 cup of flour and 1 pint (2 cups) of sugar together with 4 beaten eggs. Over the fire mix this into 1 quart (4 cups) of scalding milk; when all is smooth and incorporated, remove it from the fire and season with the juice of 1 lemon and ½ lemon rind, grated. When cool, cut the cakes open, add the cream and replace their tops.***

KISSES (mid-1800s)—Beat the whites of 9 fresh eggs to a froth, then mix with it 15 tablespoons (1 scant cup) of finest white sugar and 5 or 6 drops of essence of lemon. Drop them on buttered paper with a teaspoon, sift sugar over them and bake in a slow (275°F.) oven for 15 minutes.*

COCOANUT PUFFS—One grated cocoanut, a little over ½ pound (1¼ cups) of pulverized sugar stirred in the whites of 3 eggs, beaten light. Drop in small cakes on a greased dripping pan. Bake in a very quick (425°F.) oven and watch closely.—Anon.

GERMAN PUFFS—Mix 1 pint (2 cups) of cold sweet milk with 5 tablespoons of flour moistened in a little of the milk; add 1 tablespoon of melted butter and 6 beaten eggs, leaving out the whites of 3. Bake in buttered cups, half filled, 20 minutes in a hot (450°F.) oven.***

PUFF SAUCE—Beat the whites of 5 eggs to a stiff froth and whip in 1½ gills (¾ cup) of powdered sugar, plus the juice of 2 oranges. Turn the puffs from the cups on to a platter and cover them with the sauce just before sending to the table.—Mrs. H. M. Brewer

CHESS CAKES—Peel and grate 1 cocoanut. Take 1 pound (2¼ cups) of sugar and ½ pint (1 cup) of water, and boil them 15 minutes; stir in the whole of the grated cocoanut and boil the whole 15 minutes longer; while the mixture is still warm stir in ¼ pound (½ cup) of butter, then add the yolks of 7 well-beaten eggs. Bake in patty pans lined with a rich paste (see Index) in a fast moderate oven (375°F.) until the pastry is brown. These will keep some time and mix prettily in a basket of cake. The small oval patty tins are prettier than scallops.—Anon.

FINGER CAKES—Three eggs, beaten very light, to which add a cup of granulated sugar (excepting a tablespoonful); sift in a very small teaspoon of cream of tartar, half as much soda, a little salt and a good-sized teaspoon of vanilla extract; stir in flour enough for a stiff dough. Roll the dough very thin and sprinkle it with the tablespoon of sugar kept back from the cupful, giving it a light roll; cut the dough in strips of finger width; do not let them touch in the pan. Bake in a quick (400°F.) oven, watching them, as they readily scorch.—Mrs. Lamkin

WINE CAKES—One pint (2 cups) of sweet milk, 3 eggs well beaten, enough flour to make a thick batter. Have hot lard ready and fry them as you would other fried cakes. Drop the batter in by the spoonful and let your hand shake as you let the batter fall into the lard. Serve warm with ½ cup of heated wine mixed with 1 tablespoon of confectioners' sugar turned to the thickness of thin cream with 1 heaping teaspoon of moist arrowroot.

CHOCOLATE TREATS (late 1800s)—Grate 3 ounces of chocolate (usually 3 squares, or ¾ cup when grated) and mix it well with ¾ pint (1½ cups) of flour and a pinch of salt; add ½ pint (1 cup) each of brown sugar and chopped nut-meats, 1 beaten egg, a good gill (heaping ½ cup) of flour. When all is beaten together, pour the mixture into a shallow, buttered baking pan; bake in a moderate to fast (375°F.) oven for about 25 minutes. Cut into squares while still hot.*

COCOANUT COOKIES (late 1800s)—Cream 1/3 cup of butter with 1 cup of sugar; beat; add 1 egg and 2 tablespoons of cold milk. Mix and sift 2¼ cups of flour, 1 rounded teaspoon of cream of tartar, ½ teaspoon of baking soda and a little salt; when it is done, stir in 1 cup of grated or dried and shredded cocoanut (see Index). Combine all the ingredients, drop spoonfuls on buttered tins and bake in a not too slow (300°F.) oven for about ½ hour.*

ORDINARY COOKIE BATTER (late 1800s)—Cream 1 cupful of butter with 2 of sugar. Stir in 1 quart (4 cups) of flour slowly; add 1 egg, beaten, and

1 teaspoon of baking soda. Flavor with vanilla, almond or cinnamon, cocoanut or chocolate; chopped nuts are also good. Roll thin, cut out into cookies and bake quickly in a hot (400°F.) oven.*

MUSTER GINGERBREAD (mid-1800s)—In a bowl mix 6 tablespoons of boiling water with 1 gill (½ cup) of butter, 1 cup of molasses, a pinch of salt and 2 teaspoons of ginger; stir in 1½ pints (3 cups) of flour; add 1 beaten egg and, after that, 1 teaspoon of baking soda. Roll to ¼ inch thickness and cut into strips or squares. Wet the tops lightly with milk; mark with lines with the tines of a fork. Bake in a moderate (350°F.) oven for 25 to 30 minutes.*

FRUIT JUMBLES (mid-1800s)—Work 1 pound (2¼ cups) of sugar into ¾ (1½ cups) of softened butter; beat 5 whole eggs and add them with 1 small teacup (½ cup) of milk; mix in ¼ pound of plumped currants and ½ wineglass (¼ cup) of red wine. Mix ½ teaspoon of baking soda with 1¼ pounds (5 cups) of flour, sift them twice, and add to the other ingredients, making a smooth dough. Drop on buttered tins with a spoon and bake in a rather quick (400°F.) oven for 15 to 25 minutes.

SPONGE COOKIES (late 1800s)—Beat 3 eggs; add 1 cup of sugar; stir 1 heaping teaspoon of cream of tartar into 1 heaping cup of flour; mix this with the rest and, on completion, stir ½ teaspoon of baking soda into the batter. Drop by teaspoonfuls on a buttered tin about 3 inches apart and bake in a quick (400°F.) oven for a very few watchful minutes.*

GINGER SNAPS (late 1800s)—Sift 3 cups of wheat flour, 1 heaping tablespoon of ginger, 1½ teaspoons of salt and 2 saltspoons (½ teaspoon) of baking soda into a bowl and blend well. Bring 1/3 cup of butter and 1 cup of light-brown molasses to a quick boil; take it from the fire, stir in the flour-ginger mixture and let it stand 8 to 9 hours or over night. Add 2 beaten egg yolks. Roll the dough out thinly on a lightly floured board, cut into round shapes and bake in a low to moderate (325°F.) oven for about 10 to 12 minutes on a greased baking tin.*

JUMBLES (mid-1800s)—Beat 2 cups of sugar and 1 cup of fresh butter to a cream; then add 4 eggs, well beaten, 1 cup of raisins or walnuts chopped fine, 1 cup of sweet milk; mix; add 3 cups of flour into which 1 teaspoon of cream of tartar and ½ teaspoon of baking soda have been thoroughly combined. Bake quickly in tins 1 inch deep in a quick (400°F.) oven; grate nutmeg and sprinkle sugar over the Jumbles when they are out of the oven.*

QUICK-AS-A-WINK COOKIES (mid-1800s)—Beat ½ pint (1 cup) of sugar and ½ pound (1 cup) of fresh (unsalted) softened butter to a cream with the yolk of a large egg; add the juice and grated rind of ½ large lemon; follow with 1 pound (3-2/3 cups) of flour and 1 gill (⅛ cup) of chopped almonds that have been blanched and dried (see Index). Roll the batter to the thickness of the tip of your little finger and place it on an unbuttered baking pan. For a nice color, touch the top with the white of egg, but only lightly beaten, and a thin sprinkling of nutmeg. This bakes from 12 to 15 minutes in a low to moderate (325°F.) oven. Cut into diamond shapes before it cools or the cookies will ravel around the edges.*

HERMITS (late 1800s)—Cream 1 cup of brown sugar with 1 ditto of butter; add 2 beaten eggs. In a separate bowl, measure and blend 1 saltspoon (¼ teaspoon) each of powdered nutmeg, cinnamon, ginger and cloves with 1½ pints (3 cups) of flour, ½ teaspoon of cream of tartar and 2 saltspoons (½ teaspoon) of salt; have ready 1 cup of plumped and seeded raisins. Blend them and all the other ingredients and add, when this is done, 1 teaspoon of saleratus (baking soda) melted in 1 tablespoon of boiling water. Cut out the Hermits with a cookie cutter and bake a short ¼ hour in a moderate (350°F.) oven on a buttered baking pan. Some persons place a blanched almond in the center of each cookie.*

BOILED COOKIES—Boil 1 cup of milk, 2 of sugar, 3 of flour; cool the mixture off; then add 1 teaspoon of baking soda and the yolks of 3 eggs. Cut the dough into rounds and bake in a quick (400°F.) oven 12 minutes. —Mrs. F.

EVERLASTING COOKIES— Two cups of sugar, 1 of butter, ¾ of sweet milk, 2 teaspoons of baking powder; season to taste. Rub the butter and sugar together; then add 2 eggs, the milk and enough flour to make a soft dough. Roll it thin, cut out the cookies, sprinkle a little sugar over the top and bake with frequent checks in a quick (400°F.) oven.—Mrs. John Edwards

CARAWAY COOKIES—One cup of butter, 2 of sugar, 1 of sour cream, 1 teaspoon of soda, 2 of cream of tartar, 3 eggs, 2 tablespoons of caraway seed, a little nutmeg, flour enough to form a soft dough. Roll the dough out thin, cut out the cookies and bake in a quick (400°F.) oven.—Mrs. Russell

SAND TARTS—One pound (2¼ cups) of sugar, ¾ pound (1½ cups) of butter, 2 eggs, flour enough to make a very stiff dough. Roll it out, cut out the tarts and wet the tops with whites of eggs, then put 2 almonds on each one; sprinkle over them cinnamon and sugar. Bake 8 to 12 minutes in a faster than moderate (375°F.) oven.—Anon.

SUGAR DROPS—One pound (4 cups) of flour, ¾ pound (1-2/3 cups) of sugar, ½ pound (1 cup) of butter, 4 eggs, a gill (½ cup) of rose water. These are to be baked slowly on paper, in a (325°F.) low moderate oven. This will make 60 drops.—Mrs. H. M. Buell

NO MATTERS—Three cups of sour milk, 3 tablespoons of cream or butter; add enough flour to make a moderately stiff dough and roll each one out to about the size of a plate; fry in hot lard; cover each with nicely seasoned apple sauce; lay them one over the other.—M. A. Bingham

17. Pies, Pastries and Pandowdies

ABOUT CRUSTS AND FILLINGS (mid-1800s)—There is hardly another article of food in which so much is sacrificed to mere appearance as in pastry. And yet everybody likes a light crust, a little brown and not excessively rich, rather than one that is too rich and sits too heavily upon the stomach. A good thickness is that of a dinner plate (⅛ inch).*

In making fillings, use minimum amounts of tapioca, flour, cornstarch or eggs to thicken them; of all thickenings, eggs or yolks are the best, but also the most expensive. For almost all kinds of pies, good brown sugar is nice enough. In making certain cream pies, as in making custards, have the milk at scalding heat when it is mixed with the eggs; this tends to produce a crisp instead of a soggy undercrust.*

If the crust is tough, you are using either too much water or too little shortening; or you failed to cut the shortening into the flour thoroughly before the water was added; also, dough will toughen if handled too much after the water is in it. For a glossy brown crust, brush pies with milk or slightly beaten egg whites just prior to baking.*

The uses of left-over pie dough include making patty cases by rolling thin circles of paste and placing them on the buttered exteriors of gem or muffin pans; bake them in a hot (450°F.) oven just long enough to brown and use for creamed dishes and desserts. Some housewives make left-over dough from trimmings into pie crust; this is almost sure to turn out tough. One way to use it is to save it until next pie time and incorporate the old dough with the new.*

PIE LININGS IN LATE 1880s—Clever pie makers have learned that pie pan bottoms that have been holed with the point of a small awl, improve the crispness of the undercrust. Have the paste ¼ inch thick for very wet pie, ⅛ inch thick for drier pies. The usual practice is to make the crusts 1 inch larger than the plate, unless you cut ¾-inch-wide strips of crust wherewith to seal the pie's edges. The upper crust should extend about ¼ inch beyond the edge of the plate. It is always well to chill pie crusts before using them; it is also good practice to bake shells for soft or cream pies ahead of time in a very hot (450°F.) oven for about ¼ hour. One cannot overestimate the value of having pie crusts closely joined; this is done by wetting the edge of the undercrust with water and flour and pressing the edge of the upper crust firmly upon it.*

RICH PUFF PASTE—For every pound (4 cups) of well-sifted flour have ¾ pound (1½ cups) of chilled butter, the yolk of 1 egg and some ice-cold water; chop half the butter into the flour with a knife, then stir in the yolk; with the aid of the ice water, work all into a dough; roll it out thin, spread dabs of butter over the surface, fold it closely (butter side in) and roll again; do this about 6 times until all the butter has been used up. Place the paste, rolled in a cloth, in a cold spot until it is wanted.—Mary Abbott

FINE PUFF PASTRY—One pound (4 cups) of flour, a little more for the rolling pin and board, ½ pound (1 cup) of butter and ½ pound of lard. Cut the butter and lard through the flour (which should be sifted) into small thin shells and mix with sufficient ice water for it to roll easily. Avoid kneading it and use the hands as little as possible in mixing.—Mrs. William K. Watson

CHOPPED PASTE (late 1800s)—Chill ½ gill (¼ cup) each of butter and lard until firm; have ready ¾ pint (1½ cups) of flour sifted with 2 salt-spoons (½ teaspoon) of salt and a small pitcher of water chilled with pieces of ice. Cut the shortenings into the flour in small shavings and chop until the flour becomes granular; sprinkle just enough ice water—about ½ gill (¼ cup)—on it gradually to make a stiff paste. Put the paste on a molding (bread) board; roll it into a square about ¼ inch thick; fold it twice and roll again, always from the center outward, and strive to have the paste form a circle. Mend splits along the edges by pinching them firmly together.*

CHOPPED PIE PASTE (early 1800s)—Place 1 quart (4 cups) of sifted flour, 1 pint (2 cups) of butter, ½ pint (1 cup) of lard, 1 teaspoon of salt and 1 tablespoon of white sugar into the chopping tray. Chop all together until the shortening is thoroughly mixed with the flour; then add 1½ gills (¾ cup) of ice water slowly as you continue chopping. When it is well mixed, sprinkle your board with flour, turn the paste on it and roll it into a flat piece. Place it in a pan on ice. The paste can be used as soon as it is mixed but it will be nicer if it stands a while.*

CHOP CRUSTS FOR PIES (mid-1800s)—Sift 1 pint (2 cups) of flour with ½ teaspoon of salt, twice, into a large basin; work in ½ gill (¼ cup) of butter or lard—which must be hard and cold—until it is blended into the flour. Use your fingers and spare neither time nor energy in doing it right. Next, pinch in, dab by dab, ½ gill (¼ cup) of washed (unsalted) butter, equally cold and hard. The job is done when the pastry looks like a mess of grey-white peas. Now, for a crisp, brown crust, mix 3 tablespoons each of iced milk and iced water. Add as much of this as you need to the flour— from 4 to 6 tablespoons. Do it spoon by spoon with one hand as, with a wooden fine-pronged fork, you "lift" the liquid into the flour with the other. "Lift" is the word for this motion. It goes from the bottom up; "lift" swiftly, yet gently. You will wreck the dough if you stir it or use a spoon. The trick is to moisten, and not to soak, every little pea of dough. Test this by feel as you go along adding the liquid to the dough. As for rolling the dough, divide it into two equal portions. But each, in turn, on a flouring board covered by a fine flurry of flour shaken through a sifter. Many pie makers use linen-covered rolling pins to prevent sticking. Follow the usual pie dough practice of rolling from the middle outward and hold the rolling pin lightly as you work. Roll up and down and sideways until the bottom shell is a disk 11 inches in diameter and ⅛ inch thick. Put this bottom crust into an ungreased pan and bounce the pan lightly against the table so that the crust rests upon the bottom, leaving no air holes. Paint the crust with an egg white slightly stirred with a fork—not beaten. This makes a moisture-resistant crust.

In filling the shell, it is vital that the filling lies slightly higher in the center than at the edge of the dish; this is because the top crust must rest on a solid base. Put the top crust into place, trim it to fit the edges, by crimping the crust onto the rim of the pan with thumb and forefinger. Cut steam vents in the crust before baking.*

POTATO PIE CRUST (mid-1800s)—Boil 6 good-sized mealy potatoes and mash them fine; add a good pinch of salt, a tablespoon of butter and 2 of boiling water while they are hot or put in 3 tablespoons of cream and no butter and water. Then work in enough flour to make a paste that can be rolled out. This is an especially good crust for pot pies.*

POTATO TOP CRUST FOR MEAT AND FISH PIES (late 1800s)—Sift 1 pint (2 cups) of flour into a bowl with 1 dessertspoon (2 teaspoons) of baking powder, a good pinch of salt and a small one each of white pepper and grated nutmeg. Cut in 1½ gills (¾ cup) each of nice white lard and butter, both of the same softness; work in a good ½ pint (1 cup) of mashed potatoes and turn the mixture into a paste by adding a very little water or milk. Roll into a thickish crust on your flour board. When the crust is in place over the pie—any kind from beef to poultry to fish—make a hole in the center so that steam can escape.*

THE TIME IT TAKES TO BAKE PIES (mid-1800s)—Periods of baking usually run from 45 minutes to an hour, depending upon the thickness and nature of the pies. The heat required for soft pies varies from that needed for fruit pies in that soft pies should be baked in a quick (400°F.) oven as against a rather faster (425–50°F.) heat for the fruit kind. The thing to remember in pie baking is to give the oven a firm bottom heat. Naturally, there are exceptions to these general rules.*

BAKING PIE SHELLS BEFOREHAND (late 1800s)—For nearly all kinds of soft and custard pies, it pays to bake the undercrust or shell before the fillings are made. Place the undercrust in the pan to be used and bake it in a very hot (450°F.) oven for 10 to 12 minutes.*

CARROT PIE (late 1800s)—Cut 3 or 4 large carrots into quarters the long way, boil them until tender and wipe their skins away with a rag; mash them to a pulp and rub them through a sieve. Make a medium Cream Sauce (see Index). Mix enough of it into the carrots to give them the texture of heavy custard; season to taste with brown sugar, pepper and salt. Heat the carrots in a saucepan over hot water and, when they are hot, blend in 3 egg yolks, one at a time and thoroughly; let it all cool. Whip the 3 egg whites and put them into the filling, pour it into an unbaked pie shell and bake 1 hour in a quick (400°F.) oven.*

CHOCOLATE PIE (late 1800s)—Grate 4 ounces (4 squares) of chocolate very fine (¾ cup when grated) and stir in 3 saltspoons (¾ teaspoon) of vanilla extract; separate 5 eggs, blend the yolks into ½ pint (1 cup) of white sugar and add this to the chocolate; beat the 5 whites to a stiff froth, add them to the rest and pour the filling into a pre-baked shell (see Index). Bake in a fast (400°F.) oven about 45 minutes. Cool; cover with whipped cream; dust the top of the latter with finely grated chocolate.*

VINEGAR PIE—One cup of sugar, ½ cup of vinegar, 2 teaspoons of flour, 1 of butter, 1 of cinnamon, 2 cups of water. Boil all together until thick, and bake as you would a Custard Pie.—Ella Guild

TRANSPARENT PIE—Divide ½ pound (1 generous cup) of sugar; beat half of it into 1/3 pound (2/3 cup) of butter and the other half with the yolk of 5 eggs; combine these; then add the beaten whites, 3 tablespoons of cream and ½ teaspoon of vanilla extract. Prepare the crust in two pie plates, pour the mixture in and bake in a slow (300°F.) oven until brown and done. —Mrs. P. H. Smith

LEMON PIE—Two lemons, 5 eggs, 1 cup each of sugar and water, 8 table-spoons of pulverized sugar, 2 tablespoons of cornstarch. Grate the outside of the 2 lemon rinds into a dish, then cut the lemons in half and remove the seeds, scooping the pulp and juice into the dish with a silver spoon; add 1 cup each of sugar and water, first wetting 2 tablespoons of starch with some of the water; mix the cornstarch into the lemon-water with 5 yolks and 1 white of an egg, both well beaten first. Pour into two tins lined with pastry (see Index) and bake in a quick (400°F.) oven for 45 minutes; beat the remaining 4 whites just before baking is completed; gradually stir in 8 tablespoons of pulverized sugar and, when the pies are done, spread the snow over them and replace them in the oven until brown.—Miss Annie Slocum

RICE PIE—One quart (4 cups) of milk, boiled, 1 small teacup (½ cup) of rice flour mixed in a little cold milk; add to the boiling milk 2 tablespoons of butter; when the mixture is cold, add 5 eggs well beaten; sweeten to taste, flavor with vanilla and bake.—Mrs. A. S. Ewing

ACID PIE—One cup of soft bread or crackers, 1 cup of sugar, 2 cups of water, a little lemon, 1 egg, 1 teaspoon of tartaric acid.—M. A. Bingham

COCOANUT CUSTARD PIE (late 1800s)—Bake a shell beforehand (see Index). Make a custard with 3 beaten egg yolks strained into 1 pint (2 cups) of milk; add 2 tablespoons of cornstarch rubbed smooth in a small amount of the milk and 1 tablespoon of melted butter; add 1 gill (½ cup) of sugar (white), the juice and grated rind of a small lemon, 1 saltspoon (¼ teaspoon) of salt; when blended, stir in ½ pint (1 cup) of freshly shredded cocoanut (if dried, see Index); lastly, beat the whites of the eggs; stir them into the filling. Fill the shell and bake from 45 to 60 minutes in a quick (400°F.) oven.*

CUSTARD PIE (mid-1800s)—For this pie, use a Chopped Paste (see Index) twice the ordinary thickness (of ⅛ inch); also, to get a nice fluting, allow about 1¼ inches of the lining to extend beyond the edge; this is doubled back upon itself along the edge and pinched into flutings with the fingers (see Chop Crusts for Pies, above). Beat 3 eggs together with ½ gill (¼ cup) of white sugar, 1 tablespoon of melted butter, 1 saltspoon (¼ teaspoon) of vanilla extract, a large pinch of salt and a small one of nutmeg; when well beaten, add, slowly, 1 pint (2 cups) of scalded milk; beat the mixture and pour it into pie dish. Bake in a quick (400°F.) oven a short hour until it sets. For evenness, turn the pie around once or twice while it is baking. Powder the top with nutmeg or cinnamon.*

NO LUMP CUSTARD PIE (mid-1800s)—Beat the yolks of 3 eggs into a cream. Stir 1 tablespoon of sifted flour into 3 tablespoons of sugar; this separates the particles of flour so that there are no lumps; add the beaten yolks to this and put in a little salt and ½ teaspoon of nutmeg; beat the whites of the eggs and cut them in; have ready 1 pint (2 cups) of scalded milk that has been cooled—the milk must *not* have come to a boil—and add it to the mixture. Dust the top with nutmeg through a sieve. Put the filling into a baked (see Index) pastry shell and cook it in a not too fast (400°F.) oven about ¾ hour until set.*

LEMON PIE (late 1800s)—Make a nice light paste (see Index) and lay it into two medium-sized pans for 2 pies. Then sweeten the juice and rind of 2 lemons to taste with white sugar; melt a piece of butter the size of an egg (4 tablespoons) very slowly; also beat and strain 3 eggs. Stir these items together, then add 1 pint (2 cups) of thin cream into which 3 dessertspoons (2 tablespoons) of cornstarch have been dissolved; stir the cream in rapidly. Fill the plates and bake in a fast (400°F.) oven for 45 to 55 minutes or until the pie is set. For Meringue for Toppings, see below.*

MERINGUE FOR TOPPINGS (late 1800s)—The general rule for making a meringue is 2 tablespoons of sugar for each white of egg; a better rule, however, is to weigh the whites and to use the same weight of sugar as there is of whites. To insure well-beaten whites, add 1 saltspoon (¼ teaspoon) of salt before you beat them; add also 2 saltspoons (½ teaspoon) of vanilla extract and 2 tablespoons of sugar from the sugar to be used. Beat the whites for 5 minutes; add the remaining sugar slowly and in similar quantities; beat steadily the while. Spread the meringue over the top of the pie in even thickness and create a wave effect by pressing the surface with a tablespoon. A good way to bake the meringue is in a hot (450°F.) oven for 2, 3 or 5 minues, but a better one is to bake it for 12 to 15 minutes in a slow to moderate oven (325°F.).***

PUMPKIN CREAM PIE (late 1800s)—Have ready 1½ cups of cold cooked mashed sieved pumpkin; mix this with 1½ cups of whole milk, ¾ cup of white sugar, 1 tablespoon of cornstarch, ¼ teaspoon each of salt, nutmeg, ginger, cinnamon and white pepper (all ground). When these are blended, add the beaten yolks of 2 eggs; whip the mixture until it is smooth as butter. Pour it into a pie pan lined with Plain Paste (see Index) and bake in a quick (400°F.) oven for a good ¾ hour.*

SOME POINTERS ON FRUIT PIES (early 1800s)—Some people differ in regard to the proper thickness of crusts for fruit pies. In one rule the fruit constitutes 1/3 of the thickness and the two crusts the other 2/3; although it may look fine, this pie is neither so healthful nor so good as one made with thinner crusts and more fruit.

For apple, peach and pumpkin, crusts should be as thin as a common earthen plate (about 1/8 inch); for juicy fruits, such as berries, cherries, currants, plums and mince, it should be just a little thicker.

In making berries into pies, use deep dishes, and be careful not to fill them full, as the syrup will boil over and thus much of the richness of the pie will be lost. There is one way effectually to prevent the loss of syrup. After you have laid in the fruit, or mince, and rolled out the upper crust, wet the rim of the undercrust all around with cold water, not omitting a single spot—if you do, the syrup will escape at that spot—sprinkle a very little flour upon the rim of crust, lay the upper crust in place and press it gently down upon the rim. The flour and water acts as a paste to bind the two crusts together. Prick the top 8 to 10 times with the tines of a fork. It is a good idea to invert a small teacup in the center of a juicy fruit pie.

To avoid clammy lower crusts, which are neither good nor digestible, never fill pies made of moist materials until just before putting them into the oven; such pies should not be allowed to stand longer than it takes to put the top crust into place. Many like to dust bottom crusts with sifted bread or cake crumbs to keep them crisp.

When fruit pies are baked to perfection, the tops will generally be swelled all over and will, in moving, tremble like jelly; if not done, the middle will look like a thick liquid.*

PINEAPPLE PIE—A grated pineapple and its weight in sugar, half its weight in butter, 5 eggs, the whites beaten to a stiff froth, 1 cup of whipped cream. Cream the butter and beat it with the sugar and yolks until very light; add the cream, the pineapple and the whites of the eggs. Bake in pie plates lined with pastry (see Index) in a quick (400°F.) oven. To be eaten cold.—M. S. W.

RHUBARB AS A BERRY-STRETCHER (mid-1800s)—If, in making berry pies, you find yourself short of berries but with plenty of rhubarb in your garden, stew and add enough rhubarb to fill your needs and no one will know the difference; this is due to the peculiar faculty of rhubarb to discard its own taste and assimilate that of other fruits with which it is cooked.*

DRIED APPLE, PEACH OR APRICOT PIE (mid-1800s)—Wash the apples in 2 or 3 waters and put them to soak in rather more water than will cover them, as they absorb a great deal. After soaking 2 hours put them into a kettle with the same water and a lemon or orange cut up; boil them until very tender; when they rise, do not stir them but push them down with a skimmer; stirring makes them tasteless, as does over-night soaking. When they are tender, add brown sugar to taste and a small piece of butter and cook another 15 minutes. Nutmeg and cloves are good spices to use. Dried peaches and apricots are handled the same way, but omit the lemon or orange and spice. Put the fillings on an undercrust in a deep pie dish, cover with the top crust, prick it and bake in a quick (400°F.) oven for 3/4 hour.*

UPSIDE DOWN FRUIT PIE (mid-1800s)—Bake this pie in a 2-quart (8-cup) basin; to give it the right shape the basin must be of nearly the same size top and bottom. First make a nice pie crust (see Index). Put a layer of it in the bottom, but not around the sides of the dish; then a layer of chopped raisins; sprinkle sugar over this, pieces of butter and any spice you like— cloves and nutmeg are nice; make more layers of crust, fruit, etc., until your dish is full; put a crust on top. Bake in a slow (275°F.) oven for 2 hours; when it is done, turn it bottom upwards on a plate, and before putting it on the table sprinkle fine sugar over it. It is quite as good when warmed again as when first baked. It takes 1 pound of raisins, 10 to 12 good-sized apples and 2 large cups of sugar—more if you like.*

BLACKBERRY AND BLUEBERRY PIES (mid-1800s)—Wash and dry enough berries to fill the pie pan less than full when they are poured on the undercrust. Sift 5 tablespoons of white sugar all over the berries and dredge a little flour over the sugar through a sifter before you lay on the upper crust, which is make of a Chop Crust (see Index). Close the edge with special care (see Some Pointers on Fruit Pies, above) and bake in a quick to very quick (425–50°F.) oven from 50 to 60 minutes.*

APPLE POT PIE (early 1800s)—Make and roll a plain pie crust (see Index). With half of it line the sides, but not the bottom, of a stew-pan, having a close-fitting cover. Fill the center with peeled and sliced apples and add to them 1 teacup (1 cup) of maple syrup, a big pinch of ground cinnamon, another of salt and a little butter cut into bits, enough to spread over the surface. Be sure to have the stew-pan only two-thirds full to have room for the pie to rise. Wet the edge of the remaining crust and fit it over the top of the apples—not over the top of the pot; put the lid on and let the dish simmer on top of the stove for 1 hour without lifting the lid once. Be careful that it does not stand in a place so hot that it will burn. At serving time, remove the top crust and cut it according to the number of servings; lay it aside; dish the apples; lay the crust from the sides of the pot, also equally divided, on serving plates. Spoon the apples onto this and put the top crust over all; serve while hot.*

CHERRY PIE (mid-1800s)—All cherries, except the sweet ones, are good for pies; but the common red cherry makes the best. The method is to leave the pits intact; pour 1 quart (4 cups) of cherries into a deep dish lined with paste (see Index) after they have been mixed with a small pint (scant 2 cups) of white sugar; dredge 3 dessertspoons (2 tablespoons) of flour (or cornstarch) over this mixture; lay on the upper crust and seal it with care. Bake 45 to 60 minutes in a fairly hot (425–50°F.) oven.*

GOOSEBERRY PIE (early 1800s)—Remove the tops and tails from 1 quart (4 cups) of gooseberries. Wash the gooseberries and stew them until tender in a sugar syrup made of ½ pint (1 cup) of white sugar, powdered, and 1 gill (½ cup) of boiling water. Lay the gooseberries upon an undercrust in a deep pie dish with strips of puff pastry placed diagonally across the top. Bake in moderate to fast (375°F.) oven about 1 hour.*

TEMPERANCE MINCE MEAT (mid-1800s)—Take 8 pounds of round meat; chop it raw; now chop 1 pound of suet, 4 pounds of raisins, carefully seeded, ½ pound of citron and ¼ pound of candied orange peel; add this to the meat. Now chop as many apples as necessary to provide twice the bulk of the meat; to these add 1 pint (2 cups) of boiled soft cider and 3 pounds (6¾ cups) of sugar. Simmer apples, meat and all for 2 hours over a slow fire. Toward the end, season with powdered cinnamon, nutmeg, allspice, cloves and lemon juice to taste. Put away the mince meat in well-covered jars and let it stand at least 10 days before using. Add whole raisins and bits of butter when making the mince pies.*

OX-TONGUE MINCE MEAT PIE (early 1800s)—Chop 1 cooked beef tongue very fine; do likewise with 7 large cored and peeled apples and put them together. To 1 quart (4 cups) of wine or boiled cider add 1¼ pounds (generous 2¾ cups) of loaf sugar, pulverized; boil it up so as to skim off the top. Remove this from the fire and, as it cools, mix 1 pound of minced suet into the meat; add 1 pound each of stoned raisins and currants; ½ pound of chopped citron; the juice, pulp and grated rind of a lemon; 1 teaspoon of powdered cinnamon and 3 saltspoons (¾ teaspoon) each of powdered nutmeg and cloves. When all is well mixed, add the wine or cider; be careful in pouring it not to disturb any sediment there may be from the sugar if you use the ordinary brown kind. That which comes from Havana is seldom clean; Porto Rico and Santa Cruz are considered best. The New Orleans is almost too sweet. Place in a lined and rather deep pie pan; bake in a very fast (425–50°F.) oven for ¾ hour.*

FILLINGS FOR LARGE MINCE PIES—Large 6 pounds of lean fresh beef boiled tender, and when cold, chopped fine; a pound of beef suet chopped fine, 5 pounds of apples, chopped, 2 pounds of raisins, seeded, 2 pounds of currants, ½ pound of citron, 2 tablespoons of powdered cinnamon, 1 tablespoon of grated nutmeg, 1 tablespoon of powdered cloves, 1 tablespoon of allspice, 1 tablespoon of salt, 3 pounds (6¾ cups) of brown sugar, a quart (4 cups) of wine, a pint (2 cups) of brandy and the liquor the meat is boiled in. Mix all together. Keep in a stone jar tied over with a double paper. It should be made at least the day before it is used, and when you make pies add a little more wine to the mince meat you take out for the pies and more chopped apples—Mrs. Pulsifer.

FILLING FOR SMALL MINCE PIES—Three pints (6 cups) of peeled and chopped apples, 1 pint (2 cups) of lean boiled and minced beef, ½ pint (1 cup) of butter or beef drippings, 1 pint (2 cups) of molasses, ½ pint (1 cup) of water, 1½ teaspoons of allspice, 1 teaspoon of cinnamon, 1 teaspoon of salt, ¾ teaspoon of cloves, 2½ tablespoons of brandy, ½ nutmeg (all the spices ground). Young housekeepers will find this recipe a great comfort.—C. Kennicott

POTATO PIE—Boil until white, mealy and very tender enough baking potatoes to make a pint (2 cups) when rubbed through a colander. While the potatoes are still hot, add ¼ pound (½ cup) of butter, and mix well;

beat the yolks of 6 eggs well with 1 pound (2-1/3 cups) of fine sugar; add the grated rind and juice of 1 lemon and then the beaten egg whites; stir these lightly in. Bake in pie plates lined with paste (see Index) in a moderate (350°F.) oven 30 minutes. Eat cold.—Anon.

FRESH PEACH PIE (late 1800s)—Pare the peaches by dipping them rather quickly into boiling water and skinning them with the back of a knife; the freestones are the best peaches because they are the most tender; the clingstones require longer cooking; cut the peaches into eighths until they fill a pint (2-cup) measure. Melt 2 dessertspoons (4 teaspoons) of butter in 2 tablespoons of boiling water; blend 1 tablespoon of moistened cornstarch into ½ pint (1 cup) of white sugar with 1 saltspoon (¼ teaspoon) of salt and 2 ditto (½ teaspoon) of ground ginger. Mix all the ingredients and pour them into a baked shell (see Index). Cover with a crust or place strips of paste like lattice work across the top; alternatively, cover with whipped cream after it has baked and cooled. If an upper crust is used, perforate it with a fork. Seal the edges with a little flour and water; brush the top with milk. Bake a short hour in a more than quick oven (425–50°F.).*

PRUNE PIE (mid-1800s)—Soak and pit 1¼ pounds of prunes; boil them until they are mushy, then rub them through a sieve or colander and let them drain without pressing them if they are very wet; stir in 1 tablespoon of lemon juice and 1 saltspoon (¼ teaspoon) of grated rind of lemon with a little vanilla essence and powdered allspice or cloves. Pour this mixture into a deep dish with the crust (see Index) in place; cover it with dabs of shaved butter and sprinkle a tablespoon of flour, into which a little salt has been mixed, over it. Bake in a hot (425–50°F.) oven for 45 to 60 minutes. Whip 1½ gills (¾ cup) of cream and spread it over the pie when it is cool.*

STRAWBERRY PIE (mid-1800s)—Hull, wash and dry 1 quart (4 cups) of berries and place them on the crust in a pie pan. Beat an egg smooth with a fork and strain it into ½ pint (1 cup) of granulated sugar; when this has been creamed, stir in 1 heaping teaspoon of flour and spread this mixture evenly over the strawberries. The advantage of this procedure is that the juices will be well distributed throughout the pie. Use a Puff Paste (see Index) for the strips to be placed criss-cross over the pie. Bake about 1 hour in a moderate to fast (375°F.) oven.*

PANDOWDIES (mid-1800s)—For those unfamiliar with this great autumnal dish of New England—which our grandmothers took so much for granted that they seldom described it in detail—let me explain that a pandowdy is made up of about 6 very tart apples of medium size. After being pared and cored, they were cut into 8 sections, put in a deep, buttered baking dish and crowned with ¼ pint (½ cup) of brown sugar or molasses, pinches of cinnamon and dashes of nutmeg and a little salt. As a final benediction, about 5 ounces (10 tablespoons) of hot butter was poured over the seasoned apples. Next, a Biscuit Dough (see Index) was put over the entire batch and it was placed in a low to medium baking oven (325°F.) for about ½ hour. Then came the "break up" and "push under" of the crust (see A Fine Apple Pandowdy, below) and about ½ hour longer in the oven. It was served with milk or cream. This version of the old breakfast dish stands up well, but I recommend Hard Sauce (see Index) instead of milk or cream.*

A FINE APPLE PANDOWDY (mid-1800s)—Soak 1 tablespoon of cornstarch in 4 tablespoons of cold water taken from a ½-pint (1-cup) measure of water. Now mix 1 saltspoon (¼ teaspoon) each of salt and powdered cinnamon and nutmeg into 1 pint (2 cups) of good brown New Orleans sugar with what remains of the water and 3 saltspoons (¾ teaspoon) of vinegar. Heat it over a slow fire; when it steams, add the moistened cornstarch; stir, but do not let it boil. When it is smooth, remove it, stir in a piece of butter as large as an egg (4 tablespoons) and let it cool. Have ½ dozen good tart Baldwin or Winesap apples cored and peeled and thickly sliced in a basin of cold water seasoned with lemon juice or vinegar so that the apples do not turn brown. Make a Baking Powder Biscuit Crust with ½ pint (1 cup) of white flour mixed with 2 teaspoons of baking powder and 2½ saltspoons (generous ½ teaspoon) of salt; cut in a piece of butter the size of a walnut (1 rounded tablespoon) with a knife until the dough pebbles; add 1½ gills (¾ cup) of fresh milk and knead it in with your fingers, but not so smoothly that no lumps are left. Drain the apple slices and put them in a greased baking pan; pour the sugar mixture over them and cover this, in turn, with a neatly rolled blanket of dough, which should cover the edges of the pan closely on all sides. Bake the Pandowdy in a moderate (350°F.) oven just under 1 hour, then break the topping with a fork and work it down among the apples. Bake another 10 minutes and serve. Many wives give cream or syrup with this as a breakfast dish; but they use a Hard Sauce (see Index) if it is offered as dessert.*

APPLE PANDEEDIE (mid-1800s)—Take 6 to 8 sweet apples; pare and core them; cut them into eighths. Put them into a lined pie pan; sprinkle them richly with sugar and moisten with ½ gill (¼ cup) of water. Put the apples in the oven, and, when they are tender, cover them with marshmallows. Return them to the oven for browning; brown delicately.*

OPEN TARTS (mid-1800s)—There is joy and pride of accomplishment in serving the variety of desserts made possible by delicious open tarts. The ingredients needed are 10 ounces (2 cups) of flour, 5 ounces (10 tablespoons) of butter, 1½ gills (¾ cup) of cold water, ½ teaspoon of yeast powder, a few teaspoons of preserves or cooked fruit of any kind and a pinch of salt.

First measure the butter and flour and salt in a bowl; mix them together lightly and add the yeast powder. Mix and make a nice dough and use as little of the 1½ gills of water as possible. The quantity of water is determined by the quality of the flour; a fine grade of the latter absorbs the greatest quantity of the former. Roll out the dough on a floured board and cut it into circular pieces that will fit a muffin tin with a cake cutter. The remainder of the dough is rolled out again and smaller circular pieces cut out; with the dough that is left make small, narrow strips. Wet muffin tins with cold water and press the large circular pieces into place; fill the center with jams, preserves or even fresh fruit. Wet the edges of the tart with a barely beaten white of egg, lay the narrow strips across the top and crown them with small circular pieces of dough; bake in a hot (425°F.) oven for 25 minutes.*

A VARIETY OF TARTS (late 1800s)—Make a puff or plain paste (see Index). Roll the paste halfway between ⅛ and ¼ inch in thickness; cut it into the desired sizes; put the tarts into buttered fluted tins. Set them in the ice chest to chill and then add the filling; bake them in a hot (450°F.) oven for about ¼ hour. Varnish them with cream or the beaten yolk of an egg after 10 minutes of baking.

To fill tarts with preserves, heap them full with any kind of berry preserve and cover with whipped cream seasoned with vanilla or almond extract.

To fill tarts with pie fillings, use the recipes for the various kinds of fruit pies (see Index).

Custards can be used in tarts with whole preserved fruits, such as strawberries, cherries, etc. Many housewives who happen to have custard on hand when making tarts place 1 teaspoon on the bottom of each tart and spread one over the top.*

JELLY TARTLETS—Roll some good Puff Paste (see Index) out thin; cut it into 2½-inch squares; brush each square over with the white of an egg, then fold down the corners so that they all meet in the middle of the piece of paste; slightly press two pieces together. Brush them over with the egg; sift sugar over them; bake in a quick (400°F.) oven for ¼ hour. When they are done make a hole in the middle and fill it with jam or jelly.*

LEMON TARTS—Mix well together the juice and grated rind of 2 lemons, 2 cups of sugar, 2 eggs and the crumbs of sponge cake; beat it all together until smooth. Put this into twelve patty pans lined with paste; bake until the crust is done.—Mrs. M. A. Greene

18. Puddings, Dumplings and Flummery

EVE'S PUDDING

"If you want a good pudding, mind what you are taught;
Take eggs, six in number, when bought for a groat;
The fruit with which Eve her husband did cozen,
Well pared, and well chopped, at least half a dozen;
Six ounces of bread, let Moll eat the crust,
And crumble the rest as fine as the dust;
Six ounces of currants, from the stem you must sort,
Lest you break out your teeth, and spoil all the sport;
Six ounces of sugar won't make it too sweet,
Some salt and some nutmeg will make it complete;
Three hours let it boil without any flutter.
But Adam won't like it without wine and butter."

—ANCIENT RHYME

SOME GENERAL PUDDING POINTERS—(mid-1800s) The eggs for all sorts of puddings in which they are used should be well beaten, then strained.

If hot milk is used, the eggs should, generally, be added after all other ingredients.

Milk for pumpkin, squash, cocoanut, tapioca, ground rice, arrowroot and sweet potato puddings should be boiled; for bread and plum puddings also, unless the bread is soaked in milk over night.

When suet is used in puddings, it should be properly cleaned (see Index) and chopped fine as possible.

A flour pudding is much lighter when the materials are all beaten together than if the eggs are done separately.

When berries or cherries are to be used, put them in last.

A buttered earthen bowl with a cloth tied close over it is a very good thing in which to boil a pudding so long as the water does not rise above it in the kettle.

To cut a boiled pudding without making it heavy, lay both sides of the knife upon the pudding so as to heat the blade.

In boiling milk for puddings, it should always, as in making custards, be boiled in a pail set into a kettle of hot water (double boiler). Puddings are more delicate when milk is done that way than when it is boiled in a saucepan; besides, there is no danger of it being burned.

To make and use a pudding bag: Real pudding experts declare that puddings are lightest when boiled in a cloth or bag instead of being baked or boiled in a mold.

To make a cloth, cut a large square of thick tow or hemp cloth or stout unbleached muslin; lard or butter and flour it as you would a bag (see below). Place the pudding in the center of cloth; gather the rest of the material above it and tie it firmly with good twine.

To make a bag, use your own discretion as to size, but make it of the tightest weave of muslin you can get; a good all-around bag is one that is 18 by 12 inches; but it should be so cut that the bottom is several inches narrower than the top; the corners should be rounded. The seam should be stitched close with coarse thread on one side, and turned and stitched again on the other; this in order to secure the pudding from the water. A yard-long piece of clothesline should be sewed at the middle of the seam, about 3 inches below the top of the bag.*

TO USE A PUDDING BAG—Turn it inside out—the outside of the bag is that with the raw edge—and wring it in cold water; cover it thoroughly with lard or butter; then rub in flour; turn the floured side of the bag *inside;* lay it in a dish. Pour the batter in and tie the bag up quickly, drawing the cord as tight as possible; always allow a little room for the pudding to swell. All puddings swell more or less, but an Indian Pudding made with cold milk swells more than any other.—Mrs. Charles Pearce

TO BOIL A PUDDING—Have a commodious kettle with enough rapidly boiling water to cover the pudding completely. Lay the pudding in the water immediately; after 10 minutes turn it over to prevent the flour from settling on one side. If there is fruit in the pudding, it should be turned 3 or 4 times in the first ½ hour. To keep the pudding covered by water, add boiling water from a kettle and be certain that the water does *boil,* not merely *simmer,* steadily. Have plenty of wood on hand to keep your fire high. If the water does not boil, the pudding will turn watery; if the water sinks below the top, the pudding will crust. When you take the pudding up, plunge it for a moment into a suitable pail of cold water; then pour the water off, untie the cord and gently lay back the top of the bag. Have a dish ready and turn the pudding upon it.—M. H. C.

STEAMED BLACKBERRY, BLUEBERRY AND RASPBERRY DUMPLINGS (mid-1800s)—The procedure for middling-sized dumplings is to cut 2 dessertspoons (4 teaspoons) of butter into 1 pint (2 cups) of flour sifted with 1 tablespoon of baking powder and 1 teaspoon of salt; make it pebbly, as you do a pie crust; add 1½ gills (¾ cup) of milk as you work. Have a buttered baking vessel at hand; into this put 1 quart (4 cups) of berries and mix in 1 pint (2 cups) of sugar; then stir in 1 dessertspoon (2 teaspoons) of vinegar. Roll the paste into a suitable size to cover the berries. Put it into place and steam, tightly covered, for 1 hour in steadily boiling water that stands high enough along the sides of the dish to cook the dumpling without reaching above the top of the dish.*

BOILED APPLE DUMPLINGS (early 1800s)—It is better to make one or two large dumplings than many small ones, because drawing up the cloth must necessarily make folds in it which, when the dumplings are boiled, will leave ridges in the crust. Make a large circular Potato Crust (see Index) because it is by far the healthiest; let the middle of it be nearly 1/3 inch thick; but roll the edges thin for the reasons above mentioned. Wring a thick square pudding cloth (see Index) in water, rub it with lard and sprinkle the lard with flour; lay it into a deep dish and lay the crust into it. Mix 1 quart (4 cups) of chopped apples that have been cored and peeled with sugar and cinnamon to taste; lay the apples in the crust; put the crust together and draw the cloth around it. Tie the string so tightly that there is no room for swelling. Boil the dumpling as you would a pudding (see Index) for about 2 hours; then plunge it into cold water, untie it, turn it into a dish and serve. Serve with butter and molasses, in about equal proportions. Be sure to boil the molasses, as that, in some degree, takes away the strong taste.*

BAKED AND BOILED BATTER PUDDINGS (mid-1800s)—Baked: have 1 quart (4 cups) of cold milk in a basin; use part of it to stir 1 gill (½ cup) of flour smooth; into this put 4 unbeaten eggs; beat them well with the mixed flour. This done, stir in the rest of the milk and ½ teaspoon of salt; pour the batter into a buttered dish and bake it in a moderate (350°F.) oven about 1 hour or until set like custard. When it is done, the whole top will have risen up; so long as there is a little sunken spot in the center, it is not baked enough. A flour pudding will not be light unless it is placed in the oven immediately on being made.

Boiled: Use the same proportions as for Baked Batter Pudding; butter a tin pudding pan having a close cover and put in the mixture. Set it at once into boiling water that comes high enough around it to boil the pudding without boiling quite up to the top. Replace water that boils away with boiling water.*

A VENERABLE XMAS PLUM PUDDING (early 1800s)—Stone and cut into halves 2 pounds of raisins; add 1-2/3 pounds of currants and ½ pound of citron, the latter minced or finely sliced; mix 2 pounds (16 cups) each of bread crumbs, white and light, of the finest moist brown sugar, of fresh and minced suet; 2 teaspoons each of cinnamon and nutmeg, freshly pulverized, and 1 tablespoon of pounded bitter almonds. Combine all the foregoing ingredients; beat 16 eggs and strain them into the mixture; stir; add 1 gill (½ cup) of fine old brandy. When all is thoroughly mixed, butter and flour a good stout pudding bag; put the pudding into it; tie it down. Boil from 6 to 8 hours and serve with Brandy Sauce (see Index). A few sweet almonds, blanched and cut into strips, ornament it prettily when served. The above pudding is of rather party dimensions; it can be divided for smaller families.*

COLD CHOCOLATE PUDDING (late 1800s)—From 1 pint (2 cups) of cold milk take enough to moisten 4 tablespoons (¼ cup) of cornstarch; heat the remaining milk in a double boiler and add 3 tablespoons of sugar; melt 2 ounces (squares) of chocolate (½ cup when grated) in 3 tablespoons of simmering water and stir this into the milk, followed by the cornstarch. Cook this about ½ hour; then remove it from the fire and let it stand to cool. When the mixture has cooled, whisk the whites of 2 eggs with a large pinch of salt and 1 saltspoon (¼ teaspoon) each of almond and vanilla extract and add them to the mixture. Pour this into a mold and serve with a sweet sauce (see Index), or cover the pudding neatly with whipped cream over which a little nutmeg or cinnamon has been grated.*

COCOANUT PUDDING (mid-1800s)—Grate a cocoanut and save the milk for other use; boil 1 quart (4 cups) of milk and pour it upon the cocoanut. Beat 1 gill (½ cup) of sugar into 5 beaten and strained eggs; add 2 tablespoons of melted butter, 2 of rose water and a large pinch of salt; add the milk and cocoanut. If you have plenty of cream and eggs, use cream instead of milk and add 3 more eggs. Spice the mixture with powdered cinnamon, allspice or ginger. Bake in a buttered dish a good hour in a low to moderate (325°F.) oven or until it is firm.*

ICE CHEST COTTAGE PUDDING (late 1800s)—Set an envelope (1 tablespoon) of gelatine into ¼ cup of cold milk and scald 1¾ cups of whole milk; add ½ cup of maple syrup or ditto white or brown sugar, a pinch of salt and the milk-gelatine mixture to the scalded milk. Beat 2 whole eggs; strain and blend them into 1½ pints (3 cups) of decrusted and cubed bread slices, which should be rather stale. Add this to the scalded milk mixture, stir well and set all to cook in the top of a double boiler; keep stirring until the pudding has a smooth consistency, then remove it from fire, add ¾ teaspoon of vanilla extract and ½ teaspoon of cinnamon. Pour it into a mold, chill and serve with Orange Sauce (see Index).*

FLUMMERY (early 1800s)—Lay some Sponge Cake (see Index) in a deep dish; pour on enough white wine to moisten without soaking it; chop some seeded raisins and slice some almonds fine; sprinkle them over the cake; then spread over it a layer of jelly and turn over it a custard made with the yolks of 4 eggs (see Egg Yolk Custard for Flummery, below). Beat the 4 reserved whites to a crisp froth with 4 tablespoons (¼ cup) of pounded loaf sugar and spread them over the custard. Put a dash of red currant jelly over the top here and there. Slices of orange, dipped in sherry and dried, make a very good garnish for this splendid dessert.*

EGG YOLK CUSTARD FOR FLUMMERY (early 1800s)—Scald 1 pint (2 cups) of milk; mix, separately, 4 egg yolks, ½ gill (¼ cup) of sugar and a large pinch of salt; add the scalded milk; cook over boiling water until the mixture is smooth and creamy. Strain the custard into a cold dish and flavor it with lemon juice as it cools. Should the custard start to curdle during the cooking, set it at once into a basin of cold water and whisk it vigorously.*

POTATO STARCH FLUMMERY (early 1800s)—To 1 quart (4 cups) of milk, boiling in a pail in a kettle of water (double boiler), add 4 tablespoons (¼ cup) of potato starch, first made smooth in a little milk; stir; add a little salt; beat 4 eggs; stir them into the milk and boil the whole 1 minute more. Pour it into a mold wetted with cold water; eat the Flummery cold with a Quick Sour Cream Sauce (see Index).*

ROLY POLY PUDDING (early 1800s)—Make a Potato Pie Crust (see Index); roll it narrow and long; spread it with raspberry jam or apple sauce, but take care that the filling does not come too close to the edges of the crust. Roll it up and close the ends and sides as tightly as possible by wetting the edges of the crust with cold water and dusting with flour to make a sealing paste. Sew it up in a piece of larded and floured pudding cloth (see Index) and boil it, according to its size, from 1½ to 2 hours.*

SQUASH, PUMPKIN AND SWEET POTATO PUDDINGS (mid-1800s)—Have a large coffee cup (1 cup) of cooked and strained squash, pumpkin or sweet potato. First, mix 3 saltspoons (¾ teaspoons) of cinnamon and 2 ditto of ginger and salt into the vegetable pulp; then beat 2 whole eggs with 3 tablespoons of butter and boil 1 pint (2 cups) of milk with a piece of butter no larger than a hazelnut (1 rounded teaspoon); stirring fast, add the milk to the pulp; next, the eggs. Butter a cold dish with cold butter and sprinkle the bottom and sides with sifted cracker dust; pour the mixture in; grate nutmeg over the top and then sprinkle it with pounded crackers and sift white sugar over it. Bake in a good (350°F.) oven for 40 to 45 minutes. In baking these puddings, it is unprofitable to make them too large, as the edges become too dry before the center is cooked.*

PRETTY PUDDING—Wet 1 tablespoon of flour with ½ cup of cold milk; beat and sieve the yolks of 3 eggs; measure 1 small (6-ounce) cup of sugar; mix these together. Put 1 quart (4 cups) of milk in a kettle and set it in boiling water (double boiler); when the milk is at the boiling point, stir in the above mixture with vanilla or rose flavoring; stir until it begins to thicken, then take it off and let it cool a little; pour it into a pudding dish or cups. Then beat the whites of the eggs to a stiff froth with ½ gill (¼ cup) of fine white sugar and drop this on the top of the custard in rounds about as large as an egg; put a small spoon of currant, or other tart jelly, on the center of each round. Serve cold.—Mrs. Charles Bradbury

DAN'L WEBSTER'S PUDDIN'—One cup of molasses, 1 cup of milk, 1 cup of suet, ½ cup of brandy, or wine if you like, 1½ teaspoons of baking powder, 1 teaspoon of cloves, 1 teaspoon of cinnamon, ½ nutmeg (the spices all ground), 2 cups of currants, 1 teaspoon of salt; mix as soft as Pound Cake and steam it 2 hours. Serve with Hard Sauce (see Index).—Mrs. O. L. Wheelock

BAKED INDIAN PUDDING—"SPLENDID"—Into 2 quarts (8 cups) of scalded milk stir 1½ cups of Indian meal (yellow), 1 tablespoon of ground ginger and ½ teaspoon of salt; let this stand 20 minutes. Add 1 cup of molasses, 2 beaten eggs, a piece of butter the size of a common walnut (1 rounded tablespoon). Bake 2 hours in a buttered pan in a slow to moderate (325°F.) oven. If you have no eggs, do this: just as you put the pudding into the oven, stir in 1 gill (½ cup) of cold water, which will produce the same effect as eggs.—Mrs. A. W. D.

AMHERST PUDDING—Three cups of flour, 1 of suet, 1 of milk, 1 of molasses, 2 of raisins, salt and spice to your taste, 1 teaspoon of baking powder; boil in a bag 3 hours. For sauce: 1 cup of sugar, ½ of butter, 1 egg.—Mrs. F. M. Cragin

BREAD PUDDING—Soak a pint (2 cups) of bread crumbs in milk for an hour, then squeeze them with the hands to a pulp and mix well with a gill (½ cup) of milk; then add 3 tablespoons of sugar, ¼ pound of raisins, ¼ pound (½ cup) of melted butter and the yolks of 4 eggs; then beat the whites of the eggs to a froth and mix them with the rest. Turn the mixture into a greased dish and bake about ¾ to 1 hour in a moderate to fast (375°F.) oven. Serve with Wine Sauce (see Index), hot or cold, according to taste.—Mrs. Freeman

BREAD PUDDING—Put a pint (2 cups) of scalded milk to a pint (2 cups) of bread crumbs and add the yolks of 4 eggs well beaten, ½ pint (1 cup) of sugar, a piece of butter the size of an egg (4 tablespoons) and the grated rind of a lemon. Bake in a slow oven (300°F.) for 1½ to 2 hours. Then beat the whites of the eggs into a cup of powdered sugar and the juice of 1 lemon; cover the pudding with it and set it in a fast (400°F.) oven until it is a golden brown.—Mrs. C. M.

BROWN BETTY—One cup of bread crumbs, 2 of chopped apples (tart), ½ cup of sugar, 1 teaspoon of ground cinnamon, 2 tablespoons of butter cut into small bits. Butter a deep dish; put a layer of chopped apple at the bottom; sprinkle with sugar; add a few bits of butter and cinnamon. Proceed in this order until the dish is full; make a layer of crumbs on top. Cover closely and steam ¾ hour in a moderate (350°F.) oven; then uncover and brown quickly. Eat with sugar and cream. This is a plain, but very good, pudding, especially for the children.—Mrs. L. M. Angle

HARVARD PUDDING (early 1800s)—One-half pound of crackers, pounded, ¼ pound of currants, washed, ¼ pound of suet, shredded fine, ½ tablespoon of fine sugar; some grated nutmeg; mince it all together. Then take the yolks of 4 eggs and make it up into balls as big as turkey eggs. Fry them in fresh butter to a fine light brown.***

APPLE SAGO PUDDING—One cup of sago (tapioca) soaked for 1 hour in 1 quart (4 cups) of tepid water with a pinch of salt, 6 or 8 apples, pared and cored, quartered and steamed tender. Put the apples in the pudding form. Boil and stir the sago with 3 tablespoons of brown sugar and a dash of cinnamon until clear, adding water to make it thin, and pour it over the apples. This is good, hot with butter and sugar, or cold with cream and sugar.—Mrs. K.

BLACKBERRY OR OTHER BERRY PUDDING—One and one-half pints (3 cups) of sifted flour; blend one-quarter of this into 1½ pints (3 cups) of fresh berries. To the balance of the flour add salt sufficient to season and 1 even teaspoon of baking soda dissolved in 1 tablespoon of sweet milk; then add 1½ gills (¾ cup) of maple syrup or molasses and stir all into a smooth batter; lastly add the berries; mix lightly so as not to break the fruit. Put the mixture into a buttered mold and place it in boiling water that does not quite reach the top of the mold. Do not let it stop boiling for an instant. It must boil *at least* 2 hours. Serve with a boiled sauce (see Index).—M.

FIG PUDDING—One-half pound of figs, ¼ pound (2 cups) of grated bread, 2½ ounces (6 tablespoons) of powdered sugar, 3 ounces (6 tablespoons) of butter, 2 eggs, 1 teacup (1 cup) of milk. Chop the figs small and mix them first with the butter, then with all the other ingredients by degrees. Butter a mold, pour in the pudding, sprinkle it with bread crumbs, cover it tight and boil for 3 hours.—E. M. Walker

STEAMED FRUIT PUDDING—Place in a 2-quart (8-cup) tin basin fruit of any kind (raspberries, peaches and apples are the best); put some sugar over them, and a little water; if peaches are used put them in after paring them, whole. Have ready a biscuit crust made of 1 pint (2 cups) of flour, with a small piece of butter or lard, a little salt, 2 teaspoons of baking powder and enough water or milk to make a dough; then roll out crust and place it over the top of your fruit in the tin. Cover with another 2-quart (8-cup) basin, to give room for the crust to rise, and set it on the stove; as the fruit stews the crust will steam done. Serve with cream and sugar.—Mrs. Harriet N. Jenks

CHERRY PUDDING—A pint (2 cups) of bread crusts or soft crackers scalded in a quart (4 cups) of boiling milk, a piece of butter the size of an egg (4 tablespoons) 1 teaspoon of salt, 3 eggs, a pinch of pulverized cinnamon, a quart (4 cups) of stoned cherries, 1½ teacups (1½ cups) of sugar if eaten without sauce, and if with sauce a tablespoon of sugar. Bake about 40 to 50 minutes in a 425°F. oven.—Mrs. Harriet N. Jenks

TAPIOCA PUDDING (late 1800s)—Measure a short 1½ gills (2/3 cup) of tapioca; do not wash it, because the fine powder is the nicest part, but pick it over carefully; soak it over night in 1 pint (2 cups) of milk. The next day add 1 pint (2 cups) of milk and set it to boil in a pail in a kettle of hot water (a double boiler); stir it often until the tapioca jells. Meanwhile, beat 5 to 6 eggs into ½ pint (1 cup) of sugar. Remove the tapioca from the fire and stir in the eggs while it is still hot; add 1 dessertspoon (2 teaspoons) of butter, 1 teaspoon of salt and the filtered (strained) juice of 1 lemon with half the grated rind. Put the pudding into a baking dish. It will bake in ¾ hour in a moderate (350°F.) oven.*

WIDOW'S PLUM PUDDING (early 1800s)—Pare, core and mince apples to the weight of 4 ounces (¼ pound); add to these 4 ounces (¼ pound) of well-washed currants and a like quantity (2 cups) of grated bread and 2 ounces (scant ¼ cup) of sugar; whisk 3 eggs and beat them up with the other items, together with some minced lemon rind, 2 saltspoons (½ teaspoon) of salt and a little grated nutmeg. Put the pudding into a buttered basin, tie it down with a cloth, set it in a pan of water and boil it for 3 hours.*

POTATO PUDDING WITH CHEESE (mid-1800s)—Boil, peel and grate potatoes as required. For each pound of potatoes be prepared to use ¼ pound (1 cup) of grated cheese, ½ gill (¼ cup) of butter and about 1 pint (2 cups) of milk, depending on the mealiness of the potatoes. Cook these articles in a stew-pan over an easy fire and stir until they become a thick mixture. If too thick, add more milk. Set this aside in a bowl to cool; then beat the yolks of 4 eggs in ¼ cup of light cream and blend them into the potato mixture. Butter a pudding mold, dust it with fine cracker crumbs and check your oven with a piece of ordinary newspaper to make sure it is only moderate (350°F.). Now whisk the whites of 4 eggs into a snowy mountain and put it into the potato mixture. Place the pudding mold in a shallow pan of hot water and bake it, tightly covered, ½ hour.*

COLD RICE PUDDING (late 1800s)—Boil ¼ pound (scant 2/3 cup) of washed and rubbed rice in 1 quart (4 cups) of unsalted water; never stir the rice while it cooks. After about 20 minutes press a rice grain between your fingers; if it flattens it is right. Drain the rice and set it to dry in a warm place; later, transfer it to a crystal bowl. Meanwhile, boil ¼ pound (scant ¼ cup) of sugar in ½ cup of water; it should be a simple syrup in 15 to 20 minutes. Beware lest you burn it. Let it cool, add 1 wineglass (½ cup) of Jamaica rum and pour it all over the pudding. Decorate with preserved, fresh or canned fruits. Serve cold.*

HOT RICE-CHOCOLATE PUDDING (late 1800s)—Have ready 1½ gills (¾ cup) of cooked rice heating over hot water. Blend into this 1½ gills (¾ cup) of stoned and plumped raisins, 1 gill (½ cup) of granulated white sugar, 4 dessertspoons (8 teaspoons) of butter, 2 ounces (squares) of finely grated chocolate (½ cup when grated) and ¾ teaspoon of salt. When the chocolate and sugar are melted remove them from the fire; cool them and stir in 1 gill (½ cup) of whipped cream, next the whites of 2 eggs, well beaten, and ¾ teaspoon of vanilla extract. Pour the mixture into a buttered dish and bake about 25 minutes in a moderate (350°F.) oven. A snow of 2 beaten egg whites mixed with 1½ gills (¾ cup) of sugar is a popular topping for this pudding, which, commonly, is served without a sauce.*

CIVIL WAR PLUM PUDDING—One pound of currants, 1 pound of stoned raisins, 1 pound (2¼ cups) of sugar, 1 pound of suet, 2 pounds of grated or soaked bread, 6 eggs, ½ teaspoon of baking soda, 1 teaspoon of salt and 1 grated nutmeg. Crumb the soft part of the bread fine; soak the crust with boiling milk, or water will do; beat up the eggs and put all together, mixing thoroughly with the hands. Pour the pudding into a greased form and put it into a pot of boiling water; boil 5 hours; as the water boils away, keep adding more.—Mrs. H. S. Bristol

KISS PUDDING—One quart (4 cups) of milk, 3 tablespoons of cornstarch, the yolks of 4 eggs, ½ cup of sugar and a little salt. Put part of the milk, salt and sugar on the stove and let it boil; dissolve the cornstarch in the rest of the milk and stir it into the boiling milk; while it is still boiling, add the yolks. Flavor with vanilla. Frosting: The whites of 4 eggs beaten to a stiff froth, ½ cup of sugar; flavor with lemon. Spread all but a little of the frosting on the pudding and put it into the oven to brown. Moisten the top with the saved frosting and put on grated cocoanut, giving it the appearance of snowflakes.—Mrs. F. B. Cole

SARATOGA PUDDING—Mix 4 tablespoons of cornstarch in 1 quart (4 cups) of cold milk; stir until it boils. When it is cool, stir in 2 tablespoons of white sugar and 6 eggs, whites and yolks beaten separately. Put the mixture in a large pudding dish; place it in a pan of water; boil 1½ hours. Sauce: 1 cup of sugar, ½ cup of butter, the yolks of 2 eggs, 1 glass (4 ounces) of wine. Rub the sugar and butter to a cream; and the eggs and half the wine. Put the dish in boiling water and stir for 10 minutes, add the rest of the wine and serve.—Mrs. A. G. Beardsley

OSWEGO PUDDING—One quart (4 cups) of milk, 3 tablespoons of cornstarch, 4 eggs. Beat the yolks and mix them with a little of the milk and flour; sweeten the mixture and flavor with vanilla; scald the rest of the milk and add to it the other ingredients. Boil 3 minutes; pour the pudding into a dish and set it away to cool. Beat the whites with 4 teaspoons of sugar. Cover the pudding with a layer of currant jelly and spread the beaten whites over the whole.—T. A. G.

CORNSTARCH LEMON PUDDING—Grate the rind of 2 lemons; add the juice and rind of 6 ounces (1 scant cup) of sugar and 3 ounces (9 tablespoons) of cornstarch. Stir this well into some cold water, sufficient to make it smooth. Place 3 pints (6 cups) of milk on the fire; when it is boiling add the above, stirring all the time until it thickens. Remove it from the fire and add 1 ounce (2 tablespoons) of butter and 4 eggs. Stir again over the fire, taking care not to allow it to boil or burn; as soon as it becomes thick, remove it and fill some small cups or forms, previously dipped in cold water. Place them aside; in 1 hour they will be fit to turn out.

Sauce: Moisten 1 ounce (3 tablespoons) of cornstarch in a little cold milk; blend until smooth; then pour a pint (2 cups) of boiling milk on it. Beat the whites of 4 eggs in 3 ounces (7 scant tablespoons) of sugar, stir in 1 glass (2 ounces) of brandy; add this to the sauce and allow it to remain on the fire a short time, stirring all the while. The sauce can be served hot or cold and may be flavored with anything to fancy.—F. T. D.

ORANGE PUDDING—Peel and cut 5 sweet oranges into thin slices, taking out the seeds; pour over them ½ pint (1 cup) of white sugar. Let 1 pint (2 cups) of milk get boiling hot by setting it in a pot of boiling water; add the strained yolks of 3 eggs, well beaten and 1 tablespoon of cornstarch, made smooth with a little cold milk; stir all the time; as soon as the liquid has thickened stir in the oranges. Beat the egg whites to a stiff froth, adding 2 tablespoons of sugar and ½ teaspoon of lemon extract; spread this over the top for frosting. Set in a slow (275–300°F.) oven for a few minutes to harden. Eat cold or hot (better cold) for dinner or supper. Whole berries or sliced peaches can be substituted for oranges.—Mrs. J. G. Hamilton

PINEAPPLE PUDDING—A grated pineapple and its weight in sugar, half its weight in butter, 5 eggs, the whites beaten to a stiff froth, 1 cup of cream. Cream the butter and beat it with the sugar and yolks until very light; add the cream, the pineapple and the whites of the eggs. Bake in pie plates lined with pastry in a low to moderate (325°F.) oven. To be eaten cold.—M. S. W.

CRACKED WHEAT PUDDING—Cook cracked wheat enough for two meals; stir in, a few minutes before taking it up from the fire, raisins, dates or any other dried fruit. Next day prepare a custard as usual (see Index), stir it thoroughly through the wheat and bake just long enough to bake the custard. Thus you have two desserts with but little trouble. Very palatable and nutritious.—Mrs. A. M. Lewis

COLD TAPIOCA PUDDING—One cup of tapioca, 5 cups of water, 1 teaspoon of salt, 1 cup of sugar and 1 lemon. Wash and drain the tapioca; add the water; put it in a tin pail in a kettle of water (a double boiler); let it boil 2 hours or more until it is perfectly clear. Just before taking it up from the fire, add a teaspoon of salt, 1 cup of sugar and the rind and juice of a lemon; stir thoroughly; put it aside to cool. Eat with cream and sugar. —Mrs. H. F. Waite

DELMONICO PEACH PUDDING—Beat the yolks of 5 eggs until light; then add 6 tablespoons of sugar and beat again until the mixture is very light; mix 3 tablespoons of cornstarch with a little cold milk; mix all together and stir into it 1 quart (4 cups) of milk just on the point of boiling, having added a little salt; stir it until it has thickened well. Pour it into a dish for the table and place it in a moderate (350°F.) oven until it is thick. Then place over the top a layer of ripe skinned, sliced, sugared peaches. Beat the 5 egg whites to a stiff froth with 2 tablespoons of white sugar to each egg; pour them onto the pudding; then put it into a very fast oven (425°F.) until it is a light brown.—Mrs. De Forest

QUEEN'S PUDDING—Scald 1 quart (4 cups) of sweet milk and assemble 1 pint (2 cups) of bread crumbs, 5 separated eggs, 1 teaspoon of moistened cornstarch, the juice and grated rind of 1 large or 2 small lemons, ½ pint (1 cup) each of common and pulverized sugar. Pour the hot milk over the bread crumbs and let it cool; beat the yolks of the eggs and the cup of common sugar together; mix in the cornstarch also, but wet it first in cold water. Just before putting the pudding in to bake add the grated lemon rind; bake 30 to 35 minutes in a fast (400°F.) oven. Beat the whites of the eggs and the cup of pulverized sugar together and add the lemon juice; when the pudding is done, put this on the top and set it in the oven again for a few minutes to brown. To be eaten cold.—Mrs. F. M. Cragin

BLACK MOLASSES PUDDING (mid-1800s)—Mix ½ pint (1 cup) each of butter and sugar to a cream; add 4 eggs well beaten, then ½ pint (1 cup) of molasses, then 1 grated nutmeg, then 1 pint (2 cups) of flour and ½ pint (1 cup) of sour milk; last, 1 teaspoon of baking soda dissolved in a little warm water; steam in a buttered form for 3 hours. This pudding can be made Saturday and heated over again for Sunday. Sauce for the pudding: 1 gill (½ cup) of butter, and ½ pint (1 cup) of sugar, worked thoroughly together to a cream; put 2 gills (1 cup) of water in a saucepan, and, when it boils, thicken with 2 tablespoons of flour wetted in a little cold water to the consistency of cream. Take it from the fire and stir rapidly into it the butter and sugar; it will be like white foam; flavor to taste with brandy.—Mrs. James Wheaton

BIRD'S NEST (BAKED APPLE PUDDING)—Pare 6 or 8 large apples (Spitzenburgs or Greenings are best) and remove the core by cutting from the end down into the middle, so as to leave the apple whole except where the core has been removed; place them as near together as they can stand, with the open part upward in a deep pie dish. Next make a thin batter, using 1 quart (4 cups) of sweet milk, 5 eggs and 4 tablespoons of cornstarch and pour it into the dish around the apples, also filling the cavities in them. Bake them in a slow oven (275°F.) for 2 hours and eat them with butter and sugar.—Mrs. F. M. Cragin

A QUICK PUDDING—One-half pint (1 cup) of milk, ½ pint (1 cup) of cream, 3 eggs (the whites and yolks beaten separately), a little over ½ pint (1 cup) of flour; season with lemon or vanilla. Heat to boiling point, simmer for 15 minutes, stirring steadily, and serve.—Mrs. A. W. D.

ICED APPLE PUDDING (early 1800s)—Peel, core and quarter 24 apples; simmer them to a jelly without water if you can; then add a small pot of apricot jam and some small pieces of loaf sugar on which the rind of an orange has been rubbed; when the sugar has melted, push all through a sieve and put it into your freezing pail to cool. Stone ½ gill (¼ cup) of raisins and a like amount of Preserved Cranberries (see Index); simmer these together for a few moments in the juice of the cherries, let them cool and add them to the apple mixture; add 1 gill (½ cup) of hard cider or—lacking it—half of that of white Havana rum; also 2 ounces (scant 1/3 cup) of slivered almonds and 1 ounce (2 tablespoons) of minced citron, plus ½ teaspoon of pulverized cinnamon; whip and add, when the mixture is quite cool, 1 pint (2 cups) of cream. Put the lid on and plunge the pail into the ice tub; cover it with a wet cloth and pounded ice and salt-petre. Serve with Imperial Cream for Apple Dishes (see below).*

IMPERIAL CREAM FOR APPLE DISHES (early 1800s)—Boil 1 quart (4 cups) of cream with the thin peel of 1 lemon; then stir it until nearly cold. Have ready in the dish in which the cream is to be served the juice of 3 lemons, strained, with as much crushed loaf sugar as will sweeten the mixture (about 1 cup) according to your taste. Pour the cream into the dish from a teapot or pitcher, holding it high and moving it about so as to mix the cream thoroughly with the juice. Do not stir it. It should sit on crushed ice some 6 hours before being served. This also gives a fine air to apple pie.*

ICED CHOCOLATE WITH SHERRY (late 1800s)—Beat 3 egg yolks and put them into a saucepan with 1½ gills (¾ cup) of sugar and 5 table-spoons of dry sherry; add a pinch of salt and a little vanilla essence. Heat slowly and stir as it thickens; melt 2½ cakes of chocolate (¾ cup when grated) in the saucepan, stirring continually; when it is thickened, remove the chocolate from the fire. Beat 3 egg whites until stiff; stir them into the mixture when it is cool; add the strained juice and grated rind of 1 large or 2 small lemons; lastly, whisk 1½ gills (¾ cup) of whipping cream and blend it into the mixture. Have the serving dish to be used stand empty but covered in a bed of ice and salt over night; in the morning pour the concoction into it, cover with a cloth, and let it stand 3 to 4 hours before taking it to table.*

19. A Miscellany of Sweet Dishes

MOSS BLANCMANGE (early 1800s)—Gather the moss, but if it is old and dry moss, more should be used than if it is fresh and moist; as little moss should be used as will harden the milk. Allow 1 gill (½ cup) of moss for 1 quart (4 cups) of milk. Wash the moss and soak it over night; in the morning, tie it in a piece of muslin and boil it in the milk with a stick of cinnamon or 2 or 3 peach leaves. Boil it gently 20 to 35 minutes. Then put in a large pinch of salt and strain the milk upon ½ pint (1 cup) of crushed loaf sugar; wet a mold with cold water and pour the mixture into it without drying the mold. When firm, eat it with sugar or maple syrup and milk or cream.***

CALF'S FOOT BLANCMANGE (early 1800s)—Put 4 calf's feet into 4 quarts (16 cups) of water, season with cinnamon or lemon peel and a little salt; boil the water away to 1 quart (4 cups), strain the liquid through muslin and set it aside in a pan; when it is cool, remove all the fat; when it is hard, cut the jelly out of the pan, but be sure to avoid any sediments. Put the jelly into 1 quart (4 cups) of new milk and sweeten it with sugar, ½ pint (1 cup) or more or less, according to taste. Season with pounded almonds (sweet) or use a few peach leaves. Boil this mixture 10 minutes, strain it through muslin in a hair-sieve into a basin and stir it until it is nearly cold. Then put it into molds. Note: Be sure to scald the calf's feet first, but only enough to extract the hairs; too much scalding will extract the juice.***

RENNET IN MAKING CUSTARDS, ETC. (early 1800s)—While rennet is used mainly in the making of cheese, it also has its uses in the making of jellied desserts and is easier to do with than making Calf's Foot Jelly. While ordinary rennet is a salted-down piece of the stomach lining of a calf, the best is really the curd that is found in the calf's stomach; this curd is formed by the last milk eaten by the calf. See that the curd is clean and return it to its place in the rennet. Soak the rennet in a quart (4 cups) of water, then salt it and hang it up to dry; use pieces of the lining as necessary; keep the water in a jar for such uses as you may make of it. One-half teaspoon of curd or 1-inch-square piece of rennet is usually enough to thicken 1 quart (4 cups) of scalded milk that is cooling to lukewarm.***

RENNET WINE FOR CUSTARD (early 1800s)—Wash about 1/3 of a fresh rennet; wipe it dry and put it into a bottle of wine. The wine will be fit to use for thickening custard the next day. To keep the remainder of the rennet until more is needed, put it into a strong brine and cover it close.***

STAINED FROTH FOR CUSTARDS (mid-1800s)—Take the whites of 3 or 4 eggs, cut them into a stiff froth, then beat them into the syrup of any highly colored preserve. This makes an elegant topping for a dish of soft custard, even custard pies. Some persons, when making custards, lay the beaten whites of eggs upon the top of the scalding milk for a minute or two to harden; when the custard cups are filled, a piece of such froth is laid upon the top of each.*

CORNSTARCH REPLACES EGGS IN CUSTARDS (late 1800s)—Thrifty housewives have learned that when custards call for numerous eggs, they can omit a few by substituting ½ tablespoon (1½ teaspoons) of cornstarch for each egg omitted (see Cornstarch Custard, below).*

COLONIAL BOILED CUSTARD (pre-1800s)—Put 1 quart (4 cups) of milk into a tin pail (double boiler) that holds more than 2 quarts (8 cups); set it over the fire in a kettle of hot water. Tin is better than earthenware, because it heats so much quicker. Put in a stick of cinnamon or 3 peach leaves. When the milk foams up, nearly boiling, stir in 6 eggs which have been beaten with 2 tablespoons of crushed white sugar; stir it every instant until it appears to thicken a little; then take the pail out of the water and pour the custard immediately into a *cold* pitcher, because the heat of the pail will cook the part of the custard that touches it too much, so that it will curdle. Pour the custard into cups or glasses; cover with whipped cream when it is solid. This is a very easy way of making custards and none can be better. You may make them as rich as you choose. A pint (1 cup) of milk, a pint (1 cup) of cream and 8 eggs will make it rich enough for any epicure. So, on the other hand, they are very good with 3 to 4 eggs only to 1 quart (4 cups) of milk. For good custards, attend to nothing else until they are finished.*

BAKED CUSTARDS (mid-1800s)—Boil 1 quart (4 cups) of milk with a stick of cinnamon in it; then set it off from the hot part of the stove, and, while it cooks a very little, beat 5 or 6 eggs with 5 tablespoons of white sugar; then stir the milk and eggs together and pour the mixture into custard cups, or into a single dish that is large enough. If you bake it in a brick oven, it is a good idea to set the custard into it after the bread and other things have been baked; they will become hard in a few hours and very delicate. If you bake in a stove or range oven, it is best to use a dish and bake the custard in a very moderate heat (325°F.), else it may turn, in part, to whey.*

RICE CUSTARD—To ½ cup of rice add 1 quart (4 cups) of milk and a little salt; steam this 1 hour or until quite soft; beat the yolks of 4 eggs with 4 tablespoons of white sugar; add this just before taking off the rice; stir it in thoroughly, but do not let it boil any more; flavor with vanilla. Beat the whites of the eggs to a stiff froth with sugar; after putting the mixture into the pudding dish in which you serve it, put the whites over it and let it brown slightly in the oven.—Mrs. G. M. Dickerman

RICH CUSTARD— One quart (4 cups) of cream, the yolks of 6 eggs, 6 ounces (1 scant cup) of powdered white sugar, a small pinch of salt, 2 tablespoons of brandy, 1 tablespoon of peach water, ½ tablespoon of lemon brandy, an ounce of blanched almonds pounded to a paste. Mix the cream with the sugar and the yolks of the eggs well beaten; scald them together in a tin pail in boiling water (double boiler), stirring all the time until the custard is sufficiently thick. When it is cool, add the other ingredients and pour it into custard cups.—Mrs. Morgan

CORNSTARCH CUSTARD (late 1800s)—Measure 1 quart (4 cups) of cold milk; from this take 3 tablespoons to smooth 1 tablespoon of cornstarch in a cup. Bring the remaining milk, with a pinch of salt, to near boiling point in the top of a double boiler. Stir the cornstarch in and cook it slowly for 8 to 10 minutes until thick and smooth; stir often; add 3 tablespoons of white sugar and also 2 well-beaten eggs, and, lastly, ¼ teaspoon each of vanilla and almond extract. Transfer to a china dish and serve cold under a layer of Stained Froth (see Index).*

CHOCOLATE CUSTARD—Prepare a soft custard with 3 pints (6 cups) of milk, the yolks of 5 eggs and the white of 1. Dissolve 3 squares of chocolate (¾ cup when grated) in ½ pint (1 cup) of milk and heat it to boiling point; when cool, sweeten it with 2 tablespoons of brown sugar and flavor with 3 saltspoons (¾ teaspoon) of vanilla extract; combine the two mixtures, pour the whole into a dish and cover it with the 4 remaining egg whites beaten stiff with 4 tablespoons of white sugar; brown slightly and serve cold.— Mrs. Higgins

SAGO CUSTARD— Three tablespoons of sago boiled in a little water until clear; add 1 quart (4 cups) of milk; let it come to a boil, then add 5 or 6 well-beaten eggs and 1 gill (½ cup) of sugar. Put the vessel containing the custard in a kettle of boiling water (double boiler); stir the custard briskly until it thickens a little; flavor with vanilla after it has partly cooled. —C. D. Adams

APPLE CUSTARD (mid-1800s)—Pare, core and quarter 1 dozen tart apples, strew into them the grated rind of 1 lemon; stew them until tender in very little water; then mash them smooth with the back of a spoon. To 1½ pints (3 cups) of warm, strained apple add 1¼ pounds (2¾ generous cups) of sugar; leave it until cold. Beat 6 eggs light and stir them alternately into 1 quart (4 cups) of milk with the apples. Put the mixture into a buttered dish and bake it 20 minutes in a moderate (350°F.) oven. To be eaten cold. —Mrs. F. B. Orr

CARAMEL CUSTARD— One quart (4 cups) of milk, 1 cup of white and 1 of brown sugar, 2 tablespoons of cornstarch, 4 eggs, a pinch of salt and some vanilla extract. Place the milk with the white sugar and salt in a farina (heavy) kettle over the fire; if you have not such a kettle, a tin pail set in a pot of hot water (double boiler) will answer the purpose. Beat the eggs without separating them in a large bowl and wet the cornstarch with a little cold milk; put the brown sugar in a tin pan and set over the fire; stir it until it is thoroughly scorched but not burned. Then turn the scalding milk on the eggs; put the mixture in the kettle again over the fire; stir in the cornstarch until it thickens; lastly, stir in the scorched sugar and remove the kettle from the fire; then add a generous amount of vanilla. The scorched sugar falls into the custard in strings, but these will dissolve with vigorous stirring, after removal from the fire. Turn the mixture into custard glasses and serve cold.—Mrs. Perry Smith.

RENNET CURD—Take a piece of dried rennet 2 inches square; wash off the salt; put it into 2 quarts (8 cups) of lukewarm milk with a thread attached to it so that it can be easily removed; let it remain until the milk begins to thicken, then remove it and place the milk where it will become cold and solid. To be eaten with rich cream, sweetened and flavored to taste.—Anon.

APPLE TAPIOCA—One cup of tapioca soaked in 1½ pints (3 cups) of warm water 3 hours. Peel and core 8 tart apples; fill the apples with brown sugar, grating in a little nutmeg or moistening them with wine. One hour before the dish is needed, pour the tapioca over the apples and bake in moderate (350°F.) oven. Serve in the dish it is baked in. The addition of the whites of 4 well-beaten egg whites spread over the top and browned slightly improves it.—Mrs. E. V. Case

MELANGE—Line a deep pie dish with pie crust and spread on it a thin layer of tart apple sauce, then a layer of buttered bread; and on this another layer of apple. Bake until the crust is done; when it is done, spread on the whites of 2 eggs beaten to a froth and sweetened; brown slightly. Serve with a sauce of butter and sugar stirred to a cream and seasoned with lemon—Mrs. W. Guthrie

LEMON SPONGE—One package of gelatine; pour over it ¼ pint (½ cup) of cold water; let it stand 15 minutes; add ½ pint (1 cup) of boiling water and ¾ pound (1½ generous cups) of white sugar. Heat this until the sugar melts, then take it from the fire. Let it cool; add the juice of 4 lemons. When the gelatine is cold, but before it begins to get firm, add the well-beaten whites of 3 eggs; beat the whole 15 minutes until the mixture is quite white and begins to thicken. Then put it in a mold first wet in cold water.—Mrs. Lamkin

SNOW WHITE'S DELIGHT—One tablespoon of gelatine, soaked 10 minutes in ¼ pint (½ cup) of cold water; add ¾ pint (1½ cups) of boiling water, the juice of 2 good-sized fresh lemons, 1½ cups of powdered sugar. Allow this to stand over a slow fire only a few moments; strain it through a flannel bag into your pudding dish and set it away to become a jelly. Then make a smooth custard of the yolks of 5 eggs with 1½ tablespoons of moistened cornstarch; sweeten it to taste and cook it a few minutes in a tin pail set in a kettle of boiling water (double boiler), stirring all the while. When it is sufficiently cooked and partially cooled, flavor with vanilla extract, and, when entirely cold, pour this custard over the jelly already in the dish. Beat to a stiff froth the whites of the 5 eggs, adding a little sugar, and pour them over the top of the custard. It is then ready to serve. This is considered an excellent and delicate dessert, if properly and carefully made.—Mrs. L. H. Smith

CHARLOTTE RUSSE—Whip 1 quart (4 cups) of rich cream to a stiff froth and drain it well on a nice sieve. To 1 scant pint (2 cups) of milk add 6 eggs beaten very light; make the mixture very sweet and flavor it strongly with vanilla. Cook it over hot water (double boiler) until it is a thick custard. Soak 1 full ounce of gelatine in a very little water and warm it over hot water. When the custard is very cold, beat in lightly the gelatine and the whipped cream. Line the bottom of your mold with buttered paper and the sides with Sponge Cake (see Index) or Lady-Fingers (see Finger Cakes in Index) fastened together with the white of an egg. Fill the mold with the cream; put it in a cold place or, in summer, on ice. To turn it out, dip the mold for a moment in hot water. In draining the whipped cream, all that drips through can be re-whipped.—Mrs. A. M. Gibbs

CHOCOLATE CREAM—Soak 2 tablespoons of gelatine (in cold water sufficient to cover it) ½ hour; boil 1 quart (4 cups) of milk; scrape 2 ounces of chocolate (½ cup when grated); mix with 8 spoons of white sugar; moisten this with 3 spoons of boiling milk. Then stir the gelatine and the yolks of 10 well-beaten eggs into the milk; stir 3 minutes briskly; take off, strain the mixture and add 1 teaspoon of vanilla extract; strain the cream and put it in molds to cool. Serve with sugar and cream.—Mrs. T. Kingsford

TWO FANCY CREAMS, COFFEE AND ORANGE—Coffee: Soak a package of gelatine in a little cold water ½ hour; then place it over boiling water and add 1 gill (½ cup) each of strong coffee and sugar. When the gelatine is well dissolved, take it from the fire; stir in 3 gills (1½ cups) of cream and strain the mixture into your mold. Be sure that the mold has been previously wet with cold water. Orange: Make this according to the above rules for Coffee Cream, but omit the coffee; instead add 1 gill (½ cup) of orange juice and the grated rind of ½ orange; let the latter soak in the orange juice while the gelatine is dissolving over the boiling water; add the beaten yolks of 2 eggs when you take the gelatine off the fire and while it is still quite hot.—Anon.

BAVARIAN CREAM—One pint (2 cups) of milk, the yolks of 4 eggs, ¼ pound (generous ½ cup) of sugar, 1 tablespoon of soaked gelatine. Put all over the fire and stir it until the gelatine is dissolved; then strain the mixture through a fine sieve and when it is cool, add 1 pint (2 cups) of cold whipped cream; flavor with vanilla.—Mrs. Charles Cuffield

FLOATING ISLAND (late 1800s)—One tumbler (1 cup) of currant jelly, 1 pint (2 cups) of powdered sugar, 5 egg whites. Beat the egg whites very stiff before putting them in the jelly; then beat well again; add the sugar gradually and beat the mixture perfectly stiff. Chill it thoroughly on the ice and serve in a glass dish half filled with cold milk; cover the island with spoonfuls of whipped cream standing in peaks. Serve with plain cream.*

FRUIT FLOAT (late 1800s)—Crush a pint (2 cups) of very ripe red raspberries with a gill (½ cup) of sugar. Beat the whites of 4 eggs to a stiff froth and add gradually a gill (½ cup) of powdered sugar. Press the raspberries through a strainer to clear them of seeds and by degrees beat in the juice with the sugar and egg whites until the mixture is so stiff that it stands in peaks. Serve as Floating Island (above) in milk covered with spoonfuls of whipped cream.—Mrs. E. S. Miller

ORANGE FLOAT—Heat 1 quart (4 cups) of water with ½ pint (1 cup) of sugar; when this is boiling add to it 4 tablespoons of cornstarch mixed in cold water; let it boil, stirring it, 15 minutes. When it is cool add the juice of 2 lemons and pour the mixture over 4 or 5 sliced and peeled oranges; over the top spread the beaten whites of 3 eggs, sweetened, and flavored with a few drops of vanilla. Eaten with cream.—Mrs. M. E. Kedzie

BRANDY WHIPPED CREAM—Mix 1 pint (2 cups) of cream with 9 tablespoons of fine sugar and 1 gill (½ cup) of good brandy or wine in a large bowl; whip these with the cream dasher, and, as the froth rises, skim it into the dish in which it is to be served. Fill the dish to the top and ornament the cream with Kisses or Macaroons.—Anon.

A DISH OF SNOW (early 1800s)—Select very juicy apples; pare, core and stew them in a very little water until they are sponge soft; strain them through a sieve and sweeten with powdered sugar to which just a mite of cinnamon has been added. Chill this ice cold in a deep glass dish. Next, use the white of 1 egg for each apple you cooked; beat the egg whites, with 1 tablespoon of sugar for each egg, to a stiff froth; mix this into the apples. Serve with Whipped Cream Sauce (see Index).*

APPLE BEACONS (mid-1800s)—Make a simple syrup of ½ pint (1 cup) of boiling water, a stick of cinnamon bark and 1 pint (2 cups) of sugar. As this cooks, butter a cold baking dish with cold butter; wash and core 6 to 8 tart cooking apples; place them, well separated, in the dish. When the syrup is ready, remove the cinnamon from it and pour it over and into the apples. Bake them, covered, in a high moderate oven (375°F.) for ¾ to 1 hour. See to it that the apples do not break their skins or lose their roundness by overbaking. Remove them from the oven; place them where they will keep hot; reduce the syrup to half its volume by simmering it. Heat any kind of preserves and use them to stuff the apples, which are placed on a hot serving platter; pour the syrup over them. Have 1 gill (½ cup) of rum heated on the stove; pour this over the apples, ignite the rum so that each apple becomes a beacon and bring them to table.*

BANANA SOUFFLÉ (late 1800s)—Begin a custard by cooking 1 pint (2 cups) of milk and ½ cup of sugar; when the milk simmers, remove it from the fire; stir in 3 egg yolks and 2 teaspoons of cornstarch dissolved in a little cold milk; let this thicken over a low fire or in a double boiler and stir all the time; take it from the fire when thick and smooth. After it is cool, beat 3 egg whites snow white and blend them into the mixture. Season the custard with 1 teaspoon of vanilla extract and pour it over 5 sliced raw bananas. Top with 1 cup of whipped cream, if so desired.*

CRANBERRY DELIGHTS (late 1800s)—Open a tumbler (1 cup) of Cranberry Jelly (see Index); cut the jelly into bits and add 5 tablespoons of orange juice and a pinch of salt. Whip ¼ pint (½ cup) of good top cream and add 1 teaspoon of lemon juice just as it reaches solidity; blend this with the cranberry mixture, pour it into serving glasses and chill it on ice.*

RICE CHARLOTTE—Blanch ¼ pound (2/3 cup) of rice and boil it in 1 quart (4 cups) of milk with a little sugar and vanilla; when it is soft, let it cool, and then mix it with 1 pint (2 cups) of whipped cream. Oil a mold and fill it with a layer of rice and a layer of preserves or marmalade, alternately; let it stand until stiff and then turn it out.—E. M. Walker

FRUIT BLANCMANGE—Stew nice fresh fruit (whatever you may please, cherries and raspberries being the best), strain off the juice and sweeten it to taste. Place it over the fire in a double kettle until it boils; while it is boiling, stir in cornstarch wet with a little cold water, allowing 2 tablespoons of starch for each pint (2 cups) of juice; continue stirring until it is sufficiently cooked. Then pour it into molds wet in cold water; set them away to cool. This, eaten with cream and sugar, makes a delightful dessert.—Mrs. T. V. Wadskier

BLANCMANGE ARROWROOT—Boil 1 quart (4 cups) of milk, reserving 1 gill (½ cup) cold to wet your arrowroot with; when it boils up, stir in 2½ tablespoons of arrowroot and after a few minutes add 1 tablespoon of crushed sugar, 1 tablespoon of rose water and a little salt. Pour into molds. —Anon.

JELLIED GRAPES—A very delicate dish is made of 1/3 of cup (2 ounces) of raw rice, 2 cups of pitted grapes, ½ cup of water and 2 tablespoons of sugar. Sprinkle the rice and sugar among the grapes while placing them in a deep dish; pour on the water. Cover the dish close and simmer 2 hours in a slow (275°F.) oven. Serve cold as pudding; if served warm as pudding, increase slightly the proportion of rice and sugar.—Mrs. A. M. Lewis

LEMON OMELET (mid-1800s)—Break 6 egg yolks into a bowl and whisk them until they are thick. Now blend in gradually 1/3 pound (¾ cup) of white sugar and the strained juice of 2 lemons. The next step is to whip the egg whites, but not so stiff that they stand in tall spires when lifted. Fold these into the lemon mixture with a two-pronged kitchen fork and pour the mixture into a liberally buttered baking dish, so large that it does not reach more than two-thirds to the top, to allow space for rising. Bake in a moderate (350°F.) oven about 20 minutes. Serve with Fruit Foam (see below). A fine party dessert.*

FRUIT CREAM (mid-1800s)—Mash 2 cups of fruit—strawberries or raspberries are best, but any other will do. Strain through a sieve, but rub as much of the pulp through as possible; add ¾ pound (scant ¾ cup) of white sugar; beat well with an egg beater; next, add 1½ pints (3 cups) of heavy cream and beat hard for 15 minutes. When all is a thick foam put it into goblets for dessert or spoon into tart or puff pastry patty shells.*

FRUIT FOAM (mid-1800s)—Have a well-chilled bowl and beat in it the whites of 6 eggs; when they are stiff, add 2 tablespoons of powdered sugar, ½ teaspoon of cinnamon, ½ teaspoon of vanilla extract and 3 tablespoons of raspberry, currant, grape or gooseberry jelly. Even cranberry jelly is good with this, but, if this is used, leave out the vanilla and cinnamon and use 4 tablespoons of jelly.*

PRUNE WHIP (mid-1800s)—Sweeten to taste and stew ¾ pound of pitted prunes; when they are perfectly cold, add the whites of 4 eggs beaten stiff; stir all this together until it is light. Put it in a dish and bake in a moderate (350°F.) oven 20 minutes; chill and serve in a large dish covered with whipped cream.*

QUICK AND READY SNOW CREAM (late 1800s)—Beat 2 cups of heavy cream; in 3 tablespoons white wine dissolve a large cube of sugar rubbed on three sides against an orange and on three sides against a lemon. Mix the flavored wine into the whipped cream. Now, at the last minute, whip the whites of 2 eggs stiff and blend them into the cream mixture. This dessert is as delicious as it is wholesome and time-saving.*

TROPICAL FRUIT SNOW (late 1800s)—For a party, peel 8 sweet oranges, divide them into sections and remove the seeds and tough membranes; put a layer of oranges in a deep glass dish, flavor them with a little lemon juice and dust with powdered white sugar. Have ready 2 trimmed and sliced pineapples, 1 grated cocoanut and 6 peeled and sliced bananas; place layers of banana, cocoanut and pineapple, in that order, over the oranges; repeat the process and dust the layers freely with powdered sugar; also season with lemon juice, of which you will need about ¼ cup. The top layer is to be heaped high in the center and sprinkled liberally with sugar and cocoanut; place sliced bananas in a circle around this peak. Housewives very often sprinkle the layers with crumbled macaroons for added charm and use rum, brandy, sherry or liqueurs instead of lemon juice.*

RICE SNOW BALLS—Boil a pint (2 cups) of rice in 2 quarts (8 cups) of water with a teaspoon of salt until quite soft, then put it in small cups, having them quite full; when the cupfuls of rice are perfectly cold, turn them into a dish. Take the yolks of 3 eggs, 1 pint (2 cups) of milk, 1 teaspoon of cornstarch; flavor with lemon and cook this as you do soft custard. Turn it over the rice ½ hour previous to eating it. This is a nice dessert in hot weather. Sweetmeats are a good accompaniment.—Anon.

LEMON JELLY—Grate the outsides of 2 lemons and squeeze out the juice; mix 1 cup of sugar, ½ of butter, the yolks of 3 eggs; beat the 3 last ingredients thoroughly, then add the juice and grated rind; put the mixture over fire, stirring until it is thick; mold the jelly according to your fancy.—Jennie June

ORANGE JELLY—Soak 2 packages of gelatine in ½ pint (1 cup) of cold water for 1 hour; add the juice of 3 lemons, 2 pounds (4½ cups) of sugar and 1 pint (2 cups) of boiling water; when all are dissolved add 1 pint (2 cups) of orange juice. Strain the liquid carefully and set it on ice until ready for use. Eight oranges usually make it.—Mrs. J. P. Hoit

SUGARED FRUITS—Beat the whites of eggs just enough to break them up; dip fine stems of cherries or currants into the egg and then into powdered sugar; dry them on a sieve.—Anon.

AMBROSIA (ORANGES AND COCOANUT)—Take 1 dozen sweet oranges, peel off the skins and cut them in slices. Take a large-sized fresh cocoanut; grate it on a coarse grater. Then put alternate layers of the orange and grated cocoanut in a glass dish; sprinkle pulverized sugar over each layer of the cocoanut. This makes a beautiful and palatable dish.—Mrs. S. W. Cheever

BAKED APPLES—Pare as many apples as you wish of some nice variety, neither sweet nor sour; core them by using an apple corer or a steel fork; set them in biscuit tins and fill the cavities with sugar, a little butter, and some ground cinnamon, if you like. Set them in a hot (400°F.) oven and bake until done.**

BAKED PEARS—Place in a stone jar first a layer of pears (without paring them), then a layer of sugar, then more pears, and so on until the jar is full. Then put in as much water as it will hold. Bake in a slow (300°F.) oven 3 hours.—Mrs. J. B. Stubbs

BAKED QUINCES—One dozen nice quinces, cored and well rubbed. Put them in baking pans and fill the centers with pulverized sugar. Bake in a slow (300°F.) oven about 2 hours and serve cold, with or without cream. —Anon.

20. *Sweet Sauces for Sweet Dishes and Puddings*

ALMOND-VANILLA CREAM (mid-1800s)—Blanch, chop and mince ½ pint (1 cup) of sweet almonds and 1 tablespoon of bitter almonds. Take ½ pint (1 cup) of thick cream flavored with 1 teaspoon of vanilla extract; whip it stiff and cut into it ¼ pint (½ cup) of fine sugar; blend the almonds into this and serve with slices of Two-Four-Eight Sand Cake (see Index) that have been soaked in brandy.*

BROWN SUGAR SAUCE (early 1800s)—Stir ¼ cup of cream into 1 cup of brown sugar; soften a piece of butter as big as an egg (4 tablespoons) in the palms of your hands; when it is ready, stir this into the sugar-cream. Flavor with nutmeg, cinnamon, ginger.*

FROZEN CIDER APPLE SAUCE (mid-1800s)—Pour 4 quarts (16 cups) of cored and pared sweet apples into 2 quarts (8 cups) of boiling cider and cook, covered, to a thick pulp. Add 2 teaspoons of cinnamon and 1 of vanilla extract and sweeten to taste. Make enough of this sauce as will fill a well-scrubbed firkin; cover it up with a well-fitting lid, store in a cold place and use it from time to time. (Some New Englanders did, and still do, let this apple sauce ferment into Hard Cider Sauce; they let it freeze and dish it out by the chunk.)***

CARAMEL SAUCE (late 1800s)—Melt as many caramels as you will need in the top of a double boiler; add rich milk or cream until you have the right consistency. Season with a little salt and flavor with almond or vanilla extract to suit your liking.***

CRANBERRY SAUCE (early 1800s)—Wash and pick 1 quart (4 cups) of cranberries and boil them until they are very soft in water just enough to cover them. Then strain them through a hair-sieve, weigh them and mix equal quantities of the pulp and fine white sugar. Boil the mixture gently, and with care that it does not burn, for about 15 to 20 minutes. This can also be used as filling for Cranberry Pies (see Index).*

CRANBERRY SAUCE (mid-1800s)—Cook together 1 cup each of water and sugar about 5 minutes. Add 2 cups of cleaned and picked cranberries; let them cook about 5 minutes or until the berry skins are broken. Let the sauce stand until cool and serve.*

WHIPPED CREAM SAUCE FOR COLD DESSERTS (early 1800s)—Mix ½ pint (1 cup) of heavy cream with ¼ pint (½ cup) of fine white sugar and 1 teaspoon of lemon juice. Whip together without skimming off the broth. Beat the white of 1 large egg separately and stir it into the whipped cream.*

FOAM SAUCE FOR DESSERTS (late 1800s)—Take 1 cup of sugar and beat it together with 1 whole egg. Thicken ½ pint (1 cup) of boiling water with 1 heaping teaspoon of wetted cornstarch and add a piece of butter the size of a walnut (1 rounded tablespoon). Pour this mixture on the egg and sugar; beat to a fare-thee-well and flavor with vanilla.*

HARD SAUCE FOR PUDDINGS, RICE, ETC. (early 1800s)—Take 2 gills (1 cup) of brown sugar, ½ gill (¼ cup) of butter; stir these together until they are light; flavor with 2 tablespoons of rum or the juice of a lemon; smooth the top with a knife and grate nutmeg over it.*

EASY HARD SAUCE FOR HASTY PUDDING (mid-1800s)—Cream 1/3 cup of butter and add 1 cup of brown sugar or molasses; beat in 2 tablespoons of orange juice and 1 teaspoon of grated orange peel and whip until fluffy. Serve cold.*

HARD SAUCE FOR HOT DESSERTS (late 1800s)—Beat the white of 1 egg. Cream ½ cup of butter; add the egg white and enough powdered sugar to make the mixture quite stiff; flavor with vanilla. Water will do, but the egg makes it more creamy.*

HOT MAPLE SYRUP SAUCE (mid-1800s)—To ½ pint (1 cup) of maple syrup add 3 tablespoons of very hot water; stir well; put in a piece of butter as big as a pullet's egg (3 tablespoons); flavor with 1 saltspoon (¼ teaspoon) each of cloves and cinnamon, a pinch of nutmeg and a small teaspoon of vinegar; boil it all up; stir in 1 rounded teaspoon of cornstarch melted in 1 tablespoon of cold water. When the sauce is thick, remove it from the fire, beat it well and strain it into a sauce boat.*

MOUNTAINTOP SAUCE (mid-1800s)—This cold sauce is begun by separating 2 eggs; beat the yolks yellow, add 1½ gills (¾ cup) of white sugar slowly and stir well; follow with ¼ cup of melted butter that has been allowed to cool and ½ teaspoon of vanilla extract. For a rich sauce, blend this into 1 cup of whipped cream; for a simpler sauce, whip the whites of the 2 eggs and bind the mixture with them.*

ORANGE SAUCE (mid-1800s)—Dissolve 1 rounded teaspoon of arrowroot in a little cold water. Set 1 gill (½ cup) of whole milk to heat; when it is hot, add ½ gill (¼ cup) each of white sugar and orange juice and the grated rind of ½ orange; let the mixture cook for 5 minutes; remove it from the fire, add the arrowroot and stir while the sauce thickens. Taste for sweetness; add white sugar or apple jelly if more sweetness is wanted. Excellent with Cottage Puddings (see Index).*

RAISIN SAUCE FOR BAKED HAM (early 1800s)—When the ham is done, empty the baking pan of basting juices and skim off 2 dessertspoons (4 teaspoons) of drippings; in a skillet blend these with 2 dessertspoons (4 teaspoons) of moistened cornstarch and thin it out with 1 pint (2 cups) of hot cider in which ½ pint (1 cup) of stoned raisins has been plumped; make a smooth gravy, and, if it chances to be too thick, add as much champagne or brandy as may be needed.*

WINE SAUCE (late 1800s)—Two ounces (¼ cup) of butter, 2 teaspoons of flour, ¼ pound (scant ½ cup) of sugar, 1 gill (½ cup) of wine and ½ nutmeg grated. Mix the flour and butter together; add ½ pint (1 cup) of boiling water and the sugar and wine; just before serving, add the grated nutmeg. Serve hot.*

WINE PUDDING SAUCE—One cup of sugar, ½ cup of butter, ½ cup of red wine, 1 egg. Beat butter, sugar and eggs together; set the mixture on the stove and heat it; pour in the wine; add a little nutmeg. Pour it from one dish to another a few times and send it to the table.—Anon.

SOFT BRANDY SAUCE (early 1800s)—One gill (½ cup) of butter; stir it to a cream; beat 2 eggs very light; stir all together; add 1 small teacup (½ cup) of brandy and mix it in. Set the sauce to warm on top of a tea kettle of boiling water, not on the stove.*

CURRANT JELLY SAUCE—Brown 1 cup of sugar and a piece of butter the size of a hen's egg (4 tablespoons) in a saucepan; pour 10 tablespoons of boiling water slowly over the mixture; heat it when you are ready to serve and add ½ cup of currant jelly.—Mrs. Pulsifer

COTTAGE PUDDING SAUCE (early 1800s)—Four tablespoons (¼ cup) of white sugar, 2 tablespoons of butter, 1 tablespoon of flour; beat all to a cream and add the white of 1 egg well beaten; then add 1 gill (½ cup) of boiling water; stir well; flavor to taste.*

FOAMING PUDDING SAUCE—One-half teacup (½ cup) of butter, the same of sugar; beat them to a froth; put them into a dish and set it in a pan of hot water (double boiler); add a tablespoon of hot water, or, if preferred, a little vanilla; stir the mixture, always in the same direction, until it comes to a very light foam.—Mrs. A. R. Scranton

RASPBERRY SAUCE FOR FRUIT FRITTERS (mid-1800s)—Wet 1 teaspoon of cornstarch in cold water and stir it into 2 gills (1 cup) of gently boiling water until it thickens; when the cornstarch has cooked 10 minutes add ½ cup of raspberry preserves and 3 tablespoons of rum; take it from the fire. Rub ¼ cup of butter into a cream; add 1 cup of powdered sugar gradually, 1 beaten egg and 1 saltspoon (¼ teaspoon) of grated nutmeg. When the sauce base has cooled a bit, pour the whole into the butter-egg-sugar mixture, stir until it is mixed well and bring it to table. One can make various fruit fritter sauces. Rum goes well with apples and pears; brandy fits apricots and peaches.*

WINE SAUCE FOR DESSERTS (mid-1800s)—Depending on the kind you want, use 1 cup of red or white wine. The better the wine, the better the sauce. In a basin, mix 2 raw egg yolks with 1 whole egg; stir in 2 tablespoons of white sugar. In a little of the wine, blend 1 dessertspoon (2 teaspoons) of flour and stir this into the egg mixture. Lastly, add the rest of the wine. Place the sauce over a medium fire and, with whisk or egg beater if you have one, whip steadily until it thickens; beware of scorching.*

WINE PLUM PUDDING SAUCE (pre-1800s)—Make a Cream Sauce based on 2 tablespoons of flour to a scant 2 ounces (1/4 cup) of butter, diluted with 2 tablespoons of milk followed by 2 tablespoons of cold water. Add a large wineglass (1/2 cup) each of sherry and brandy, 2 teaspoons of pounded sugar and a very little grated lemon peel. Thin with hot water or hot milk to suit if too thick.*

HOT ALMOND SAUCE (mid-1800s)—Stir 1/2 pint (1 cup) of sifted sugar into 1/2 pint (1 cup) of cream whipped with 3 saltspoons (3/4 teaspoon) of almond and 1 (1/4 teaspoon) of vanilla extract. Put 1/2 gill (1/4 cup) of butter in a pail placed in boiling water (double boiler); when it has melted, add the rest of the ingredients. Always prepare this just before serving time, otherwise it may become too thin.*

QUICK SOUR CREAM SAUCE (early 1800s)—Put together 3/4 pint (1 1/2 cups) of sour cream and 1/2 pint (1 cup) of sugar (white); beat the mixture 5 to 8 minutes and grate some nutmeg over it. Specially appropriate for Indian and Plum Puddings.*

COLD SAUCE FOR PUDDINGS (mid-1800s)—Mix 3 tablespoons of softened butter with 6 tablespoons of white sugar and stir them to a cream; whip the white of 1 egg and combine it with the butter, etc. Add rose water, a few drops of lemon juice or a spoonful of boiled but cold cider.*

SHERRY PUDDING SAUCE (late 1800s)—Cream 1/4 cup of butter with 1/2 cup of sugar; beat 2 egg yolks lemon-colored and thick; add them to the sugar and butter; whip 1/2 cup of cream until stiff; stir it into the mixture and set it to thicken in the top of a double boiler. When the sauce is ready, blend 1/4 cup of sherry into it and serve while hot.*

21. Coffee, Cordials and Cups That Cheer

TO MAKE FAR FROM INSTANT COFFEE (early 1800s)—To have good coffee you must use equal quantities of Mocha and Java beans; since there are often little stones or pebbles in them, pick them carefully. If you have no coffee roaster, put one kind of bean—do not mix them before roasting—into a round-bottomed iron kettle and let it be where it will be hot for an hour or two without burning; then put it where the beans will brown and stir them constantly until they are done. Do the same with the other beans. If they are left over the fire even half a minute, the beans next to the kettle may burn black; this is enough to injure all the rest. Before you take the beans up, stir a piece of butter the size of a small nut into each batch. Now put the beans, while still hot, together in a tin box with a close cover and mix them with your coffee scoop.

In a small family, not more than 2 pounds should be roasted at once to retain freshness and fragrance. For the same reason, beans should be ground only as they are wanted.***

TO BREW COFFEE (early 1800s)—Put a large coffee cup (8 ounces) of ground beans into a pot that will hold 1 quart (4 cups) of water; add the white of an egg, or 2 or 3 clean eggshells, or a bit of well-cleaned and well-dried fish skin (cod or haddock) of the size of a nine-pence. Pour upon it 3 pints (6 cups) of boiling water and boil 10 minutes. Then pour out a little coffee from the spout, in order to remove the grains that may have boiled into it; strain this back into the coffee pot. Let the coffee stand 8 to 10 minutes where it will keep hot, but do not boil it; boiling coffee a great while makes it strong, but not so lively and agreeable.***

REAL PARISIAN CHOCOLATE (late 1800s)—Scrape 2 sticks of chocolate (½ cup when grated) and boil them in ½ cup of water. Stir the chocolate to a paste; make it very smooth. Sweeten ½ pint (1 cup) each of milk and cream with loaf sugar to taste and, when this is boiling, pour it upon the chocolate; let them boil together a few seconds, stirring them well. Serve immediately, topped with whipped cream.*

COCOA BEST WHEN CRACKED (mid-1800s)—When you cook cocoa in the shell, put 2 heaping tablespoons to 3 pints (6 cups) of boiling water. Boil it a great while—about 2 or 3 hours. It is a good idea to change the water every hour; skim off the oil and add 3 gills (¾ cup) of scalded milk; boil it up again and set it aside until next day, as all the oily substance can best be removed when the cocoa is cold. Reheat it slowly.***

TEA—When the water in the tea kettle begins to boil, have ready a tea steeper; pour into the tea steeper just a very little of the boiling water and then put in tea, allowing 1 teaspoon of tea to each person. Pour boiling water over this until the steeper is a little more than half full; cover tightly and let it stand where it will keep hot but not boil. Let the tea infuse for 10 or 15 minutes and then pour it into the tea urn, adding more boiling water in the proportion of 1 cup of water for every teaspoon of dry tea which has been infused. Have boiling water ready in a water pot and weaken each cup of tea as desired. Do not use water that has boiled long for tea. Spring water is best for tea, and filtered water next best.—Anon.

TEA À LA RUSSE—Pare and slice fresh, juicy lemons; lay a piece in the bottom of each cup, sprinkle it with white sugar and pour hot, strong tea over it. Or the lemon may be sent around in slices with the peel on. No cream is used.—Anon.

ICED TEA À LA RUSSE—To each glass of tea add the juice of ½ lemon; sweeten the tea and add pounded ice.—Anon.

LEMONADE WITH THAT OLD LANG SYNE FLAVOR (mid-1800s)—This is a very important drink during our hot summer seasons. If freely used in the spring, like sulphur and molasses, there would be far less of billiousness and fevers of which to complain. Lemonade is more wholesome when only moderately sweet. Roll the lemons, cut them in halves and squeeze their juices into your lemonade pitcher; next, slice the halves, drop them into the pitcher and dust them with granulated sugar. Let the sugar and lemons lie for a full hour, as this extracts the flavor from the rinds. A bit of ice laid on top of the lemons during this period improves the lemonade. After an hour or so, add what water you want for lemonade, stir well for 5 minutes and then it is ready for drinking, all the oil and acid of the fruit being set free. A good rule to go by is ¼ pint (½ cup) of sugar to ½ pint (1 cup) of lemon juice and 1 quart (4 cups) of water. If ice water is used as well as ice it makes for a better lemonade.*

HOME-MADE WINES ARE LEGAL—if you do not make more than 200 gallons in a calendar year and if they are meant for your own household consumption only; but the law requires that you inform the Alcohol Tax section of your Internal Revenue office of your intentions. There are no taxes to pay; but you are in trouble if you sell as little as 1 tiny pint.—H. L. A.

ELDERBERRY WINE (mid-1800s)—The old, slow but best method is to figure on 5 pounds of sugar for every 12 pounds of elderberries that have been carefully culled and washed; put them in a crock or firkin, mash them with a potato pounder and stir in the sugar. Next add 2 gallons of cold well water. Put the vessel in a warm kitchen corner and cover it with muslin; stir every Saturday and Wednesday morning over a period of 6 weeks. Then run the wine twice through a muslin-lined strainer or a very fine hair-sieve; rinse the container; return the wine to it; let it stand, covered as before, for 2 weeks, then bottle it; let the corks sit loosely for 1 week, then cork well.***

CURRANT WINE (early 1800s)—Put 1 quart (4 cups) each of sugar, water and currant juice—or more in similar proportions—into a tight keg with a faucet. Leave out the bung for 2 or 3 weeks, and then put it in loosely so that if the wine ferments longer, the keg will not burst. After the fourth week, put the bung in tight. Let it stand for 1 year, then draw it off and bottle it.***

CURRANT SHRUB (mid-1800s)—For every pint (2 cups) of currant juice, add 1 pound (2¼ cups) of white, crushed sugar; boil the juice and sugar together. Stir constantly while it cools, and when cold, bottle it. A spoonful or two of this in a tumbler of water affords a refreshing beverage.*

ELDERBERRY CORDIAL (mid-1800s)—This great household standby is usually made in small quantities and taken in small nips. Pick and choose 6 quarts (24 cups) of berries; wash them, cover with water and let them simmer until mushy; strain them thoroughly through a flannel bag, but do not press it. To each pint (2 cups) of juice add ½ pint (1 cup) of sweet brown New Orleans sugar; return the juice to the kettle and have ready a muslin spice bag that contains 1 dessertspoon (2 teaspoons) each of whole cloves and allspice and ditto pieces of cinnamon bark. Let this simmer with the elderberry-sugar mixture for about ½ hour. Remove the kettle from the fire, discard the spice bag and turn the juice into a pan. Measure it carefully and, to each pint (2 cups) of syrup, add 1¼ (2½ cups) of good brandy or aged-in-the-barrel corn whiskey. This can now be bottled and used at any time.*

FISHERMAN'S RUM TODDY (early 1800s)—Heat a pewter or china mug. If it holds 8 ounces, fill half of the mug with boiling water; add a lump of butter as big as a scallop and 1 teaspoon of sugar; stir until both melt, then fill the mug to the brim with rum.*

DANDELION WINE (early 1800s)—To 1 gallon (16 cups) of dandelion blossoms, picked just after dawn, add 1 gallon of boiling water and let this stand for 3 to 4 days to steep; then strain off the flowers. Add 4 pounds (9 cups) of sugar, also 4 medium oranges and 2 large lemons, all peeled, seeded and chopped; lastly, add ½ pint (1 cup) of good yeast. After it has been working for 3 weeks, strain the wine and bottle it; place corks in the bottle necks, but do not drive them down until a full week has passed.***

GINGER BEER (early 1800s)—Pour 1 gallon (16 cups) of boiling water upon 1½ ounces (7½ tablespoons) of ground ginger roots, 1 ounce (3 tablespoons) of cream of tartar, 1 pound (2¼ cups) of clean and sifted brown sugar and 2 fresh lemons sliced thin. It should stand for 24 hours with ½ pint (1 cup) of good yeast, then should be strained through muslin or a hair-sieve, bottled and corked. This beer improves with age and will keep several weeks unless the weather is very hot.***

MAPLE BEER (early 1800s)—To 4 gallons of boiling water add 1 quart (4 cups) of maple syrup and 1 small tablespoon of essence of spruce. When it is about milk warm, add 1 pint (2 cups) of yeast and, when it is fermented, bottle it.***

CRANBERRY DRINK (mid-1800s)—Put ½ pint (1 cup) of mashed cranberries into ½ pint (1 cup) of water and press them well. Boil 2 quarts (8 cups) of water with 1 heaping tablespoon of oatmeal and a bit of lemon peel; stir the cranberry-water mixture into this when the oatmeal is cooked; add ½ pint (1 cup) of white wine and sugar to taste—not too much sugar, or the fine sharp taste of the cranberries will be destroyed. Boil for ½ hour, let it cool and strain.*

RHUBARB CORDIAL (mid-1800s)—Wash and chop 10 pounds of rhubarb and let it stand 3 days in 2½ gallons of water with the grated rinds of 5 lemons. Run through a hair-sieve into a jug and add 7 pounds of light-brown Havana sugar. Do not cork the jug, but cover its mouth with cheesecloth. Have it remain undisturbed for 14 days. Then put the cork into place and give it a month in which to ripen.***

CIDER PUNCH (early 1800s)—Place a large piece of ice in a punch bowl and lay upon it a rind of lemon peel cut in a thin spiral, a slice of cucumber ¼ inch thick and peeled, 3 tablespoons of light-brown sugar, ½ teaspoon of freshly grated nutmeg and 1 saltspoon (¼ teaspoon) of pounded ginger. Pour upon this 1 quart (4 cups) of cider and 1 pint (2 cups) each of brandy and sherry; it makes no difference if the cider is sweet or hard. Mix well with a ladle.*

XMAS MILK PUNCH (early 1800s)—Add the thin skins and juices of 12 lemons and 1¾ pounds (4 generous cups) of pulverized loaf sugar to 2 quarts (8 cups) of cold water and 4 quarts (16 cups) of light-colored rum; mix well; stir in 2 quarts (8 cups) of scalded milk and let it all stand, covered, in a cold place for 24 hours, when it is ready for use. For small families, this recipe can be reduced in equal proportions. Always sprinkle the surface of the punch with grated nutmeg at the time of serving.*

EGG FLIP (mid-1800s)—Beat up 3 whole eggs with 4 ounces (scant ½ cup) of moist brown sugar in a saucepan; add ½ teaspoon of nutmeg and 1 gill (½ cup) of rum. Set a quart (4 cups) of ale (or beer) to boil; when it does, stir it gradually into the eggs and rum until quite smooth, then serve in pewter tankards.*

HOT MULLED WINE (early 1800s)—Work 5 egg yolks into ½ gill (¼ cup) of heavy cream. Beat the whites well. Boil 24 whole cloves in 1½ pints (3 cups) of water for 10 minutes; strain the water and stir it into the cream and eggs slowly but steadily. When this is thick, add 1 quart (4 cups) of red or white wine—dry, not sweet—with 2 dessertspoons (4 teaspoons) of strained lemon juice; whip the stiff egg whites into the hot wine swiftly; sweeten as desired and serve.*

SODA CREAM—Two and a half pounds (4½ cups) of white sugar, ⅛ pound of tartaric acid, both dissolved in 1 quart (4 cups) of hot water. When this is cold, add the beaten whites of 3 eggs, stirring well. Bottle for use. When you come to drink it, put 2 large spoons of this syrup in a glass of cold water and stir in it ¼ spoon of bicarbonate of soda. Any flavor can be put in the syrup. An excellent drink for summer.—Mrs. M. G. Rand

RASPBERRY ACID—Dissolve 5 ounces of tartaric acid in 2 quarts (8 cups) of water; pour it upon 12 pounds of red raspberries in a large bowl; let it stand 24 hours; strain it without pressing. To a pint (2 cups) of this liquor add 1 pound (2¼ cups) of white sugar; stir until dissolved. Bottle, but do not cork for several days, when it is ready for use. Two or 3 tablespoons in a glass of ice water will make a delicious beverage.—Mrs. G. W. Pitkin

RASPBERRY VINEGAR—To 4 quarts (16 cups) of red raspberries put enough vinegar to cover them and let them stand 24 hours; scald and strain the liquid; add a pound (2¼ cups) of sugar to each pint (2 cups) of juice. Boil it 20 minutes and bottle it. It is then ready for use and will keep years. To 1 glass of water add a great spoonful. It is much relished by the sick. Very nice.—Mrs. W. S. Walker

BLACKBERRY SYRUP—To 1 pint (2 cups) of juice put 1 pound (2¼ cups) of white sugar, ½ ounce (2¼ tablespoons) of powdered cinnamon, ¼ ounce of mace, and 2 teaspoons of cloves; boil all together for ¼ hour, then strain the syrup, and add to each pint (2 cups) a glass of French brandy. Fine for drinks and griddle cakes.—Mrs. Blackburn

LEMON SYRUP—Pare off the yellow rind of the lemon, slice the lemon and put a layer of lemon and a thick layer of sugar in a deep plate; cover the plate close with a saucer and set it in a warm place. This is an excellent remedy for a cold.—Mrs. DeForrest

HOP BEER—One handful of hops; boil them an hour, strain them, and add 1 pint (2 cups) of molasses and enough water to make 2 gallons (16 cups). When milk-warm, add 1 cup or cake of yeast; let it all stand over night; skim and pour it off from the yeast carefully. Add 1 tablespoon of wintergreen and bottle for use.—Mrs. Dickinson

TO TEST THE QUALITY OF ALCOHOL OR WHISKEY (mid-1800s)—Pour a little into the hollow of your hand; let it evaporate without rubbing it; when your palm is dry, sniff the spot where the stuff has been poured; if the odor is unpleasant, the article is undesirable.***

22. *Sweet, Sour, Spicy Pickles and Other Items*

NEVER KEEP PICKLES IN POTTER'S WARE (early 1800s)—Arsenic and other poisonous substances are used in the glazing, and this is often decomposed by vinegar. Whole families have been poisoned this way, and where fatal effects do not follow, a deleterious influence may be operating upon the health from this cause, when not suspected. Pickles should be made with cider vinegar.***

OLD-TIME MUSTARD PICKLE (early 1800s)—Have ready 1 pint (2 cups) each of raw plucked cauliflower, peeled and sliced green tomatoes, cucumbers and ½ pint (1 cup) of the small white onions called buttons, peeled and washed. Put 1 pint (2 cups) of vinegar, the best to be had, on the stove with 1 gill (½ cup) of dark-brown New Orleans sugar; skim the liquid until it is clear; then add ½ gill (¼ cup) each of minced green and red pepper, 2 tablespoons of grated horse-radish, a like amount of mustard seed and 1 tablespoon each of tumeric (optional) and celery seeds. Let this simmer 10 minutes, add the vegetables and allow it to cook, as slowly as possible, until it is a thick pickle.*

CELERY AND CABBAGE PICKLE (late 1800s)—Chop 1½ quarts (6 cups) each of celery and cabbage and put them into a saucepan with 2 quarts (8 cups) of wine vinegar; add 2 dessertspoons (4 teaspoons) each of mustard and celery seeds, also 2 teaspoons of salt and 3 whole black peppers. Let all simmer until tender, put the pickle into jars and cover well.*

BEETS, HOW TO PICKLE (mid-1800s)—Simmer a number of large dark-red beets with unbroken skins for about 2 hours with their tops and root stubs left on as a precaution against the beets' bleeding. With a toothpick determine when they are fully cooked. Drain, cool and peel them and cut them into slices from ½ to ¼ inch thick, as you like them. Have some shredded horse-radish ready as well as a stone or china crock with a well-fitting cover. Put the beets down in layers, with a sprinkling of horse-radish, tiny bits of blades of mace or laurel (bay) leaves and a few peppercorns on each layer; cover completely with steaming hot vinegar; if you can afford the best, use wine or cider vinegar; otherwise ordinary vinegar will do.*

PEPPERS VERSUS CUCUMBERS (early 1800s)—For pickled green peppers, take those that are fresh, glossy and hard; soak them in salt and water, about ½ pint (1 cup) of salt to 1 quart (4 cups) of water, for 9 days; change the brine each day; let them stand in a warm place. Then put them into cold vinegar. If you wish them very hot, leave in the seeds. If not, take out the seeds of the greater part of them.

If peppers are put into the same jar with cucumbers, the entire strength of them will go into the latter; they themselves will become utterly tasteless. On the other hand, a crock of cucumbers is improved by 5 or 6 green peppers.*

PICKLED NASTURTIUM SEEDS (early 1800s)—Many persons consider these seeds better than capers; gather them while green, let them lie a few days to dry, then throw them into cold vinegar; being very spicy, they need no seasonings other than a little salt; drain them and boil enough vinegar to cover them. They should be kept 6 months, covered close, before they are used.*

PICKLED MUSKMELONS (early 1800s)—The common kind are much better for this purpose than cantaloupes; with a sharp knife make a smooth incision so as to cut a half-moon out of one side of the melon. Remove the seeds with a teaspoon; fill the hole with an equal mixture of cloves, mustard seed, chopped onions, peppercorns and shredded horse-radish. Sew on the piece you took out with a needle and coarse thread. Lay the melons in a jar and pour boiling vinegar, with a little salt in it, over them. Repeat this 2 or 3 times in as many days with the same vinegar; finally, lay them in fresh vinegar and cover them close.***

OUDE SAUCE—One pint (2 cups) of green tomatoes, 6 red peppers (not large), 4 onions. Chop these together, add 1 cup of salt and let them stand over night. In the morning, drain off the water; add 1 cup of sugar, 1 cup of horse-radish, 1 tablespoon of ground cloves, 1 tablespoon of cinnamon. Cover with vinegar and stew gently all day.—C. Kennicott

MY MOTHER'S FAVORITE PICKLES—One quart (4 cups) of raw cabbage chopped fine, 1 quart (4 cups) of boiled beets chopped fine, 2 cups of sugar, 1 tablespoon of salt, 1 teaspoon of black pepper, ¼ teaspoon of red pepper, 1 teacup (4 ounces) of grated horse-radish. Cover the pickles with cold vinegar and keep them from the air.—Mrs. Savage

FRENCH PICKLES—One peck (8 quarts) of tomatoes sliced, 6 large onions, some cauliflower (as much or as little as you prefer). Sprinkle a pint (2 cups) of salt over all of them at night, the resulting liquor to be drained off in the morning. Then boil the tomatoes, onions, etc., in 2 quarts (8 cups) of water and 1 quart (4 cups) of vinegar 15 or 20 minutes. After boiling them, put the vegetables in a colander and drain the liquid off. Put into a kettle 7 pints (14 cups) of vinegar, 2 pounds (4½ cups) of brown sugar, ½ pound of white mustard seed, 2 tablespoons of ground allspice, 2 of cloves, 2 of ginger, 2 of cinnamon, 2 of ground mustard, ½ tablespoon of cayenne. Put all the tomatoes, etc., into the kettle and boil them 15 or 20 minutes; stir the pickle and be careful not to burn it.—H. N. Jenks

MIXED PICKLES—Three hundred small cucumbers, 4 green peppers sliced fine, 2 large or 3 small heads of cauliflower, 3 heads of white cabbage shaved fine, 9 large onions and 1 large root of horse-radish sliced, 1 quart (4 cups) of green beans cut ½ inch long and 1 quart (4 cups) of green tomatoes sliced. Put this mixture in a pretty strong brine 24 hours; after rinsing, let it drain 3 hours, then sprinkle in ¼ pound of black and ¼ pound of white mustard seed, also 2 teaspoons of ground black pepper. Let it all come to a good boil in just vinegar enough to cover it, adding a little alum. Drain again, and, when cold, mix in ½ pint (1 cup) of ground mustard. Cover the whole with a fresh batch of boiling cider vinegar; add tumeric enough to color it, if you like.—Mrs. F. M. Cragin

WEST INDIA PICKLE—One crisp white cabbage, 2 heads of cauliflower, 3 heads of celery, 1 quart each of small green plums, peaches, grapes, radish pods, nasturtium seeds, artichokes, tomatoes and string beans, the green part of a watermelon next to the rind, 1 quart of small onions parboiled in milk, 100 small cucumbers about an inch or so long, a few green peppers and 3 limes or green lemons. Cut fine the cabbage, cauliflower, celery, pepper and limes and add green ginger; mix these well with the rest, then pour a strong hot brine over them and let them stand 3 hours and take them out and let them drain over night. Mix 1 ounce of tumeric powder with a little cold vinegar, add 1 bottle of French mustard, ground cinnamon, allspice, 2 nutmegs, black pepper, 4 pounds of white sugar and 1 gallon of vinegar. Pour this mixture boiling hot over the pickle; if there is not sufficient liquid to cover it nicely, add more vinegar.—Mrs. Edward Ely

HYANNIS CRANBERRY RELISH (mid-1800s)—Cull and clean 1 pint (2 cups) of cranberries. Only the nicest will do, because they will be served raw. Have a nice tart Winesap apple; pare it, core it and cut it into quarters; put the apple into a basin with the berries. Take a large orange and a small lemon; peel both; slice and remove the seeds; add ¾ pint (1½ cups) of white sugar. Chop and stir all these items until they are well minced and thoroughly united. Chill until dinner time. If any remains after the meal, put it into an air-tight jar and keep it on ice; even so, the relish has poor lasting qualities.*

SPICED PEACHES (late 1800s)—Put 3 pounds (6¾ cups) of brown sugar, 1 pint (2 cups) of vinegar, 1 tablespoon of cinnamon bark, 1 tablespoon of allspice to boil. Meanwhile, scald and peel 5 pounds of peaches; leave them whole, but insert 5 cloves in each. Cook until tender and can them—without removing the cloves—in their own syrup while hot.*

SPICED PEARS (late 1800s)—Put 4 pounds (9 cups) of the best brown sugar to boil with 1 quart (4 cups) of cider vinegar or other good, plain vinegar. Tie the following spices in a bag in the amount of 1 teaspoon of each: mixed whole spices, bark of cinnamon, cassia buds, allspice, plus ½ teaspoon of cloves. Boil them with the vinegar and skim often. In 10 minutes add 8 pounds of whole pared pears; leave stems on; cook 10 minutes or until tender. Skim out the fruit and put it into stone jars; boil the syrup 10 minutes longer and pour it over the fruit. The next day, pour the syrup off and boil it again; do this 3 consecutive mornings. Keep the bag of spices in the syrup until the last boil-up.*

CHINESE PICKLED EGGS (early 1800s)—Boil the eggs 12 minutes, throw them into cold water and peel them. For 12 eggs, boil a large red beet until very soft; peel and mash it fine. Add enough boiling vinegar so that it and the beet, combined, will cover the eggs in the crock for which they are intended; add 1 tablespoon of salt, ½ teaspoon each of ground black pepper, grated nutmeg and cloves. When this mixture is cold pour a little of it, well stirred, into the bottom of the crock; put the eggs in the remaining hot mixture over them. Cover the crock tightly with a suitable bladder. The eggs are good after the first week, better after second, splendid after a month.***

PICKLED OYSTERS (early 1800s)—Open 100 oysters and let them simmer slowly in their own juices for 8 to 12 minutes, depending on how large or small they are; remove them and lay them, one by one, into small jars. While they cool, make a pickle as follows. Measure the oyster liquor, add a similar volume of vinegar and put these into a saucepan; for each pint (2 cups) in the pan, put in 1 blade of mace (pounded), a ½-inch-wide strip of lemon peel and 12 black peppercorns. After boiling this 5 minutes, take it away to cool and, when cold, pour the pickle upon the oysters. Tie the jars down closely. This pickle will keep only during the cold months. Small jars must be used, because unless the contents are eaten at once, the oysters will spoil.***

PICKLED CHERRIES—Five pounds of cherries, stoned or not, 1 quart (4 cups) of vinegar, 2 pounds (4½ cups) of sugar, ½ ounce (2¼ tablespoons) of cinnamon; ½ ounce (2 tablespoons) of cloves, ½ ounce of mace; boil the sugar and vinegar and spices together (grind the spices and tie them in a muslin bag), and pour the hot liquid over the cherries.—Mrs. J. B. Adams

PICKLED PLUMS—To 7 pounds of plums, 4 pounds (9 cups) of sugar, 2 ounces of stick cinnamon, 2 ounces of cloves and 1 quart (4 cups) of vinegar add a little mace. Put in the jar alternately a layer of plums and a layer of spices. Scald the vinegar and sugar together; pour it over the plums. Repeat 3 times for plums (only once for cut apples and pears); the fourth time scald all together. Put them into glass jars and they are ready for use.—Mrs. Meek

PICKLED APPLES—For 1 peck (8 quarts) of sweet apples take 3 pounds (6¾ cups) of sugar; season 2 quarts (8 cups) of vinegar with ½ ounce (2¼ tablespoons) of cinnamon and ½ ounce (2 tablespoons) of cloves; pare the apples, leaving them whole; boil them in part of the vinegar and sugar until you can put a fork through them; take them out, beat the remainder of vinegar and sugar and pour it over the apples. Be careful not to boil them too long, or they will break.—Mrs. Watson Thatcher

PICKLED PEACHES—Take 5 pounds (11¼ cups) of brown sugar to 1 gallon (16 cups) of pure cider vinegar; put in a bag containing 1 stick of cinnamon and 24 cloves; boil it hard for 30 minutes, skimming off the scum until the liquid is clear. Meanwhile, dip the peaches quickly in boiling water; rub them with a flannel cloth, sticking 4 cloves in each peach. If the peaches are clingstones put them into the boiling syrup for 15 or 20 minutes; if freestones do not do this. Lay the peaches in the jar in layers and pour the syrup over them while it is hot; then put a small plate over them to keep them from rising and cover tightly with cloth or paper. In 4 days look at them, and, if necessary, boil the syrup and pour it over the peaches again while hot. Keep them in a cool place while the weather is hot to prevent their souring. The White Sugar Cling is nice for pickling, and the Blood Peach is very rich, but dark. Small pears can be pickled in the same manner, if the skin is taken off.—Mrs. C. D. Howard

PICKLED MELONS—Take 12 ripe melons, wash them, pare them and take out the seeds; cut them in slices; put them in a stone jar, cover them with vinegar and let them stand 24 hours. Take out the melon and to each quart (4 cups) of fresh vinegar add 3 pounds (6¾ cups) of brown sugar, 3 ounces (generous ¾ cup) of cinnamon, 2 (½ cup) of cloves, 2 (generous ½ cup) of allspice. Boil the sugar and spices in the vinegar; skim it well; then put in the melon and boil for 20 minutes; let the syrup boil a few minutes after taking the melon out, then pour it over them.—Mrs. Wicker

PICKLED CAULIFLOWER—After cutting off all the green leaves, put the cauliflowers into boiling water with a good supply of salt and boil them from 3 to 5 minutes; take them out of the salt and water, dip them in clear cold water 1 minute to send the heat to the heart of the cauliflower and cut them in pieces convenient to put in jars. Then make a mixture of 1 tablespoon of mace, 1 of cloves, 1 of allspice, 1 of ginger, 2 of white mustard seed and a red pepper pod to each gallon (16 cups) of vinegar. Let the mixture boil and pour it upon the cauliflower, cover them closely and let them stand 1 week. Then pour off the vinegar, scald it and return it hot again to the cauliflower; put the cauliflower and vinegar in jars ready for use. The best cider vinegar should be used, and if it is not perfectly clear it will injure the cauliflower.—Mrs. Anna Marble

TO PICKLE MARTINOES OR MARTYNIAS—Pick them when soft enough to run a pin through, or from 2 to 3 inches long. Soak them in clear water 1 night, or longer if very salty, then scald them in weak vinegar. Skim them out and throw them in cold water; then pour over them (after draining them from the water) scalding hot vinegar and sugar in the proportion of 5 pounds of sugar to each gallon of vinegar, a handful of cloves and cinnamon, or whatever spices desired, scalded in the vinegar. If the martinoes are not tender enough the scalding can be repeated.—Mrs. E. S. Chesebrough

GOOSEBERRY SOY—Take 6 pounds of gooseberries that are nearly ripe and 3 pounds (6¾ cups) of sugar, 1 pint (2 cups) of best vinegar, and boil all together until quite thick; season to suit your taste with ground cloves and cinnamon. To be eaten with meats; will keep good a long time.— M. A. Bingham

TO STORE CUCUMBERS (mid-1800s)—If you are striving to collect, for pickling, 200 to 300 small cucumbers of uniform size and face difficulties in doing so, you can obtain them gradually and put them in a crock with a gallon of brine made by boiling 1 pint (2 cups) of kitchen salt to the gallon (16 cups) of water; skim the brine as it cooks for a good 10 minutes after it boils up. Do not pour the brine into the crock until it is cool. As you salt the cucumbers away, wash them gently, but do not trim their stems. Make sure that there is always brine enough to cover them. Before you pickle these cucumbers, it is necessary to soak the salt out of them in fresh, cold water.*

BRINE FOR CUCUMBERS (early 1800s)—Three pails water, 2 quarts of coarse salt (rock is good). Heat the water to simmering point and add enough rock salt so that the liquid will float an egg; skim well. Dissolve in the hot brine 1 pound of alum and pour it all into a jar or a keg.***

CONGRESS PICKLES—Wash the cucumbers. Take 1 pint (2 cups) of fine salt to 100 medium-sized cucumbers and sprinkle it over them; pour on enough boiling hot water to cover them; let them stand 48 hours. Take them out of the brine, wipe them, put them in jars and pour over them 1 quart (4 cups) of scalding hot vinegar with 3½ cups of sugar and a bag of any spices you like. If the vinegar becomes tasteless, put them into fresh vinegar before using them. Keep them covered tight.—Henrietta Jackson

PICKLED CUCUMBERS—Wash your cucumbers with care and take care you do not break the little prickles upon them, as the effect will be to make them soft; place them in jars. Make a weak brine of a large handful of salt to 1 gallon of water. When it is scalding hot, turn it over the cucumbers and cover them; repeat this process three mornings in succession, taking care to skim the liquid thoroughly. On the fourth day have ready a porcelain kettle of vinegar, to which has been added a piece of alum the size of a walnut. When the vinegar is scalding hot, put in as many cucumbers as the vinegar will cover; do not let the cucumbers boil, but skim them out as soon as they are scalded through and replace them with others, adding each time a small piece of alum. When this process is through, throw out the vinegar and set what you need of cider vinegar or white vinegar aboiling, with ginger root, allspice and cloves, mustard seeds and red peppers. Meanwhile, sort the pickles to size, place them in stone or glass jars, and turn over them the hot spiced vinegar. Seal the jars and put them away in a cool place. —Mrs. Hugh Adams

CHILI SAUCE (late 1800s)—Scald, skin and chop 12 large tomatoes; chop 2 small onions, 2 red peppers and 2 green peppers. Simmer these with 2½ cups of vinegar, 5 heaping tablespoons of sugar and 1½ tablespoons of salt from 2 to 3 hours; put into air-tight containers that have been scalded with boiling hot water and left bottom-up to dry.*

CURRY POWDER, TO MAKE (mid-1800s)—Housewives have learned to their grief that many of the curry powders available today are adulterated with red lead. To avoid them, here is a recipe brought home from Curry's homeland by a skipper in the East Indian trade. Take ½ pound (4 cups)

each of turmeric and coriander seed, 2 ounces (8 tablespoons) of fenugreek, 1 ounce (4 tablespoons) each of mustard, cinnamon and ginger, ½ ounce (2 tablespoons) each of cayenne, ground black pepper and salt and ¼ ounce (1 tablespoon) of allspice. Pound and blend all these ingredients exceedingly fine in a mortar and sift them in a hair-sieve. This is a richly aromatic and full-flavored curry and should be used in the proportion of 1 teaspoon to ¼ pint (1 cup) of sauce (see also Index).*

CHUTNEY (mid-1800s)—Soak and chop 1 quart (4 cups) of dried apricots; peel, core and chop 2 ripe pears; take ¼ pound (½ cup plus 2 tablespoons) of pitted dates and a like amount (about ¾ cup) of seeded raisins; chop an onion fairly fine; mash a clove of garlic. Blend all this together. Next, stir in 4 teaspoons of ginger powder, 2 tablespoons of fenugreek, 1 teaspoon of salt, 1 gill (½ cup) of sugar and ½ gill (¼ cup) of light-brown sugar. Put the mixture to boil in a good heavy kettle; remove it to a place where it can simmer, well-covered for 1 hour. Keep the lid closed during this time to prevent any and all evaporation of flavors. Some folks like a thick Chutney, others prefer it thinned down. The Chutney can be thinned with a little cider; if it is hard, so much the better.*

CHUTNEY (late 1800s)—This great ingredient with boiled rice is not always easy to buy, but it takes little time and trouble to prepare. However, it calls for a lot of chopping. Chop enough green tomatoes to make 1 quart (4 cups), enough tart apples and seeded raisins to make 1 pint (2 cups) of each, 2 onions and 1 red pepper. Into a proper pot pour 1 quart (4 cups) of vinegar and ditto of sifted brown sugar; add 3 tablespoons of salt and ditto of fenugreek, a small piece of ginger root (1 inch) and ½ teaspoon of ground pepper. There are persons whose copper-lined throats permit them to enjoy a whole teaspoon of cayenne instead of the ground pepper. When these items approach the simmering point, add all the chopped ingredients. The secret of a good Chutney is that it has cooked slowly 1 entire day from breakfast to supper. Skim when necessary. Let it cool. The next morning, give it a full 5-minute boil-up, which requires constant stirring—bottle and cork. It is always better to use many small bottles than a few large ones.*

PICCALILLI (late 1800s)—Mince 2 small heads of cauliflower and 2 of cabbage very fine; wash, drain and chop 50 carefully selected tiny cucumbers; extend the same treatment to 4 red and 4 green peppers, but be sure to remove the seeds. Cover the vegetables with salted water; use about ¼ gill (2 tablespoons) of salt per quart (4 cups) of water. Let them stand all day or all night; drain them; cover them with boiling vinegar in which 3 tablespoons of mustard seed, a small piece of ginger root, 12 black peppercorns and 1 blade of mace have been cooking. Let the vegetables stand 24 hours. Then 3 times, at 24-hour intervals, drain off the liquid, reheat it and pour it over the vegetables; after the last dousing the Piccalilli is ready for sealing into jars, jugs or crocks.*

CRANBERRY CATSUP (mid-1800s)—To make about 1 quart (4 cups) of catsup, pour 2 pounds of cranberries and ½ pint (1 cup) each of vinegar and water into an iron kettle; boil until the berries are pulped; rub them through a sieve and return them to the kettle with 1 pint (2 cups) of dark-brown molasses and ½ teaspoon each of ground nutmeg, cinnamon, allspice, cloves and salt. Let the catsup boil 5 minutes and be alert lest it sticks to the kettle.*

MUSHROOM KETCHUP (early 1800s)—Clean, skin and slice the mushrooms. Place layers of mushrooms and fine table salt in a fitting stone crock; let it stand in a warm place from sunset to past sunrise. Rub the mushrooms through a sieve and add any liquor that has gathered in the crock. Measure this and add 1 pint (2 cups) of vinegar and 2 tablespoons each of pulverized cloves, mustard, allspice and mace or nutmeg for each quart (4 cups) of mushroom pulp and juice. Put all this into a preserving kettle and cook slowly until it acquires ketchup thickness. The best way to keep it is in small, wide-mouthed bottles stoppered by new and well-fitting corks.*

GOOSEBERRY CATSUP—Eight pounds of ripe or partially ripe fruit, 4 pounds (9 cups) of brown sugar, 1 pint (2 cups) of good vinegar, 2 ounces each fine cloves and cinnamon tied in a bag. Boil the berries and sugar for 3 or 4 hours; then add the spice; boil them a little more. Put the catsup in a jar and cover it well. It will keep 2 years if occasionally you scald the liquor and add a little vinegar and spice.—Mrs. R. Harris

TOMATO CATSUP (late 1800s)—Take as many ripe tomatoes as you need, wipe them clean, cut them up and cook them until soft; strain them through a sieve. To every gallon (16 cups) of tomato add 1 pint (2 cups) of vinegar, 1 scant teaspoon of red pepper, ¼ cup of salt, 3 tablespoons of sugar. Add, tied into a bag, 1 tablespoon of black peppercorns, 2 of dry mustard, 3 of cinnamon, 2 of cloves and ½ tablespoon of mace. Boil very slowly 4 to 5 hours. Remove the spices. Bottle while hot.*

CUCUMBER CATSUP—Take a dozen large ripe cucumbers; pare them, cut them open and take out all the seeds; then grate them. Make a bag like a jelly bag of some thin muslin cotton, and hang the cucumbers up in it to drain over night. Chop 2 or 3 onions and 2 or 3 green peppers; add 1 tablespoon of salt and boil it, with the cucumber jelly left in the bag, with a quart (4 cups) of best vinegar; simmer the catsup until you can rub all through a colander and bottle.—Mrs. Warren Hastings

GREEN TOMATO SAUCE—One peck (8 quarts) of green tomatoes cut in very thin slices; sprinkle them with salt; press them with a plate and leave them to drain 24 hours. Then place them in a porcelain kettle in layers with the following mixture: 6 large onions cut in slices, ½ gill (¼ cup) of mustard, ¼ pound of mustard seed, 2 teaspoons of cloves, 4 teaspoons of black pepper, 2 teaspoons of ginger, 4 teaspoons of allspice. All the spices should be ground. Cover this with vinegar and simmer 2 hours or until the tomato looks clear. Pour the sauce into jugs when cold and cover with oiled paper or melted, not hot, lard.—Mrs. Houghteling

CHILI SAUCE—One peck (8 quarts) of ripe tomatoes boiled ½ hour and drained; add a cup of salt, 1 quart (4 cups) of vinegar, 1 ounce of whole cloves, 1 ounce of cinnamon, 1 ounce of allspice, 1 ounce of ground white mustard, 1 quart (4 cups) of sliced onions, a little celery, a little horse-radish, ½ pound (1 generous cup) of sugar, 6 red peppers. Boil all 1 hour.—Etta C. Springer

ROSE VINEGAR FOR SALADS (mid-1800s)—To every ¼ pound (2 cups) of rose leaves put 2 quarts (8 cups) of good vinegar; use a large jar with a firmly fitting cover. Allow this to infuse until a fine tincture is obtained; then strain off the infusion. If you have to collect the rose petals slowly, let them accumulate in a jar between thin layers of salt; the latter must be wiped or washed off before the infusion begins.*

ROSE WATER FOR BAKING, ETC. (mid-1800s)—Follow the method described under Rose Vinegar for Salads, above. But, instead of vinegar, use only 1 pint (2 cups) of warm water that has been boiled. Rose water obtained by this method serves well, but it is not very lasting.*

CELERY VINEGAR—Soak 1 ounce of celery seeds in ½ pint (1 cup) of vinegar; bottle it well and use for soups, gravies and salads.—Mrs. Monroe Heath

CIDER-HONEY VINEGAR, TO MAKE (early 1800s)—Mix cider and honey, in the proportions of 1 pound of honey to 1 gallon of cider. Let it stand in an unbunged keg for some months, and vinegar will be produced so powerful that water must be mixed with it for common use.***

WINE VINEGAR, TO MAKE (mid-1800s)—Take any sort of home-made wine that has gone through fermentation; put it into a cask that has had vinegar in it. Then take some of the fruit or stalks of which the wine has been made and put them, wet, in an open-headed cask with a coarse cloth over it, in the sun, for 6 days, after which put them in the wine-vinegar; stir it well about and put it in a warm place with a stone over the bung. When the vinegar is sour enough and fine, rack it off into a clean cask, bung it up and put it into the cellar for use.***

FRUIT VINEGARS, TO MAKE (mid-1800s)—Thrifty housewives make vinegar from the pulp and husks of grapes, gooseberries, currants and other berries after wine has been made from the juice. Add half its weight in sugar to the left-over pulp; let it stand in a keg or crock; when it starts to ferment, add 1 gallon water for every 2 pounds of total weight; stir it well and let it steep for 2 days; then strain it. When it is cool, ferment it with yeast for a week and then put it into a barrel with 1 pint of vinegar and 2 ounces of white sugar for every gallon. Lay a loose tile or a piece of slate over the bung; keep it in a warm place for about 3 months; bung it and use the vinegar.***

CELERY SALT, TO MAKE (early 1800s)—Save the root of the celery plant and dry and grate it; measure it and mix in 1/3 as much salt. Keep it in a bottle well corked. This is delicious for soups, oysters, gravies and hashes.*

PARSLEY SALT, TO MAKE (early 1800s)—Dry sprigs of parsley over night in a bake-oven after baking is done (200°F.). Next morning strip the leaves off the stalks, pound them to a powder in a mortar and mix in salt to taste.*

SPICED SALT FOR SOUPS, GRAVIES AND STUFFINGS (late 1800s)—Assemble in a large bottle 4 ounces (¼ cup plus 2 tablespoons) of salt, 2 ounces (3 tablespoons) of celery salt, 1 ounce (4½ teaspoons) each of white pepper, ground thyme, marjoram and summer savory; add 1 saltspoon (¼ teaspoon) of cayenne pepper, ½ teaspoon each of powdered cloves, allspice and mace. Shake the bottle every time you use it and keep it well corked in between.*

FRENCH MUSTARD, TO MAKE (early 1800s)—Mince and pound a medium onion in a bowl; cover it with good vinegar; add to it a pinch of cayenne pepper, ½ teaspoon of salt, 1 tablespoon of sugar, and dry mustard enough to thicken it and mix all together. Set the mustard on the stove and stir until it boils. Rub it through a sieve and use it. Very hot, strong and pungent.***

MADE-MUSTARD—Pour a very little boiling water over 3 tablespoons of mustard; add 1 saltspoon (¼ teaspoon) of salt, a tablespoon of olive oil, stirred slowly in, and 1 teaspoon of sugar; add the yolk of an egg, beaten well, and pour in vinegar to taste. It is best eaten next day.—Phoebe Jane Chapin

23. Preserves, Butters, Marmalades and Canning

WHEN FRUIT IS SEALED IN GLASS CANS—Wrap paper of two or three thicknesses around the cans or put them in a dark closet. The chemical action of light will affect the quality of the preserves even when their containers are perfectly air-tight. With this precaution, glass cans are preferable to any other for preserving fruit.—Anon.

FOR CANNING THE LARGER FRUITS—as peaches, pears, etc.—place them in a steamer over a kettle of boiling water, laying first a cloth in the bottom of the steamer; fill this with the fruit and cover tightly. Let them steam until they can be easily pierced with a fork. Make a syrup of sugar; the thickness of maple syrup is the right consistency. As the fruit has been steamed, drop each for a moment in the syrup, then place it in the can; have each can half full of fruit. Then fill the can up with the hot syrup, cover and seal.—Anon.

HINTS ON PRESERVES (late 1800s)—To present glass jars from cracking owing to the use of boiling syrups, put any type of silver tableware into the glasses and tumblers and they will not crack even when red hot preserves, etc., are poured into them.

Add a small dab of butter to syrups that return to sugar and heat them over a low fire; they become a soft sugar that can be used in cake icing and fillings.

Reheat fermented preserves and add a little sugar, then use them in sweet sauces, pies and other desserts.

Syrups will not go candying if 1 teaspoon of vinegar is added to them while still hot in the kettle.*

BOILING SWEETMEATS (early 1800s)—Do this very gently lest the syrup should burn, and also so that the fruit may become thoroughly penetrated with the sugar. Furious boiling breaks small and tender fruits. Too long boiling makes sweetmeats dark, and some kinds are rendered hard and tough. When sweetmeats are cold, cover them close, and if they are not to be used soon, paste a paper over the top, and with a feather brush over the paper with the white of an egg.**

MAKING SYRUP FOR PRESERVES (mid-1800s)—Put in a kettle a large common teacup (1 cup) of water for every pound (2¼ cups) of sugar. As the sugar begins to heat, stir it often. When it rises toward the top of the kettle, put in a small teacup (½ cup) of cold water; repeat this process again; then set the kettle aside. If the sugar is perfectly pure, there will be no scum on the top. If there is scum, take it off carefully. It is not necessary to strain the syrup if it looks clear.*

TO CLARIFY SUGAR (early 1800s)—The common method is to put in a beaten white of egg for each 2 pounds (4½ cups) of sugar and use ½ pint (1 cup) of water for each pound (2¼ cups) of sugar. After the syrup has boiled enough remove it from the fire and let stand 10 minutes; then skim away the scum and pour off the syrup so gently as not to disturb the sediment. Have the kettle washed, return the syrup to it, reheat it and add the fruit. Persons who strain sugar through flannel bags should always wring them dry in hot water to prevent waste by sugar coatings on the bags.***

PRESERVING (late 1800s)—Put the jars into cold water; let them boil over a fire 30 minutes; fill the jars with cooked fruit and pour in syrup to overflowing; adjust rubbers and covers. Invert the jars and let them stand on a folded cloth until they are cold; if there are no air bubbles, place the jars in a cool dark closet to keep. If air bubbles are present, remove the covers from the offending jars, reheat the contents and add enough hot syrup to drive off the air.*

TO PRESERVE APPLES (early 1800s)—Weigh equal quantities of Newtown Pippins and the best of sugar; allow 1 sliced lemon for every pound. Make a syrup (see Index) and then put in the whole apples. Cook them until they are tender; then lay them into the jars and boil the syrup until it becomes a jelly; use just enough water to cook the apples adequately. To be sure, other sour, hard apples are very good preserved, but none keep as well or are as handsome as Newtown Pippins.**

CRABAPPLES (early 1800s)—Weigh the apples and put them into water almost enough to cover them, but not quite. Take them out when they have boiled 3 to 5 minutes and put into the water as many pounds of sugar as you have fruit. Boil this syrup until it is clear; then set it aside until it is cold; skim it; return the fruit to the kettle and put it again on the fire; the moment it actually boils, take it off. Lay the fruit into jars with care so as not to break it and cover with the syrup.***

BLACKBERRY PRESERVE (mid-1800s)—High blackberries are not good, but to 1 pound of the low-running blackberries allow 1 pound of fine sugar. Put them together in the preserving kettle, the fruit first, the sugar on top. These berries are so juicy that water is not necessary; but they must begin to stew very slowly, and boil most gently 1 hour.***

CRANBERRY PRESERVE (early 1800s)—Pour scalding water upon the cranberries, as this makes it much more easy to separate the defective ones from the good than if they are washed in cold water. Measure the fruit and allow 2 quarts (8 cups) of sugar for 5 (20 cups) of fruit. Boil the cranberries until they are soft in 2½ quarts (10 cups) of water; stir them often. When they are ready, add the sugar and boil them as gently as you can for 30 minutes more. Tend them carefully, as they are liable to burn.*

CRANBERRY-QUINCE PRESERVE (late 1800s)—Put 1 quart (4 cups) of white sugar, ¾ quart (3½ cups) of cranberries and 1 pint (2 cups) each of chopped apples and quince into a saucepan with ¼ pint (½ cup) of orange juice and the minced outside skin of a whole orange; stir and let the preserve cook slowly over a low heat until it sets. Pour it into tumblers and cover.*

CRANBERRY DELIGHT (early 1800s)—Clean 1 quart (4 cups) of cranberries, discard the poor berries and set the good ones to boil in ½ pint (1 cup) of boiling water; stir for 4 to 6 minutes to prevent them from scorching. Add ½ pint (1 cup) of sugar; when it becomes a syrup add the juice of ½ quart (2 cups) of whole Preserved Strawberries (see Index); when it is hot, add the strawberries. Cook only until the strawberries are heated; stir lightly to avoid mashing them. Most people prefer this cold. (This preparation can also be used as filling for Cranberry Pies, for which see Index.)*

GOOSEBERRY PRESERVE (mid-1800s)—Buy 6 pounds of gooseberries; trim each berry top and bottom; wash and drain them. Take 5 oranges and grate their rinds; peel them and be sure to remove the pith; divide the oranges into sections; take away the seeds and cut the sections into small pieces. Plump (see Index) and stone 1½ pounds (4½ cups plus 2 tablespoons) of raisins. Make a syrup in a kettle of 5 pounds (11¼ cups) of sugar and 2 pints (4 cups) of water; keep the syrup at simmering point and stir in all the ingredients. Let the preserve bubble, very slowly, for several hours until it is thick as oatmeal, then put it into scalding hot (see Preserving, above) jars at once.*

BRANDIED PEACHES (late 1800s)—To give them a fine finish, pour boiling water over the peaches to be canned and polish them with a piece of toweling to remove the fuzz. Next, roll each peach in powdered sugar; place them in quart-sized, patent-topped, air-tight jars. Cover them with sugar and fill each jar to the brim with a good grade of French brandy. Seal them at once and serve on special occasions. Do not use cooking brandy, as this seldom has the required flavor and strength.*

PRESERVED CHERRIES—Stone the fruit, weigh it, and for every pound take ¾ pound (1½ generous cups) of sugar. First dissolve the sugar in water in the proportion of 1 pint (2 cups) of water to 1½ pounds (3¼ cups) of sugar; then add the fruit and let it boil as fast as possible for ½ hour until it begins to jell. As soon as it thickens put it in pots, cover them with brandied paper and then cover closely from the air. This method applies to all kinds of small fruits.—Jennie June

PRESERVED PEACHES—Select firm peaches of fine quality. If too ripe they are not likely to keep perfectly. Pare or skin them (see Index), place them in a steamer over boiling water and cover it tightly; an earthen plate placed in the steamer under the fruit will preserve the juices which afterwards may be strained and added to the syrup. Let them steam for 15 minutes or until they can be easily pierced with a fork. Make a syrup (see Index) of the first quality of sugar; the thickness of maple syrup is the right consistency; as the fruit is steamed, drop each peach into the syrup for a few seconds; then take it out and place it in the can; when the cans are almost full, pour the hot syrup over the fruit and seal them immediately. Inexperienced housewives will do well to remember that the syrup should be well skimmed before being poured over the fruit. We prefer the proportions of ½ pound (1 generous cup) of sugar to a pound of fruit for canning, although many excellent housekeepers use more, others use less. This method is excellent for all of the large fruits, such as pears, quinces, apples, etc.—Jennie June

PRESERVED QUINCES—As you peel and core the quinces, throw them in cold water; strain them out of the water and make a syrup. To every pound of fruit put a pint (2 cups) of water and a pound (2¼ cups) of sugar. When the syrup boils, put in the fruit and boil it until soft. Boil the syrup down as usual for other preserves.—Mrs. Anna Marble

PRESERVED PLUMS—Allow to every pound of fruit ¾ pound (1½ generous cups) of sugar; put into stone jars alternate layers of fruit and sugar and place the jars in a moderately warm (250°F.) oven. Let them remain there until the oven is cool; if prepared at tea time let them remain until morning. Then strain the juice from the plums and boil and clarify it, or try 6 hours in a warm (275°F.) oven. Remove the fruit carefully to glass or china jars, pour over it the hot syrup and carefully cover with brandied paper, or thick white paper pasted, or a bladder tied closely down.—Jennie June

SPICED PEACHES OR PEARS—For 10 pounds of good mellow peaches, use 5 pounds (11¼ cups) of sugar, 1 pint (2 cups) of good vinegar, a dozen whole cloves or a 3-inch stick of cinnamon. Take the sugar, vinegar and cloves, and let them come to a boil and turn them over the fruit. This do 3 days in succession, and the last day put the fruit into the syrup, a few at a time, and let them just boil up.—Mrs. Henry M. Knickerbocker

GINGERED PEARS (mid-1800s)—Make a syrup with 1 pound (2¼ cups) of white sugar and a little water (½ cup). Peel and core 2 pounds of pears; cut them into quarters and slice them fine; put them into the syrup. Peel 2 lemons as you would oranges, divide them into halves and discard the seeds; cut the halves into ⅛-inch slices and quarter the slices; add these to the pears; mince ¼ pound of candied ginger and put it with the pears, etc. Let this cook in a pail in boiling water (double boiler) for 3 to 4 hours and then pour it into jelly glasses.*

EGG PLUMS (early 1800s)—To make the most elegant of all plum sweetmeats, take the Duane or the Egg plums, ripe, but not very ripe. The skin can usually be pulled off; if not, pour boiling water over them in a colander and remove the skins at once. Allow equal quantities of plums and sugar and, for 6 or 8 pounds of fruit, use 1 pint (2 cups) of water. Make a syrup of sugar and water; skim the syrup and lay in a few plums at a time; let them boil 5 minutes; lay them into a jar as you take them from the kettle, and, when all are done, pour the boiling syrup over them. After 2 days, pour the syrup off; boil it again and pour it upon the plums again; do this every 2 or 3 days until the plums look clear. Then, if you wish the syrup to be very thick, boil it ½ hour and, when cold, pour it upon the plums.***

TO PRESERVE STRAWBERRIES WHOLE (late 1800s)—Take equal cup measures of berries and sugar; moisten each cup of sugar with ¼ cup of cold water; pour the sugar into the empty preserving pan, which should be set over a pot of boiling water; the water helps the sugar to melt; when the sugar is liquid, put it over a direct fire as usual and let it boil into a syrup; watch closely, lest the sugar foams up suddenly and boils over before you can stop it; stir it with a wooden spoon whenever it starts to rise; let it simmer until it forms little beads. The berries, washed, hulled and dried, are then put in; be sure to add 1 pint (2 cups) of freshly made red-currant juice if you can; it helps so much. Let all boil 5 minutes, then lift the berries into jars with a small sieve; boil the syrup 5 minutes longer and pour it over the berries. These berries would win prizes at any county fair.*

PRESERVED STRAWBERRIES (mid-1800s)—Take large strawberries, not extremely ripe; weigh equal quantities of fruit and best sugar (white); put them together over night to extract the berry juices. The next day boil the strawberries long enough to scald them without shrinking them, 6 to 8 minutes after they commence boiling. Skim them out and cook the syrup for ½ hour; then pour it, hot, upon the strawberries.***

CURRANT AND RASPBERRY PRESERVE (early 1800s)—Take 3 pounds each of raspberries, currants (9¾ cups) and sugar (6¾ cups). Wash the berries. Strip the currants from their stems and squash them with a potato pounder; leave the currants for ½ hour in boiling water and strain them through a sieve lined with several layers of thin muslin. Simmer the currant juice and sugar in a saucepan for ¼ hour; add the raspberries, let it all boil up and remain boiling to the count of 10; remove the mixture from fire; pour it into tumblers.*

JAMS, HOW TO KEEP (mid-1800s)—Always keep jams in a cool, dry place. If they are stored in a closet, leave the door open frequently, that air may blow upon the jars. In a hot place, jams will ferment; in a cold and damp one, they may become moldy.*

A FEW HINTS ON MAKING JAMS (mid-1800s)—If you must buy your fruits in stores or from hucksters, never buy them if it has been raining; berries should always be picked in dry weather and, better yet, be wholly free from dew at the time of picking. Scan berries one by one and reject all that are bruised or decayed.

Sugar for canning should not be the powdered kind, for that makes the jam thick and turbid-looking. Loaf sugar should not be in large lumps, because it will be so long in dissolving; break loaf sugar into lumps the size of hazelnuts and dry it in front of the fire before it is put with the fruit.

Jam is and looks better when the sugar is added only after the berries have reached the point where they begin to "fall" or break.

Remember the fire must be bright and clear, not too fierce, or it may burn the fruit; not too gentle, or the fruit will be too long aboiling. The preserving pan must never be placed flat upon the fire, but should be hung on a trivet; if not, the fruit will be sure to become scorched.

Apple Jam or Jelly is improved by placing a leaf of rose geranium on the top of the apples before you seal each glass.*

OLD NEW ENGLAND APPLE JAM (early 1800s)—Always choose apples that will fall easily; weigh them after they are pared, cored and thinly sliced. Put the apples in a jar and set the jar in a pot of boiling water; let it stand until the apples are soft; now put the apples into a pan over a fire with 3 pounds (6¾ cups) of sugar and the juice and grated peels of 2 lemons for every 4 pounds of apples; add also a few small bits of white ginger. The latter is essential to this jam's peculiar excellence. Stir and skim it as it comes to a boil; from that moment on, let it simmer 30 minutes; then transfer it to crocks and cover tightly.***

NEW NEW ENGLAND APPLE JAM (late 1800s)—Pare, core and simmer 6 pounds of apples (about 18 medium ones) with ¾ quart (3 cups) of cold water and 1 tablespoon of cinnamon. Make a simple syrup of 1½ pounds (3¼ cups, plus 2 tablespoons) of sugar by boiling it slowly; add the apples, when tender, to the syrup and the thin, chopped rinds of 2 lemons; place the apples in sterilized jars and set them in a cool place until cool; then keep them in a dark and dry closet.*

BLACKBERRY JAM (early 1800s)—Do not use overripe berries and be sure they are picked in dry weather. To each pound of well-picked berries add ¾ pound (1¾ cups) of pulverized white sugar. Put these in the kettle and have a slow fire going from the time you put the boiler on the stove; the moment when the bubbles from the first boil-up appear, lift the kettle from the fire and transfer the jam to glasses and crocks.*

CRANBERRY JELLY (early 1800s)—Boil 1½ quarts (6 cups) of cranberries in 1 quart (4 cups) of water, strain this through a jelly bag, without pressing, into a basin and measure it. Heat the cranberry liquid and add ¾ pint (1½ cups) of white sugar for each pint (2 cups) of liquid when it starts to boil; skim and stir constantly. After 5 minutes of lively boiling, drip a drop of the jelly liquid onto a cold plate. If the jelly hardens, it is done; if not, continue cooking until it jells. When it is done, fill the tumblers and cover them well with good white paper that has been soaked in brandy; seal tightly by running a string around each tumbler. This jelly does not keep very well over a long run. Make it in small quantities and often.*

RAW CRANBERRIES, TO KEEP (early 1800s)—Raw cranberries have great lasting powers. One can keep ½ peck (4 quarts) in the cellar weeks on end; just keep them in a tub of water which is changed every week or so.*

FANCY LEMON BUTTER—Beat 6 eggs, ¼ pound (½ cup) of butter, 1 pound (2¼ cups) of the rind and juice of 3 lemons. Mix all together and set it in a pan of hot water to cook. Very nice for tarts, or to eat with bread.—Mrs. D. S. Munger

PEACH BUTTER—Take pound for pound of peaches and sugar; skin and slice the peaches and cook them in very little water until they become soft; then put in one-half the sugar and stir for ½ hour, then the remainder of the sugar and stir 1½ hours. Season with cloves and cinnamon.—Mrs. M. L.

TOMATO BUTTER—Nine pounds peeled tomatoes, 3 pounds (6¾ cups) of sugar, 1 pint (2 cups) of vinegar, 3 tablespoons of cinnamon, 1 tablespoon of cloves, 1½ tablespoons of allspice; boil 3 or 4 hours until quite thick, and stir often that it may not burn.—Mrs. Johnson

APPLE JELLY—Take juicy apples (Baldwins, if possible); take the stems and tops off and wash them nicely; then cut them up in quarters and put cold water on them, just enough to cover them; boil them soft. Afterward strain them through a jelly bag. Then take 2 pints (4 cups) at a time with 2 pints (4-2/3 cups) of crushed sugar; boil these 20 minutes; then do the same with the rest of the juice. Don't strain so close but that you can, by adding a little more water, use the apples for sauce or pies.—Mrs. N. P. Iglehart

CURRANT JELLY—Use the currants when they first ripen; pick them from the stems and put them on the stove in a stone jar, bruising them with a wooden spoon; then when they are warm, squeeze them through a coarse cloth or flannel and put the juice on the fire in a new tin pan or porcelain kettle; 1 quart (4 cups) of juice requires 2 pounds (4½ cups) of sugar, or a pint to a pound; boil 15 minutes. To be a nice color, the currants should not come in contact with iron spoons or tin dishes, unless new and bright. The jelly should be made quickly. It never fails to jell well if the currants are not too ripe. The same method is to be used for jam, only do not strain the currants, but mash them well. Currants should not be dead ripe for jelly or jam.—Mrs. C. Wheeler

GOOSEBERRY JELLY—Boil 6 pounds of green unripe gooseberries in 6 pints (12 cups) of water (they must be well boiled, but not burst too much); pour them into a basin and let them stand covered with a cloth for 24 hours. Then strain them through a jelly bag, and, to every pint (2 cups) of juice add 1 pound (2¼ cups) of sugar. Boil the jelly 1 hour; then skim it and boil for ½ hour longer with a sprig of vanilla.—Mrs. E. M. Walker

COFFEE JELLY (late 1800s)—One pint (2 cups) of clear coffee as strong as it is generally drunk; sugar to taste. Pour 1 gill (½ cup) of cold water on a tablespoon of gelatine and let it soak 15 minutes; pour off the water and put the gelatine when well dissolved in the hot coffee; wet a mold and pour the jelly into it through a strainer.*

CIDER JELLY—Take and mix 2 tablespoons and 1 dessertspoon (2-2/3 tablespoons, in all) of gelatine, the grated rind of 1 lemon and the juice of 3; then add ½ pint (1 cup) of cold water and let it all stand 1 hour; then add ¼ pound (generous ½ cup) of sugar, 1 pint (2 cups) of boiling water and 1 pint (2 cups) of cider; put the jelly into molds and set them in a cool place.—Mrs. George Frost.

CRABAPPLE JELLY (mid-1800s)—Cover the fruit, stemmed, washed, wiped and quartered, with cold water in a heavy iron kettle; let it simmer gently until the apples are done. Transfer the fruit to a jelly sleeve (bag); let the juice drain off, but do not use pressure. Put the juice over a gentle fire and for each pint (2 cups) add 1 pound (2¼ cups) of sugar when it boils. It is well to have the sugar heated in the oven; skim as needed. After the sugar has melted, let the syrup boil until it jells, usually about 5 minutes, and pour it into glasses. Let the jelly harden before you cover it.*

QUINCE MARMALADE—Boil your fruit in as little water as possible until it is soft enough to break easily; pour off all the water and rub the fruit with a spoon until entirely smooth. To 1 pound of the quince add 10 ounces (1½ scant cups) of brown sugar and boil 20 minutes, stirring often.—P. B. A.

ORANGE MARMALADE—One dozen Seville oranges, 1 dozen common oranges, 1 dozen lemons. Boil the oranges and lemons whole in water for 5 hours. Scoop out the insides, removing the seeds; cut the peel into thin slices with a knife and add to every pound of pulp and peel 1 pint (2 cups) of water and 2 pounds (6½ cups) of sugar. Boil 20 minutes.—Mrs. J. Young Scammon

ORANGE MARMALADE—Wash and boil, unpeeled and slowly, 14 oranges and 10 lemons for 2 or 3 hours. Throw away the water and open the oranges. and lemons, taking out the seeds and preserving all the pulp and juice possible; cut the rinds in small strips or chop them, but cutting in strips is better. Weigh it all, when this is done; then put 3 pounds (6¾ cups) of sugar to every 2 pounds of the pulp and boil it slowly until it is clear.—Mrs. William Brackett

TO CAN TOMATOES—Wash your tomatoes and cut out any places that are green or imperfect; then cut them up and put them over the fire to cook with a little salt; boil them until perfectly soft; then strain them through a colander; turn them back to cook, and, when they have come to boiling heat, pour them into stone jugs (1- or 2-gallon jugs, as you prefer). They will keep a day or two in winter if all are not used at a time; put the cork in; have some canning cement hot and pour it over the cork. The jug must, of course, be hot when the tomatoes are poured in.—Mrs. Edward Ely

CANNED PINEAPPLE—For 6 pounds of fruit when cut and ready to be canned, make a syrup with 2½ pounds (5½ generous cups) of sugar and nearly 3 pints (6 cups) of water; boil the syrup 5 minutes and skim or strain it. Then add the fruit and let it boil up; have cans hot; fill and shut them up as soon as possible. Use the best white sugar. As the cans cool keep tightening them up.—Mrs. F. L. Bristol

CANNED STRAWBERRIES—After the berries are pulled, let as many as can be put carefully in the preserve-kettle at once be placed on a platter. To each pound of fruit add ¾ pound (1½ generous cups) of sugar; let them stand 2 or 3 hours until the juice is drawn from them. Pour the juice in the kettle, let it come to a boil and remove the scum which rises; then put in the berries very carefully. As soon as they come thoroughly to a boil, put them in warm jars and seal them while boiling hot. Be sure the cans are air-tight.—Miss Blaikie

CANNED CHERRIES—Prepared in the manner of Canned Strawberries (see Index), allowing but ½ pound (1 generous cup) of sugar to a pound of fruit. After putting the fruit into the syrup let it scald (not boil hard) for 10 or 15 minutes and then can and seal it. A few of the cherry stones put in a muslin bag and put into the syrup to scald with the fruit imparts a fine flavor; they should not be put in the jars with the fruit. This method works well with all the small fruits, such as strawberries, raspberries and also plums.—Jennie June

24. Ice Creams and Ices

TO MAKE ICE CREAM (mid-1800s)—An ice-cream freezer can be more ornery than one would believe possible if it is not treated right. *First,* keep the gears well oiled; *second,* make sure that the freezing can sits well in the freezer; *third,* use cracked ice the size of nuggets; for each pint (2 cups) of cracked ice add 1 pint (2 cups) of rock salt and make sure that they are well mixed; *fourth,* always put the freezing can *empty* into the freezer and pack the ice-salt well around it; let it stand for 10 minutes of chilling before the can is filled; *fifth,* wait 5 minutes after the can is filled before you work the freezer; *sixth,* for first 10 minutes turn the handle slowly, as this is a decisive period; after that, churn increasingly rapidly until your arm tells you that the cream is frozen; *seventh,* without removing the can from the ice, take the dasher out, scrape the cream from sides of the can with a spoon and, using a tumbler with a flat bottom, press the cream into a solid pack. Cover the cream and let it stand in ice about 20 minutes so it may ripen.*

AFTER FREEZING ICE CREAM (mid-1800s)—Save the salt by pouring all the contents of the ice tub into a sack. When the ice has melted and the water run off, nearly all the salt is left in the sack and can be used again.*

WHEN WHIPPING CREAM (mid-1800s)—It is a good idea to use a round, straight-sided 2-quart metal measure or some similar cooking vessel. Before you whip the cream, chill this article with chunks of ice that can be pounded later for the freezing. Also, put your cream whisk upon the ice for a good chilling. Wipe all articles dry before the whipping begins.*

SPOON-WHIPPING CREAM FOR ICE CREAM (mid-1800s)—If you have not a whisk such as is made expressly for whipping cream, it can be easily, though not quickly, done with a spoon. Beat the cream, not over and over as you do the yolks of eggs, but back and forth, and keep the spoon below the surface; as fast as the froth forms, take it off and lay it into a dish. It will not return to its liquid state if whipped in this manner.*

DANGERS IN EATING ICE CREAM (early 1800s)—The aged, the delicate and children should abstain from eating it; even the strong and healthy should partake of ice cream in moderation. It should be eaten immediately after the repast, or some hours after, because the taking of these substances *during* the hours of digestion is apt to provoke indisposition.***

CHOCOLATE ICE CREAM (late 1800s)—Cook 2 ounces of grated chocolate (½ cup when grated) with ½ pint (1 cup) of white sugar and 3 tablespoons of rapidly boiling water; stir the while. Remove this from the fire and, while it cools, whip and add 1 quart (4 cups) of cream; also add 3 teaspoons of vanilla extract. Put into freezer.*

CUSTARD VANILLA ICE CREAM (mid-1800s)—Take 3 eggs and separate them. Scald ½ pint (1 cup) of rich milk in a pail in boiling water (double boiler) and dissolve therein ½ pint (1 cup) of sugar (white) and 2 dessert-spoons (4 teaspoons) of cornstarch dissolved in 2 tablespoons of cold milk; toss in a pinch of salt and stir as this thickens. Beat the 3 yolks lemon-yellow in a bowl and pour the cream sauce over them; stir relentlessly; return the mixture to the pail and cook it again over hot water until thick; remove it from the fire to cool. Whip and add 1¼ quarts (5 cups) of cream; ditto the beaten whites of the 3 eggs and 1 dessertspoon (2 teaspoons) of extract of vanilla. Run this through a strainer before freezing it.*

CHOCOLATE FIG ICE CREAM (late 1800s)—Soak 1½ cups of minced figs in ½ cup of sweet or hard cider; rub away all the fig lumps in a sieve. Make a syrup of ¾ cup of white sugar and 4 squares of bitter-sweet chocolate (1 cup of grated chocolate); cool it; add 2/3 cup of whipped heavy cream, 1 teaspoon of vanilla extract and 1 saltspoon (¼ teaspoon) of salt. Add the figs and let all stand until freezing time. To keep the figs from settling at the freezer's bottom, it is necessary to open the freezing can occasionally and stir the figs into the mixture.*

FRENCH ICE CREAM (late 1800s)—Beat 6 egg yolks yellow; blend 2 cups of milk and 1 cup of sugar into the yolks; make this into a soft custard over boiling water in a saucepan; let it cool. Add ¼ teaspoon of salt and 2½ tea-spoons of vanilla extract. Chill the custard; whip and add 1 pint (2 cups) of heavy cream when the custard is cold. This makes a good 1½ quarts of ice cream.*

LEFT-OVER BROWN BREAD ICE CREAM (late 1800s)—In a low oven heat and dry crumbed Boston Brown Bread; roll the crumbs and sift them until you have ½ pint (1 cup); then stir them into the mixture prepared for French Ice Cream (see above).*

PHILADELPHIA ICE CREAM (late 1800s)—Like Joseph's coat of many colors, this recipe is the source of many shades of ice-cream blendings. The Philadelphia method is to have 1 quart (4 cups) of whipping cream, ½ pint (1 cup) of granulated sugar and 1 teaspoon of vanilla extract handy. Of the cream, ½ pint (1 cup) is heated and the sugar added when the cream is hot enough to melt it; it is cooled, whereupon the vanilla is stirred in and, after that, the remaining cream, thoroughly whipped.*

OTHER ICES FROM PHILADELPHIA ICE CREAM (late 1800s)—
Strawberry: Mash 1 pint (2 cups) and incorporate them into Philadelphia cream.*
Coffee: Chill ¼ pint (½ cup) of black unsweetened coffee and add it to Philadelphia cream.*
Banana: Pound 4 bananas, after removing brown patches, with 3 dessert-spoons (2 tablespoons) of strained lime juice and add this to Philadelphia cream.*

Peach: Stew enough skinned peaches to make ½ pint (1 cup); pound them to a pulp and add them to Philadelphia cream.*

FROZEN RUM SYLLABUB (mid-1800s)—Let the cream be frozen; then— just before removing it from the freezer—crank in 2 gills (1 cup) of fine old Medford rum that has been around the Horn and back with Yankee Whalers.**

COFFEE WITH BRANDY NOGGIN (mid-1800s)—Take 1 quart (4 cups) of cold, strong coffee unsullied by sugar or cream. Add to that ¾ pint (1½ cups) of sugar; whip ¾ pint (1½ cups) of cream with a heaping saltspoon (¼ teaspoon) of salt and stir it into the coffee. Work the mixture in the freezer until it becomes a thickly congealed mass; do not let it freeze solid. Let each individual stir in brandy to suit his liking.*

MAPLE SYRUP ICE CREAM (early 1800s)—Place a tin pail with ½ pint (1 cup) of cream in a kettle of boiling water (double boiler); when it is hot add ½ pint (1 cup) of heated maple syrup and set it aside. When the mixture is cool add 1 teaspoon of strained lemon juice; whip 1½ pints (3 cups) of cream and add it. Cover the tin pail tightly; place it in a tub with a good layer of heavily salted crushed ice on the bottom; pack salted ice around and over the pail; let the latter stand under a piece of sailcloth. Some folks think that ice cream freezes better with salt-petre instead of plain rock salt.*

STRAWBERRY ICE CREAM—Mash with a potato pounder in an earthen bowl 1 quart (4 cups) of strawberries with 1 pound (2¼ cups) of sugar; rub this through the colander, add 1 quart (4 cups) of sweet whipped cream and freeze it. Very ripe peaches or coddled apples may be used instead of the strawberries.—Mrs. Harland

VANILLA ICE CREAM—One pint (2 cups) of milk, the yolks of 2 eggs, 6 ounces (generous ¾ cup) of sugar, 1 tablespoon of wetted cornstarch. Scald this mixture until it thickens; when it is cool, add 1 pint (2 cups) of whipped cream and the whites of the 2 eggs, beaten stiff; sweeten and flavor with vanilla to taste and freeze.—M.

PISTACHIO CREAM—Make a nice vanilla ice cream. Have ready pistachio nuts, which have been prepared by pouring boiling water over them and letting them stand in it a few moments, then stripping off the skins; pound them to a paste in a mortar; mix them with the cream. Freeze.—Mrs. Charles C. Crary

FROZEN PEACHES—Make a syrup of a pound (2¼ cups) of sugar and ½ pint (1 cup) of water; when boiled and skimmed place in it 5 or 6 large peaches, peeled and halved, with the blanched kernels. Let them boil gently until clear, being careful not to break them. Skim them from the syrup and leave them to drain. Squeeze the juice of 6 lemons and add it to the syrup with gelatine which has been soaked ½ hour and melted over boiling water. The gelatine must be used in the proportion of 1 tablespoon for each pint (2 cups) of syrup. Wet a mold, pour in the jelly to the depth of ½ inch and let it harden on the ice; then fill the mold with peaches and half-formed jelly and place it on the ice. Do not disturb it until perfectly stiff.—Bella Lyon

MACEDOINE OF FRUIT—Cider Jelly (see Index) and fruit in alternate layers frozen together. The fruit may be of any and all sorts, and may be candied or preserved, or slices of pear, apple, etc. It must be boiled in syrup and then drained. The mold must be filled after the jelly has begun to form, but before it is stiff, and the first layer should be of jelly. When filled, place the mold in salt and ice prepared as for freezing ice cream; cover it closely, and let it remain several hours.—Mrs. Andrews

ORANGE AND LEMON ICES—The rind of 3 oranges grated and steeped a few moments in a little more than a pint (2 cups) of water; strain 1 pint (2 cups) of this liquid on a pound (2¼ cups) of sugar and then add 1 pint (2 cups) of orange or lemon juice. Pour the mixture into the freezer, and, when it is half frozen, add the whites of 4 eggs beaten to a stiff froth.—Bella Lyon

ICES OF FRESH FRUITS AND BERRIES (late 1800s)—To 1 quart (4 cups) of boiling water add 1 pint (2 cups) of white sugar; when this thickens to a syrup let it cool. Add 1 pint (2 cups) of the juices of pulped and strained fruit; mix in the juices of 1 orange and 1 lemon, strained; beat the white of 1 egg until it peaks and blend it in. Freeze this as you would ice cream. These dishes are also called Sherbets in the aping of the French manner.*

CHOCOLATE ICE CREAM SAUCE (late 1800s)—Grate and melt ½ gill (¼ cup) of chocolate; add ½ gill (¼ cup) of boiling water and 1½ gills (¾ cup) of milk; when the mixture shines remove it from the fire. Whip ½ pint (1 cup) of heavy cream; add the chocolate mixture when it is cool; with ½ saltspoon (a pinch) of salt beat the white of 1 egg; stir this into the sauce with 1 teaspoon of essence of vanilla. Serve hot or cold with Chocolate or Vanilla Ice Cream.*

FLAMING SAUCE FOR ICE CREAM (late 1800s)—Stone 2 pounds of sweet cherries; boil them with 1 pound (2¼ cups) of sugar and add a small amount of arrowroot (½ teaspoon) moistened in water to thicken the cherry sauce. Next, add ½ wineglass (2 tablespoons) of good Madeira or sherry or a similar amount of currant jelly. This sauce should be served very hot, in a deep chafing dish if possible; just before serving, pour 6 tablespoons of heated brandy over the sauce, ignite it and bring the sauce to the table while it is flaming.*

STRAWBERRY SAUCE FOR ICE CREAM (mid-1800s)—Soften ½ gill (¼ cup) of butter (see Index) and cream it with ½ pint (1 cup) of sugar; take an egg white, cut it to a stiff froth and stir it into the butter mixture; have ready ¾ pint (1½ cups) of mashed strawberries and whip them into the sauce, which is served cold.*

25. Hard, Soft and Pull Candies

SIMPLE SECRETS OF CANDY-MAKING (mid-1800s)—First, it will be necessary to understand the action of heat upon sugar. The first step in this process is the reduction of sugar to a syrup, which is done by adding water to sugar in the proportion of 1½ pints (3 cups) of water to 3½ pounds (6¾ cups) of sugar. When this boils up in the kettle we have simple syrup. A few more minutes of boiling reduces the water which holds the sugar in a perfect solution.

At this stage, if the syrup is allowed to cool, the candy crystallizes on the sides of the dish, and we have rock candy. If, instead of allowing it to cool at this point, we allow it to reach a higher degree of heat, we shall find, in putting a spoon into the syrup, when drawing it out, a long thread of sugar will follow the spoon. It is to this point that confectioners bring the syrup for the greater number of candies produced.

The greatest skill is required on the part of the candy maker to push the boiling sugar to this point without allowing it to reach the caramel state, when it becomes bitter and dark and is no longer fit to use as a confection. If you add 1 teaspoon of cream of tartar to the 3½ pounds of sugar and 1½ pints of water, it will prevent the tendency of the sugar to assume a granular condition.

To test the candy drop it into cold water. When this becomes at once hard and brittle the vessel should be removed from the fire.

Flat sticks are formed by pouring the candy into long flat pans and, when it is cooling, creasing the mass so that it will readily break into sticks when cold.*

TO MAKE ROUND STICKS OF CANDY—Roll it into pencil-thick sticks with the hands when cool enough to handle and yet warm enough to mold.

To make Barber's Poles, take small portions of candy while it is cooling; color half of them red with an edible dye; leave the remainder white; roll them into sticks and twist 1 red and 1 white stick together.
—Mrs. Henry G. Griswold

SYRUP FOR CRYSTALLIZING (late 1800s)—For every 3 pounds (6¾ cups) of sugar allow 1 pint (2 cups) of water and boil the syrup until it will thread; it is then in the proper state to produce a fine crystal. When the syrup has boiled sufficiently, remove it from the stove and leave it undisturbed in the pan or kettle until quite cold; then sprinkle a little water over it to dissolve the thin crystal film which has formed over the top. Place the candies to be crystallized in shallow pans slightly inclined and pour the syrup carefully over them. Cover the candies with a damp cloth, allowing the cloth to rest on the syrup so that it will take up the crust of sugar which forms on the syrup. In 3 hours drain off the syrup, leaving the candies to dry.*

CHECKERMINTS (late 1800s)—One pint (2 cups) of white sugar, 1 table-spoon of glucose (dextrose), ½ pint (1 cup) of boiling water. Boil the mixture 3 or 4 minutes, then test it by dipping the thumb and finger into cold water, then into the syrup and rubbing the syrup that adheres to the fingers; if it forms a soft, creamy ball (not sticky) it is done. Take it off the fire and beat it until it grows white; then add 1/3 teaspoon of pink coloring and 1 teaspoon of essence of checkerberry.**

MOLASSES CANDY—One cup of molasses, 1 cup of sugar, ½ cup of water, 1 tablespoon of vinegar, a piece of butter the size of an egg (4 table-spoons). Boil (but do not stir) the mixture until it hardens when dropped in cold water; then stir in a teaspoon of (baking) soda and pour it on buttered tins. When cool, pull it and cut it in sticks.—Julia French

BUTTERSCOTCH CANDY—Four cups of brown sugar, 2 of butter, vinegar to taste, 2 tablespoons of water and a little soda. Boil the mixture ½ hour; drop a little in hot water, and, if crisp, it is done.—Mrs. K. North

SUGAR TAFFY—Three pounds (6¾ cups) of best brown sugar, 1 pound (2 cups) of butter, enough water to moisten the sugar. Boil the mixture until crisp when dropped into cold water, then pour it into pans, or upon platters, as thin as possible. It usually requires to boil fast, without being stirred, ¾ hour.—Mrs. Joseph B. Leake

LEMON CANDY—Put into a kettle 3½ pounds (7 scant cups) of sugar, 1½ pints (3 cups) of water and 1 teaspoon of cream of tartar. Let it all boil until it becomes brittle when dropped in cold water. When it is sufficiently done, take it off the fire and pour it into a shallow dish which has been greased with a little butter; when it has cooled so that it can be handled, add a teaspoon of tartaric acid and the same quantity of extract of lemon and work them into the mass. The acid must be fine and free from lumps. Work this in until evenly distributed, and no more, as too much working will tend to destroy the transparency of the candy. Pour the candy onto a tin; cool and cut it. This method may be used for preparing all other candies, as pineapple, etc., using different flavors.—Hannah Jones

CREAM CANDIES—Three and one-half pounds (7 scant cups) of sugar to 1½ pints (3 cups) of water; dissolve in the water before putting it with the sugar ¼ ounce of fine white gum arabic, and when these have been added to the sugar put in 1 teaspoon of cream of tartar. The candy should not be boiled quite to the brittle stage. The proper degree of doneness can be ascertained if, when a small skimmer is put in and taken out, when you blow through the holes of the skimmer, the melted sugar is forced through in feathery filaments. Remove the syrup from the fire at this point and test it by rubbing against the sides of the dish with an iron spoon. If it is to be a chocolate candy, add 2 ounces (½ cup) of chocolate finely sifted and such flavoring as you prefer—vanilla, rose or orange. If you wish to make cocoanut candy, add the cocoanut while the syrup is soft and stir until it is cold.—Anon.

CANDY FOR PULLING—One pound (2¼ cups) of sugar, 1½ cups of water, 3 tablespoons of rose water. Boil 20 minutes, then pull.—Anon.

MAPLE CANDY—One and one-half pounds (3½ generous cups) of sugar, ½ cup of maple syrup, a piece of butter the size of a walnut (1 tablespoon). Add a little water to the syrup and have the sugar thoroughly dissolved. To try it, drop a spoonful in a glass of ice water; if brittle, it is done. —Carrie A.

GUM DROPS—Place in a kettle 3 pounds (6¾ cups) of sugar, a pint (2 cups) of water, ¼ pound of dissolved gum arabic and a few drops of lemon. Cook until the syrup, on being tested, will form a soft ball (see Checker-mints, above); then remove it from the stove and run the syrup, by means of a funnel, into starch prints. Sift a little starch powder over the top and set the tray away for 24 hours. The drops may then be removed from the starch and crystallized (see Index).—Mrs. Abner Hudson

CREAM CANDY—One pound (2½ cups) of white sugar, 1 wineglass of vinegar, 1 tumbler (1 cup) of water, a dash of vanilla. Boil the candy 1½ hours and putt it if you choose.—Anon.

COCOANUT DROPS—To 1 grated cocoanut add half its weight of sugar and the white of 1 egg cut to a stiff froth; mix thoroughly and drop on buttered white paper or tin sheets. Bake 10 minutes in a hot (400°F.) oven. —Anon.

KISSES—One egg, 1 cup of sugar, ½ cup of butter, ½ cup of milk, 1 teaspoon of cream of tartar, ½ of soda, flour enough to make a stiff dough. Form the dough into balls, place them on tins and sprinkle them over with powdered sugar. Bake in a quick oven (400°F.) until a light golden brown.—E. S. P.

PEANUT CANDY (late 1800s)—Boil 1 cup of sugar and ¼ cup of water until it ropes from the spoon. Add ½ teaspoon of cream of tartar and 1 cup of shelled peanuts. Turn immediately into buttered tins.*

BROWN SUGAR CREAMS (mid-1800s)—One pint (2 cups) of brown sugar, 1 tablespoon of butter, ½ pint (1 cup) of cream, 1 teaspoon of vanilla extract. Boil the mixture until it is quite crisp when tried in water. When it is done, beat it until it begins to crumble, then make it into balls with an almond in each.*

CHOCOLATE CARAMELS—Two cups of brown sugar, 1 cup of molasses, 1 cup of chocolate grated fine, 1 cup of boiled milk, 1 tablespoon of flour; a piece of butter the size of a large English walnut (1 rounded tablespoon). Let the mixture boil slowly; pour it on flat tins to cool; mark it off while warm.—E. C. S.

CHOCOLATE CARAMELS (late 1800s)—Three pounds (6¾ cups) of brown sugar, ½ pound (1 cup) of butter, ½ pound (8 squares) of chocolate grated fine (2 cups when grated), 1 pint (2 cups) of cream or milk. Melt all these together with care and boil 20 minutes or ½ hour, stirring constantly. Just before taking the candy off the fire, flavor it with vanilla and add a small cup (½ cup) of granulated sugar. Pour it into a buttered tin; when partly cool, mark it in pieces about an inch square.*

CRYSTALLIZED POPCORN (late 1800s)—One cup of sugar, 3 tablespoons of water, a piece of butter the size of a walnut (1 tablespoon). Boil until it is ready to candy, then pour it over 3 quarts (6 cups) of popcorn. Stir well. (To test for "candying," drop a small amount into very cold water.)*

CARAMELS (late 1800s)—One cup of molasses, ½ cup of milk, 1 cup of sugar, 1 teaspoon of flour, a piece of butter half the size of an egg (2 tablespoons), ¼ pound of chocolate (1 cup of grated chocolate). Boil the caramel until it turns hard in water; add a teaspoon of vanilla extract; turn it into a pan and mark it into squares.*

CREAM FOR WALNUTS AND DATES (early 1800s)—Take 1 pint (2 cups) of sugar, ½ pint (1 cup) of water. Boil this until it threads when dropped from a fork. Don't stir until it is nearly cold, then beat until it is white and creamy. Flavor with lemon juice and mold it with the hands.*

STRAWBERRY DROPS (mid-1800s)—Mix strained strawberry pulp with pounded loaf sugar until a stiff paste is formed. Put the paste in a bright tin saucepan and stir until it boils. Then drop it slowly onto a shallow tin baking dish; when cold set in warm (250°F.) oven with door open, to dry.*

PEPPERMINTS (late 1800s)—Two cups of sugar, ½ cup of water, 1 tablespoon of glucose (dextrose, available in drug stores). Boil 5 minutes. When nearly cold beat it to a cream and add 1 teaspoon of peppermint with a small amount of green coloring. Drop by the teaspoonful on buttered paper. In testing for readiness, follow directions for Checkermints (above).*

GRANDMOTHER'S FUDGE (late 1800s)—Use a heavy copper or similar metal saucepan and have a steady fire of glowing embers. Over this, in the pot, melt 2 ounces (2 squares) of chocolate (½ cup of grated chocolate) and 2 tablespoons of maple syrup with ½ pint (1 cup) of sugar and a good ½ cup of half cream, half milk; add also a good pinch of salt. Stir all the while, until you have a smooth liquid. Stop stirring, but watch until the fudge reaches the point where it can be rolled into small, soft balls. Then add, but do not mix in, 1 teaspoon of vanilla extract and remove the pan to a spot on the stove where it will merely keep warm. By tasting, discover when the fudge is lukewarm; then add 2 tablespoons of melted fresh (unsalted) butter. Whip the mixture to a creamy consistency; if too thick, warm a little cream to thin it down; when it changes from shiny to dull, pour the fudge into a well-buttered square baking tin, but do not cut it into squares until it is quite cool.*

INDEX